# COPYRIGHT USER RIGHTS

# Copyright User Rights

*Contracts and the Erosion of Property*

PASCALE CHAPDELAINE

*BCL, LLB, LLM, PhD*

*Associate Professor, University of Windsor, Faculty of Law,*
*of the Bar of Ontario and le Barreau du Québec*

OXFORD
UNIVERSITY PRESS

OXFORD
UNIVERSITY PRESS

Great Clarendon Street, Oxford, OX2 6DP,
United Kingdom

Oxford University Press is a department of the University of Oxford.
It furthers the University's objective of excellence in research, scholarship,
and education by publishing worldwide. Oxford is a registered trade mark of
Oxford University Press in the UK and in certain other countries



First Edition published in 2017

Impression: 1



Published in the United States of America by Oxford University Press
198 Madison Avenue, New York, NY 10016, United States of America

British Library Cataloguing in Publication Data
Data available

Library of Congress Control Number: 2017945340

ISBN 978–0–19–875479–4

Printed and bound by
CPI Group (UK) Ltd, Croydon, CR0 4YY

Pour Trudo, Rafaël, et Albéric

# *Acknowledgements*

This book builds on the theoretical framework that I developed in my PhD Thesis *The Copyright Consumers' Bargain: Defining the Rights to Commercial Copies of Copyright Works* (Osgoode Hall Law School, Canada, 2013). Chapter 7 is based to a large extent on parts of Chapter 6 of my thesis, while parts of Chapters 3 and 5 build on various sections of my thesis. Parts of Chapters 1 and 4 build on an article published in 2015: 'The Undue Reliance on Physical Objects in the Regulation of Information Products', while parts of Chapter 2 build on an article published in 2013 'The Ambiguous Nature of Copyright Users' Rights'.

It is a difficult task to thank in only a few lines the many friends, colleagues, students, family members who have accompanied me as I was working on my book. I will likely forget many along the way. Special thanks to friends and colleagues who have provided detailed comments on the whole manuscript: David Vaver whose breadth of knowledge and perspicacity continue to amaze me, and Séverine Dusollier, for providing thoughtful and detailed comments and for bringing to my attention areas of EU law and of European national laws that I was less familiar with. Many thanks to my partner Trudo Lemmens, and colleagues who have provided comments on other portions of the manuscript: Ariel Katz, Jeffery Berryman, and Myra Tawfik.

I thank the University of Windsor, Faculty of Law for providing generous financial support for my research, with special thanks to Dean Chris Waters and former Dean Camille Cameron for their encouragement on every step of the way. I thank the University of Windsor law librarians including Annette Demers and Vicki Jay Leung for their insights and guidance. Nick Kawar (Windsor Law JD 2017) Vagmi Patel (Windsor Law JD 2016) Diana Lee (Windsor Law JD 2015) and Marit Peters (Law graduate, K.U. Leuven) provided excellent research assistance. The students in my copyright law and international intellectual property law classes in the past years inspired me as we sought to make sense of the numerous inconsistencies and intricacies of copyright law together.

I am grateful to the organizers and participants of conferences and seminars where I presented work that has made its way into the book. Pamela Samuelson and Laura Heymann, in particular, made detailed comments on a paper selected at the Annual Junior Scholars in Intellectual Property Workshop, Michigan State University College of Law in 2013. I thank the organizers and participants of the International Association of Consumer Law conference, University of Amsterdam in 2015, as well as Peter Yu, other organizers and participants at the Texas A&M University School of Law IP Scholars Roundtable in 2015, and colleagues at the Faculty of Law, University of Windsor, and the University of Ottawa where I presented my work at Seminar series in 2014 and 2016.

As my book builds on parts of my PhD work and more generally on the theoretical framework that I developed in my thesis, I owe special thanks to my thesis committee starting with my supervisor Giuseppina D'Agostino and committee members David Vaver and Geraint Howells, and to the department of Graduate Studies at Osgoode Hall Law School for their invaluable support. The Social Sciences Humanities Research Council (SSHRC) as well as York University provided generous financial support which made the completion of my thesis possible. Lisa Austin encouraged me to look into James W. Harris, *Property and Justice*, which became a significant source of inspiration in my thesis. Graeme Dinwoodie provided thoughtful comments on my thesis work and shared valuable insights as I was writing my book, while Peggy Radin shared many words of wisdom and advice as I started working on my book.

I thank the editors at Oxford University Press for their guidance and advice throughout the publication process, including Ruth Sullivan, Louise Summerling, Gemma Parsons, and Natalie Patey. Special thanks are further owed to Janet MacMillan, Janelle Bowman, Raffaella Rullo, and Nancy Rebecca for their insightful and meticulous editing work.

Many friends, family members, and colleagues have forgiven me for my limited availability as I was writing this book. Above all, I thank my partner Trudo and our sons Rafaël and Albéric for their love, patience, and for the continuous source of joy and inspiration that they provide me.

The book reflects research on the relevant legislation and case law as of January 1, 2017.

# *Table of Contents*

# *Table of Cases*

# *Table of Legislation*

## NATIONAL (STATE AND PROVINCIAL) LEGISLATION

### Australia



### Belgium



### Canada

*Federal Legislation*

***Provincial Legislation***

# *List of Abbreviations*

| | |
|---|---|
| ACTA | (Anti-Counterfeiting Trade Agreement) |
| ALRC Report | Australian Law Reform Commission Report (2013) |
| *Austl CA* | *Australia Copyright Act* |
| *Belgium WER/CDI* | Belgium Wetboek van economisch recht/Code de droit economique |
| *Canada CA* | *Copyright Act* (Canada) |
| *Canada CMA* | *Copyright Modernization Act* |
| CCQ | Civil Code of Quebec |
| CRTC | Canadian Radio-Television and Telecommunications Commission |
| DMCA | *Digital Millennium Copyright Act* |
| EU | European Union |
| France *CPI* | *Code de Propriété Intellectuelle* (France) |
| HADOPI | Haute autorité pour la diffusion des œuvres et la protection des droits sur Internet |
| *OCPA* | *Consumer Protection Act* (Ontario) |
| *OSGA* | *Sale of Goods Act* (Ontario) |
| TPMs | technological protection measures |
| TRIPS | Trade Related Aspects of Intellectual Property |
| UCC | Uniform Commercial Code (US) |
| *UKCDPA* | *Copyright, Designs and Patents Act 1988* (UK) |
| *UKCRA* | *Consumer Rights Act 2015* (UK) |
| *UKSGA* | *Sale of Goods Act 1979* (UK) |
| US *UCC* | *Uniform Commercial Code* (US) |
| USC | 17 USC |
| WIPO | World Intellectual Property Organization |
| WTO | World Trade Organization |

# Introduction

## Do Copyright Users Have Rights?

### Preliminaries

Do copyright users have rights? Can they reproduce a book, create a new work from an existing song, transfer the copy of software to someone else, or work around a digital lock that blocks access to a film? What are the societal norms and values that we promote through copyright law permissions and restrictions? What place should users have in copyright law? These are the central questions of this book.

Copyright user rights and interests are getting more and more public attention, and feature more prominently than ever in copyright law and policy debates. Uses and methods of dissemination of digital copyright works stretch our imagination, whether through e-book downloads, music streaming, social media or other sharing platforms, virtual worlds or interactive video games, or through 3D printing. The drastic change of the technological environment in which users access and enjoy copyright works, and the tensions that arise between users' expectations on the one hand, and copyright holders' desire to protect their works on the other, explain to a large extent the increasing attention to copyright users.

Until recently, multilateral intellectual property conventions dealt with copyright user interests sporadically, as an incident to the exclusive rights of copyright holders. The *Berne Convention*,[1] *TRIPS*,[2] and the *WIPO Internet treaties*,[3] focus predominantly on defining the rights and remedies of copyright holders, and deal with the interests of users mostly through the 'three-step test', which sets parameters on how member states may restrict copyright holders' exclusive rights.[4] This changed in 2013: the *Marrakesh Treaty to Facilitate Access to Published Works for Persons Who Are Blind, Visually Impaired, or Otherwise Print Disabled*[5] (*Marrakesh*

[1] *Berne Convention for the Protection of Literary and Artistic Works*, 9 September 1886, 828 UNTS 221.

[2] *Agreement on Trade-Related Aspects of Intellectual Property Rights, Marrakesh Agreement Establishing the World Trade Organization, Annex 1C*, 15 April 1994, 1869 UNTS 29, 33 ILM 1197.

[3] *WIPO Copyright Treaty*, 20 December 1996, WO033EN; *WIPO Performances and Phonograms Treaty*, 20 December 1996, WO034EN.

[4] See Chapter 2: 'Exceptions to copyright infringements and international obligations.'

[5] 27 June 2013, online: <http://www.wipo.int/treaties/en/text.jsp?file_id=301016> accessed 4 February 2017.

*Treaty*) is the first multilateral instrument that centres on the interests of a defined class of copyright users, mandating member states to facilitate the availability of works in accessible format through copyright limitations and exceptions. In some cases, the Marrakesh Treaty goes one step further by requiring member states to impose obligations on copyright holders[6] for the benefit of the users as defined in the treaty.[7]

At the regional and national levels, an important body of jurisprudence, copyright policy reports, and civil society movements have created a momentum around the promotion of the interests of copyright users. In 2004, the Supreme Court of Canada, in the unanimous judgment in *CCH Canadian Ltd v Law Society of Upper Canada* [*CCH*],[8] made a statement which resonates to this day: copyright exceptions are not mere loopholes in the *Copyright Act* but are more properly understood as users' rights.[9] Several judgments by the Supreme Court of Canada following *CCH*, expanded the understanding of the purpose and scope of copyright users' rights as they were established in *CCH*.[10]

Other events, studies, or initiatives signal a profound dissatisfaction with the right-holder-centric regulation of intellectual property rights and its impact on users and the public interest. For example in the US, there was significant push-back in 2012 against the proposed *Stop Online Piracy Act* [*SOPA*],[11] introduced in the US House of Representatives, and against the proposed *Protect Intellectual Property Act* [*PIPA*][12] introduced in the US Senate. Both bills were subsequently abandoned.[13] In the EU, the rejection of the ratification of the 2011 *Anti-Counterfeiting Trade Agreement* [*ACTA*][14] by the European Parliament in 2012,[15] reflects the same discontentment. Policy papers worldwide, studying the impact of the digital economy on copyright, and making recommendations for legal reform have focused their attention to the interests of users.[16]

Most of the literature on copyright users looks at their interests from a macro-level perspective. 'Macro level' refers to the broader regulatory design of copyright: the

[6] ibid, art 7. [7] ibid, art 4. [8] 2004 SCC 13 [*CCH*]. [9] ibid at para 48.

[10] See Chapter 2: '"User rights" as a rule of interpretation.'

[11] US, Bill HR 3261, *Stop Online Piracy Act*, 112th Cong, 2011.

[12] US, Bill S 968, *Preventing Real Online Threats to Economic Creativity and Theft of Intellectual Property Act of 2011*, 112th Cong, 2011.

[13] Jonathan Weisman, 'After an Online Firestorm, Congress Shelves Antipiracy Bills', *The New York Times* (20 January 2012), online: <http://www.nytimes.com/2012/01/21/technology/senate-postpones-piracy-vote.html> accessed 4 February 2017; Stephanie Condon, 'PIPA, SOPA put on hold in wake of protests', CBS News (20 January 2012), online: <http://www.cbsnews.com/news/pipa-sopa-put-on-hold-in-wake-of-protests/> accessed 4 February 2017.

[14] 1 October 2011, online: <http://www.international.gc.ca/trade-agreements-accords-commerciaux/topics-domaines/ip-pi/acta-text-acrc.aspx?lang=eng> accessed 4 February 2017. *ACTA*'s signatory members include Canada, the EU and its Member States, the US, Japan, and Australia. The treaty requires at least six ratifications to come into force.

[15] Charles Arthur, 'Anti-piracy agreement rejected by European Parliament, but Acta could be revived by European Commission', *The Guardian* (4 July 2012), online: http://www.guardian.co.uk/technology/2012/jul/04/acta-european-parliament-votes-against accessed 4 February 2017.

[16] See e.g., Austl, Commonwealth, Law Reform Commission, *Copyright and the Digital Economy* (Report No 122) (Sydney: ALRC, 2013).

public policy arguments that need to be considered, how copyright holders' exclusive rights should be limited through exceptions to copyright infringement (e.g., fair use, fair dealing, educational purposes), or otherwise (e.g., limiting the term of copyright with longer or shorter terms based on the nature of the work, or limiting the scope of derivative rights, or having greater resort to compulsory licences to increase access to copyright works). A macro-level approach to copyright user rights includes applying human rights law to copyright to justify when the exclusive rights of copyright holders should be limited for the benefit of users.[17] The approach also involves the application of competition law and policy on copyright holders' exclusive rights for the benefit of users and for consumer welfare.[18]

The scope of copyright, the broader considerations of public policy in copyright law, and how copyright law interacts with human rights, constitutional law, and competition law, play a determinant role in shaping the rights and interests that copyright users may have. At the same time, looking at the interests of users through these means does little in defining what the precise scope of user rights are or should be. This approach is somewhat passive towards copyright users and is removed from the practical issues users face, at the ground level, and on a day-to-day basis. A macro-level approach to copyright user rights may, therefore, produce more limited results when it comes to effectively promoting and developing those rights at a substantive level.

This book takes a radically different approach. In contrast to the macro-level perspective to user rights, I define the contours of copyright user rights as private rights through property, contracts, copyright law, and remedies, without hereby neglecting the constant interaction between private law and public law.[19] This exercise changes the focus of the conversation that we have had so far around the proper scope of copyright protection in the face of constant technological change. Giving shape and substance to the rights of users displaces the exclusive and privileged position that the state grant of copyright has enjoyed in the law and policy arena. New questions arise and they demand answers: what if users also have property rights and entitlements in the copyright work produced by authors and not just the physical embodiment? What happens when we apply the prevailing theoretical justifications supporting copyright grants to the rights of users? Does the law provide adequate remedies to users against copyright holders that restrict their legitimate uses and enjoyment of copyright works?

Through a systematic exercise of defining copyright user rights as private rights, double standards start to emerge in how legal concepts, values, and ideals are applied to users and copyright holders, generally for the benefit of the latter. Why and how

[17] See Chapter 7: 'The contributions of property and other theories.'

[18] See e.g., Gustavo Ghidini, *Innovation, Competition and Consumer Welfare in Intellectual Property Law* (Cheltenham: Edward Elgar, 2010).

[19] See Michel Rosenfeld, 'Rethinking the Boundaries Between Public Law and Private Law for the Twenty-First Century: An Introduction' (2013) 11 Intl J Constitutional L 125; Alain Supiot, 'The Public-Private Relation in the Context of Today's Refeudalization' (2013) 11 Intl J Constitutional L 129.

is that so? A meticulous observation of copyright user private rights also reveals another important insight: our (mis)conceptions about tangibility and intangibility shape what user rights are and will become to a large extent. For instance, the tangibility and intangibility dichotomy impacts how we define goods, services, sales, and licences. How we apply concepts of tangibility and intangibility touches a sensitive nerve of copyright user rights that I probe through different scenarios in this book.

Approaching copyright user rights through private law, and in particular tangible personal property, may appear to be somewhat constraining and counterintuitive. Some may be tempted to criticize this approach as traditionalist, and as one that will do little to address the unique nature and challenges of copyright regulation in an ever-changing technological environment. I will demonstrate, however, that the rewards for taking this approach are high.

Indeed, it may appear counterintuitive to look at copyright user rights through property. The property rights that users have in the supporting medium and copy of a copyright work—the book, the CD, the DVD—seem insignificant, compared to the intellectual property rights that copyright holders have in the work itself.[20] From that viewpoint, the intellectual property rights of copyright holders should dictate what users may and may not do with their copies of the work.[21] While this is true to some extent, this book provides a counter narrative to this view by analysing the scope of property rights users (should) have in copies of copyright works. The fact that the personal property rights in copies of copyright works have been trivialized in the past does not mean they ought to be treated as such. A careful examination of what the scope of those property rights should be within the greater framework of copyright and private law sheds light on their significance and calls for more attention on how to mediate user personal property rights with the rights of copyright holders.

Approaching user rights through the property rights users have in copies of copyright works may also appear to be too constraining. Some may argue it fails to address the challenges posed by ongoing technological change to copyright's subsistence. In a digital environment, users decreasingly experience copies of copyright works through individualized copies they own, and increasingly through services. Having property rights in copies of copyright works is, therefore, becoming less commonplace. While this is true to a large extent, physical individualized copies of copyright works (books, music CDs, film DVDs, paintings, architectural works, tattoo art) will continue to co-exist with digitized works that have no physical embodiments. Further, the analysis of the treatment of the tangible and intangible dichotomy in law, as well as the essential requirements of ownership, reveal that the lack of a physical embodiment should not displace per se users' ownership rights in digital copies of copyright works.[22] Also, my account of copyright user rights does not focus exclusively on property. The private rights of users derive from other bodies of law including contract and copyright law. Finally,

[20] See Chapter 1. [21] ibid. [22] See Chapters 1 and 4.

the traditionalist critique only serves too well exceptionalism in copyright law, an approach I denounce as working against the rights of users and ultimately resulting in a de-legitimization of copyright.[23] *Au contraire*, copyright law has much to gain through greater alignment with general and more traditional concepts of property and contracts.

This book looks at copyright user rights from an international copyright law perspective, as well as from a multijurisdictional perspective. There is a significant body of jurisprudence on copyright user rights that emanates from the Supreme Court of Canada. It is, therefore, befitting that a book on copyright user rights focuses particularly on Canadian copyright law. The other jurisdictions include the United States, the European Union, the United Kingdom, France, and Australia.

## Terminology

Depending on the context, 'user rights' or 'copyright user rights' will be used either (i) by referring to the way courts use these terms (regardless of whether this reference accurately reflects 'rights' in the legal sense of the term), (ii) in the legal sense of the term, or (iii) as a normative account of what 'user rights' should mean in copyright law.

When I use 'copyright users' or 'users', I refer to the broadest range and category of users, from seemingly more passive users to active user-authors, and from individual users to institutional users (e.g., broadcasters, libraries, educational institutions). In some cases, 'copyright users' or 'users' will refer more specifically to individual users, for example when I discuss the interaction between copyright law and consumer law. By doing so, I recognize that individual users are in many ways in a different position than institutional, large entity users. Having more limited bargaining power, more limited access to resources and information, are some of the aspects that may set individual users apart from institutional users.[24] At the same time, individual and institutional users share common aspirations and interests: legal certainty, having powers and privileges over copyright works that meet their reasonable expectations, in keeping with the technologies that empower how users experience those works and the broader purpose of copyright.

For ease of reference, and unless the context indicates otherwise, 'copyright works' refers to all subject matter that is protected by exclusive rights under copyright law, and thus includes works (i.e., original literary, dramatic, musical, and artistic works)[25] and other subject matter protected by copyright (e.g., performer's

[23] See Chapter 8.

[24] For a discussion on the various types of copyright users and their interests, see Pascale Chapdelaine, *Copyright Consumers' Bargain, Defining the Rights to Commercial Copies of Copyright Works* (PhD Thesis, York University Graduate Program in Law, Osgoode Hall Law School, 2013) at 45–49 [unpublished].

[25] See e.g., *Copyright Act* (Canada), RSC 1985, c C-42, s 5(1) [*Canada CA*].

performances, sound recordings, communication signals, all of which are often referred to as 'neighbouring rights' or 'related rights').

The term 'copyright holders' includes all persons who hold the exclusive rights conferred by copyright, whether they are corporate or other entities or individuals (including authors). In mass-market environments, copyright holders (who are not the original authors) are often the owners of the copyright and distributors of copyright works. The all-encompassing expression 'copyright holders' does not imply that the interests of copyright holders (who are not the authors) and authors are the same. Often, their interests are not aligned.[26] It is beyond the purpose and scope of this book to discuss the divergence of interests between copyright holders (who are not authors) and authors.[27]

'Commercial copies of copyright works', 'copies of copyright works', and 'information products' refer to those products that are the object of a legal transaction between users and copyright holders (or their distributors), as opposed to copies of copyright works made by persons in possession of copyright works (which may or may not be lawful reproductions of the copyright works). 'Personal property' refers to the property rights users have in copies of copyright works they purchased, generally in a mass-market environment, and acknowledges that in some limited cases users may have real property rights in the copy of the copyright work (e.g., architectural works). For ease of reference, 'personal property', which is the terminology employed in the common law tradition, also includes 'movable property', the terminology employed in the civil law tradition.

Depending on the context, 'Technological protection measures' or 'TPMs' refers either to the technology copyright holders use to protect access to or use of their works, or to legal provisions enacted in national and regional jurisdictions to confer additional protection to copyright holders who make their copyright works available with technological measures. 'Technological measures' is another expression used to designate the technologies employed by copyright holders to protect access or use of their works when there is a need to contrast the technological mechanisms of protection with the regime of legal provisions that protect these mechanisms.

## Overview

This book is divided into three parts. Part I 'In search of copyright user rights' (Chapters 1 to 3) looks into the nature and meaning of copyright user rights, and how they concomitantly operate on two distinct planes: the personal property

[26] See Giuseppina D'Agostino, *Copyright, Contracts, Creators, New Media, New Rules* (Cheltenham: Edward Elgar Publishing, 2010) on the protection of freelance authors in copyright law, in particular, in relation to the misalignments between the interests of authors and copyright holders and how the rights and interests of authors can be better protected, see pp 201–89.

[27] ibid, for a discussion of the divergence between the interests of authors and copyright holders and how they are addressed in copyright law.

rights in copies of copyright works and statutory exceptions to copyright infringement. I uncover three major weaknesses of copyright user rights and important discrepancies between how courts, policy-makers and commentators refer to 'user rights', and the legal meaning of 'rights'.

In Chapter 1, I look at the peculiar nature of the personal property rights of copyright users who own copies of copyright works, and how those rights fare poorly compared to other forms of personal property on the ownership spectrum as elaborated by James W Harris in *Property and Justice*.[28] The personal property of copyright users is unique because it is largely defined by its interaction with copyright, and significantly shaped by well-established commercial practices of copyright holders and distributors, some of which weaken the personal property of copyright users. The progressive dematerialization of commercial copies of copyright works adds another layer of complexity and uncertainty and has led to an inconsistent regulation of copies of copyright works as goods, as services, or *sui generis*. While it is true that not all users own copies of copyright works, those who do (or who should be recognized as owners of copies), are left with a watered down version of ownership. The account of copyright user personal property rights in Chapter 1 reveals the first weak strain of user rights.

Chapter 2 looks at the nature of exceptions to copyright infringement (e.g., fair use, fair dealing, and exceptions for librarians, museums, and archives) and at how copyright user rights are often assimilated, at times even exclusively to exceptions to copyright infringement. I discuss whether copyright user rights should be better understood as a rule of interpretation of copyright exceptions, rather than giving rise to 'rights' in the legal sense. I further investigate the nature of, and consequences of exceptions to copyright infringement consisting of rights or privileges, and whether they are, or should be mandatory (i.e., that exceptions may not be waived by contract). I look at the mechanics of exceptions to copyright infringement and at the shortcomings of this regulatory tool within the broader framework of copyright law. Noting the damaging effect of the legal uncertainty that surrounds the nature of exceptions to copyright infringement, I conclude that they are probably more properly characterized as privileges than rights, and that, unless expressly stated otherwise, they are not mandatory and may be waived by contract. This account of exceptions to copyright infringement reveals the second weak strain of copyright user rights.

Chapter 3 further probes the nature of copyright user rights as rights or privileges, this time from the perspective of the remedies users may have against copyright holders when they are restricted in how they use copyright works. Given the prevailing absence in copyright statutes of obligations of copyright holders and of user remedies, copyright users need to base their claims and remedies in other bodies of law. I map out how users could construct claims for restricted uses of copyright works on the basis of a breach of contract, sale of goods law, consumer law, or as a breach of the obligation of good faith, or in tort. The exercise proves

[28] Oxford: Clarendon Press, 1996.

to be fraught with uncertainty and obstacles to how users may assert claims under those various bodies of law outside copyright law. Among those uncertainties and obstacles, the nature of copyright user rights is one. Whether copyright exceptions are mandatory or may be waived by contract is another. Finally, the treatment of immaterial copies of copyright works as goods, services, or *sui generis* undermines the strength and potential success of copyright user claims and remedies against copyright holders. These obstacles may explain in part the relatively few cases involving copyright user claims. This account of copyright user remedies reveals the third weak strain of copyright user rights.

In Part II 'Rethinking tangibility and intangibility' (Chapters 4 to 6) I argue that the inconsistencies and weaknesses of the current state of copyright user rights identified in Part I can be explained in large part by the confusion around tangibility and intangibility, and by how legislatures and courts struggle to properly regulate the treatment of copies of copyright works, goods, services, sales, licences, and digital locks in an increasingly immaterial world.

In Chapter 4, I tackle the misconception of the requirement of a physical object to decide whether commercial copies of copyright works are goods, services, or *sui generis*, and the ripple effects of that misconception on how courts construe sales and licences. This misconception has significant consequences for the regulation of information products and user rights. Factors including individuality, scarcity, physical control, and exclusivity should inform a more cohesive regulation of copyright user rights and be the determining factors to define copies of copyright works as goods, services, or *sui generis*, rather than somewhat arbitrary considerations based on the misconstrued effects of the presence of a physical object.

Chapter 5 further illustrates, through the evolution of the doctrine of copyright exhaustion or the first sale doctrine, how courts and lawmakers struggle with concepts of tangibility and intangibility. The difficulty of applying the exhaustion or first sale doctrine to digital works reflects similar difficulties identified in Chapter 4 on how to adapt traditional concepts of personal property, goods, services, sales, and licences to information products, in an ever-changing technological environment. I question the extent to which the doctrine of exhaustion or first sale will remain relevant as users increasingly experience copyright works through services and decreasingly through the possession of individualized copies.

Chapter 6 delves further into the tangible versus intangible divide and looks at the effect of digital locks on a larger pool of users than just traditional copyright users: more specifically, those inadvertent copyright users who buy, for example, a car or piece of equipment, without necessarily suspecting that it embeds copyright works (e.g., software), let alone digital locks blocking access to and use of important components of the physical object. I argue that the progressive intrusion and enforcement of digital locks in the world of physical objects will either provide the silver lining to users by triggering favourable legal reform, or will further hollow out their rights. I also explore the changing role of technological protection measures in light of the shift from accessing copyright works through individualized digital copies to experiencing works through services.

In Part III 'Rethinking user rights through property, rights, and privileges' (Chapters 7 and 8) I reframe copyright user rights through a normative analysis that situates users and their rights as they relate to the function of personal property and the broader objectives of copyright law. In Chapter 7, I draw from property theory, and from the most influential theories related to copyright to justify the existence and scope of copyright user rights at a normative level. The variety of identities and interests of copyright users, as well as the different means by which users experience copyright works, that is, through their property in the copy of the work, as service users, or as public-space-users, call for a pluralistic theoretical approach to justify the existence and scope of user rights. Starting with the *prima facie* normative status of all ownership freedoms developed by Harris, in *Property and Justice*,[29] I also refer to the instrumentalist theories of economic efficiency to justify the raison d'être and scope of user personal property rights in copies of copyright works. The influential instrumentalist theories to incent the creation and dissemination of works provide a strong basis to define the contours of user rights beyond the instances where users have property rights in copies of copyright works. The popularity of utilitarian and instrumentalist theories to justify the existence of the exclusive grant conferred by copyright, and to some extent pragmatism motivate my choice to apply these theories to justify user rights. In doing so, I take the utilitarian/instrumentalists arguments a few steps further and show how those arguments must equally apply to the rights of users if the copyright system relying upon those foundations is to retain its credibility.

Building on the substantive analysis of copyright and user rights presented in Part I and Part II, and on the theoretical justifications of user rights developed in Chapter 7, Chapter 8 proposes two main principles that should guide copyright law and policy and the further development of user rights. The first one calls for more cohesion between copyright law, private law, and public law, and for less exceptionalism in copyright law. The second principle requires that the balance in copyright law be adjusted for its future application as a mediation tool between the competing interests of copyright holders, users, intermediaries, and the public. Instituting positive obligations for copyright holders in relation to users and steering freedom of contract toward the objectives of copyright law are necessary regulatory changes to rectify ongoing imbalances. Technological neutrality should guide the judiciary toward promoting a balance between competing interests in the midst of ever-changing technological environments. The two guiding principles that I propose here lead to the creation of a taxonomy and hierarchy of copyright user rights—from user-copy-owners, to service users, to public-space-users—that reflect their degree of proximity to property rights and which take into account the myriad ways users experience copyright works.

I conclude by reflecting on the challenges that copyright law will continue to face in regulating older forms together with newer forms of works and methods of dissemination.

[29] ibid.

At a time where the regulation of copyright comes increasingly under attack and scrutiny, failing to substantiate copyright user rights and to give users the place they deserve in copyright law will be done at the peril of copyright law's legitimacy and sustainability. The exercise of substantiating copyright user rights as I do in this book is a timely one, with application and ramifications that extend in other areas of law and beyond the future of copyright law and policy.

# PART I

# IN SEARCH OF COPYRIGHT USER RIGHTS

# 1

# User Rights to Commercial Copies of Copyright Works

## A Peculiar Form of Personal Property

The nature of commercial copies of copyright works is much less explored than the nature of copyright.[1] Looking at copyright statutes for clarification on the nature of commercial copies of copyright works would be looking in vain as there is only the occasional reference that distinguishes ownership in the copy from copyright, as is the case in the US and in France.[2] Copyright laws generally define the exclusive rights and remedies of copyright holders and provide exceptions for certain acts that can be performed on copyright works without the authorization of copyright holders. Even with respect to exceptions to copyright infringement commonly referred to as 'user rights', the legal relationship between the user performing the

[1] The literature on the nature of copyright is abundant. For example see: Wendy J Gordon, 'An Inquiry into the Merits of Copyright: the Challenges of Consistency, Consent, and Encouragement Theory' (1989) 41 Stan L Rev 1343; L Ray Patterson & Stanley W Lindberg, *The Nature of Copyright: A Law of Users Rights* (Athens: University of Georgia Press, 1991); Mark A Lemley, 'Property, Intellectual Property and Free Riding' (2005) Texas L Rev 1031; Carys J Craig, 'Locke, Labour and Limiting the Author's Right: A Warning Against a Lockean Approach to Copyright Law' (2002) 28 Queen's LJ 1; Neil Weinstock Netanel, *Copyright's Paradox* (New York: Oxford University Press, 2008); Michael Spence, *Intellectual Property* (Oxford: Oxford University Press, 2007) at 12–50; Séverine Dusollier, *Droit d'auteur et protection des oeuvres dans l'univers numérique*, 2nd ed (Bruxelles: Larcier, 2007) at 309–28. Authors discussing the nature of rights to copies of copyright works include Joseph P Liu, 'Owning Digital Copies: Copyright Law and the Incidents of Copy Ownership' (2001) 42 Wm & Mary L Rev 1245; Dusollier, ibid at 377–418; Brian W Carver, 'Why License Agreements do not Control Copy Ownership: First Sales and Essential Copies' (2010) 25 BTLJ 1887; Aaron Perzanowski & Jason Schultz, 'Reconciling Intellectual & Personal Property' (2014) 90 Notre Dame L Rev 1.

[2] *Copyright Act*, 17 USC § 202 [*USC*]: 'Ownership of a copyright, or of any of the exclusive rights under a copyright, is distinct from ownership of any material object in which the work is embodied. Transfer of ownership of any material object, including the copy or phonorecord in which the work is first fixed, does not of itself convey any rights in the copyright work embodied in the object; nor, in the absence of an agreement, does transfer of ownership of a copyright or of any exclusive rights under a copyright convey property rights in any material object.' In France, *see* art L.111-3 CPI, which makes the distinction between ownership of copyright as intangible property and ownership in the material object that embeds the copyright work. Other copyright acts make no reference to the nature and scope of rights in commercial copies of copyright works: see e.g., the UK *Copyright, Designs and Patents Act 1988*, c 48 [*UKCDPA*], Canada's *Copyright Act*, RSC 1985, c C-42 [*Canada CA*], and Australia's *Copyright Act 1968* (Cth) [*Austl CA*].

Copyright User Rights: Contracts and the Erosion of Property. First Edition. Pascale Chapdelaine.

permitted acts and the copy of the work is not clearly spelled out.[3] The application of some of the exceptions to copyright infringement requires that the acts be performed on a copy that the user *owns*, or on a *lawfully acquired copy*.[4] However, the rights to copies of copyright works are left largely undefined, although there are some fragmented implications that can be derived from what copyright exclusive rights do not already cover. This is where property law and theory need to step in to augment understanding of the nature of commercial copies of copyright works and the rights users have to them.

A book, a music CD, a film, or video game DVD have long been recognized forms of personal property.[5] A tattoo protected by copyright and affixed on a human body would also qualify as the personal property of the person wearing it.[6] What is peculiar about copies of copyright works is that they embed two distinct sets of rights. When users buy a book, a music CD, or a video game DVD, they become the rightful owner of the chattel with powers and privileges to use and enjoy the copyright work that it embodies. Users do not become the owners of the copyright work per se.[7] The copyright holder is the owner of the copyright therein, which is a distinct form of intangible personal property.[8] Copyright also confers on copyright holders remote limited non-ownership proprietary interests to commercial copies of copyright works.[9] While copyright holders cannot use the physical

[3] For example, in *Canada CA* (n 2), this is the case for the application of the fair dealing provisions (ss 29–29.2), the non-commercial user-generated content provision (s 29.21), the private copying regime (ss 79–88), exceptions with respect to educational institutions and libraries, archives, and museums, although for some of the permitted uses it is implicit that the copy of the work from which they are allowed to perform acts without the authorization of copyright holders is under the control and power of the educational institution or library, archives, and museums (ss 29.4–30.5). The later listening or viewing exception requires that the programme to be recorded was received legally (s 29.23(1)(a)). See also: *UKCDPA* (n 2) ss 28A–31, 32–44A, 70–71; *USC* (n 2) §§ 107, 108(a)–(c), (f)–(i), 110, 121.

[4] For example in the *Canada CA* (n 2), this is a requirement for the application of the reproduction for private purposes exception (s 29.22), the backup copies' exception (s 29.24), the exception applying to computer programs (s 30.6). *USC*, (n 2) §§ 108 (d)–(e), 109(a), 109(d), 117. See also: *UKCDPA* (n 2), s 56, ss 31A–31C (requiring 'lawful possession' or 'lawful use').

[5] Numerous cases in Canada, the US, and the UK have recognized that copies of information products embedded in a physical medium are 'goods', often in cases involving the application of sale of goods law implied obligations. In the US, see *RRX Industries Inc v Lab-Con Inc*, 773 F (2d) 543 (9th Cir 1985); in the UK, see *St Albans City & District Council v International Computers Ltd*, [1997] FSR 251 (CA) [*St Albans*]; *Kingsway Hall Hotel Ltd v Red Sky IT (Hounslow) Ltd*, [2010] EWHC 965 (TCC). In Canada, see *Gerber Scientific Instrument Co v Bell-Northern Research Ltd* 17 BLR (2d) 21, 1994 CarswellOnt 1029(OCA).

[6] Yolanda M King, 'The Enforcement Challenges for Tattoo Copyrights' (2014) 22 J Intell Prop L 29 on the tension between the intellectual property rights of the tattoo artist and the owner of the copy of the tattoo.

[7] *USC* (n 2) § 202; art L.111-3 CPI (France). As noted by Julie E Cohen, 'Overcoming Property: Does Copyright Trump Privacy?' (2002) U Illinois J L Technology & Policy 375 at 378: 'Conditions imposed on would-be users of things embodying copyright works far outstrip any conditions imposed on would-be users of other kinds of things.'

[8] Although some property scholars and courts view copyright as personal property, whether copyright is property is the subject of ongoing debate. See Pascale Chapdelaine, 'The Property Attributes of Copyright' (2014) 10 Buffalo Intellectual Property L J 34.

[9] ibid at 61–64.

embodiment of their work (unless they simultaneously own the physical embodiment of the copyright work together with the copyright),[10] copyright holders control to a large extent the economic activity that revolves around that physical embodiment of the copyright work owned by consumers and other users.[11]

The personal property in copies of copyright works is often forgotten, including by courts and legislators.[12] The prominence of the literary, musical, or artistic work that forms the essence of the book, musical recording, computer program, or video game trivializes the physical medium that supports it and the rights that come with it, making them relatively insignificant in comparison.[13] In that respect, copyright's predominance on the commercialized products embodying copyright works is different from other intellectual property rights such as trademarks or patents that tend, in commerce, to be more incidental to the product to which they are associated.[14] The online distribution of copyright works reinforces the trivialization of the physical embodiment in contrast to the creative work because the transfer of a physical component to users with the work becomes less apparent.[15] As commentators aptly remarked: 'the copy is now a concept plagued by uncertainty'.[16]

The dichotomy between the personal property of the copy of the work embedded in the chattel (e.g., the book, the video game DVD) and the copyright that protects the work has been traditionally presented as the distinction between the tangible and the intangible, with the former being the copy of the copyright work and its physical embodiment owned or possessed by the user, and the latter being the bundle of exclusive rights as they relate to the work as materialized, that is, owned by the copyright holder.[17] The competing property interests of copyright holders and user-copy-owners are somewhat more apparent in presence of a physical embodiment of the copy of the work, and raise distinct issues when the physical embodiment is the human body, as is the case with tattoo art.[18]

As I discuss in Chapters 4 and 5, as copies of copyright works dematerialize, the distinction between tangibility and intangibility is an increasingly misleading and unsatisfactory dichotomy in the regulation of copyright user rights. One example

[10] E.g., when a sculptor or painter still owns the sculpture or the painting that they created.

[11] David Lametti, 'The Concept and Conceptions of Intellectual Property as Seen Through the Lens of Property' in G Comandé & G Ponzanelli, eds, *Scienza e Diritto nel Prisma del Diritto Comparato* (Torino: Giappichelli, 2004) at 281–82. For example, the exclusive reproduction and rental rights.

[12] See generally Carver (n 1).

[13] However, Dusollier (n 1) at 379 notes that, in theory, there is no hierarchy between the two competing rights.

[14] In the case of the commercial copy of a copyright work, the main object of the transaction is the work, to which the exclusive rights of copyright holders are related. In the case of other goods to which a trademark or patent are related, they are not the main object of the commercial transaction but incidental to it.

[15] By contrast, in a transaction that involves a music CD or film DVD, the digital copy is embedded in a physical medium that is normally sold.

[16] Perzanowski & Schultz (n 1) at 38.

[17] On the rights of copyright holders to the work, see Chapdelaine, 'Property Attributes of Copyright' (n 8) in particular at 55–59.

[18] See King (n 6). See Chapter 7: 'The Contributions of Property and Other Theories.'

is the struggle that legislators and courts have to define copies of copyright works not embodied in a physical object.

## Sometimes a 'Good' . . . and Sometimes Not

The nature of commercial copies of copyright works as 'goods' is a separate inquiry from their nature as personal property: while goods are usually personal property, many forms of personal property (e.g., debt, liquidated damages, promissory notes, shares, copyright) are considered 'choses in action',[19] which typically disqualify them as goods under sale of goods law.[20] Here, the existence of a physical object in which the copyright work is embedded often determines whether the user in possession of the copy of a copyright work may or may not invoke sale of goods and consumer law protection traditionally afforded to owners of goods.

In *St Albans City & District Council v International Computers Ltd* [*St Albans*][21] Sir Iain Glidewell of the Court of Appeal (of England and Wales) stated in a frequently cited *obiter dictum* that the presence or not of a physical medium to supply the copy of the computer software would be the decisive factor to determine whether a computer program qualified as a good or not.[22] Sir Iain made the distinction between the transfer of a computer disc for money, which would trigger the application of warranties under the applicable sale of goods law,[23] and transactions involving software without the transfer of a disc, which would not trigger such application.[24] However, in this case, the mere provision of a computer program would not, even though a disc was involved in the arrangement, have triggered the application of sale of goods implied warranties of quality and fitness for purpose because the installer had himself transferred the program onto the computer but had retained the disc.[25] The characterization that computer software

[19] WH Hastings Kelke, *An Epitome of Personal Property Law*, 3rd ed (London: Sweet & Maxwell, 1910) at 5–6.

[20] E.g., The *Sale of Goods Act 1979* (UK), c 54, s 61(1) [*UKSGA*], defines 'goods' as including 'all personal chattels other than things in action and money, and in Scotland all corporeal moveables except money'. In the US, the *Uniform Commercial Code*, (2002), online: <www.law.cornell.edu/ucc/ucc.table.html> accessed 4 February 2017 [*US UCC*], § 2-105 (1) defines goods as all things 'which are movable at the time of identification to a contract for sale', but excludes 'things in action'; Ontario *Sale of Goods Act*, RSO 1990, c S-1 [*OSGA*], s 1(1) defines goods as 'chattels personal' other than 'things in action'; Ontario *Consumer Protection Act*, SO 2002, c 30, schedule A [*OCPA*], s 1, has a broader definition of goods as 'any type of property'. In the EU, EC *Parliament and Council Directive 1999/44/EC of 25 May 1999 on certain aspects of the sale of consumer goods and associated guarantees*, [1999] OJ, L 171/07 at 12 [*Directive 1999/44/EC*], art 1(2)(b) defines goods as any 'tangible' movable item, with some limited exceptions.

[21] *St Albans* (n 5).

[22] ibid at 265–66. The defendant was under an express contractual obligation to provide the plaintiffs with software that would enable them to accomplish certain functions. It was therefore not necessary to consider the legal ground (e.g., statutory or common law) under which implied obligations would apply. Nourse LJ indicated concurrence with the *obiter dictum*: ibid at 259.

[23] As the allegedly defective instructions (e.g., the code in the computer program) were part of the disc, and would have made the disc (i.e., a good) defective: ibid at 265–66.

[24] ibid at 265–66. See also *Southwark LBC v IBM UK Ltd*, [2011] EWHC 549 (TCC).

[25] *St Albans* (n 5) at 266.

without a physical supporting medium is not a good, as suggested by Sir Iain's remarks, was applied or accepted in subsequent judgments,[26] while not followed in others.[27] Courts in the US and Canada have also been more readily inclined to find that commercial copies of copyright works are goods when a physical object is handed over,[28] and less consistently so in the absence of a physical supporting medium.[29]

Given the typical use and enjoyment of copyright works, the need for a physical object to qualify such works as a good is perplexing. For a large portion of copyright works, for example, software, books, musical recordings, the physical medium (i.e., the disc, the DVD, the book cover, and the paper) in/on which they are embedded has never been a defining component. It is the literary, functional,

[26] See *Horace Holman Group Ltd v Sherwood International Group Ltd* 2000 WL 491372 (TCC). See also *Southwark LBC v IBM UK Ltd* (n 24) at paras 96ff, where in an *obiter dictum* Akenhead J stated that software could constitute goods under *UKSGA* (n 20) but in the context of the transfer of a supporting physical medium such as a CD; *Gammasonics Institute for Medical Research Pty Ltd v Comrad Medical Systems Pty*, [2010] NSWSC 267 at paras 24–47: software downloaded from the Internet was not a good for Sale of Goods Act purposes. See *Your Response Ltd v Datateam Business Media Ltd*, [2014] EWCA Civ 281 (English CA); *Fern Computer Consultancy Ltd v Intergraph Cadworx & Analysis Solutions Inc*, [2014] EWHC 2908 (Ch).

[27] *The Software Incubator Ltd v Computer Associates UK Ltd* [2016] EWHC 1587 (QB) at paras 47–54.

[28] See *Gerber Scientific Instrument Co v Bell-Northern Research Ltd* (n 5); *Lalese Enterprises Inc v Arete Technologies Inc* (1994), 59 CPR (3d) 438, 1994 CarswellBC 1220 (WL Can) (SC); *Western Engineering Service Ltd v Canada Malting Co*, [1994] OJ No 2026 (QL) (Gen Div); *Classified Directory Publishers Inc v Image Management Technologies Inc*, 1995 CarswellOnt 2449 (WL Can) (Gen Div); *Michael's Pizzeria Ltd v LP Computer Solutions Inc* (1996), 139 Nfld & PEIR 295, 433 APR 295, 1996 CarswellPEI 31 (WL Can) (SC (TD)); *Villeseche v Total North Communication Ltd*, 1997 CarswellYukon 53 (WL Can) (CA); *WJ Caul Funeral Home Ltd v Pearce* (1997), 153 Nfld & PEIR 252, 1997 CarswellNfld 11 (WL Can) (TD); *Saskatoon Gold Brokers Inc v Datatec Computer Systems Ltd* (1986), 55 Sask R 241, 1986 CarswellSask 401 (WL Can) (QB); in the US, see *RRX Industries Inc v Lab-Con Inc*, 773 F (2d) 543 (9th Cir 1985). Courts tend to approach contracts for the supply of computer hardware and computer software as a whole as sale of goods: see Barry B Sookman, *Computer, Internet, and Electronic Commerce Law* (Toronto: Thomson Carswell, 1988) (loose-leaf at para 2.17(b)). In *Arvic Search Services Inc v Foam Shop Ltd*, 2008 ABPC 256, the court, in an *obiter dictum*, stated that software did not constitute goods. In that case, the issue of the application of implied obligations under the Alberta *Sale of Goods Act* did not need to be addressed as the issue to be tried revolved around the consequences of non-performance of the contract by both parties.

[29] In Canada, see e.g., *Arvic Search Services Inc v Foam Shop Ltd* (n 28) where the court in *obiter dictum* stated that software did not constitute goods. But see *PCM Technologies Inc v O'Toole*, 2012 ONSC 2534, 217 ACWS (3d) 581, where the court treated software as goods, even though software was not embodied in a physical medium. The issue of whether the software contracted for should be a good or service was not considered, and the analysis proceeded on the assumption that it was a good, with the court applying *Sale of Goods Act*, s 15. In the US, courts have been willing to consider software alone as involving a transaction in goods. See e.g., the frequently cited case *Schroders Inc v Hogan Systems Inc*, 522 NYS 2d 404 (NY Sup Ct 1987) at para 3 where the *US UCC* (n 20) (as adopted in the state of New York), was held to apply to software licences even if no hardware was being transferred; *Shema Kolainu-Hear our Voices v Providersoft, LLC*, 832 F Supp (2d) 194, 2010 WL 2075921 (EDNY Dist Ct 2010), where the court refers to case law supporting treatment of a software licence as a good under the *US UCC*, noting uncertainty in the area. In that case, the parties had agreed to treat the software licence agreement as 'goods'; *Gross v Symantec Corporation*, 2012 WL 3116158 (ND Cal) at 9 where the court held that software delivered online with no physical supporting medium qualified as goods under the California UCC; *Rottner v AVG Technologies USA Inc*, 943 F Supp (2d) 222 (D Mass 2013) treating malware downloaded from the internet as goods.

and artistic quality of the copyright works that users experience when buying such products, just as consumers buy lemonade or soda not for the bottle but for the drink it contains. The drink does not stop being a good because it is outside the bottle. In *Beta Computers (Europe) Ltd v Adobe Systems (Europe) Ltd*,[30] a judgment preceding *St Albans*,[31] Lord Penrose acknowledged the artificiality of making the supporting medium as the determining factor to qualify the object of the transaction of computer software as goods:

> It appears to emphasize the role of the physical medium, and to relate the transaction in the medium to sale or hire of goods. It would have the somewhat odd result that the dominant characteristic of the complex product, in terms of value or of the significant interests of parties, would be subordinated to the medium by which it was transmitted to the user in analyzing the true nature and effect of the contract. If one obtained computer programs by telephone, they might be introduced into one's own hardware and used as effectively as if the medium were a disk or CD or magnetic tape.[32]

And yet, the Court in *Beta Computers* refused to treat the supply of computer software as a sale of goods.[33] Courts' willingness to qualify copies of copyright works as goods when there is no physical supporting medium is variable. In a recent judgment by the High Court of England and Wales, Judge Waksman held that software was goods under the *Regulation 17(2) of the Commercial Agents (Council Directive) Regulations 1993*, noting the oddity of the requirement of a physical embodiment to qualify software as goods.[34]

The ambivalence on the treatment of copies of copyright works as goods in absence of a physical embodiment persists in more recent waves of regulation of 'digital content' both at the international and domestic levels. For instance, the Trans-Pacific Partnership (2016)[35] leaves it up to member states to determine whether trade of digital products through electronic transmission involves trade in goods or services.[36] Another approach to digital content is to regulate it (or at least some of it) as a *sui generis* category, that is, neither as goods or services. This is the case of EU *Directive 2011/83/EU*,[37] and of the proposal of an EU directive for the supply of digital content,[38] and at the domestic level, of the UK *Consumer Rights Act*.[39]

[30] 1996 SLT 604 (Outer House) [*Beta Computers*].

[31] *St Albans* (n 5).

[32] *Beta Computers* (n 30) at 608–09.

[33] ibid. In that case, Lord Penrose qualified the software licence agreement as a *sui generis* contract.

[34] *The Software Incubator Ltd v Computer Associates UK Ltd* (n 27).

[35] 4 February 2016, online: www.international.gc.ca/trade-agreements-accords-commerciaux/agr-acc/tpp-ptp/text-texte/toc-tdm.aspx?lang=eng accessed 4 February 2017. Signatories include Australia, Canada, Chile, Japan, Mexico, US, and Vietnam.

[36] ibid, art 14.1, n 3.

[37] EC, *Council and Parliament Directive 2011/83/EU of 22 November 2011 on consumer rights, amending Council Directive 93/13/EEC and Directive 1999/44/EC of the European Parliament and of the Council and repealing Council Directive 85/577/EEC and Directive 97/7/EC of the European Parliament and of the Council*, [2011] OJ, L 304/64 [*Directive 2011/83/EU*].

[38] EC, Commission, *Proposal for a Directive of the European Parliament and of the Council on certain aspects concerning contracts for the supply of digital content*, COM (2015) 634 final 2015/0287 (COD).

[39] *Consumer Rights Act*, 2015 (UK), c 15.

Chapter 4 critiques the requirement of a physical supporting medium exchanged hand-to-hand for commercial copies of copyright works to qualify as 'goods', and takes a closer look at more recent waves of regulation that create a *sui generis* category for digital content distinct from goods or services, in both cases through the tangibility and intangibility dichotomy.

## Do Users Own the Copies of Copyright Works They Buy?

The question whether users own the copies of copyright works they buy is a rather strange one: 'buying' or 'purchasing' something involves a sale, the essence of which is to transfer ownership from the seller to the buyer. And yet, determining whether users own the copies of copyright works they purchased is becoming increasingly complex, and its proper resolution is in my view critical to a large segment of copyright users.

Beyond ownership of commercial copies of copyright works (through purchase, gift, or bequest), users access copyright works through different legal relationships: they may borrow the copy from a library or from a friend or they may rent it (typically for a fixed period of time at the expiry of which possession is transferred back to the owner of the copy, e.g., in the days of video rentals). Copyright users may also view the work (e.g., through Internet streaming services) without ever being in possession or control of the copy. In a non-commercial context, users may download copies of copyright works when there is an express or implied licence authorizing them to do so, in which case they become the owner of the copy they have downloaded.

Whether users own the copies they buy determines whether they can benefit from important exceptions to copyright infringement or 'copyright user rights', including the first sale or exhaustion doctrine,[40] and from exceptions relating to computer programs.[41] Whether users own the copies they buy is a complex question for at least three reasons. First, the prevailing commercial practice under which copyright holders *license the copy* of the work (in addition to the copyright in the copy) is giving rise to inconsistent treatment by courts and significant confusion. Some courts have treated such transactions as a transfer of ownership to the user-buyer, regardless of the terms of the contract, while other courts have enforced terms licensing the copy without transferring ownership to buyers.[42] Second, the uncertain nature of copies of copyright works as goods, as discussed above, may have rippling effects on how courts characterize the commercial transaction through which users access copyright works, blurring the line between goods and services and consequently transforming a contract of sale into a contract

[40] 17 USC § 109(a),(d); *Canada CA* (n 2) ss 3(1)(j), 15(1.1)(e), 18(1.1)(b); *UKCDPA* (n 2) ss 18(3)(a).

[41] See e.g., *Canada CA* (n 2) s 30.6, 30.61; *USC* (n 2) § 117; *UKCDPA* (n 2) ss 50A–50D; *USC* (n 2) § 117.

[42] See Chapter 4: 'Ripple Effects on Sales and Licences'.

of services.[43] Third, even in a straightforward sale of the copy of a copyright work occasioning transfer of title in the copy to the user, the presence of copyright holders' exclusive rights to the work embedded in the copy requires a closer look at the requirements of ownership and the extent to which they are actually met for the copyright-user-buyer. The extent to which users own the copies they buy is an important question from a legal and normative perspective in the broader context of the progressive expansion of the scope of copyright holders' exclusive rights in the last century.

## Copyright users and the ownership spectrum

In *Property and Justice*,[44] James W Harris defines the essence of every property institution as the twin manifestation of trespassory rules[45] and the existence of an ownership spectrum.[46] These various forms of ownership have in common: (i) a juridical relation between a person and a resource, which implies the ability to identify each and a separateness between the two;[47] (ii) privileges and powers that are open ended;[48] and (iii) that authorize self-seekingness by the owner.[49] Self-seekingness refers to the intimate relationship between the owner and the resource determining how they choose to dispose of the resource, with *prima facie* no duty to account to any one for the merit or rationality of that preference.[50] While 'full-blooded ownership'[51] is the strongest illustration of all three characteristics on the ownership spectrum, at the other end, mere property embraces 'some open-ended set of use-privileges and some open-ended set of powers of control over uses made by others'.[52] For instance, full powers of transmission may not be present in the case of mere property, while it is *prima facie* the case in full-blooded ownership.

Harris's detailed articulation of the heterogeneous nature of property, the ownership spectrum, the operation of property limitations, as well as his characterization of intellectual property is particularly helpful to better understand the nature of rights users have in copies of copyright works. Lawfully acquired copies of copyright works are a unique form of personal property that is heavily subject to the

[43] ibid. [44] James W Harris, *Property and Justice* (Oxford: Clarendon Press, 1996).

[45] ibid at 25, 86: 'trespassory rules' refer to all rules which, by reference to a resource, impose obligations (negative or positive) upon an open-ended range of persons, with the exception of some privileged individual, group, or agency (i.e., the owner(s)). They are open-ended, and give rise to various civil or criminal remedies such as damages, possessory recovery, injunction, or restitution. They presuppose the existence of a separate, reasonably identifiable resource.

[46] ibid at 5: the ownership spectrum spans from 'mere property' to 'full-blooded ownership'.

[47] ibid at 332; James E Penner, *The Idea of Property in Law* (Oxford: Clarendon Press, 1997) at 105–28.

[48] E.g., art 947 CCQ defines the right of ownership as 'the right to use, enjoy and dispose of property fully and freely, subject to the limits and conditions for doing so determined by law.'

[49] Harris (n 44) at 5. [50] ibid at 65.

[51] ibid at 30, defines 'full-blooded ownership' as the relationship between a person (or persons) and a thing such that he (or they) have *prima facie* unlimited privileges of use or abuse over the thing and *prima facie* unlimited powers of control and transmission, so far as such use or exercise of power does not infringe some property independent prohibition.'

[52] ibid at 29.

exclusive rights of copyright holders. The *ownership spectrum* and the gradation of rights that Harris describes help break down the powers and privileges of copyright holders over their intangible resource (copyright), as well as the powers and privileges of the personal property owners of the tangible resource (the commercial copy) embedding the copyright work.

To what extent are the features on Harris's ownership spectrum present with respect to commercial copies of copyright works? To what extent do commercial copies of copyright works give rise to trespassory powers? In answer to the second question, owners of commercial copies of copyright works have trespassory powers similar to owners of other forms of personal property, powers that give rise to legal remedies, including revesting of the personal property in case of theft.[53]

To answer the first question, that is, the extent to which commercial copies of copyright works share the characteristics that are common to all ownership interests, I will apply each of the three features on the ownership spectrum to determine the extent to which consumers *own* the commercial copies of copyright works they purchase.

### *Juridical relation between a person and a resource*

The requirement of a juridical relation between a person and a resource on the ownership spectrum implies that the person and the resource can be identified, as well as separateness between the two.[54] Every form of property also implies a scarcity in resources and an exercise of wealth allocation.[55] In the case of consumers of commercial copies of copyright works embedded in physical objects, the requirement of a juridical relation between a person and a resource is easily fulfilled. The user and the commercial copies of copyright works are identifiable and each one is separate. The requirement in some jurisdictions of fixation, for a work to be protected by copyright, imposes that separateness between the author and their work and subsequently between the author (or copyright holder) and users of the work.[56] Fixation enables the creation of an identifiable and perceptible work product that persists in time beyond its moment of creation or interpretation.[57]

As I discuss in Chapter 4, the juridical relation between users and copyright holders may be less obvious when the work is accessed online with no physical supporting medium. Depending on the transaction, the user may be acquiring a

[53] E.g., see British Columbia *Sale of Goods Act*, RSBC 1996, c 410, s 29.

[54] This is a requirement for any property institution: Harris (n 44) at 332; James E Penner (n 47) at 105–28.

[55] Harris (n 44) at 24.

[56] *Berne Convention for the Protection of Literary and Artistic Works*, 9 September 1886, 828 UNTS 221 art 2(2) leaves it to member states to impose a requirement of fixation for eligibility of protection. In some jurisdictions, copyright law imposes a requirement of fixation for works of authorship to be protected: see *Théberge* v. *Galerie d'art du Petit Champlain inc*, 2002 SCC 34, at para 145: 'The work is, so to speak, the physical outcome of the creative process. Fixation of the work in a medium is a condition *sine qua non* of the production of a work.'

[57] In that sense and to some extent, the requirement of fixation in copyright law shares a common preoccupation with the qualification of 'goods' in sale of goods law (and consumer law).

product or using a service that will give rise to a different juridical relation between the user and the copy.[58] Nevertheless, in each case there is separateness between the user and the copyright work. We can safely assume that the first requirement on the ownership spectrum of a relationship between a person and a resource is easily met in the case of users and commercial copies of copyright works.

### *Open-ended privileges and powers*

The second feature common to all ownership interests on the ownership spectrum is that the privileges and powers that a person has with respect to a resource are *prima facie* open-ended.[59] The open-ended texture of powers and privileges sets property interests apart from other non-ownership proprietary interests that confer specific privileges and powers.[60] The infinite ways by which a person can *prima facie* interact with a resource distinguish ownership interests in a resource from those in a product, the use of which would be entirely governed by the terms of a contract, as is sometimes the case in virtual worlds.[61] The significance of *prima facie* open-ended powers and privileges to define ownership of a resource is sometimes overlooked in property theory.[62]

In principle, users' powers and privileges in relation to commercial copies of copyright works should allow consumers to perform any act that is not exclusively reserved to copyright holders[63] (or restricted by contract), any act that has been authorized by the copyright holder, and any act that falls under one of the exceptions to copyright infringement.[64]

In the realm of copyright users' *prima facie* open-ended privileges and powers, consumers and other users may read, listen to, view, or play permanent copies of a book, musical recording, film, or computer program that they own as often as they please. Consumers can play the musical recording as part of a performance or skit

58 See Chapter 4: 'Misconceptions about Tangibility and Intangibility in Defining Information Products.'

59 Harris (n 44) at 5.

60 ibid at 55–58 (e.g., easements would fall under the category of non-ownership proprietary interests).

61 On the rights of members to virtual world sites largely defined by contracts see generally Joshua AT Fairfield, 'Virtual Property' (2005) 85 BUL Rev 1047; and Greg Lastowka, *Virtual Justice* (New Haven and London: Yale University Press, 2010) at 193.

62 On various conceptions of property, see Chapdelaine, 'Property Attributes of Copyright' (n 8) 52–53. On the effects that a specific view of property as being 'an infinitely malleable bundle of rights' has in the online world and intersection between contract and property, see Perzanowski & Schultz (n 1) at 19, 27–32.

63 I.e., the exclusive right to produce or reproduce the work, to communicate it to the public, to perform it in public, to rent computer programs and musical recordings, to authorize the first sale of each copy of copyright works (e.g., see *Canada CA* (n 2) ss 3, 15, 18, 21, 26), and in some jurisdictions, to create derivative works (see e.g., *USC* (n 2) §106 (2)).

64 Liu, 'Owning Digital Copies' (n 1) at 1287 notes, regarding the unlimited ability to read copies of copyright works (in a US context): 'The legal "source" of this unlimited ability to read, to the extent there is one, can be found in the gaps in the *Copyright Act*. Section 106 of the Act, as several commentators have noted, does not include in the bundle of copyright rights the right to control the reading of a given copy.'

in the privacy of their home, can mark the commercial copies of copyright works with their name, can restore them,[65] or can lend the copies to friends. All these acts are not exclusively reserved to copyright holders and should therefore be part of the *prima facie* open-ended powers and privileges of copy owners.

The permanent possession of the copy of a copyright work and the power to transfer the title to the copy are important open-ended powers and privileges that are characteristic of ownership.[66] Permanent possession and the physical control of the copy withstand the open-endedness of copyright users' other powers and privileges. The power of permanent possession and the power to transfer title of the copy differentiate ownership from a lease, or a loan, or accessing a service under which the right to possess and the right to transfer title are either temporary or non-existent.

As a result of rights exclusively reserved to copyright holders under copyright law, users may not reproduce any copyright work and cannot play a musical recording or film in public,[67] including at a neighbourhood fair,[68] during a public performance in a park, or at the corner store where they work part-time, without obtaining the authorization of the copyright holders or paying royalties to the relevant copyright collective body.[69] Users may not create derivative works from the work, telecommunicate to the public any substantial portion of their book, musical recording, or film, including posting it on Facebook, YouTube, or on their personal website, without the prior consent of the copyright holders (which may be implied), or unless it falls under one of the exceptions to copyright infringement.[70] The list of usage restrictions imposed on copies of copyright works goes on and on.

On the ownership spectrum, the ability to generate revenue from commercial copies of copyright works is one of the most constrained powers and privileges of users. The commercial character of the use will bar or lessen users' ability to invoke exceptions to copyright infringement.[71] There are qualifications: for example, except for computer programs, cinematographic works, or other types of works which may be specified in domestic copyright law, users may generally rent out

[65] Copy owners have rights to make modifications and repair at common law: David Vaver, *Intellectual Property Law Copyright, Patents, Trademarks*, 2nd ed (Toronto: Irwin Law, 2011) at 219–20.

[66] Tony Honoré, 'Ownership' in Tony Honoré, ed, *Making Law Bind, Essays Legal and Philosophical* (Oxford: Clarendon Press, 1987) 161 at 166–79.

[67] However, they can recite in public 'a reasonable extract from a published work': *Canada CA* (n 2) s 32.2(d).

[68] Unless the use would fall under one of the limited exceptions to copyright infringement for educational institutions: ibid ss 29.4–30.

[69] Either directly or through the relevant collective agency that is administered by the Copyright Board under ibid ss 2 (see 'collective society') and 67(a).

[70] See Chapter 2.

[71] The commercial character of the acts performed on a work is a bar to the application of the non-commercial user-generated content exception to copyright infringement (*Canada CA* (n 2) s 29.21). The commercial character of the use and the potential impact on the market of the copyright work are among the factors to consider (although not determinant) to assess whether the dealing in a work is fair under the fair use and fair dealing exceptions to copyright infringement: see *USC* (n 2) § 107; *CCH Canadian Ltd v Law Society of Upper Canada*, 2004 SCC 13 at paras 53ff.

the commercial copies of copyright works they own, as long as doing so does not involve a reproduction of the work, an act reserved to copyright holders.[72]

The open-endedness of copyright users' powers and privileges over their commercial copies of copyright works increasingly diminishes as copyright holders' exclusive rights continue to expand.[73] As one commentator observes, it is as if the fear of weakening copyright as intangible property justifies each time increasing the powers of property in other things (e.g., commercial copies) through which it takes form.[74] Quite apart from the duration of copyright, which has progressively increased over time,[75] the addition of exclusive rental rights,[76] the right to prevent parallel imports and the exclusive right of distribution,[77] the creation of new access-control rights,[78] and the less than certain application of exhaustion or first sale doctrine to digital copies distributed online with no physical supporting medium,[79] are examples of copyright holders' exclusionary powers that directly interfere with copy owners' powers and privileges beyond the traditional right to control the reproduction of works and their performance in public.[80] The distinction between the exclusive rental or distribution right and other exclusive rights is disappearing when works are embedded in digital copies. As users are increasingly empowered technologically in relation to their uses of copyright works, restrictions

[72] The *Agreement on Trade-Related Aspects of Intellectual Property Rights, Marrakesh Agreement Establishing the World Trade Organization, Annex 1C*, 15 April 1994, 1869 UNTS 29, 33 ILM 1197 art 11 requires member states to confer to copyright holders the exclusive right to authorize rental of computer programs and cinematographic works, with some exceptions; *Canada CA* (n 2) s 3(1)(i) (exclusive right to authorize rental of sound recordings embedding musical recordings). But see *Directive 2006/115/EC* (n 76) on the broader exclusive right to authorize rental in the EU.

[73] Jessica Litman, *Digital Copyright* (Amherst: Prometheus Books, 2001) ch 3, in a US context, on the shift toward more protection of right holders accelerated since the mid-seventies; Chapdelaine, 'Property Attributes of Copyright' (n 8) at 34–35; On the progressive expansion of copyright protection at the international level and in Canada, see Pascale Chapdelaine, *Copyright Consumers' Bargain, Defining the Rights to Commercial Copies of Copyright Works* (Doctor of Philosophy Thesis, York University Graduate Program in Law, Osgoode Hall Law School Library, 2013) at 149–54.

[74] Cohen (n 7) at 379.

[75] Chapdelaine, *Copyright Consumers' Bargain* (n 73) at 149–54.

[76] In Europe, EC, *Parliament and Council Directive 2006/115/EC on rental right and lending right and on certain rights related to copyright in the field of intellectual property*, [2006] OJ, L 376/28 art 3, requires all Member States to provide the exclusive right to copyright holders to authorize the rental of copies with respect to all copyright works and other subject of copyright with limited exceptions (i.e., it does not apply to buildings and to works of applied art). The Directive repeals EC, *Council Directive 92/100/EEC on rental right and lending right and on certain rights related to copyright in the field of intellectual property*, [1992] OJ, L 346/61, which already provided for the application of the exclusive rental right to a similar broad range of copyright works and other subject matter of copyright. For the US, see *USC* §§ 106(3), 109(b)(1)(A). In Canada, the exclusive right to authorize the rental of copies of copyright works applies to computer programs and to sound recordings of musical works: *Canada CA* (n 2) s 3(1)(h)–(i).

[77] E.g., *Canada CA* (n 2) s 27.1; s 3(j) confers the exclusive right to copyright holders 'in the case of a work that is in the form of a tangible object, to sell or otherwise transfer ownership of the tangible object, as long as that ownership has never previously been transferred in or outside Canada with the authorization of the copyright owner.'

[78] See Chapter 6. [79] See Chapter 5: 'The thorny question of digital exhaustion.'

[80] E.g., the rental right involves no copy being made of copyright works and is closely associated with the right to transfer the copy of the work, which through the application of exhaustion or the first sale doctrine is within the exclusive domain of copy owners: see Chapter 5.

on the right to reproduce or on the ability to make digital copies available to the public are becoming as intrusive on the property rights of the digital copy owner as restrictions on the right to transfer or rent the digital copy. While there is an increase of copyright holders' control over privileges and powers that were traditionally reserved to copyright users, the reverse is also true: some legislatures increase the acts users can do without the authorization of copyright holders by adding new exceptions to copyright infringement.[81]

The restrictions imposed by copyright on commercial copies of copyright works go to the heart of the open-ended privileges and powers of consumers. A comparison of an electronic book protected by copyright with an electronic book in which all copyright has expired after the copy was purchased illustrates that point. In the latter case, consumers should, in principle, be allowed to make as many copies as they wish for time- or space-shifting purposes, give the copies to friends, or post copies on the Internet. They can convert the work into a play or reproduce substantial parts and incorporate the copy in other works. All these acts would be restrained if the copyright had not expired.[82] The list of powers and privileges is open-ended and neither do users need to ask permission of anyone, nor is there any contract that tells them that they can perform all of these acts. They simply can do them, as owners or possessors of the copy of the electronic book, *in which copyright has expired.*

Even the most basic *prima facie* open-ended privileges and powers of users—to play, view, listen to, or read commercial copies of copyright works—are increasingly falling under the control of copyright holders, particularly when the works are distributed online with no physical supporting medium. An expansionist view of copyright, that is one under which copyright holders' exclusive powers and privileges should allow them to control access and uses of their works in their entirety,[83] has favoured the adoption at the international and national levels of legal regimes strengthening the effects of technological measures that copyright holders apply to their works to protect their access and use.[84] Restrictions of use dictated through non-negotiated standard end-user agreements also increase copyright holders' control over their works.[85]

The open-ended power and privilege to transfer title to commercial copies of copyright works is also increasingly under threat. Traditionally, consumers could

[81] See Chapter 2.

[82] Subject to the application of specific limitations to the exclusive rights of copyright holders, including fair dealing.

[83] See e.g., Jane C Ginsburg, 'Essay: From Having Copies to Experiencing Works: The Development of an Access Right in US Copyright Law' (2003) 50 J Copyright Society USA 113 at 120–21: 'the right to control the manner in which members of the public apprehend the work. The concept is distinct from reproduction or communication to the public to the extent that I may communicate a copy of my work to the user's hard drive, or the user may purchase a digital copy such as a CD ROM, but the user may not "open" the work to apprehend (listen to, view) its contents, unless the user acquires the "key" to the work. And the key may vary with the nature and extent of enjoyment of the work.'

[84] See Chapter 6.

[85] See Pascale Chapdelaine, 'The Ambiguous Nature of Copyright Users' Rights' (2013) 26 IPJ 1 at 26–28.

sell, donate, otherwise dispose of, or destroy the commercial copies of copyright works they purchased. However, contract terms restraining consumers' ability to transfer or assign their commercial copies of copyright works have been held valid in spite of the exhaustion or first sale doctrine. The application of the doctrine is even less certain when digital copies are distributed online with no physical supporting medium.[86] As a result, the ability of consumers to transfer their commercial copies of copyright works—one of the fundamental open-ended powers and privileges on the ownership spectrum—is also under threat.

In the case of commercial copies of copyright works, the second feature on the ownership spectrum by which the powers and privileges of the resource are open-ended is much more constrained than most other forms of personal property.[87] The review conducted here of open-ended powers and privileges and the limitation thereto reveals that the restrictions on commercial copies of copyright works are substantial and increasingly so. I shall now examine the extent to which the privileges and powers related to commercial copies of copyright works authorize consumers' self-seekingness.

### *Privileges and powers that authorize self-seekingness on the part of the owner*

The third feature common to all ownership interests on the ownership spectrum is that the privileges and powers that a person has in the resource confers privileges and powers that authorize self-seekingness on the part of the owner.[88] Self-seekingness is the intimate relationship between the owner and the resource as to how the owner chooses to dispose of the resource, with *prima facie* no duty to account to anyone about the merit or rationality of that preference.[89]

The self-seekingness component common to all ownership interests is particularly significant for consumers of commercial copies of copyright works, although also present within the broader category of users. Consumers, as typically defined by law, perform acts within their personal and intimate sphere of interest and not for business purposes.[90] On that terrain, the constraints on consumers' open-ended powers and privileges have repercussions on the extent to which the commercial copies of copyright works they own authorize self-seekingness.[91] The limitations on consumers' open-ended powers and privileges related to the commercial copies of copyright works they own are not trivial: they go to the heart of the uses that consumers increasingly want to make of copyright works.[92]

[86] See Chapter 5.

[87] As Cohen (n 7) at 378, notes: 'The expansion is particularly dramatic in the case of things embodying works, and not just because the bundle of rights conferred by copyright is particularly limited to start with. Conditions imposed on would-be users of things embodying copyright works far outstrip any conditions imposed on would-be users of other kinds of things.'

[88] Harris (n 44) at 5. [89] ibid at 65.

[90] See definition of 'consumer' under *Consumer Rights Act 2015* (UK), c 15, s 2(3); *US UCC* (n 20) § 1-201(b)(11); *OCPA* (n 20) s 1.

[91] See above: 'Open-ended privileges and powers.'

[92] For a review of consumer uses and expectations of copyright works, see e.g.: Center for Democracy & Technology, 'Evaluating DRM: Building a Marketplace for the Convergent World'

They directly and materially impede the *prima facie* self-seekingness that ownership in copies of copyright works should include.[93] The situation in relation to copyright works is reversed: consumers are, to a large extent, *a priori* banned from the self-seekingness aspect of their property rights in the commercial copies of the copyright works they own. As a corollary to the important limitations on consumers' open-ended powers and privileges, the ability of commercial copies of copyright works to authorize self-seekingness is also compromised in comparison to other forms of personal property.

## Commercial Copies of Copyright Works and the Standardization of Property

The standardization of property or *numerus clausus* is the principle by which there is a fixed and closed list of property interests recognized by law. *Numerus clausus* is generally understood to be part of the civil law tradition, although the doctrine is not applied consistently,[94] and in some jurisdictions there is serious doubt as to the extent to which the principle still reflects the state of the law.[95] Civil law defines property interests through entitlements of ownership[96] and its possible dismemberments.[97] Restriction of 'the exercise of the right to dispose of property' is explicitly prohibited except in limited circumstances,[98] and is subject to specific conditions.[99] There is a growing recognition that a similar

(2006) at 7–8, online: <www.cdt.org/copyright/20060907drm.pdf> accessed 4 February 2017; see also Pamela Samuelson & Jason Schultz, 'Should Copyright Owners Have to Give Notice of Their Use of Technical Protection Measures?' (2007) 6 J Telecommunications & High Technology L 41 at 44–45.

[93] Joseph P Liu, 'Copyright Law's Theory of the Consumer' (2003) 44 Boston College L Rev 397 at 412, refers to copyright works as not only being individual consumer goods but as also being social goods: 'to make sense of and interpret many copyright works meaningfully, it is sometimes necessary to communicate with others about the works; to share viewpoints, to debate, and to argue. Although some works can certainly be consumed alone, by an individual consumer, many works are suited to social consumption. The ability to communicate about copyright works enriches our understanding of those works and enables us to get much more out of them.'

[94] David Lametti, 'Concept of Property: Relations through Objects of Social Wealth' (2003) 53 UTLJ 325 at 360–61, on the application of *numerus clausus* in the Québec civil law system.

[95] See *Société la Maison de la Poésie* v. *Société des Auteurs et Compositeurs dramatiques (SACD)*, Cass civ 3$^{e}$, 31 October 2012, (2012) Bull civ III, No 84, where the French cour de cassation recognized the creation of a *sui generis* real right with respect to immovable property (building) other than the real rights listed in the French civil code.

[96] Art 947 CCQ enumerates the rights of ownership as 'the right to use, enjoy and dispose of property fully and freely.'

[97] Art 1119 CCQ lists the dismemberments of ownership as 'usufruct, use, servitude and emphyteusis' and confirms that they are real rights.

[98] Art 1212 CCQ imposes this prohibition, except if it is done by gift or will.

[99] ibid: it needs to be in writing and it is only valid 'if it is temporary and justified by a serious and legitimate interest.' Art. 1214 CCQ provides that 'it may not be set up against third persons uses unless it is published in the proper register.'

principle exists in the common law,[100] although this recognition is not without controversy.[101]

One consequence of *numerus clausus* is to set important limitations on freedom of contract by restraining how owners can alter the nature of their property rights as they transfer them to others.[102] The *numerus clausus* principle flows from the *opposability to all* feature of property and, as some commentators argue, serves to reduce the overall information costs with respect to similar rights.[103] Merrill and Smith explain the dynamics at play when applying *numerus clausus* as the need to constrain the information-processing costs of parties that are not privy to a contract that creates another species of property rights:

> by allowing even one person to create an idiosyncratic property right, the information processing costs of all persons who have existing or potential interests in this type of property go up. This external cost on other market participants forms the basis of our explanation of the *numerus clausus*.[104]

As a result, this feature of the property institution reflects the need to reach the optimal standardization of property law.[105] The need to standardize forms of property rights is as much the prerequisite of an essential characteristic of property as being 'opposable to all' as it is the rectifying tool to preserve it. How can a right efficiently be opposable to all if it can always be subject to innumerable customizations and alterations? And how can this distinctive feature of property survive without maintaining that standardization?

The efficiency rationale invoked by Merrill and Smith to justify maintaining a uniformity of property interests is a compelling justification that benefits all community members who have similar ownership rights to the ones of the owner who alters them through one transaction, and also benefits future transferees of the resource to which the ownership rights have been altered in an unconventional manner.

Commentators debate the existence of the *numerus clausus* principle in the common law tradition.[106] First, the principle is hard to reconcile with the need to adapt property rights to the various needs of property owners.[107] Second, the notification of terms can in fact reduce information costs without the standardization of property.[108]

The first argument invoked against *numerus clausus*, that favours tailored property interests to suit individual needs over the standardization of property has some merit when it can be established that users have a broad range of needs with respect

[100] Thomas Merrill & Henry Smith, 'Optimal Standardization in the Law of Property: The Numerus Clausus Principle' (2000) 110 Yale LJ 1: the authors conducted a survey on the common law of property to demonstrate that the same principle exists in this legal tradition, although not uniformly and without bearing any specific appellation; see Henry Hansmann & Reinier Kraakman, 'Property, Contract, and Verification: The Numerus Clausus Problem and the Divisibility of Rights' (2002) 31 J Leg Stud 373. See also Hanoch Dagan, *Property Values and Institutions* (Oxford: Oxford University Press, 2011) at 4, on why the author supports the *numerus clausus* principle within the institutions of property.

[101] E.g., see Glen O Robinson, 'Personal Property Servitudes' (2004) 71 U Chicago L Rev 1449.

[102] Merrill & Smith (n 100) at 5–6.

[103] ibid at 8.

[104] ibid at 27.

[105] ibid at 40.

[106] E.g., see Robinson (n 101).

[107] ibid.

[108] ibid at 1487.

to specific products and that the market is able to respond to those individual preferences. Obviously, the argument of choice and preferences is relevant only to the extent that the preference of the user is one that the application of the standardization of property would restrict. It seems that the non-application of *numerus clausus* would do the exact opposite: enable copyright holders to constrain users' increasingly threatened power to transfer the copies they lawfully possess.[109] The non-application of *numerus clausus* also sits well with a broad application and interpretation of the exclusive right to authorize the distribution of copyright works, giving carte blanche and much control to copyright holders as to how they make their works available (including by creating a *sui generis* property right in the commercial copy). Also, in consumer transactions of commercial copies of copyright works, there are indications that at least some of the restrictions imposed on the commercial copies are widespread rather than varied and individualized, for example, restrictions on alienation of the commercial copy or on the ability to produce derivative works from the work embedded in the commercial copy.[110] Restrictions on the alienation of commercial copies increase the power and control of copyright holders over the commercialization of their works and are unlikely to be in place to respond to specific consumer needs.[111] While the restrictions on alienation of the commercial copy would typically fall within the purview of contractual clauses that the application of the *numerus clausus* principle could set aside, the application of the *numerus clausus* principle would not set aside restrictions such as the prohibition of the creation of derivative works. The right to create derivative works is part of copyright holders' exclusive rights, while the right to control the subsequent transfer of copies of copyright works, is not typically so.[112]

The second argument against *numerus clausus*, that is, that notification can reduce information costs without resorting to the standardization of property depends on the ability of the notification to effectively communicate a new property interest.[113] Even assuming that a notice meets the standard of effective communication that implies that consumers will understand its meaning and ramifications, it is questionable that notices could ever reduce information transaction costs to the same extent that the standardization of property can. A limited list of forms of property will always, conceptually, be more efficient than notifications giving potentially rise to different forms of property interests for each new transaction. Even if a new form of property interest becomes an industry norm, consumers

[109] See below: 'If neither owned by the copyright user nor a good, then what?'

[110] Chapdelaine, 'Ambiguous Nature of Users' Rights' (n 85) at 26–28.

[111] A distinction needs to be made between the rental of a commercial copy that would restrict alienation powers while at the same time responding to specific consumer needs and a transaction that would resemble a sale in all other material aspects except for the restriction on alienation of the commercial copy.

[112] See Chapter 5. Some may criticize that view on the basis that the exclusive distribution right effectively allows copyright holders to retain control over copies of copyright works and to shape the transaction accordingly.

[113] E.g., a prominent notice on packaging of a commercial copy of copyright work would more effectively reduce information costs than a clause in lengthy standard terms and conditions.

would never know for sure because it could always be subject to change and remain within the control of suppliers.

The scepticism about the standardization of property can be justified to some extent when the *numerus clausus* principle implicates a trade-off: more standardization gives rise to greater efficiency for the collectivity of owners of similar interests; however, it may reduce some choices (assuming that consumers have myriad preferences for a particular product, that the market adequately responds to individual user preferences, and that the choices in question would be of a nature to be limited through the standardization of property). In the case of mundane consumer transactions of commercial copies of copyright works, it is not clear that the standardization of property would limit choices for users. In the context of the mass commercialization of information products, reasons in addition to economic efficiency may support the application of the *numerus clausus* principle, for example the need to rectify various asymmetries between suppliers and purchasers.[114]

Commentators who doubt the existence of the *numerus clausus* principle, or question its raison d'être, seem to minimize the *in rem*, or opposable to all distinctive feature of property. In that view, property and contracts are two forms of private ordering and, on that basis, sceptics question why courts should give precedence to property over contracts by refusing to enforce contract clauses that go against, *inter alia*, the standardization of property.[115] To accommodate individual needs, the freedom of contract of private parties should prevail over broader collective implications and the standardization of property.[116]

Commercial copies of copyright works do not fare so well on the terrain of the *numerus clausus* principle compared to other forms of property, and arguably, even less so than copyright as a form of intangible property.[117] On the one hand, the limitations imposed on the open-ended powers and privileges of consumers by copyright holders' exclusive rights could be viewed as not derogating from the *numerus clausus* principle. On that view, limitations imposed by copyright on commercial copies of copyright works illustrate the flexibility of property and the endless variations of ownership interests that exist on the ownership spectrum. In the same vein, the progressive expansion of copyright holders' exclusive rights is merely moving commercial copies of copyright works further down on the ownership spectrum, without disqualifying the ownership proprietary interest users have in them.

On the other hand, commercial copies of copyright works may be outliers to the *numerus clausus* principle in important respects. The complex relationship between

[114] There may be other issues: see Molly Shaffer Van Houweling, 'The New Servitudes' (2008) 96 Geo LJ 885 at 924–49, where the author raises concerns on contractual restrictions on information products' uses, which the author calls 'the new servitudes', by looking at three main areas of concern that arise with respect to real property and personal property servitudes, i.e., notice and information costs, the problem of the future, and externalities.

[115] Robinson (n 101) at 1477–78.

[116] ibid.

[117] Chapdelaine, 'Property Attributes of Copyright' (n 8) at 64–67.

the exclusive rights of copyright holders and the ownership rights of users to commercial copies of copyright works may lead the judiciary to misinterpret the scope of copyright holders' exclusive rights, and in turn lead to greater discrepancies in the homogeneity of the rights pertaining to commercial copies of copyright works than with respect to other forms of personal property.[118]

Commercial copies of copyright works do not conform to the *numerus clausus* principle when copyright holders restrict, through widespread licensing practices, consumers' and other users' rights to transfer copies of copyright works.[119] To the extent that these rights are enforced by contract or otherwise, the restriction of the power to alienate potentially disqualifies commercial copies of copyright works from being the personal property of copyright users. Similarly, the non-applicability of the exhaustion doctrine to digital copies of copyright works distributed online with no hand-to-hand exchange has the same effect.[120] The restriction on users' power to alienate commercial copies of copyright works while having indefinite powers of possession[121] creates a *sui generis* form of property interest that does not equate to any known dismemberments of ownership. This is precisely what the *numerus clausus* principle seeks to prevent or even forbid.

## If Neither Owned by the Copyright User Nor a Good, Then What?

The changing nature of copies of copyright works, from 'goods' to legally undefined, or *sui generis* products, and the decline if not vanishing of users' ownership of copies of copyright works, is the untold story about copyright user rights. These changes have been happening in parallel to the more publicized way copyright has expanded under international conventions and national laws over the last century, and they are progressively eroding the powers and privileges of copyright users.

The practice of licensing the copy of the copyright work rather than selling it begs two important questions: what precise property rights does the user-recipient of the copy of the copyright work have and what rights does the copyright-holder-supplier retain in the copy? At first sight, it seems that in a scenario of licensing copies of the copyright work, neither the copyright-holder-supplier nor the recipient-user owns the personal property that comprises the commercial copy. The user-recipient typically has permanent possession and physical control of the copy, but they are restrained from transferring title to it. The copyright-holder-supplier usually reserves transfer of title in the copy but does not retain ownership of the copy either, the user-recipient being vested with permanent possession and

[118] E.g., see Pascale Chapdelaine, 'The Undue Reliance on the Physical Object in the Regulation of Information Products' (2015) 20 J Tech L & Pol'y 65 at 96–100, on the confusion that subsists between the intellectual property rights in the copyright work and the personal property rights in the copy.

[119] See Chapter 5: 'The commercial practice not to sell copies.'

[120] See Chapter 5.

[121] See below: 'If neither owned by the copyright user nor a good, then what?'

physical control of the copy.[122] Does this result make any sense? [123] Is the creation of a new property interest justified and for what purpose, considering its impact on users, on balancing competing interests in copyright law, on legal certainty, economic efficiency, and other issues identified in this chapter on the merits of the standardization of property?[124]

How have we moved from the long-standing non-controversial proposition that commercial copies of copyright works are the personal property of their owner-recipients to users not really owning the copies they acquire with their basic power to transfer title being stripped away? And how did we get to commercial copies of copyright works not being recognized as 'goods' by law when the copyright work is not embedded in a physical object?

Unlike other forms of property, whereby the exclusionary powers associated with ownership mean that the owner has the power to set the agenda,[125] in relation to the ownership of copies of copyright works, we have come to accept that this agenda is to be almost exclusively set by the copyright holder. In a new copyright era, where copyright work access-controls merge with the control of acts reserved to copyright holders, a double standard exists on the forms of intrusions that are acceptable to consumers and other users versus the ones that are acceptable on copyright holders' exclusive rights.[126]

As methods of exploitation evolve toward the online distribution of copies of copyright works with no supporting physical object, the meaning of ownership—as opposed to no ownership—and the degree of privileges and powers that it entails are even more critical questions than they ever were before.[127]

A proper mapping of copyright user rights needs to consider the property rights in commercial copies as well as the permissions of use conferred by copyright law. Having looked at property and sale of goods law as the first step to determine the rights users have to commercial copies of copyright works, the next chapter looks at the nature of exceptions to copyright infringement (commonly referred to as 'user rights') and how often they operate independently of the user's proprietary interests in the commercial copy of the copyright work.

[122] As per the three elements common to all ownership proprietary interests discussed above in this chapter: i.e., (i) the relationship between a person and a resource; (ii) the *prima facie* open-ended powers and privileges; and (iii) powers and privileges that authorize self-seekingness on the part of the owner.

[123] See Chapter 5: 'The commercial practice not to sell copies.'

[124] See above 'Commercial copies of copyright works and the standardization of property.'

[125] Larissa Katz, 'Exclusion and Exclusivity in Property Law' (2008) 58 U TLJ 275 at 277–78, whereby the author presents a narrower view of the power to exclude resulting from ownership, i.e., 'What it means for ownership to be exclusive is just that owners are in a special position to set the agenda for a resource.'

[126] Cohen (n 7) at 380 refers to the legal endorsement of digital rights management as applied by copyright holders as being viewed as acceptable forms of intrusion on consumers' rights in copies of copyright works on the one hand, in contrast with consumer activities related to information products (such as use of automated software for comparative pricing) as being condemned on various legal bases, on the other hand.

[127] See Chapter 4.

# 2

# The Nature and Function of Exceptions to Copyright Infringement

## Exceptions as 'User Rights'

In copyright parlance, 'user rights' often refers to statutory exceptions to copyright infringement found in copyright laws worldwide.[1] Fair use, fair dealing, private copying, educational institutions, libraries and archives, persons with perceptual disabilities, computer programs, and ephemeral recordings are among the common groups, types of uses or works, for which statutory exceptions to copyright infringement have been enacted.[2] To those, there are other targeted exceptions to copyright infringement applicable to a wide range of situations or entities, from agricultural fairs to religious organizations,[3] or works derived from architectural works, or sculptures found in public spaces.[4]

Somewhat surprisingly, the main foundation of law and theory of copyright users' rights relies on those exceptions or defences to copyright infringement, which are typically not associated to rights.[5] The copyright exception of fair use or fair dealing is more readily linked to user rights than the personal property rights of copy owners of copies of copyright works.[6] The connection of exceptions to user rights may be attributable in part to the landmark 2004 Supreme Court of Canada

[1] This is particularly true in Canada in the aftermath of the landmark judgment by the Supreme Court *CCH Canadian Ltd v Law Society of Upper Canada*, 2004 SCC 13 [*CCH*]. See Michael Geist, 'Copyright Users' Rights in Canada Hits Ten: The Tenth Anniversary of the CCH Decision' (4 March 2014), *Michael Geist* (blog), online: <www.michaelgeist.ca/2014/03/cch-anniversary/> accessed 4 February 2017.

[2] See e.g., Canada's *Copyright Act*, RSC 1985, c C-4, ss 29–29.2, 29.4–30.61, 30.8–30.9, 32, 80 [*Canada CA*]; 17 USC §§ 107–108, 112, 117, 121 (2010) [*USC*]; *Copyright, Designs and Patents Act 1988* (UK), c 48, ss 29–30, 31A–31C, 32, 37–43, 50A–50C [*UKCDPA*]; Australia's *Copyright Act 1968* (Cth), ss 40–42, 43C–44, 47B–47F, 47J, 49–52, 110AA [*Austl CA*]; art L122-5, L122-6-1 CPI [*France CPI*].

[3] See e.g., *Canada CA* (n 2) ss 32.2(2)–(3).

[4] ibid, s 32.2(1)(b).

[5] See below: 'The nature of exceptions to copyright infringement.' See M Geist, ed, *In the Public Interest: The Future of Canadian Copyright Law* (Toronto: Irwin Law, 2005) (several of the contributors focused on the implications of exceptions to copyright infringement as 'user rights'). There are notable exceptions to the theory of user rights beyond exceptions to copyright infringement. See Ray L Patterson & Stanley W Lindberg, *The Nature of Copyright: A Law of Users' Rights* (Athens: University of Georgia Press, 1991). See Chapter 7.

[6] See Chapter 1 'A peculiar form of personal property' on the lack of scholarship and clarity in copyright law on users' personal property rights in copies of copyright works.

Copyright User Rights: Contracts and the Erosion of Property. First Edition. Pascale Chapdelaine.

judgment *CCH Canadian Ltd v Law Society of Upper Canada* [*CCH*],[7] stating that fair dealing and other exceptions to copyright infringement are users' rights.[8]

There are other reasons why exceptions to copyright infringement take centre stage in the arena of user rights. With the rapid expansion of copyright in recent decades,[9] exceptions to copyright infringement have been the regulatory response and the theoretical ground of choice to counter increasingly powerful copyright holders' rights.[10] Yet, an exception is, by definition, an outlier to a rule or principle or the starting point of reference, and as such is an unbefitting legal foundation to assert and promote the interests of copyright users.

After setting out the main features of exceptions to copyright infringement and contextualizing them vis-à-vis copyright limitations and international obligations, this chapter queries the nature of exceptions as rights, whether they can be set aside or waived by contract, and regulatory trends around the use of exceptions to copyright infringement by legislatures worldwide.

## The 'Mechanics' of Exceptions to Copyright Infringement

Exceptions to copyright infringement permit users to perform acts that would otherwise require the authorization of the copyright holder, without asking permission, with or without having to give remuneration to the copyright holder. In property theory terms, exceptions act as a property-limitation rule on the rights of copyright holders. Property-limitation rules occur when *prima facie* normative claims founded on the prevailing ownership conception (here of copyright) are overridden. But for the limitation they contain (an exception to copyright infringement), the (copyright) owner would be free to do as they please, for example, applying trespassory protection powers or asking for remuneration for the use permitted under the exception.[11]

Exceptions to copyright infringement apply (i) to specific persons or entities: educational institutions,[12] libraries, archives and museums,[13] network service providers,[14] persons with perceptual disabilities;[15] (ii) for specific purposes: research and

[7] *CCH* (n 1). [8] ibid at para 48.

[9] Jessica Litman, *Digital Copyright* (Amherst: Prometheus Books, 2001) ch 3, in a US context, on the shift toward more protection of right holders that has accelerated since the mid-1970s; Pascale Chapdelaine, 'The Property Attributes of Copyright' (2014) 10 Buffalo Intellectual Property LJ 34 at 34–35; On the progressive expansion of copyright protection at the international level and in Canada, see Pascale Chapdelaine, *Copyright Consumers' Bargain, Defining the Rights to Commercial Copies of Copyright Works* (Doctor of Philosophy Thesis, York University Graduate Program in Law, Osgoode Hall Law School Library, 2013) at 149–54.

[10] See e.g., *Canada CA* (n 2) ss 29–32.2, 79–88; *USC* (n 2) §§ 107–22; *Austl CA* (n 2) ss 40–47J, 65–73; *France CPI* (n 2) art L122-5, L122-6-1.

[11] James W Harris, *Property and Justice* (Oxford: Clarendon Press, 1996) at 34.

[12] See e.g., *Canada CA* (n 2) ss 29.4–30.04.

[13] ibid, ss 30.1–30.21; Robert Burrell & Allison Coleman, *Copyright Exceptions: The Digital Impact* (Cambridge and New York: Cambridge University Press, 2005) at 136–63.

[14] *Canada CA* (n 2) s 31.1. [15] ibid, ss 32–32.01.

private study, news, criticism, parody, satire,[16] private purposes,[17] non-commercial user-generated content;[18] or (iii) to accommodate technological exigencies and developments: ephemeral works,[19] computer programs,[20] backups,[21] time- and space-shifting.[22]

The justification for exceptions constraining the powers and privileges otherwise conferred on copyright holders is to safeguard a broad range of public policy and other competing interests[23] that would be otherwise compromised by too broad copyright protection. While the computer program backup exception may fulfil the reasonable expectations of lawful users of copies of software, or the ephemeral recording accommodate technological exigencies of broadcasters, the right to reuse a work for the purposes of criticism and review may be justified on the basis of freedom of expression, while promoting the dissemination of the underlying and newly created copyright work. Another frequently invoked justification to exceptions is market failure to, for example, explicate private copying regimes.[24] At the same time, the interests promoted through exceptions to copyright infringement need to be balanced with the harm that the exceptions may cause to copyright holders' normal exploitation of their works or other legitimate interests.[25]

As copyright holders' rights expand and as technological environments and social norms evolve, exceptions to copyright infringement are one of the regulatory tools that might allow legislatures and judiciaries to keep copyright true to its 'property-specific justice reasons'.[26] The policy objectives that justify exceptions are either intrinsically linked to the objectives of copyright or external to it. The reproduction of copyright works may be necessary in any given case to encourage the creation of new works, for example, in the case of parody or satire, where the exception promotes a purpose intrinsic or *internal* to copyright. Therefore, exceptions may act as a safeguard against copyright protection undermining the very reason for which copyright was created in the first place.[27] Also, an exception allowing a reproduction for the purpose of criticism and review may be justified by the fundamental right of freedom of expression or free speech, and be required for copyright law to comply with human rights.

One defining characteristic of exceptions to copyright infringement, that is that the exceptions enable users to perform acts without the authorization of copyright holders, needs to be qualified. One qualification is that the exercise of exceptions

[16] ibid, s 29; Burrell & Coleman (n 13) at 42–79. [17] *Canada CA* (n 2) s 29.22.
[18] ibid, s 29.21. [19] ibid, ss 30.8–30.9. [20] ibid, ss 30.6–30.61.
[21] ibid, s 29.24. [22] ibid, s 29.23. [23] See Chapter 7.
[24] Jacques De Werra, 'Moving Beyond the Conflict Between Freedom of Contract and Copyright Policies: In Search of a New Global Policy for On-Line Information Licensing Transactions' (2003) 25 Colum J L & Arts 239 at 330–37.
[25] Austl, Commonwealth, Law Reform Commission, *Copyright and the Digital Economy* (Report No 122) (Sydney: ALRC, 2013) [ALRC Report] founds several of its recommendations for the adoption of a fair use model or a modified version of fair dealing on the premise that permitted uses under these exceptions to copyright infringement are unlikely to cause harm to copyright holders' markets or authors' moral rights. See e.g., paras 7.43–7.53. See below 'Exceptions to copyright infringement and international obligations.'
[26] Harris (n 11) at 168. See Chapter 7. [27] See Chapter 7.

to copyright infringement largely depends on the autonomous powers and privileges that users have on the copyright work. Users' powers and privileges over copyright works are influenced by various factors. First, a different regime applies to digital works protected by technological measures: the legal protection of such works may impair users' ability and privilege to benefit from an exception without the permission of the copyright holder.[28] Second, some exceptions to copyright infringement are only available to users who own the copy of the copyright work.[29] Third, in an environment where copyright works are increasingly accessed through services rather than through the exercise of physical control over a specific copy of the work, the relinquishment of power in favour of copyright holders is almost complete, with the result that, in practice, the user will require the assistance and consent of the copyright holder to benefit from an exception to copyright infringement that they (the user) would be normally entitled to exercise without consent. Fourth, contracts between users and copyright holders may restrict users from performing acts under an exception to copyright infringement, which they would otherwise be entitled to do.[30]

Another important qualification is that the law discriminates between copies of works embedded in physical objects from the ones that are not,[31] thereby allowing the free exercise of exceptions or limitations to copyright infringement in one case and not in another. The availability of the first sale or exhaustion doctrine is generally considered to apply only to copyright works in a physical embodiment.[32]

## Contextualizing Exceptions to Copyright Infringement

### Exceptions to copyright infringement and international obligations

The enactment, application, and interpretation of exceptions to copyright infringement take place within an elaborate web of international, regional, and bilateral intellectual property treaties. The *Berne Convention for the Protection of Literary and Artistic Works* [*Berne Convention*],[33] the *Agreement on the Trade-Related Aspects of Intellectual Property Law* [*TRIPS*],[34] and the World Intellectual Property Organization (WIPO) Internet treaties[35] are among the most important

28 See Chapter 6.

29 E.g., *Canada CA* (n 2) ownership is a requirement for the application of the reproduction for private purposes exception (s 29.22), the backup copies' exception (s 29.24), and the exception applying to computer programs (s 30.6). *Austl CA* (n 2) ss 43C, 47B–47F, 47J, 110AA. Ownership of the copy of the work is also a requirement for the exercise of the first sale doctrine: see Chapter 5.

30 See below: 'May exceptions to copyright infringement be waived by contract?'

31 See Chapter 4: 'Misconceptions about tangibility and intangibility in Defining Information Products.'

32 See Chapter 5.

33 9 September 1886, 828 UNTS 221.

34 *Agreement on Trade-Related Aspects of Intellectual Property Rights, Marrakesh Agreement Establishing the World Trade Organization, Annex 1C,* 15 April 1994, 1869 UNTS 29, 33 ILM 1197 [*TRIPS*].

35 *WIPO Copyright Treaty*, 20 December 1996, WO033EN [*WCT*] and *WIPO Performances and Phonograms Treaty*, 20 December 1996, WO034EN [*WPPT*].

multilateral treaties dealing with the protection of copyright and addressing exceptions to copyright infringement.

From its inception, the multilateral regime of copyright has focused on the protection of author and right holder works.[36] This trend has intensified under the auspice of the World Trade Organization with the adoption of *TRIPS*, and under WIPO with the *WIPO Internet treaties*.[37] As a result, norms aimed at promoting access and dissemination of works, *inter alia* through exceptions to copyright infringement, are largely absent from copyright multilateral instruments.[38] One notable exception is the *Marrakesh Treaty to Facilitate Access to Published Works for Persons Who Are Blind, Visually Impaired, or Otherwise Print Disabled* [*Marrakesh Treaty 2013*],[39] the first multilateral instrument that centres on exceptions to copyright infringement, mandating Member States to facilitate the availability of works in accessible format for beneficiaries as they are defined in the treaty.[40] WIPO initiatives may lead to the introduction of additional international instruments addressing other exceptions to copyright infringement.[41] More recent international treaties show a subtle change of tone toward a greater recognition of the need to balance the scope of copyright with competing legitimate interests.[42]

Member States of the *Berne Convention, TRIPS*, and the *WIPO Internet treaties* are not left entirely to their own devices when it comes to exceptions to copyright infringement. The *Berne Convention* provides specific mandatory and optional exceptions to copyright infringement, with or without compulsory compensation to right holders.[43] Moreover, the *Berne Convention, TRIPS*, and *WIPO Internet treaties* all include what is commonly referred to as the 'three-step test', which sets the conditions that Member States must fulfil when they impose exceptions on copyright holders' exclusive rights.[44] The three-step test provides that Member

[36] *Berne Convention* (n 33) preamble. Art 20 provides that Member States may enter into special agreements among themselves provided that they 'grant to authors more extensive rights than those granted by the Convention, or contain other provisions not contrary to this Convention'.

[37] P Bernt Hugenholtz & Ruth L Okediji, 'Conceiving an International Instrument on Limitations and Exceptions to Copyright', sponsored by the Open Society Institute (OSI) (2008), at 6–7, online: <www.opensocietyfoundations.org/reports/conceiving-international-instrument-limitations-and-exceptions-copyright> accessed 4 February 2017.

[38] ibid.

[39] 27 June 2013, online: <www.wipo.int/treaties/en/text.jsp?file_id=301016> accessed 4 February 2017.

[40] ibid, art 4.

[41] WIPO Standing Committee on Copyright and Related Rights (SCCR), 32nd session, 9–13 May 2016, Summary by the Chair, items 6 and 7, online: <www.wipo.int/edocs/mdocs/copyright/en/sccr_32/ref_sccr_32_summary_by_the_chair.pdf> accessed 4 February 2017, on current work on exceptions for libraries and archives; and for educational, teaching, and research institutions; and for persons with disabilities other than print disabilities.

[42] See *Trans-Pacific Partnership*, 4 February 2016 (not in force), online: <http://www.international.gc.ca/trade-agreements-accords-commerciaux/agr-acc/tpp-ptp/text-texte/toc-tdm.aspx?lang=eng>, art 18.66.

[43] *Berne Convention* (n 33) art 10, 10*bis* (exceptions without remuneration), 11*bis* (exceptions with remuneration).

[44] *Berne Convention* (n 33) art 9(2); *TRIPS* (n 34) art 13; *WCT* (n 35) art 10; *WPPT* (n 35) art 16. The three-step test is limited to reproduction rights in the case of the *Berne Convention*, ibid, and applies to all exclusive rights in the case of *TRIPS, WCT*, and *WPPT*. See Sam Ricketson & Jane C

States shall confine limitations or exceptions on copyright holders' exclusive rights to: (i) special cases, (ii) which do not conflict with a normal exploitation of the work, and which (iii) do not unreasonably prejudice the legitimate interests of copyright holders.[45] The test has been incorporated *en bloc* in regional instruments and some national laws.[46] Like the treaties from which it emanates, the three-step test is copyright-holder-centric. Its criteria focus the analysis on the possible effects of the exceptions on right holders' exclusive rights. *A priori*, they evoke no legitimate constraints on copyright holders' private rights to pursue valuable public interest goals, such as the dissemination of works to the public, and adequate levels of access to users.

In theory, the three-step test establishes a mandatory framework for how national Member States should address exceptions to copyright infringement in their laws. In practice, it is questionable whether the broad wording of the three-step test provides much guidance to national legislatures and regional organizations.[47] Unlike other international intellectual property convention norms prescribing the adoption of unequivocal standards (e.g., the duration of copyright set to a minimum of 50 years),[48] the effects of the three-step test on exceptions to copyright infringement remain uncertain and controversial. There is little jurisprudence at the international level to guide its interpretation, and national courts' interpretations of the test have given rise to important discrepancies in the application of the three-step test.[49] Opinions vary greatly on the exact purpose and scope of the three-step test.[50]

The *TRIPS* version of the test was discussed in the Panel Report, *United States–Section 110(5) Copyright Act*, of the World Trade Organization Dispute Settlement

Ginsburg, *International Copyright and Neighbouring Rights, The Berne Convention and Beyond*, 2nd ed (Oxford: Oxford University Press, 2006) at 755–878, analyzing the exceptions to copyright holders' exclusive rights under each of the three conventions.

45 *Berne Convention* (n 33) art 9(2); *TRIPS* (n 34) art 13; *WCT* (n 35) art 10; *WPPT* (n 35) art 16. The language varies between the three conventions, but the substance of each of the three requirements is similar, except for the *Berne Convention* (n 33) art 9(2), which applies only to the exclusive reproduction rights of copyright holders.

46 See e.g., at the European level, EC, *Directive 2001/29/EC of the European Parliament and the Council of 22 May 2001 on the harmonisation of certain aspects of copyright and related rights in the information society*, [2001] OJ, L 167/10 [*Directive 2001/29/EC*], art 5(5). In France, see e.g., *France CPI*, art L122-5, L122-6-1 V, & L 331-9. Commentators view the national incorporation of the test with scepticism, and as adding more legal uncertainty to the application of copyright exceptions. See e.g., Christopher Geiger, 'The Three-Step Test, a Threat to a Balanced Copyright Law' (2006) 37 Int Rev Intellectual Prop & Comp L 683; Séverine Dusollier, *Droit d'auteur et protection des oeuvres dans l'univers numérique*, 2nd ed (Brussels: Larcier, 2007) [Dusollier 2007] at 435–47; European Parliament, DG for Internal Policies, Policies Department: Citizens' Rights and Constitutional Affairs, *The Relations between Copyright Law and Consumers' Rights from a European Perspective* by Séverine Dusollier (Brussels: European Parliament, 2010) at para 2.1.3.

47 Unlike other international intellectual property norms, e.g., the obligation pursuant to *TRIPS* (n 34) to protect computer programs as literary works, or the obligation to secure exclusive rental rights on computer programs, and, optionally, on cinematographic works (ibid, arts 10–11).

48 *TRIPS* (n 34) art 12.

49 Hugenholtz & Okediji (n 37) at 21.

50 See below in this section.

Body.[51] The Panel Report is a frequently cited legal authority[52] on the application of the three-step test to copyright.[53] The opinion in the Panel Report is that the three-step test is cumulative.[54] The first component of the test confining an exception or limitation to 'special cases' means that it 'must be limited in its field of application or exceptional in scope'[55] and that it 'should be narrow in quantitative as well as a qualitative sense'.[56] The second portion of the test assesses whether the exception 'would enter into economic competition with the ways that right holders normally extract economic value from that right to the work and deprive them of significant tangible economic gains'.[57] This second portion of the test is reminiscent of one of the factors generally applied to assess whether the fair use or fair dealing exceptions apply to a use that would otherwise infringe copyright.[58] It is not clear what the third requirement—that is, the exceptions or limitations 'do not unreasonably prejudice the legitimate interests of the right holder'—adds to the second element of the test.[59] The significance of the third step of the test is largely dependent upon how one interprets the second step of the test. What would be something that would *not* deprive copyright holders of 'significant tangible economic gains' (passing the second step of the test according to the Panel) and yet unreasonably prejudice their legitimate interests, especially if 'legitimate interests' means interests protected by law?[60] Would it include moral rights (which would be irrelevant for right holders that are non-physical entities)? Compulsory licensing would pass the third element of the test, intimating that exceptions that do not provide for compensation (such as fair use or fair dealing) would need to pass an additional level of scrutiny to comply with the test,[61] but precisely what that extra step would be is not entirely clear.

Views on the effects of the three-step test—called 'the infamous test'[62] and imposing a 'limit to limitations'[63]—vary widely. In one view, the test allows for a balanced interpretation and grants flexibility to the implementation of exceptions by national jurisdictions.[64] This is the view that a group of international copyright

[51] *(Complaint by the European Communities)* (2000), WTO Doc WT/DS160/R at 31–68 [Panel Report], on the interpretation of *TRIPS* art 13. See Daniel Gervais, *The TRIPS Agreement: Drafting History and Analysis*, 3rd ed (London: Thomson Reuters, 2008) 236–48.

[52] Although panel reports only bind the parties to the dispute, they are often referred to as authoritative sources of law on the interpretation of *TRIPS* and other international agreements.

[53] See Martin Senftleben, *Copyright, Limitations and the Three-Step Test* (The Hague: Kluwer Law International, 2004); ALRC Report (n 25) at 116–22.

[54] Panel Report (n 51) at para 6.97. [55] ibid at para 6.109. [56] ibid.

[57] ibid at 48. [58] ALRC Report (n 25) at 110–12.

[59] Hugenholtz & Okediji (n 37) at 24, on how the WTO Dispute Settlement Body, in its Panel Report (n 51) seems to have collapsed the third part of the test into the second part of the test.

[60] See Gervais (n 51) at 241.

[61] Hugenholtz & Okediji (n 37) at 24, referring to the 1967 Stockholm conference when the three-step test was incorporated into the *Berne Convention* (n 33).

[62] Hugenholtz & Okediji (n 37) at 52. [63] ibid at 18.

[64] E.g., Christophe Geiger, Reno Hilty, Jonathan Griffiths, & Uma Suthersanen, Declaration A Balanced Interpretation Of The 'Three-Step Test' In Copyright Law (2010) 1 JIPITEC 119, online: <https://www.jipitec.eu/issues/jipitec-1-2-2010/2621> accessed 4 February 2017 [Declaration A Balanced Interpretation Of The 'Three-Step Test']; Andrew F Christie, 'Maximising Permissible Exceptions to Intellectual Property Rights' in Annette Kur & Vytautas Mizaras, eds, *The Structure of*

scholars advocated in the *Declaration A Balanced Interpretation Of The 'Three-Step Test' In Copyright Law*.[65] This initiative falls within broader movements that press for the recognition of, and need to make use of the flexibilities that international intellectual property conventions such as *TRIPS* contain, so as to allow Member States to adequately balance a broad range of competing interests with those of exclusive right holders.[66] From another viewpoint, the three-step test leads to interpretations that construe narrowly the permitted exceptions to copyright. This is, generally, the approach in the jurisprudence of the World Trade Organization Dispute Settlement Body.[67]

Symptomatic of the three-step test's lack of effective guidance are debates about the compliance of the United States (US) style of fair use with the test.[68] Fair use is the well-established doctrine codified in the US *Copyright Act* by virtue of which acts that otherwise infringe will be allowed, without remuneration, subject to a non-exhaustive list of criteria (i.e., the purpose and character of the use, the nature of the copyrighted work, the amount and substantiality of the portion used compared to the copyrighted work as a whole, and the effect of the use upon the potential market for, or value of, the copyrighted work).[69] The scholars signatory to the *Declaration A Balanced Interpretation Of The 'Three-Step Test'* [70] concluded that open-ended limitations and exceptions would comply with the three-step test, so long as the scope of such exceptions and limitations would be reasonably foreseeable.[71] The main point of contention about fair use compliance with the three-step test is that fair use needs to meet the first requirement of the test. Some suggest that the 'fairness' of the use is a 'special case' that would fulfill the first part of the three-step test.[72] As an open-ended judicially derived test allowing a vast panoply

*Intellectual Property Law: Can One Size Fit All?* (Cheltenham: Edward Elgar, 2011) at 121; Martin Senftleben, 'The International Three-Step Test: A Model Provision for EC Fair Use Legislation' (2010) 1 JIPITEC 67.

65 Declaration A Balanced Interpretation Of The 'Three-Step Test' (n 64).

66 The international movement toward an interpretation of *TRIPS* (n 34) that gives more flexibility to its Member States has been prevalent in the area of patents and public health issues, as reflected in WTO, *Declaration on the TRIPS agreement and public health*, WTO Doc WT/MIN(01)/DEC/2, Doha 14 November 2001. See also Christopher Geiger, 'Exploring the Flexibilities of the TRIPS Agreement's Provisions on Limitations and Exceptions' in Annette Kur & Vytautas Mizaras, eds, *The Structure of Intellectual Property Law: Can One Size Fit All?* (Cheltenham: Edward Elgar, 2011) at 287; see generally, Graeme B Dinwoodie & Rochelle C Dreyfuss, *A Neofederalist Vision of TRIPS, The Resilience of the International Intellectual Property Regime* (Oxford: Oxford University Press, 2012).

67 The three-step test has been applied by the panels constituted by the World Trade Intellectual Property Dispute Settlement Body in relation to various intellectual property rights. With respect to *TRIPS* (n 34) art 13 (three-step test for copyright), see Panel Report (n 51) at 31–68. See also on the interpretation of *TRIPS*, ibid, art 30 (three-step test regarding patents): *Canada – Patent protection of pharmaceutical products (Complaint by the European Communities)* (2000), WTO Doc WT/DS/114/R at paras 7.20ff; for a review of the interpretations of the tests applied in Panel reports, see: Graeme B Dinwoodie & Rochelle C Dreyfuss, 'Designing a Global Intellectual Property System Responsive to Change: the WTO, WIPO, and Beyond' (2009) 46 Hous L Rev 1187 at 1206ff.

68 See ALRC Report (n 25) at 116–22, reviewing the literature on the compliance of fair use with the three-step test and concluding that fair use is compliant with the three-step test.

69 *USC* (n 2) § 107.

70 Declaration A Balanced Interpretation Of The 'Three-Step Test' (n 64).

71 ibid.

72 ibid at 119, para 4.150 referring to a submission by Professor Jani McCutcheon.

of uses without remuneration, the fair use doctrine has the inherent power to significantly (re)shape the scope of exclusive rights of copyright holders. One obvious example that comes to mind is the extent to which the application of the fair use doctrine directly impacts the scope of the derivative right.[73] If open-ended tests, evolving from time to time, co-exist side by side with targeted exceptions, such as private copying, archives and museums, and reproduction for backup purposes, on the spectrum of permitted exceptions under the three-step test, what direction does the test really give on the substance of exceptions and limitations of copyright holders' rights?

International intellectual property conventions have shaped and will likely continue to shape regional and national copyright law to a large extent.[74] The harmonization objectives for the protection of intellectual property and the high level of state membership to the multilateral treaties create internal and external political pressures to comply with the international norms the treaties create.[75] Whether the justifications for invoking international conventions to change copyright law are always founded upon genuine international legal obligations rather than political grounds is debatable.[76]

Arguments that promulgate a particular course of action or interpretation in domestic jurisdictions and that are based on international conventions need to be approached with caution. Invoking the three-step test as an aid to interpret national laws calls for even more scrutiny, given the inherent vagueness and lack

[73] *USC* (n 2) § 106(2). One important element of the fair use analysis, that is the level of transformation of the protected work, which usually takes place through *deriving* the new work from the protected work, will impact on the scope of the derivative work.

[74] In the US, see e.g., US, House Judiciary Committee, *WIPO Copyright Treaties Implementation and on-line Copyright Infringement Liability Limitation* (HR Rep No 105-551) (1998), 'Purpose and Summary', online: <www.gpo.gov/fdsys/pkg/CRPT-105hrpt551/html/CRPT-105hrpt551-pt2.htm> accessed 4 February 2017: preceding the enactment of the *Digital Millennium Copyright Act*, Pub L No 105-304, 112 Stat 2860 (1998); *Directive 2001/29/EC* (n 46) Preamble. *Canada CA* (n 2) has been amended on numerous occasions to comply with international conventions: *Canada–United States Free Trade Agreement Implementation Act*, SC 1988, c 65; *World Trade Organization Agreement Implementation Act*, SC 1994, c 47; *Copyright Modernization Act*, SC 2012, c 20.

[75] See e.g., Office of the United States Trade Representative (USTR) Government's Special 301 'Watch List', which identifies US trading partners with lower levels of protection of intellectual property rights online: <https://ustr.gov/issue-areas/intellectual-property/Special-301> accessed 4 February 2017.

[76] In particular, arguments on the manner by which the *Canada CA* (n 2) needed to be amended for Canada to comply with its international obligations to implement effective technological measures under the *WIPO Internet treaties* (n 35) have been the subject of heated debate. See e.g., Michael Geist, 'The Case for Flexibility in Implementing the WIPO Internet Treaties: An Examination of the Anti-Circumvention Requirements' in Michael Geist, ed., *From 'Radical Extremism' to 'Balanced Copyright': Canadian Copyright and the Digital Agenda* (Toronto: Irwin Law, 2010) at 222; and in direct response to this article: Mihaly Ficsor, 'TPMs and Flexibility ("The Ability of *Bending without Breaking*") – Why Should the TPM Provisions of Bill C-32 Protect Access Controls and Prohibit "Preparatory Acts" ', online: Osgoode Intellectual Property Law & Technology Program <www.iposgoode.ca/2010/11/digital-locks-circumvention-and-the-copyright-reforms-proposed-by-bill-c-32/> accessed 4 February 2017. See also Canada *Copyright Modernization Act* (n 74) Preamble, which specifically refers to the need for Canada to coordinate its approach with other countries through the adoption of internationally recognized copyright norms and to amend the *Canada CA* (n 2) to comply with the *WIPO Internet treaties* (n 35).

of operational force of the test. The transformation doctrine applicable in several jurisdictions[77] requires an enabling act of the legislature to give effect to the international convention. The traditional view is that when the enabling act is in place, the international convention serves as an aid to interpret and contextualize the national law and gives effect to it and clarifies any uncertainty.[78] International treaties provide a contextual interpretation tool for the national enabling acts.[79] Given the nature of the three-step test and the wide divergence on its interpretation, its ability to effectively clarify uncertainties in the scope of exceptions to copyright infringement that might arise in domestic law is likely limited. It is noteworthy that the Supreme Court of Canada, which often resorts to international treaties to interpret Canadian laws,[80] did not refer to the three-step test when interpreting the scope of fair dealing on a few occasions.[81]

In spite of its lack of workability and normative guidance to national and regional jurisdictions, the three-step test may serve an important purpose in the future. The *Marrakesh Treaty 2013*,[82] the first international copyright instrument designed to promote specific user rights, requires Member States to comply with each version of the three-step test.[83] The comfort that the three-step test may provide to right holders' interests—attributable in part to the well-established presence of the test in multilateral intellectual property treaties[84]—may ease the way toward the adoption in the future of other international instruments that promote the interests of users, including access and dissemination of copyright works for the public interest.

[77] For example, in Canada, see *Capital Cities Communications Inc v Canadian Radio-Television Commission*, [1978] 2 SCR 141 at 171–76. International conventions are negotiated and signed by the government and do not create laws. The enabling Act of Parliament must fall within Parliament's subject matter powers.

[78] *National Corn Growers Assn v Canada (Import Tribunal)*, [1990] 2 SCR 1324, Part IV(B)(a), Gonthier J. This approach is not followed consistently. Sometimes courts resort to international conventions, even in absence of an enabling act of the legislative body giving force and effect to the international convention: see *Baker v Canada (Minister of Citizenship and Immigration)*, [1999] 2 SCR 817; *Society of Composers, Authors and Music Publishers of Canada v Canadian Assn of Internet Providers*, 2004 SCC 45, paras 65, 73, 97,108, 149–51 where the Supreme Court referred to *WCT* (n 35) to interpret *Canada CA* (n 2) at a time where Canada was only a signatory to *WCT*, ibid.

[79] Ruth Sullivan, *Sullivan and Driedger on the Construction of Statutes*, 4th ed. (Toronto: Butterworths, 2002) at 422.

[80] In a copyright context, see: *Théberge v Gallerie d'art du petit Champlain Inc*, 2002 SCC 34, [2002] 2 SCR 336 at paras 6, 71, 114; *Entertainment Software Association v Society of Composers, Authors and Music Publishers of Canada*, 2012 SCC 34, [2012] 2 SCR 231 at paras 16–20, 24, 87–97; *Rogers Communications Inc v Society of Composers, Authors and Music Publishers of Canada*, 2012 SCC 35, [2012] 2 SCR 283 at paras 25, 36–43; *Re: Sound v Motion Picture Theatre Associations of Canada*, 2012 SCC 38 at para 7.

[81] *CCH* (n 1); *Society of Composers, Authors and Music Publishers of Canada v Bell Canada*, 2012 SCC 36 [*Bell Canada*]; and *Alberta (Education) v Canadian Copyright Licensing Agency (Access Copyright)* 2012 SCC 37 [*Alberta*].

[82] *Marrakesh Treaty 2013* (n 39).

[83] ibid, art 11, requiring Member States to comply with *Berne Convention* (n 33) art 9(2); *TRIPS* (n 34) art 13; *WCT* (n 35) art 10(1) and (2).

[84] The three-step test was first introduced in the 1967 Stockholm revision of the *Berne Convention* (n 33) opened for signature 24 July 1971, [1978] ATS 5 (entered into force on 15 December 1972), and adopted in other international intellectual property treaties (n 44).

## Exceptions to copyright infringement and limitations

In contrast to exceptions to copyright infringement, which allow persons in pre-defined circumstances to perform acts that are otherwise part of the exclusive domain of copyright holders, one may think of limitations as a means to describe the structural outer limits of copyright, beyond which is out of reach of copyright holders.[85] The idea and expression dichotomy, whereby copyright protects the expression of the idea and not the idea itself,[86] and the term of copyright are examples of structural limits to copyright holders' exclusive rights.[87]

In theory, the distinction between limitations and exceptions has some appeal and may be helpful to regulators and the judiciary in their interpretation of the scope of copyright user rights. The distinction contrasts exceptions to other restraints to copyright. As a result of limitations, users are able to perform acts on copyright works because the acts are outside the scope of what copyright holders' exclusive rights protect, and through exceptions, users are allowed to enter copyright holders' exclusive rights' territory if they meet certain requirements.[88] This distinction may be useful to guide the rules of interpretation that apply to limitations and exceptions. In practice however, some restraints on copyright are hard to qualify as either limitations or exceptions.[89] Moreover, the scope of some limitations is uncertain (e.g., idea vs. expression dichotomy) with the result that limitations operate in a similar way to exceptions. They are also invoked as defences to copyright infringement claims, for example, by discrediting the existence of copyright against which the infringement is alleged, invoking the merger or *scènes à faire* doctrine.[90] International intellectual property conventions refer to *exceptions* and *limitations* in the three-step test setting parameters to restrictions on copyright holders' exclusive rights.[91] There is little guidance on the difference, if any, between 'limitations' and 'exceptions'.[92]

The substantial part doctrine under which copyright protection extends only to a substantial part of the work, leaving users free to perform acts on non-substantial parts of the work, could be a limitation as much as an exception to copyright

[85] Christie (n 64) at 123–25.

[86] *TRIPS* (n 34) art 9(2). The idea versus expression dichotomy is the general rule of the outer limit of the scope of copyright protection. Arguably, there are exceptions to that rule, such as the exclusive right to protect derivative works.

[87] Christie (n 64) at 123–24. Other views on structural limitations of copyright include one where copyright is 'a communicative act' that confines 'author's copyright to their state of participant in an ongoing dialogue': Abraham Drassinower, *What's Wrong with Copying?* (Cambridge, MA: Harvard University Press, 2015) at 181–82.

[88] ibid at 123–25. [89] See discussion below in this part.

[90] The idea versus expression dichotomy is often invoked in alleged infringement of computer software cases. See e.g., *Delrina Corp v Triolet Systems Inc* (2002), 58 OR (3d) 339 (CA).

[91] *TRIPS* (n 34) art 13, *WCT* (n 35) art 10, *WPPT* (n 35) art 16. The *Berne Convention* (n 33) art 9(2) does not refer to 'exceptions or limitations' but rather to reproductions which may be permitted under the three-step test. See above: 'Exceptions to copyright infringement and international obligations.'

[92] Hugenholtz & Okediji (n 37) at 19; Christie (n 64) at 123.

infringement.[93] The position is the same with the first sale or exhaustion doctrine, under which copyright holders cannot control the fate of a copy of a work after first sale is authorized.[94] Although in theory both the substantial part and first sale doctrines set the outer limits to copyright exclusivity (as limitations do), they are both subject to judicially developed tests or interpretations that operate in a way that is similar to exceptions to copyright infringement.[95] In relation to the difficulty of distinguishing limitations and exceptions, compulsory licences may be seen as an outer limit to copyright, as they convert copyright holders' rights from a property rule to a liability rule, thereby allowing users to perform otherwise reserved acts on works without authorization, as long as they pay proper remuneration.[96] At the same time, compulsory licences intervene within the core domain of copyright holders, tend to be specific, and may therefore not have the same structural defining qualities of copyright as the idea versus expression dichotomy or as the term of copyright, unless we would move toward a new regime that converts the property rule that generally defines copyright to a liability rule by greater use of compulsory licences.[97] Thus, exceptions and limitations are not immutable: exceptions may evolve toward limitations through legislative reform or judicial decisions as the two concepts relate to their impact on the nature and scope of copyright as defined at any given point in time.

Exceptions permitting acts that fall within the property powers and privileges of copyright holders may suggest a stricter construction of exceptions than of limitations to copyright. At times, courts have held that statutory exceptions call for a narrow interpretation.[98] Modern trends of statutory interpretation lean toward a purposive analysis.[99] The modern approach focuses on determining the underlying rationale of exceptions and exemptions and is concerned that exceptions and exemptions not be used to undermine the purpose of any given legislation.[100] On that basis, a narrow or broad interpretation may equally support legislative purpose, depending on the nature of the statute and its exceptions.[101]

In *CCH*, the Supreme Court of Canada applied a purposive analysis to interpret the scope of fair dealing and other exceptions to copyright infringement:

> [T]he fair dealing exception is perhaps more properly understood as an integral part of the *Copyright Act* than simply a defence ... The fair dealing exception, like other exceptions in the *Copyright Act*, is a user's right. In order to maintain the proper balance between the rights of a copyright owner and users' interests, it must not be interpreted restrictively.

[93] See *Canada CA* (n 2) s 3: users may reproduce, communicate to the public, etc. non-substantial parts of copyright works without copyright holders' authorization.

[94] See Chapter 5.

[95] See Chapter 5 on the uncertainty of the application of the first sale doctrine to copies of copyright works not embedded in a physical object, and on what constitutes a licence as opposed to a sale.

[96] See e.g., *Canada CA* (n 2) ss 19(1) (2a), regarding sound recordings of musical works.

[97] Lawrence Lessig, *The Future of Ideas* (New York: Random House, 2001) at 254–55, recommending increased use of compulsory licences for musical recordings.

[98] Ruth Sullivan, *Sullivan on the Construction of Statutes*, 6th ed (Markham: LexisNexis Canada, 2014) at para 15.53.

[99] ibid, at paras 9.1–100. [100] ibid, at para 15.54. [101] ibid, at para 9.76.

As Professor Vaver, *supra*, has explained, at p. 171: 'User rights are not just loopholes. Both owner rights and user rights should therefore be given the fair and balanced reading that befits remedial legislation.'[102]

The Court's interpretation of exceptions as 'users' rights' underscores the purpose given to exceptions as an essential vehicle 'to maintain the proper balance between the rights of a copyright owner and users' interests'.[103] On that basis, the Court called for a broad interpretation of exceptions to copyright infringement.[104]

In an era where 'striking a proper balance' among various competing interests has become a preoccupation of law and policy-makers and commentators,[105] exceptions to copyright infringement may be one readily available, obvious tool to achieve that goal. Given the copyright-holder-centric focus of international copyright conventions and national laws, a broad interpretation of exceptions may be necessary to attain that balance.

## The Nature of Exceptions to Copyright Infringement

Whether exceptions to copyright infringement are rights, privileges, or defences has important legal ramifications for copyright users. Based on Wesley Hohfeld's theory of jural correlatives,[106] lawful users have a legal claim against copyright holders to exercise exceptions to copyright infringement[107] if they are rights,[108] but not if they are privileges or mere defences.[109] This is particularly relevant when technological protection measures (TPMs) restrict the exercise of an otherwise permitted act.[110] By contrast, an exception to copyright infringement is a privilege

102 *CCH* (n 1) at para 48. 103 ibid. 104 ibid.

105 Declaration A Balanced Interpretation Of The 'Three-Step Test' (n 64); Reno Hilty & Sylvie Nérisson, *Balancing Copyright—A Survey of National Approaches* (Heidelberg: Springer-Verlag, 2012) at 1–78; ALRC Report (n 25) at 41–56, the 'Framing Principles for Reform' reflecting a balance among authorship, creation, incentives to create and disseminate works, and promoting fair access to content; *Marrakesh Treaty 2013* (n 39) Preamble, recital 9.

106 I.e., that a person's right implies that someone else has a duty towards that person. A privilege is the ability to do something with no correlation from anyone obligated toward it (no right). E.g., a defence to copyright infringement would qualify as a privilege to the extent that it allows a user to perform certain acts without authorization but does not require copyright holders to facilitate the exercise of these acts. See: Wesley N Hohfeld, 'Some Fundamental Legal Conceptions as Applied in Judicial Reasoning' (1913) 23 Yale LJ 16 at 30–31. See also Wesley N Hohfeld, 'Fundamental Legal Conceptions as Applied in Judicial Reasoning' (1917) 26 Yale LJ 710.

107 E.g., the right to make copies for private purposes or fair dealing.

108 Unless the exceptions to copyright infringement are not mandatory and have been restricted by the copyright holder in binding agreement.

109 See discussion below on the French cases *Warner Music: Christophe R., UFC Que Choisir/Warner Music France, Fnac* , Trib. gr. inst. 5e Paris, 10 January 2006, (2006) JurisData: 2006-292685; on appeal CA Paris, 20 June 2007, *Fnac Paris/UFC Que Choisir et autres* (2007) Juris Data 2007-337236 Confirmed by the Cour de cassation: Cass civ 1re, 27 November 2008, *UFC Que Choisir/Fnac, Warner Music France* (2008) JurisData 2008-046005. [*Warner Music*] and *Studio Canal* et al *v S Perquin and Union fédérale des consommateurs Que choisir*, CA, Paris, 4 April 2007, Gaz Pal 18/07/2007 No 199, 23; confirmed by the Cour de Cassation: Cass civ 1re, 19 June 2008 (2008) Bull civ I No 177 [*Mullholland Drive*].

110 See Chapter 6.

to the extent that it does not impose any duty on copyright holders, such as to facilitate the performance of a permitted act. A privilege leaves users free to make the permitted use as they please, unless the exceptions to copyright infringement are not mandatory and are restricted by contract or by TPMs.[111] If exceptions to copyright infringement are mandatory privileges, any attempt by copyright holders to restrain the exercise of the exceptions is not enforceable,[112] leaving users free to circumvent the TPMs without being liable for infringement.[113] As a result, mandatory (or non-waivable) user rights offer the strongest form of protection for copyright users and other users, while non-mandatory privileges offer them the weakest form of protection. Between the two poles, a mandatory privilege does not impose any obligation on copyright holders to facilitate the exercise of an act permitted under an exception to copyright infringement; but at the same time, any obstacle imposed by copyright holders restricting the performance of the said act by users is non-enforceable, leaving users free to perform an act otherwise permitted by an exception to copyright infringement. An exception to copyright infringement that may be superseded by contract is weaker in mass-market environments where non-negotiated standard end-user agreements prevail, to the extent that the exception is subject to contract terms that may negate it.[114]

The Supreme Court of Canada stated unanimously in *CCH*, and reaffirmed in three subsequent judgments,[115] that exceptions to copyright infringement are 'more properly understood as an integral part of the *Copyright Act* than simply a defence'[116] and are users' rights.[117] The Supreme Court could have referred to exceptions to copyright holders' exclusive rights,[118] but instead it explicitly referred to them as 'rights'. The Supreme Court's qualification of exceptions to copyright infringement contrasts with courts in other jurisdictions, including the US and France, that have held that exceptions to copyright infringement are defences that cannot form the basis of a legal claim,[119] while having incidentally

[111] In the case of TPMs blocking the permitted use, users would be allowed to circumvent usage-control TPMs to perform a permitted act, e.g., a fair use of the work, provided that they have the technical ability to do so: see Chapter 6.

[112] Hohfeld (n 106). On the distinction between mandatory exceptions and mandatory rights, see Dusollier 2007 (n 46) at 483–84.

[113] See below: 'May exceptions to copyright infringement be waived by contract?'

[114] For a discussion on the legal nature of exceptions to copyright infringement and on their mandatory nature see Dusollier 2007 (n 46) at 477–511.

[115] *Bell Canada* (n 81); *Alberta* (n 81); *Reference re Broadcasting Regulatory Policy CRTC 2010-167 and Broadcasting Order CRTC 2010-168*, 2012 SCC 68 [*CRTC*].

[116] *CCH* (n 1) at para 48, referring specifically to the fair dealing exception to copyright infringement.

[117] ibid; *Bell Canada* (n 81) at para 11; *CRTC* (n 115) at paras 36, 58.

[118] *Canada CA* (n 2) ss 29ff, preceding title, refers to 'Exceptions'. Exceptions or defences to copyright infringement are how these limitations of copyright holders' exclusive rights are commonly referred to: see *Berne Convention* (n 33) art 9; the *WCT* (n 35) art 10 and the *WPPT* (n 35) art 16, which also refer to 'exceptions' and 'limitations' of the exclusive rights of copyright holders.

[119] *Campbell v Acuff-Rose Music, Inc,* 510 US 569 at 590 (1994), fair use being referred to as an affirmative defence; see Civ. Bruxelles 25 May 2004 (*Test-Achats v EMI-Sony-Universal-IFPI*), AM 2004 338, affirmed on appeal: Bruxelles (9e ch.) 9 September 2005 (*Test-Achats v EMI-Sony-Universal-IFPI*) online: <http://www.crid.be/pdf/public/5259.pdf> accessed 4 February 2017. See the

and occasionally referred to fair use or other exception as a 'user right', with no further development of the issue.[120] The *UKCDPA*[121] suggests that exceptions to copyright infringement are not rights.[122] The view that exceptions to copyright infringement do not constitute rights in the sense that they involve duties on the part of copyright holders as per Hohfeld's theory of jural correlatives is also shared by copyright scholars.[123]

The French case *Warner Music* illustrates the consequences of the distinction between rights and mere defences to copyright infringement.[124] The Tribunal of first instance had ordered the rescission of the sale of CDs for digital music on the basis that the CD, which contained TPMs, could not be used on a specific kind of laptop. The CD contained a notification of the TPMs and stated that it could be read on most CD players and computers. The Tribunal held that this incompatibility with some computers constituted a latent defect under the French Civil Code.[125] The Tribunal also ordered Warner Music France to remove TPMs from the CDs it distributed, as TPMs prevented users from making private copies of the digital music. The Tribunal held that this annulled *de facto* the limit set by the legislator on the exclusive right of authors, which allowed individuals to make private copies.[126] The Court of Appeal reversed the two orders of the Tribunal outlined above.[127] It reversed the first order on the ground of deficient evidence of the existence of a latent defect.[128] It reversed the second order on the basis that the private copying exception to authors' rights was not a right but a defence.[129] Hence, it could not be the basis for the initiation of a claim.[130] The French Court of Appeal and the Cour de Cassation in the *Mulholland Drive* case adopted the

discussion below in this chapter on the French cases *Warner Music* (n 109) and *Mulholland Drive* (n 109).

120 See e.g., *Bateman v Mnemonics Inc*, 79 F (3d) 1532 at no 22 (11th Cir 1996); *Suntrust Bank v Houghton Mifflin Co*, 268 F (3d) 1257 at no. 3 (11th Cir 2001); *US v Elcom Ltd*, 203 F Supp (2d) 1111 at 1119 (ND Cal 2002); *321 Studios v Metro Goldwyn Mayer Studios Inc*, 307 F Supp (2d) 1085 (ND Cal 2004); *Whelan Associates Inc v Jaslow Dental Laboratory Inc*, 797 F (2d) 1222 (3rd Cir 1984).

121 *UKCDPA* (n 2).

122 ibid, s 28(1), states with respect to acts permitted in relation to copyright works: 'The provisions of this article specify acts which may be done in relation to copyright works notwithstanding the subsistence of copyright; *they relate only to the question of infringement of copyright* and do not affect any other right or obligation restricting the doing of any of the specified acts.' (emphasis added)

123 For a review of the literature and case law on the legal nature of exceptions to copyright infringement see Dusollier 2007 (n 46) at 477–94, in particular at 481–85 regarding the arguments against qualifying exceptions to copyright infringements as rights; Séverine Dusollier, 'Copie privée v. mesures techniques de protection: l'exception est-elle un droit?', note sous Prés. Bruxelles (cess.), (2004) 4 Auteurs & Média 338 at 342–44, where the author argues in a Belgian context that exceptions to copyright infringement are not rights; David Vaver, 'Copyright Defenses as User Rights' (2013) 60:4 J Copyright Society of the USA 661 at 669, hesitating to qualify exceptions to copyright infringement as rights with correlative duties in Hohfeld terms, or as rights that can be transferred, but acknowledging that they are nevertheless entitlements.

124 *Warner Music* (n 109).

125 Art 1641 CcF.

126 As per *France CPI* (n 2) art L 122-5, L 211-3.

127 *Warner Music* (CA) (n 109).

128 ibid.

129 ibid.

130 ibid. Confirmed by the Cour de cassation: Cass civ 1re, 27 November 2008, *UFC Que Choisir/ Fnac, Warner Music France* (2008) JurisData 2008-046005.

same approach.[131] Given the subsequent introduction under French law of procedures facilitating the resolution of complaints by any interested person deprived of their ability to perform a permitted act blocked by TPMs[132] the characterization of exceptions to copyright infringement as incapable of forming the basis of a claim no longer stands.[133]

The *Marrakesh Treaty 2013* requires Member States to ensure that TPMs implemented in their jurisdiction do not prevent beneficiaries from enjoying the exceptions to copyright infringement set out in the treaty.[134] Depending on how this obligation is implemented by the Member States of the Treaty, it may give rise to the basis of a claim for beneficiaries who are prevented to make uses of copyright works allowed under the Treaty.

Developments in Canadian jurisprudence, French legislation, and the implementation of the obligation of the *Marrakesh Treaty 2013*, have the potential to broaden the nature and scope of exceptions to copyright infringement on new grounds. As is the case in France, users deprived of the benefit of some exceptions to copyright infringement now have explicit recourse to enforce their entitlement under those exceptions. But what precisely are (or may be) exceptions to copyright infringement? What are the possible meanings of 'user rights' when referring to exceptions to copyright infringement?

## 'User rights' as a rule of interpretation

By identifying exceptions to copyright infringement as 'user rights', the Supreme Court of Canada, in *CCH* and subsequent judgments, has given new direction on the interpretation of exceptions to copyright infringements.[135] 'User rights' has become a rule of interpretation that gives increased prominence to the role of exceptions in balancing competing interests in copyright law.[136] The Supreme Court held that the allowed purposes under the fair dealing provisions called for a 'large and liberal interpretation',[137] that the purpose of 'research' included research for commercial purposes,[138] and that 'private research' could be conducted in a classroom in the presence of others.[139] Treating exceptions as users' rights also led the Supreme Court to interpret exceptions from the perspective of the user, not copyright holders.[140] From that standpoint,

[131] *Mulholland Drive* (CA) (n 109), confirmed by the Cour de Cassation (ibid).

[132] See Chapter 3: 'User claims and remedies in copyright law'.

[133] ibid; see Giuseppe Mazziotti, *EU Digital Copyright and the End-User* (Berlin: Springer-Verlag, 2008) at 205.

[134] *Marrakesh Treaty 2013* (n 39) art 7.

[135] *CCH* (n 1), *Bell Canada* (n 81), *Alberta* (n 81) and *CRTC* (n 115). For a historical account of fair dealing in Canada, see: Ariel Katz, 'Fair Use 2.0: The Rebirth of Fair Dealing in Canada' in Michael Geist, ed, *The Copyright Pentalogy, How the Supreme Court of Canada Shook the Foundations of Canadian Copyright Law* (Ottawa: University of Ottawa Press, 2013) at 93.

[136] *CCH* (n 1) at para 48; *Bell Canada* (n 81) at paras 9–11, 49.

[137] *CCH* (n 1) at para 51; *Bell Canada* (n 81) at para 15; *Alberta* (n 81) at para 19.

[138] *CCH* (n 1) at para 51.

[139] *Alberta* (n 81) at paras 19, 27.

[140] ibid at para 22; *Bell Canada* (n 81) at paras 29, 30, 34.

in *Society of Composers, Authors and Music Publishers of Canada v Bell Canada* [*Bell Canada*],[141] whether streaming music fell within the purpose of research needed to be assessed from the perspective of users and consumers.[142] When looking at the amount of music streaming to assess the fairness of the dealing, a user rights' analysis must focus on each individual user, not on the aggregate of music streaming taking place.[143] The Court held that the streaming of music by online music providers was fair and therefore not an infringement of copyright.[144] In *Alberta*, the Supreme Court held that the copying of textbooks by teachers had to be considered from the perspective of the student users and their own purpose of private study,[145] holding that the Copyright Board had misapplied *CCH* and remitting the case to the Board for its reconsideration of the fairness of the dealing.[146] In *CRTC*, the Supreme Court held that a value for signal regime set up by the Canadian Radio-Television and Telecommunications Commission (CRTC) was *ultra vires* of its powers as it, *inter alia*, effectively allowed broadcasters to control the simultaneous retransmission of works, while section 31 of the *Copyright Act*—a user's right—explicitly restricts them from doing so.[147]

In Canada, the effect of characterizing exceptions to copyright infringement as 'users' rights' has led to the development of a new rule of interpretation that calls for a broader application of exceptions and greater attention to the interest of copyright users within the larger framework of copyright.

## User rights or privileges?

Whether exceptions to copyright infringement are rights or privileges requires a closer look at their nature and function. The essence of exceptions to copyright infringement is to allow lawful copyright users to perform certain acts on copyright works *without the authorization* of copyright holders and with or without remuneration. First, as a precondition of the exercise of the exception as a right, the performance of the act being constrained by copyright holders needs to be identifiable as falling under an exception to copyright infringement. While the delineation of some exceptions is reasonably clear (e.g., private copying regime, reproduction for private purposes, backup copies, exceptions relating to computer programs), others are to be assessed on a case-by-case basis with the development and support of judge-made rules (e.g., fair dealing, non-substantial part doctrine). Second, to be able to assert that exceptions are rights giving rise to legal claims, one needs to look at provisions as they exist in some jurisdictions, that give precedence to TPMs over the existence of the exception; in other words, exceptions to copyright infringement where users are allowed to perform certain acts

[141] *Bell Canada* (n 81). [142] ibid at para 30. [143] ibid at para 41.
[144] ibid at para 49. [145] *Alberta* (n 81) at paras 22–23. [146] ibid at paras 37–38.
[147] *CRTC* (n 115) at para 69, referring to *Canada CA* (n 2) s 31.

on copies of copyright works, subject to not circumventing any TPMs applied to those works.[148]

The lack of certainty, that is whether certain acts fall within the scope of an exception to copyright infringement, should not be a bar per se to exceptions being rights giving rise to claims. For instance, the scope of copyright often leaves room for interpretation and yet does not stop copyright holders from invoking their exclusive rights as the basis of legal claims against alleged infringers. The difference between copyright and exceptions, however, is that copyright law, through its applicable statutes, typically defines what constitutes primary or secondary copyright infringement and spells out the remedies available to copyright holders.[149] With some limited exceptions, copyright law neither generally spells out any obligation on copyright holders to allow the exercise of exceptions to copyright infringement, nor includes remedies for users who wish to take benefit from the exception to copyright infringement of which they were deprived.[150] The general absence of identifiable obligations of copyright holders, legal procedures, and designated remedies under which copyright users can make a claim against copyright users is evidence against characterizing exceptions to copyright infringement as rights, more than indicating the potential lack of clarity of scope of the exceptions per se.

TPMs undoubtedly add layers of complexity when one seeks to determine the nature of exceptions to copyright infringement and the effect of the introduction of TPMs on exceptions. In some jurisdictions, TPMs effectively create a hierarchy between exceptions to copyright infringement by making the availability of some exceptions explicitly subject to the non-circumvention of existing TPMs, therefore allowing copyright holders to eliminate the application of those exceptions by controlling the access to their works with TPMs.[151] As a result, exceptions that are expressly subject to such TPM-overriding-exception provisions, are some sort of halfway right at best, or halfway privilege. The exceptions are available only for works not protected by TPMs; the exceptions to copyright infringement become non-existent with respect to works protected by TPMs.[152]

For other exceptions to copyright infringement that apply regardless of the presence of TPMs that protect the work,[153] the introduction of TPM regimes weakens both the exercise of such exceptions and the assertion that they are user rights. There are four possible interpretations or legislative models on the

[148] See e.g., *Canada CA* (n 2) ss 29.22(1)(c), 29.23(1)(b), 29.24(1)(c), subjecting the availability of the exceptions to copyright infringement to not circumventing TPMs.

[149] See Chapter 3.

[150] ibid.

[151] See e.g., *Canada CA* (n 2) subjecting the availability of the following exceptions to copyright infringement to not circumventing TPMs: reproduction for private purposes exception (ibid, s 29.22(1)(c)), fixing signals and recording programmes for later listening or viewing exception (ibid, s 29.23(1)(b)), and back-up copies exception (ibid, s 29.24(1)(c)).

[152] ibid.

[153] E.g., fair dealing, the non-substantial part doctrine, the private copying regime, computer program exceptions, exhaustion or first sale doctrine, and the non-commercial user-generated content exception: *Canada CA* (n 2) ss 3(1), 3(1)(j), 29–29.21, 30.6–30.61, 79–88.

effects of TPMs on the nature of exceptions to copyright infringement as rights or otherwise.

Under one interpretation or legislative model, the TPM provisions have the effect that for works supplied with TPMs, the TPMs override exceptions to copyright infringement (regardless of their nature as rights or privileges) to the same extent contract terms would (under the assumption that exceptions may be waived by contract).[154] Users are not allowed to circumvent TPMs to make lawful uses of works and copyright holders applying TPMs have no obligation to facilitate the exercise of the exception at the request of users or otherwise.[155] Under this interpretation or legislative model, copyright holders' use of TPMs overrides the application of the exception.

Under a second interpretation or legislative model, the TPM provisions confirm that exceptions to copyright infringement are privileges and not rights in Hohfeld terms: on the assumption that they have the technical means to do so, users are legally entitled to circumvent TPMs to perform a non-infringing act (e.g., fair use or fair dealing). At the same time, the existence of TPM provisions supports the view that copyright holders are under no obligation to take any steps to give users the benefit of the exception to copyright infringement. This could be one way to interpret the consequences of TPM regimes in the US and in Canada.[156] The non-technologically inclined are at a disadvantage compared to technologically habile users, as copyright holders have no positive obligation to facilitate the exercise of the exception. Also under this legislative model, the TPM provisions prohibit the making of circumventing devices or the provisions or circumventing services, making it even more difficult for users to circumvent TPMs.[157]

Under a third interpretation or legislative model, the TPM provisions do not negate an interpretation under which exceptions to copyright infringement are user rights in Hohfeld terms, while altering the nature of those rights significantly with respect to works protected by TPMs. Here, as for the second interpretation or legislative model presented above, users are legally entitled to circumvent TPMs to perform a non-infringing act (e.g., fair use or fair dealing). In addition, the TPM provisions, although not explicit, would also require copyright holders to facilitate permitted uses by lawful users, at users' requests. This could be one way to interpret the consequences of TPM regimes in jurisdictions such as the US or Canada, although in my view, the second interpretation on the effects of TPMs presented earlier is likely more accurate.[158] TPM provisions that have such effect would partially override exceptions to copyright infringement: users are deprived of an essential feature of exceptions by having to ask permission to exercise them, but may

[154] See below 'May exceptions to copyright infringement be waived by contract?' *Directive 2001/29/EC* (n 46) recital 39 provides that Member States' exceptions for private copying 'should not inhibit the use of technological measures or their enforcement against circumvention' which has been interpreted by some scholars as effectively overriding the exception when copyright holders protect their works with TPMs: see André Lucas & Pierre Sirinelli, 'Exceptions de copie privée et mesures techniques de protection' (2005) 16 Propriétés intellectuelles 340 at 342–43.

[155] See below 'May exceptions to copyright infringement be waived by contract?'

[156] See Chapter 6. [157] ibid. [158] See Chapter 6.

still obtain such authorization from copyright holders who would be obliged to comply if the user is entitled to the benefit of the relevant exception.

Under a fourth interpretation or legislative model, the TPM provisions impose specific obligations on copyright holders to allow users to benefit from available exceptions either by requiring copyright holders to set the proper mechanisms in place, or in response to an administrative decision.[159] In France and other jurisdictions, administrative bodies oversee the resolution of any complaint filed by any interested person who is deprived of their ability to perform a permitted act that is blocked by TPMs. This legislative model arguably elevates the status of certain exceptions to user rights.[160] The implementation of the *Marrakesh Treaty 2013* obligation to remove the obstacles created by TPMs for visually impaired beneficiaries holds the same potential.[161]

Under the four possible interpretations (or legislative models) of the effects of TPM provisions presented here, TPMs weaken, at varying degrees the availability for copyright users of exceptions to copyright infringement. TPM regimes (as further explored in Chapter 6) add a cloud of uncertainty that is detrimental to the constitutive nature and strength of copyright user rights. Chapter 8 examines solutions to reconcile TPMs and copyright holders' and users' interests.

## May exceptions to copyright infringement be waived by contract?

Whether exceptions to copyright infringement are mandatory or not (i.e., whether they may be waived by contract) is a field of inquiry distinct from that of their nature as rights, privileges, or defences discussed above, yet it is equally important to assess users' entitlements to commercial copies of copyright works. While exceptions to copyright infringement confer greater benefits on users if they constitute rights as opposed to privileges,[162] they are potentially significantly weakened if they may be waived by contract (not mandatory), especially in relation to consumer transactions subject to non-negotiated standard end-user agreements. A mandatory exception to copyright infringement makes a contract term to the contrary unenforceable, while a non-mandatory user right can be the basis of a legal claim only to the extent that it has not been overridden by enforceable contractual terms.[163]

The mandatory nature (or not) of exceptions to copyright infringement shapes the legal landscape of copyright users to a large extent: copyright works are increasingly made available with non-negotiated contract terms of use, or with TPMs which *de facto* play a similar role to contract terms in determining copyright user rights.[164] Whether copyright holders may 'contract out' of statutory

159 See Chapter 3: 'User claims and remedies in copyright law'.

160 ibid.

161 *Marrakesh Treaty 2013* (n 39) art 7.

162 See above: 'User rights or privileges?'

163 ibid.

164 See Chapter 6. An entire book examines the question of the mandatory nature of limitations to copyright holders' exclusive rights: see Lucie Guibault, *Copyright Limitations and Contracts, An Analysis of the Contractual Overridability of Limitations on Copyright* (The Hague: Kluwer Law International, 2002); see also, Jacques De Werra, 'Moving Beyond the Conflict between Freedom of Contract and

exceptions to copyright infringement involves issues of public and private interests and the vehicles through which they are promoted, a subject that is discussed in Chapter 8.[165] For now, this section looks at how the waivability of exceptions to copyright infringement and the uncertainty that surrounds it impact the nature of exceptions.

Most copyright statutes are silent on whether exceptions to copyright infringement are mandatory or whether they may be waived by contract.[166] Some copyright statutes including in France and Belgium, or regional instruments including in the European Union (EU) provide that exceptions are mandatory, or specifically single out exceptions that may not be waived by contract.[167] The consequence of the absence of explicit reference to the mandatory nature of exceptions to copyright infringement leads to diverging opinions. For some courts and commentators, silence suggests that exceptions to copyright infringement may be waived by contract,[168] subject to doctrines extraneous to copyright law, such as the common law doctrine of public policy, or copyright misuse applying to contract terms overriding exceptions to copyright infringement.[169] Other commentators, having conducted a comparative study on the mandatory nature of exceptions to copyright infringement, are of the view that no definitive conclusion can be derived from statutory silence on that question.[170] Whether exceptions to copyright infringement may be waived by contract depends on the underlying justification supporting the exception.[171] Exceptions that are justified by fundamental rights (i.e., the freedom of expression to parody a work) may not be overridden by contract, while the ones that are justified on other grounds, for example,

Copyright Policies: in Search of a New Global Policy for Online Information Licensing Transactions' (2003) 25 Colum JL & Arts 239; Dusollier 2007 (n 46) at 495–511; Estelle Derclaye, 'Copyright Contracts, Public Policy and Antitrust' in Christopher Heath & Kung-Chung Liu, eds, *Copyright Law and the Information Society in Asia*, IIC Studies (Oxford: Hart Publishing, 2006) 167; M Kretschmer, E Derclaye, M Favale & R Watt, 'The Relationship between Copyright and Contract Law: A Review Commissioned by the UK Strategic Advisory Board for Intellectual Property Policy (SABIP)', 2010 online: <http://papers.ssrn.com/sol3/papers.cfm?abstract_id=2624945> accessed 4 February 2017.

165 Chapter 8: 'Adjusting the balance.'

166 See e.g., *USC* (n 2); *Canada CA* (n 2); *UKCDPA* (n 2).

167 See e.g., *France CPI* (n 2) art L 122-6-1 in fine, listing exceptions to copyright infringement that are mandatory; Belgium *Code de droit économique*, art XI.193, listing exceptions to copyright infringement relating to computer programs that are mandatory. See also EC, *Council and Parliament Directive 2009/24/EC of 23 April 2009 on the legal protection of computer programs*, [2009] OJ L 111/16 [*Directive 2009/24/EC*] where some exceptions to copyright infringement related to computer programs cannot be limited by contract: art 5(2) and (3); *Austl CA* (n 2) s 47H (computer programs).

168 See ALRC Report (n 25) at para 20.26, acknowledging that there is no certainty on that matter. US courts have explicitly held exceptions to copyright infringement may be waived by contract. See e.g., *Bowers v Baystate Techs, Inc*, 320 F (3d) 1317 at 1325 (Fed Cir 2003); *Davidson & Associates Inc*, et al *v Internet Gateway*, 334 F Supp (2d) 1164 (ED Mo 2004).

169 See ALRC Report (n 25) at paras 20.35–20.41.

170 See Guibault (n 164) at 214–40, 263–77, 291, 296–302: based on her analysis of EU and US copyright and other laws, Guibault concluded that there is no definite means to determine whether limitations to copyright are mandatory or not, unless the relevant copyright laws explicitly state so.

171 De Werra (n 24) at 330–37 takes the position in a European context that copyright limitations that are grounded in fundamental rights (e.g., freedom of expression) may not be overridden by contract, but that most other limitations may.

public policy (education, persons with disabilities) may be.[172] The same reasoning applies to exceptions to copyright infringement that are justified by market failures, that is, they may be overridden by contract to the extent that the market failure disappears, for example, with the apparition of new technologies.[173] Relying on the underlying justifications of exceptions to copyright infringement to elucidate whether exceptions are mandatory may not be all that satisfactory given the debate and uncertainty around what the proper justifications should be.[174]

In jurisdictions promoting copyright user rights, such as is the case in Canada,[175] a reasonable argument could be made that at least some exceptions to copyright infringement may not be waived by contract in non-negotiated standard form agreements, regardless of the statute being silent on the issue.[176] In other jurisdictions such as the US, statutory silence tends to support the interpretation that exceptions to copyright infringement may be waived by contract,[177] except if contracting out of the exception would offend the doctrine of public policy, doctrine of copyright misuse, or other similar doctrine, or would validate an interpretation of the relevant copyright act that would violate constitutional rights.[178]

The extent to which exceptions to copyright infringement are held to be waivable (or non-mandatory) significantly weakens users' chances of successfully invoking the doctrine of public policy or the doctrine of copyright misuse against copyright holders' commercial practices that restrain users' uses of works. If the legislature's intent is that copyright holders can contract out of exceptions to copyright infringement, it becomes harder to argue that restrictions surrounding the exercise of exceptions to copyright infringement offend public policy or are a misuse of copyright.

The legal uncertainty that surrounds the mandatory nature (or waivability) of exceptions to copyright infringement is less than desirable for copyright users.[179] Given that exceptions to copyright infringement are an important if not the main regulatory tool for the promotion of user interests, any uncertainty surrounding the status of exceptions to copyright infringement makes copyright users more vulnerable. Chapter 8 will explore the arguments in favour and against the mandatory nature of exceptions to copyright infringement with some recommendations.

172 ibid at 335–36. See also Dusollier 2007 (n 46) at 507–09.

173 De Werra (n 24) at 336–37.

174 See Chapter 7. See also ibid at 333–35 on the debate on the theoretical justifications that withstand the right to make private copies, i.e., the extent to which it is based on the right to privacy.

175 See above: '"User rights" as a rule of interpretation.'

176 See e.g., for Canada, Pascale Chapdelaine, 'The Ambiguous Nature of Copyright Users' Rights' (2013) 26 IPJ 1 at 37–43.

177 US courts have explicitly held that exceptions to copyright infringement may be waived by contract. See e.g., *Bowers v Baystate Techs, Inc* (n 168); *Davidson & Associates Inc,* et al *v Internet Gateway* (n 168).

178 De Werra (n 24) at 330–36.

179 UK, Ian Hargreaves, 'Digital Opportunity: A Review of Intellectual Property and Growth,' 2011 at 51, online: <www.ipo.gov.uk/ipreview-finalreport.pdf> accessed 4 February 2017.

## Regulatory Design Implications and Trends

One response to the progressive expansion of copyright in subject matter, scope, and duration has been the progressive addition of specific, piecemeal exceptions to copyright infringement in national legislation and in regional instruments.[180] The result is an expansive convoluted list of exceptions, some of which overlapping others.[181] International conventions reflect a different approach, subjecting Member States' copyright limitations and exceptions for the most part to the general framework of the three-step test.[182]

While in theory the addition of exceptions should be welcomed by users, as increasing their powers and privileges over copyright works in the long run, the expansionist pattern of adding specific, piecemeal exceptions should be no panacea to the expansion of copyright as it could lead to an overly complex and fragmented regime that is quickly out of pace with technological developments.[183] Too many exceptions to the rules undermine copyright holders and users, increasing uncertainty as to their respective position. The introduction of TPMs in various jurisdictions, creating a regime of infringement and exceptions parallel to copyright does not simplify matters.[184]

The regulatory dance between copyright holders' rights and users' rights or privileges is symptomatic of a greater malaise and of weak attempts to reach a balance between competing interests, given that the exceptions are in some cases devoid of meaningful substance. Some exceptions to copyright infringement can be specifically overridden by contract or by the application of TPMs, or the status of these exceptions vis-à-vis TPMs or restrictive standard contract terms of use is unclear.[185]

The proposition by the Australian Law Reform Commission to repeal most of Australia's *Copyright Act* exceptions to copyright infringement and introduce a general US-style fair use provision may be a welcome alternative to the regulatory trend to continually add new exceptions to copyright infringement.[186] The Commission supported the regulatory design choice of a general open-ended fair-use-style exception to copyright infringement as one that promoted flexibility and sufficient certainty, technological neutrality, the public interest, transformative

[180] E.g., *Directive 2001/29/EC* (n 46) art 5, lists over 15 exceptions (with sub-exceptions); *Canada CA* (n 2) ss 29–32.2,79–88, enumerates over 25 exceptions to copyright infringement (not even counting sub-exceptions within broader categories). See also *USC* (n 2) §§ 107–22; *UKCDPA* (n 2) ss 28A–75; *Austl CA* (n 2) ss 40–47J, 65–73; *France CPI* (n 2) enumerates over 16 exceptions to copyright infringement. See e.g., art L122-5, L122-6-1.

[181] ibid.

[182] See above: 'Exceptions to copyright infringement and international obligations.'

[183] E.g., *Canada CA* (n 2) ss 79–88, private copying regime is becoming increasingly limited in its application because of its failure to adapt to new technologies, e.g., MP3.

[184] See Chapter 6.

[185] See above: 'May exceptions to copyright infringement be waived by contract?'

[186] ALRC Report (n 25) at 13–18.

uses, and alignment with reasonable consumer expectations, while protecting right holders' markets.[187]

As a regulatory model, exceptions to copyright infringement remain a vehicle that confines copyright user rights. Even in jurisdictions that are most auspicious for copyright users, the legal nature of exceptions to copyright infringement remains uncertain. Given the current state of the law, exceptions may be no more than privileges and defences to copyright infringement that impose no positive obligations on copyright holders to allow users to exercise those exceptions. Similarly, exceptions to copyright infringement may be no more than waivable commodities that are dispensed with at the will of copyright holders through non-negotiated standard terms of use. User rights cannot rest on such unstable foundations.

[187] ibid at 87–122.

# 3

# In Search of Copyright User Remedies

## Charting the Landscape of Copyright User Remedies

Exploring the remedies users may have against copyright holders in relation to restricted uses of copyright works is an important way to evaluate the nature and scope of the rights that copyright users have. Having a legal right implicates the correlative duty of another, the breach of which typically gives rise to a remedy.[1] The strength of copyright users' rights should be measured by the duties conferred upon others to honour them.[2]

There are few cases involving copyright user claims against copyright holders restricting their uses of copyright works.[3] The low level of copyright user claims against copyright holders can be interpreted as an indicator that commercial transactions involving copyright works do not give rise to important legal concerns. Conversely, it could be an indicator that various factors and obstacles that are specific to information products make it even more difficult for consumers and other users to assert their claims than in relation to other products.[4] Various studies and reports conducted on the application of sale of goods and consumer protection law to commercial copies of copyright works corroborate the latter view.[5] The

[1] See Chapter 2: 'User rights or privileges?' [2] ibid.

[3] One notable exception is France: see e.g., Trib gr inst 6e Nanterre, 15 December 2006, *Association UFC Que Choisir v Société Sony France, Société Sony United Kingdom Ltd* (2008) JCP E 3, 19; *Christophe R, UFC Que Choisir/Warner Music France, Fnac,* Trib. gr. inst. 5e Paris, 10 January 2006, (2006) JurisData: 2006-292685; CA Versailles, 30 September 2004, *EMI Music France v Association CLCV,* online: <http://www.juriscom.net/jpt/visu.php?ID=579> accessed 8 September 2016; CA Paris, 20 June 2007, *Fnac Paris v UFC Que Choisir et autres*, online: <http://www.legalis.net/jurisprudence-decision> accessed 8 September 2016; Trib gr inst 6e Nanterre, 2 September 2003, *Françoise M v EMI France, Auchan France*, online: <http://www.legalis.net/jurisprudence-decision> accessed 8 September 2016; Cass civ 1st, 27 November 2008, *UFC Que Choisir v Fnac Warner Music France*, online: <https://www.legifrance.gouv.fr/affichJuriJudi.do?idTexte=JURITEXT000019842464> accessed 8 September 2016.

[4] As a starting point, there are important obstacles to the enforcement to consumer claims generally. For a recent overview of the different theories and strategies employed for the regulation of consumer protection and enforcement issues, see Fabrizio Cafaggi & Hans W Micklitz, eds, *New Frontiers of Consumer Protection: The Interplay Between Private and Public Enforcement* (Cambridge: Intersentia, 2009), in particular Samuel Issacharoff & Ian J Samuel, 'The Institutional Dimension of Consumer Protection' at 47–62.

[5] UK, Department for Business, Innovation and Skills, Robert Bradgate, *Consumer Rights in Digital Products*, 2010, online: <http://www.google.ca/search?sourceid=navclient&ie=UTF-8&rlz=1T4ADBF_enCA275CA275&q=Bradgate%2c+Consumer+rights+in+digital+products+2010> accessed 4 February 2017; Marco BM Loos et al, 'Analysis of the Applicable Legal Frameworks and

uncertainty around the rights copyright users have[6] may explain to a large extent the relative absence of user claims against copyright holders. The near absence of government consumer agencies and consumer organizations' attention to copyright user claims in comparison to other industries is another.[7] Last but not least, as a corollary to the uncertain nature of user rights, the remedies users may have against copyright holders are limited or remain largely undefined, which is the main focus of this chapter.

In response to pleas for more specific constraints on copyright holders' exclusive rights to address legitimate interests of users, a common assumption is that contract law, sale of goods law, consumer law, competition or antitrust law are adequate to deal with the rights and interests of copyright users.[8] This chapter tests this common assumption with respect to contract, sale of goods, and consumer law, through various scenarios where the rights and interests of copyright holders are potentially in conflict with those of users. [9]

The scarcity if not lack of remedies available to copyright users against copyright holders is rarely invoked in pleas for a greater acknowledgement of copyright users and more balanced copyright regimes.[10] Statutory copyright laws provide remedies for copyright infringement as defined therein, but no such

Suggestions for the Contours of a Model System of Consumer Protection in relation to Digital Content Contracts' (2011) University of Amsterdam, Centre for the Study of European Contract Law (CSECL), Institute for Information Law (IViR), Amsterdam Centre for Law and Economics (ACLE), online: http://ec.europa.eu/justice/newsroom/consumer-marketing/events/digital_conf_en.htm accessed 4 February 2017.

[6] See Chapter 1 and Chapter 2: 'The nature of exceptions to copyright infringement.'

[7] Governmental consumer protection agency activities will generally mirror their constitutive consumer protection legislation which target specific industries that do not include the one of information products. See, e.g., the segments of the industry specifically addressed by the Office de la Protection du Consommateur (Québec), online: http://www.opc.gouv.qc.ca/en/consumer/ accessed 4 February 2017. The segments of industry that were under the scrutiny of UK Office of Fair Trading before it closed on 1 April 2014 did not include information products and were: Consumer Credit, Financial and Professional Services, Pharmaceutical and Health, Retail and Wholesale, Transport. In France, consumer organizations such as Que Choisir, online: <https://www.quechoisir.org/> accessed 4 February 2017, have been active in asserting copyright user claims against copyright holders and distributors. In Australia, see mandate of Australian Competition and Consumer Commission, online: <https://www.accc.gov.au/consumers> accessed 4 February 2017.

[8] See e.g., Austl, Commonwealth, Law Reform Commission, *Copyright and the Digital Economy* (Report No 122) (Sydney: ALRC, 2013) at 435–58 [ALRC], discussion on the appropriateness of making exceptions to copyright infringement mandatory, pointing to other legal doctrines, such as the doctrine of public policy, consumer law, the doctrine of copyright misuse, that could ensure that the rights of users are adequately protected.

[9] See below: 'User claims and remedies against restricted uses of copyright works based on breach of contract, sale of goods, or consumer law,' and 'User claims against restricted uses of copyright works for breach of obligation of good faith or in tort.'

[10] Works focusing on the copyright user perspective rarely address remedies users may have against copyright holders. See e.g., Ray L Patterson & Stanley W Lindberg, *The Nature of Copyright: A Law of Users Rights* (Athens: University of Georgia Press, 1991); Jessica Litman, *Digital Copyright* (Amherst: Prometheus Books, 2001); Robert Burrell & Allison Coleman, *Copyright Exceptions: The Digital Impact* (Cambridge: Cambridge University Press, 2005); Maria A Pallente, 'The Next Great Copyright Act' (2013) 36 Colum JL & Arts 315 at 326ff, discussing the improvement of the enforcement of copyright holders' rights, but with no discussion of addressing copyright users claims or remedies.

equivalent exists for copyright users.[11] Copyright-user-related arguments are primarily made as defences to allegations of copyright infringement.[12] Copyright statutes generally offer few if any remedies to users against copyright holders. Resorting to declaratory judgments to clarify the legal status of copyright users is one form of remedy in the broader sense that is generally available.[13] Some copyright statutes offer remedies to users in limited circumstances, which is what I explore next.[14]

## User Claims and Remedies in Copyright Law

The introduction in the World Intellectual Property Organization (WIPO) Internet treaties (1996)[15] of an international obligation to provide legal safeguards to technological protection measures (TPMs)[16] has led some jurisdictions to introduce recourses by users against copyright holders blocking legitimate uses of their works.[17] This is the case in European jurisdictions as a result of EU *Directive 2001/29/EC*.[18] The Directive imposes an obligation on its Member States to require copyright holders to make available to beneficiaries of certain exceptions to copyright the means by which to benefit from those exceptions.[19] Conferring explicit remedies in copyright statutes for users to use against copyright holders was a first in several jurisdictions putting such a mechanism in place.[20]

For example in France and Belgium, the relevant copyright statutes provide that TPMs cannot restrain the 'normal use' (or similar concept) of a copyright work.[21] A normal use relates more closely to concepts of latent defects in the civil law, to sale of goods or consumer protection law implied obligations of quality and fitness for purpose,

[11] Various international and regional intellectual property instruments require member states to provide adequate remedies for the enforcement of copyright holders' exclusive rights. See e.g., *Agreement on Trade-Related Aspects of Intellectual Property Rights, Marrakesh Agreement Establishing the World Trade Organization, Annex 1C*, 15 April 1994, 1869 UNTS 29, 33 ILM 1197; EC, *Directive 2004/48/EC of the European Parliament and of the Council of 29 April 2004 on the enforcement of intellectual property rights*, [2004] OJ, L 195/16.

[12] See Chapter 2: 'The mechanics of exceptions to copyright infringement.'

[13] See e.g., *CCH Canadian Ltd v Law Society of Upper Canada* (1999), [2000] 2 FC 451 (TD): defendant's unsuccessful counterclaim for a declaration of non-infringement of copyright; dismissed on appeal: *CCH Canadian Ltd v Law Society of Upper Canada*, 2002 FCA 187.

[14] See below: 'User claims and remedies in copyright law.'

[15] I.e., the *WIPO Copyright Treaty*, 20 December 1996, WO033EN [*WCT*] and *WIPO Performances and Phonograms Treaty*, 20 December 1996, WO034EN [*WPPT*].

[16] See Chapter 6. [17] ibid.

[18] EC, *Parliament and Council Directive 2001/29/EC of 22 May 2001 on the harmonisation of certain aspects of copyright and related rights in the information society*, [2001] OJ, L 167/10.

[19] ibid, art 6.4. See Chapter 6: 'Setting requirements for technological protection measures.'

[20] See e.g., Belgium: Séverine Dusollier, 'Les nouvelles dispositions belges en matière de protection technique des œuvres' (2005) *Auteurs & Médias*, 532, at the heading 'Les sanctions de l'absence de mesures volontaires et de l'entrave à l'utilisation normale' [Dusollier, 'Nouvelles dispositions belges'].

[21] France Code de Propriété Intellectuelle [*France CPI*], art L 331-5 (in French, *libre usage*); Belgium Wetboek van economisch recht/Code de droit economique [*Belgium WER/CDE*] art X.291 § 4 (in French, *destination normale* and in Dutch, *beoogde dool te gebruiken*).

than it does to copyright law.[22] As an import into copyright law, the normal use concept provides a broad foundation for a claim by copyright users that makes room for user property rights and interests in copyright works, in an otherwise copyright-holder-centric regime.[23] Other provisions in *France CPI* prescribe obligations in relation to the interoperability of copies of copyright works,[24] and require that copyright holders employing TPMs take adequate measures to allow users to benefit from exceptions to copyright infringement specified in the said provisions.[25] A broad exception tempers copyright holders' obligation to take 'adequate measures' to permit the benefit of certain exceptions when there is a contract between the user and the copyright holder whereby the user may access the works at a time and place they choose.[26] Depending on how broadly this exception is interpreted, it may significantly reduce copyright holders' obligation in an environment where users increasingly access copyright works through services,[27] and it is not clear whether it would also exclude only works accessed as services or whether it would exclude individualized copies downloaded from users as a result of such contract between users and copyright holders.[28]

In France, the 'Haute Autorité pour la diffusion des oeuvres et la protection des droits sur Internet' [HADOPI], a regulatory body in charge, among others, of overseeing the application of TPMs, allows any interested party under *France CPI*[29] to file a complaint in relation to TPMs interfering with designated exceptions to copyright infringement,[30] or in relation to interoperability issues surrounding copyright works.[31] HADOPI's mandate includes promoting conciliation between the parties, failing which it delivers a decision rejecting the complaint, or issuing an injunction to ensure the benefit of the relevant exception to copyright infringement.[32] HADOPI may also issue opinions ('avis') and make recommendations (e.g., amendments to laws) and also has regulatory powers.[33] HADOPI has issued opinions concerning the removal of TPMs relative to the National Library's obligations of legal deposit of works for purposes of reference and conservation,[34] the interoperability of devices for the benefit of private copying exception in the case of broadcasts,[35] and with respect to the interoperability of Blu-Ray technology.[36]

[22] Dusollier, 'Nouvelles dispositions belges' (n 20) at the heading 'l'utilisation de l'œuvre conformément à sa destination normale.' See below: 'User claims and remedies against restricted uses of copyright works based on breach of contract, sale of goods, or consumer law.'

[23] See Natali Helberger & P Bernt Hugenholtz, 'No Place Like Home for Making a Copy, Private Copying in European Copyright Law and Consumer Law' (2007) 22 BTLJ 1061 at 1096–97, pointing to the assertion of user rights within a copyright-holder-centric regime as an 'uphill struggle'.

[24] *France CPI* (n 21) art L 331-5, L 331-31-32.

[25] ibid, art L 331-7. L 331-31. See also *Belgium WER/CDE* (n 20) art X 291 § 2.

[26] France CPI (n 21), art L 331-8; *Directive 2001/29/EC* (n 18) art 6(4) provides similar exception.

[27] See below: 'Goods and services.'

[28] ibid.

[29] *France CPI* (n 21) art L 331-33.

[30] ibid, art L 331-31.

[31] ibid, art L 331-32.

[32] ibid, art L 331-35.

[33] ibid, art L 331-31,36.

[34] Avis relatif à l'exception de dépôt légal, 2013, no 2013-1 (HADOPI), online: <https://hadopi.fr/sites/default/files/page/pdf/AvisBnFs.pdf> accessed 4 February 2017.

[35] Avis relatif à l'exception de copie privée des programmes télévisés, 2014, no 2014-1 (HADOPI), online: <https://www.hadopi.fr/sites/default/files/20140911-Avisexception-copiepriveedesprogrammes.pdf> accessed 4 February 2017.

[36] Avis rendu sur saisine de l'association VideoLAN, 2013, no. 2013-2 (HADOPI), online: <https://hadopi.fr/sites/default/files/page/pdf/Avis_videoLAN.pdf> accessed 4 February 2017.

The UK *Copyrights, Designs and Patents Act* [*UKCDPA*][37] provides a mechanism allowing users to file a complaint after failing to come to an agreement with a copyright holder regarding a TPM that prevents activities permitted by one of the relevant copyright exceptions.[38] Taking into account various factors, the Secretary of State issues a decision,[39] which may include a direction to the copyright holder to make available to the complainant the means of carrying out the permitted act on the relevant copyright work.[40] This procedure excludes certain copyright works[41] and does not apply to 'copyright works made available to the public on agreed contractual terms in such a way that members of the public may access them from a place and at a time individually chosen by them.'[42]

It is difficult to evaluate the impact of the mechanisms set up in jurisdictions like France and the UK to address the obstacles TPMs may create for users. The fact that the parties must first seek to arrive at a mutually satisfactory solution, and that the access issue may thereby be resolved, may explain the low recorded recourse to these procedures to date. Such remedies illustrate the obstacles and burdens that TPMs place on users, who, without them, would be able to benefit from an exception to copyright infringement without having to ask permission of the copyright holder or having to file a complaint with the relevant administrative body.[43]

Other jurisdictions, including Canada, foresee similar mechanisms (through regulations) under which the copyright holder may be required to provide access to a work protected by TPM and for which the complainant should be granted access under the relevant statute.[44]

Except for the targeted procedures enabling users to seek the removal of TPMs blocking the benefit of exceptions to copyright infringement or the 'normal use' of the copyright work, copyright laws remain silent on the remedies users may have against copyright holders for restrictions on access or use of

[37] 1988 (UK), c 48 [*UKCDPA*]. [38] ibid, ss 296ZE and 296ZEA.

[39] Intellectual Property Office, 'Guidance on the Technological Protection Measures (TPMs) complaint process' (3 November 2014), online: <https://www.gov.uk/government/uploads/system/uploads/attachment_data/file/448277/Guidance_on_the_Technological_Protection_Measures_TMPs_Complaints_Proces....pdf> accessed 4 February 2017. So far, neither have the complaints filed under this procedure related to eligible subject matter and nor have they qualified for consideration by the Secretary of State under *UKCDPA* (n 37) s 296ZE: Intellectual Property Office, 'Complaints to Secretary of State under s 296ZE under the Copyright, Designs and Patents Act 1988' (17 July 2015), online: <https://www.gov.uk/government/uploads/system/uploads/attachment_data/file/440384/ipo-foi-2014-432-complaints-to-secretary-of-state-under-s_296ze-cdpa.pdf> accessed 4 February 2017.

[40] *UKCDPA* (n 37) s 296ZE (3).

[41] ibid, s 296ZE (2): it does not apply to computer programs. [42] ibid, s 296ZE (9).

[43] See Chapter 2: 'The "mechanics" of exceptions to copyright infringement.'

[44] E.g., Canada *Copyright Act*, RSC 1985, c C-4, s 41.21(2)(b) [*Canada CA*], the Governor-in-Council may make regulations 'requiring the owner of the copyright in a work ... that is protected by a technological protection measure to provide access to the work, ... to persons who are entitled to the benefit' of some exceptions to the application of TPMs. As of 1 June 2016, no regulations had been made to that effect.

copyright works. Mapping out the remedies users may have against copyright holders requires looking outside the confines of copyright statutes, that is, in contract law, sale of goods law, consumer law, unfair practices law, and in tort. Other avenues available in competition or anti-trust law, or in privacy law are not discussed here.

## User Claims and Remedies Against Restricted Uses of Copyright Works Based on Breach of Contract, on Sale of Goods, or Consumer Law

How are copyright holders' restrictions on uses of copies of copyright works a potential breach of contract? Does the potential breach stem from various statutory or common law implied obligations or warranties, such as quality, fitness for a particular purpose, or quiet possession? Or do usage restrictions contravene consumer statutory information disclosure requirements? And how may the restrictions give rise to unfair commercial practices?

It is beyond the scope of this book to provide a detailed analysis of statutory or common law warranties or implied obligations, information disclosure requirements, and unfair practices, which this author has presented elsewhere.[45] The following highlights some of the key features of those obligations or prohibitions pursuant to which copyright users may have a claim against copyright holders, and offers relevant points of comparison between them.

Starting with implied obligations, the application of consumer implied obligations of quality, fitness for purpose, and quiet possession to information products are the main focus of study of this chapter. For reasons I discuss further below, at least in theory, these consumer implied obligations have greater potential than others to counter copyright holders' commercial practices to block users' benefit from otherwise legitimate uses under copyright statutes.[46] Thus the idea is to explore how these seemingly more promising avenues may equip copyright users against commercial practices that block access to legitimate uses of copyright works.

Consumer protection laws have progressively constrained freedom of contract and the implied obligations of our study have significantly encroached upon the application of the maxim *caveat emptor*.[47] The consumer protection of the quality,

[45] See Pascale Chapdelaine, *Copyright Consumers' Bargain, Defining the Rights to Commercial Copies of Copyright Works* (Doctor of Philosophy Thesis, York University Graduate Program in Law, Osgoode Hall Law School Library, 2013) at 318–64 [Chapdelaine, 'Copyright Consumers' Bargain'].

[46] ibid at 324–51 where the author reviews the applicability of standard consumer law statutory warranties to copies of information products.

[47] *Caveat Emptor* would continue to apply with respect to the sale of specific goods where the buyer had a chance to inspect the goods before purchase and is deemed to have accepted the goods subject to such defects as his examinations should have revealed: Jacob S Ziegel & Anthony J Duggan, *Commercial and Consumer Sales Transactions, Cases, Text and Materials*, 4th ed. (Toronto: Edmond Montgomery Publications Limited, 2002) at 192.

fitness for purpose, or quiet possession of products is regulated through statutory implied conditions or warranties[48] to which different remedies apply in case of breach.[49] Often, the statutory implied obligations cannot be set aside by contract (i.e., they are mandatory),[50] are even considered as *ordre public* in some jurisdictions including Québec, with penal sanctions applicable in case exoneration clauses are used.[51] In other jurisdictions, implied obligations can be overridden by contract.[52] Common law implied obligations may continue to apply to certain transactions that fall outside the scope of the relevant provincial or territorial statutes.[53] For instance, this could be the case if commercial copies of copyright works distributed online were to be excluded from the definition of goods and discredited from the application of the relevant statutory warranty.[54]

The minimum protection offered by the mandatory nature of the statutory implied obligations in some of the Canadian provincial jurisdictions and elsewhere,[55] is of increasing significance for consumers accessing copies of copyright works online. The transaction of these copies is almost invariably accompanied by extensive non-negotiated terms and conditions that can easily alter and even negate the application of the statutory implied obligations.[56] Without their mandatory nature, statutory implied obligations of quality, fitness for use, or quiet possession could be seriously undermined in the online environment.

Typically, statutory implied obligations can be rebutted only in the limited cases specifically listed in the applicable statutory provisions.[57] The remedies available for breach of an implied obligation include specific performance, damages (i.e.,

[48] In most provinces in Canada, statutory implied conditions apply with respect to quality, fitness for purpose, and correspondence with description. In all provinces and territories of common law tradition in Canada, statutory implied warranties of quiet possession apply: see Chapdelaine, 'Copyright Consumers' Bargain' (n 45), 324–51.

[49] Traditionally, the breach of a warranty entitles the claimant to seek damages. The breach of a condition entitles the claimant to rescind the contract and/or to seek damages: Stephen M Waddams, *The Law of Contracts*, 5th ed (Toronto: Canada Law Book Inc, 2005) at para 586; Angela Swan, *Canadian Contract Law*, 2nd ed (Toronto: Lexis Nexis Canada, 2009) at 472.

[50] See e.g., *Consumer Rights Act*, 2015 (UK), c 15, ss 41, 47 [*UKCRA*].

[51] See e.g., Québec *Consumer Protection Act*, RSQ c P-40.1, [*QCPA*] ss 261, 277.

[52] See e.g., Alberta *Sale of Goods Act* RSA 2000, c S-2 [*ASGA*], ss 15–16; other examples include the *New Brunswick Consumer Product Warranty and Liability Act*, SNB 1978, c C-18, ss 24–26 1 [*NBCPWLA*], which restricts cases where the statutory implied warranties can be excluded by contract if for instance 'It is shown that it would not be fair or reasonable to allow reliance on such agreement' (s 25 (1)) and if the consumer suffers losses for which seller would have been otherwise liable had the contract not been made (s 26).

[53] E.g., if the supply of copies of copyright works does not qualify as a good or in some case if it does not correspond to a sale.

[54] *St Albans City & District Council v International Computers Ltd* [1997] FSR 251 (CA).

[55] See e.g., *QCPA* (n 51) ss 261, 262; Ontario *Consumer Protection Act*, SO 2002, c 30, schedule A, s 9(3) [*OCPA*]; British Columbia *Sale of Goods Act*, RSBC 1996 c 410, ss 18, 20 [*BCSGA*], *UKCRA* (n 50) ss 41, 47.

[56] Pascale Chapdelaine, 'The Ambiguous Nature of Copyright Users' Rights' (2013) 26 IPJ 1 at 26–28 [Chapdelaine, 'Ambiguous Nature of Copyright Users' Rights'].

[57] E.g., the statutory implied obligation of quality will not apply to defects specifically brought to the attention of the purchaser before the sale took place. Or the implied warranty of title will not apply with respect to facts that are specifically brought to the attention of the purchaser and that she agrees to assume.

exemplary or punitive damages), and rescission of contract,[58] and vary based on the nature of the implied obligation and the nature of the breach.[59] Although these remedies may be of limited appeal to the consumer of copyright works on an individual transaction basis, the interest of those remedies also resides in how they may shape copyright distributors' business practices to ensure compliance with the law, including acting preventively toward potential class actions.

Information disclosure requirements in consumer protection laws are the least intrusive obligations to suppliers' freedom of contract. They do not impose any minimum standard of quality or other feature of the product as is the case with statutory implied obligations, or scrutinize the fairness or conscionability of the terms imposed by suppliers, as is the case for prohibitions against unfair practices. If suppliers disclose the information in the manner prescribed, they are in compliance with the statutory consumer protection obligation. The remedies for breach of these disclosure requirements are also more limited than with respect to the statutory implied obligations and provisions against unfair terms. In the cases where the information disclosure requirement applies to a breach that touches upon the scope of permitted use of copies of copyright works, the consumer is not in a position to require that the relevant use be allowed through specific performance. Nor is the existence of information disclosure requirements likely to alter suppliers' behaviour in the marketplace, through, *inter alia*, expanding the scope of permitted use. All that the information disclosure provisions require is that the information on the rights and obligations of the contract be disclosed to consumers.

Consumer protection law statutes often prohibit unfair practices, for example, making a false, misleading, deceptive, or unconscionable representation. This is the case of several provincial jurisdictions in Canada.[60] They typically include a non-exhaustive list of practices that may be considered as unfair.[61] Among those practices, 'a representation that the transaction involves or does not involve rights, remedies or obligations if the representation is false, misleading or deceptive'[62] or a 'representation using exaggeration, innuendo or ambiguity as to a material fact or failing to state a material fact if such use or failure deceives or tends to deceive'[63] may be relevant to terms (or the absence of terms) dealing with the scope of use of copies of copyright works. Further, representations, by a person who knows or ought to know, 'that the consumer transaction is excessively one-sided in favour

[58] See e.g., Ontario *Sale of Goods Act*, RSO 1990, c S-1 ss 51–52 [*OSGA*]; *OCPA* (n 55) s 100; *QCPA* (n 51) art 272; EC, *Parliament and Council Directive 1999/44/EC of 25 May 1999 on certain aspects of the sale of consumer goods and associated guarantees* [1999] OJL 171/07 at 12, art 3 [*Directive 1999/44/EC*], lists the remedies available to consumers for goods that do not conform to the contract. They include: repair or replacement, reduction in the price, rescission of contract.

[59] Waddams (n 49); Swan (n 49).

[60] See e.g., *OCPA* (n 55) ss 14–15; *QCPA* (n 51) art 8, 10, 11 & 215ff.

[61] A representation claiming sponsorship approvals that are not true or a representation of certain attributes or quality of goods or services that are non-existent would fall under that category: *OCPA* (n 55) s 14 (2) 1 & 3.

[62] See e.g., *OCPA* (n 55) s 14 (2) 13.

[63] See e.g., *OCPA* (n 55) s 14 (2) 14.

of someone other than the consumer' or 'that the terms of the consumer transaction are so adverse to the consumer as to be inequitable'[64] may also find application with respect to transactions involving copyright works. There are similar regulations prohibiting unfair practices in consumer commercial transactions in the European Union,[65] with their national implementation counterparts in, *inter alia*, the UK[66] and France.[67] In the US, the *UCC* contains provisions conferring powers to the courts to set aside a contract or any term thereof that is held to be unconscionable.[68] In some jurisdictions including some Canadian provinces, the body responsible for overseeing the application of consumer protection laws has broad powers to intervene against unfair practices, including the authority to seek injunctive relief.[69] Competition or anti-trust laws also prohibit similar commercial practices.[70]

The prohibition of unfair practices constrains suppliers' freedom of contract to protect consumers against abuses. The prohibition specifically targets non-negotiated standard end-user agreements, including copyright notices.[71] The prohibitions against unfair practices require an element of falsehood, deceit, or unconscionability, or a practice that is misleading, which tends to limit their scope of application. In contrast, statutory warranties or implied obligations are deemed to be present in all consumer transactions, and as we saw, are often mandatory.[72]

[64] See e.g., *OCPA* (n 55) s 15 (2) e) & (f).

[65] EC, *Council Directive 93/13/EEC of 5 April 1993 on unfair terms in consumer contracts*, [1993] OJ L095, at 29 [*Directive 93/13/EEC*] under which unfair terms are non-binding on consumers: art 6, and characterizing a contract term as unfair 'if, contrary to the requirement of good faith, it causes a significant imbalance in the parties' rights and obligations arising under the contract, to the detriment of the consumer' (art 3 para 1). It also provides 'an indicative and non-exhaustive list of the terms which may be regarded as unfair' (art 3 para 3); EC, *Parliament and Council Directive 2005/29/EC of 11 May 2005 concerning unfair business-to-consumer commercial practices in the internal market and amending Council Directive 84/450/EEC, Directives 97/7/EC, 98/27/EC and 2002/65/EC of the European Parliament and of the Council and Regulation (EC) No 2006/2004 of the European Parliament and of the Council*, [2005] OJ, L 149 at 29 [*Directive 2005/29/EC*] art 6, in particular paras 1f and g regarding representations on the nature of the intellectual property rights of the trader or his agent or on the nature of the rights of consumers. The potential application of these directives to terms and conditions that restrict *inter alia* consumers' exercise of copyright limitations or use of materials that are in the public domain is discussed in: Lucie Guibault, 'Accommodating the Needs of iConsumers: Making Sure They Get Their Money's Worth of Digital Entertainment' (2008) 31 J Consum Policy 409 at 416.

[66] *Directive 93/13/EEC* (n 65) was implemented in the UK through the *Unfair Terms in Consumer Contracts Regulations 1999*, SI 1999/2083, now repealed and replaced by the *UKCRA* (n 50); *Directive 2005/29/EC* (n 65) was implemented through the *Consumer Protection from Unfair Trading Regulations 2008*, SI 2008/1277.

[67] *Code de la consommation*, art L 120-1ff deals with 'pratiques commerciales déloyales.'

[68] *Uniform Commercial Code (2002)* (US) § 2-302 and § 2A-108.

[69] See e.g., *Consumer Protection and Business Practices Act, SS 2014*, c C-30.2, s 92 [*SCPBPA*]. Regarding more generally the remedies that need to be available in each Member State, see *Directive 93/13/EEC* (n 65) art 7, and *Directive 2005/29/EC* (n 65) art 11.

[70] See e.g., Canada *Competition Act* (RSC 1985, c C-34) ss 74.01, 74.011. The Commissioner has the power to bring certain practices for review before the courts referred to in the Act. Courts have the power to issue penalties if there is a finding of a deceptive marketing practice: ibid s 74.1.

[71] This is the case of *Directive 93/13/EEC* (n 65) which specifically regulates non-negotiated consumer commercial transactions.

[72] Chapdelaine, 'Copyright Consumers' Bargain' (n 45) 324–51.

Information disclosure requirements, while they provide less effective remedies for the purpose of our discussion, also apply to a broad range of transactions that are pertinent to commercial transactions of copies of copyright works.[73]

The construction of the legal claims that I propose here emphasizes the main proposition of Chapter 1: rights in the commercial copy of the work have a legal and normative value that is distinct from statutory exceptions to copyright infringement.[74] In property theory terms, the successful user claims would act as a property limitation rule on copyright holders' exclusive rights.[75] As I demonstrate here, the path to assert user rights in contract, sale of goods, consumer protection law, or in torts,[76] remains largely undefined and fraught with uncertainty.

Copyright user claims and remedies are considered through three distinct scenarios that situate the contemplated uses restricted by copyright holders within or outside copyright holders' exclusive domain. In relation to the uses reserved to copyright holders, the scenarios further include uses that are allowed by exceptions to copyright infringement if certain conditions are met.

## Restricted uses fall within the exclusive rights of copyright holders

The restrictions of use of copyright works in this scenario are within the sphere of the exclusive property rights of copyright holders: the prohibition on making copies of the copyright work, on communicating the work to the public, on creating a derivative work from the copyright work, on performing the work in public, on authorizing the first sale, or on transferring ownership of the work where that work is in the form of a tangible object.[77] Here, the contemplated uses that are restricted are not allowed by exceptions to copyright holders' exclusive rights, such as fair dealing, fair use, the private copying regime, exceptions applying to computer programs, or non-commercial user-generated content, a situation that I discuss in the third scenario examined below.[78]

In this scenario, the question boils down to how users may assert claims against copyright holders for restrictions of uses that are the applicable default rules under the relevant copyright legislation. The obvious short answer to this question is that users do not have the right to do acts that are explicitly reserved under copyright law, that do not fall under an exception, or that have not been authorized

[73] Information disclosure requirements are required in distance contracts and Internet agreements, and in some jurisdictions for all consumer agreements: Chapdelaine, 'Copyright Consumers' Bargain' (n 45) 358–62.

[74] See Introduction and Chapter 1.

[75] I.e., when the *prima facie* open-ended privileges of ownership are overridden: James W Harris, *Property and Justice* (Oxford: Clarendon Press, 1996) at 34. See Chapter 2: 'The "mechanics" of exceptions to copyright infringement.'

[76] See below: 'User claims and remedies against restricted uses of copyright works for breach of obligation of good faith or in tort.'

[77] E.g., US *Copyright Act*, 17 USC §§ 106, 113–15, 120 [*USC*]; *Canada CA* (n 44) ss 3, 15, 18, 21, 26.

[78] See below: 'Restricted uses fall within the exclusive rights of copyright holder and are allowed by law under certain conditions.'

by copyright holders. Therefore, users would not be able to assert claims against copyright holders restricting their uses within these parameters.

I have argued elsewhere that even for restrictions of use that fall within the exclusive domain of copyright holders, copyright users might be able to assert claims against such restrictive uses but that the likelihood of success of such claims was slim.[79] For instance, the success of a claim based on the breach of an implied obligation (of quality, fitness for purpose, quiet possession) in jurisdictions that rely on users' reasonable expectations in their consumer protection law (to determine whether such implied obligation was breached), would depend on how much weight courts would place on the notification function of copyright holders' exclusive rights being opposable to all in their assessment of what consumers' reasonable expectations should be.[80] In other words, what weight does the default regime of copyright holders' exclusive rights have against other factors that would shape consumers' reasonable expectations when they buy the copy of a copyright work based on expectations users may have as owners of the copy, and the normal use that should come with such ownership (as measured by, e.g., the technological empowerment that surrounding technologies give users in their uses of copyright works, and commercial practices by other copyright holders that would allow by contract uses otherwise restricted by copyright law).[81] Courts will likely be inclined to favour explicit statutory copyright restrictions over surrounding environmental factors and social norms in their assessment of what consumers' reasonable expectations ought to be.[82]

Claims of implied licences are among the other avenues that copyright users may pursue to counter usage restrictions that are backed up by copyright holders' exclusive rights, for example when it ought to be implied by the main purpose of the contract that users should be able to perform certain acts with the copyright work in spite of restrictions by the copyright statute.[83] While arguments of implied licence and breach of implied obligations failing to meet users' reasonable expectations under consumer law may be made, users stand a far weaker chance of successful claims against the restrictions of use imposed by copyright holders than under the second and last scenarios explored further below, and that are the main focus of this chapter.

## Restricted uses fall within the exclusive rights of copyright holders and are allowed by law under certain conditions

In this scenario, copyright holders (or distributors) restrict users' ability to perform acts that are within the copyright holders' exclusive domain (such as making copies of the musical recording or telecommunicating it to the public, e.g., by posting

[79] Chapdelaine, 'Copyright Consumers' Bargain' (n 45) at 396–405. [80] ibid.
[81] ibid. [82] ibid.
[83] ibid. Implied licences are often implied in contracts where the author needs to develop a copyright work for another party and where there are no clear terms of use set out in the contract. See e.g., *Effects Associates Inc. v Cohen*, 908 F (2d) 555 (9th Cir 1990).

it on the Internet), and yet they are acts that users can perform under copyright law. A usage that is a fair dealing or fair use[84] or that is specifically allowed under the reproduction for private purposes exception[85] or other exceptions applicable to computer programs[86] would fall in that category. In property theory terms, by permitting those acts without the authorization of copyright holders in specific cases, copyright law creates a property-limitation rule on the exclusive rights of copyright holders.[87]

As discussed in Chapter 2, the nature of exceptions to copyright infringement (i.e., whether they are rights or mere defences), as well as whether they may be waived by contract, is an unsettled area of the law.[88] The introduction of TPM legal frameworks worldwide lessens the extent to which exceptions to copyright infringement effectively confer rights on users.[89]

Given the different regulation of exceptions to copyright infringement or user rights and their uncertain nature in many jurisdictions, different hypotheses need to be considered. In the first hypothesis, exceptions to copyright infringement are mandatory (may not be waived by contract), and in the second, they are not (i.e., they may be waived by contract). I discuss the different strengths of user claims and remedies and whether the exceptions to copyright infringement are considered as rights or not. This exercise underscores the impact of various copyright policy design choices on the availability of copyright user claims based on laws other than copyright law.

### *The exceptions to copyright infringement are mandatory (may not be waived by contract)*

There are various situations in which lawful users can be constrained by contract or TPMs from performing certain acts on the commercial copies of copyright works that they purchased, and that they would otherwise be authorized to do under copyright law. For instance, users may want to reuse parts of the musical recording of a song as part of an audiovisual original creation and post it on YouTube or on Facebook for non-commercial purposes. Non-negotiated standard end-user agreements typically forbid such reuse.[90] Other users may want to reproduce a non-substantial part of a film to use as part of an online discussion forum of amateur film critics or for professional purposes, but would be unable to do so without the consent of copyright holders because of the TPMs applied to their DVD. Users

[84] See Chapter 2: 'The "mechanics" of exceptions to copyright infringement.'

[85] See e.g., *Canada CA* (n 44) s 29.22.

[86] ibid, ss 30.6–30.61; USC (n 77) § 117; *UKCDPA* (n 37) ss 50A–50C.

[87] See Harris (n 75) at 34. Property-limitation rules occur when *prima facie* normative claims founded on the prevailing ownership conception (here of copyright) are overridden. But for the limitation they contain (an exception to copyright infringement), the (copyright) owner would be free to do as they please, e.g., applying trespassory protection powers.

[88] See Chapter 2: 'The nature of exceptions to copyright infringement.'

[89] ibid. See Chapter 6.

[90] Chapdelaine, 'Ambiguous Nature of Copyright Users' Rights' (n 56) at 26–28.

may want to reproduce and communicate to the public parts of a book in the context of a parody or satire but are restrained from doing so by the terms of the contract pursuant to which they purchased the e-book online. Other users may want to present portions of a musical recording at community training sessions, which would amount to a performance in public and would typically not be allowed under non-negotiated standard end-user agreements of commercial copies. And the list goes on and on.

If such exceptions to copyright infringement cannot be waived by contract (are mandatory), the contract clause or TPMs restricting the permitted use would be, at a minimum, unenforceable, thereby allowing the user to circumvent the TPM and perform the act restricted by contract or TPMs, without breaching the contract or contravening the statutory TPM.[91] If exceptions to copyright infringement are considered as rights, not only is the restriction unenforceable, but also users could possibly assert their claim through injunctive relief against copyright holders, requiring them to lift the restriction to allow users to perform the permitted use.[92]

Regardless of the nature of exceptions to copyright infringement as rights or defences, the question is how could users formulate a claim against copyright holders who are barring the exercise of an exception to copyright infringement that is mandatory (that cannot be waived by contract). The starting premise is that contractual or TPM restrictions barring the performance of acts otherwise allowed without the authorization of copyright holders (and based on the hypothesis that they are mandatory; cannot be waived) do not comply with copyright law. Each implied obligation of quality, fitness for purpose, title, or quiet possession contains, to various degrees, a requirement that the goods sold comply with law.[93] Any non-compliance with law may constitute a breach of the implied obligation unless this 'defect' was specifically brought to the attention of users.[94] Could copyright holders be in breach of those various implied obligations by restricting uses of their works otherwise permitted by copyright law?

Using a quality or fitness for purpose analysis, it is doubtful that users could establish a successful claim on the basis of an alleged non-compliance with law resulting from copyright holders' restrictions on access to the work. There will be a breach of the implied obligation if the non-compliance with law limits or impairs

[91] Certain TPM regimes allow for this possibility, making circumvention of TPMs lawful when done for the purpose of a use permitted under the relevant copyright act: see Chapter 6. However, this is not the case in all jurisdictions, ibid, trumping the lawful exercise of exceptions to copyright infringement.

[92] See Chapter 2: 'User rights or privileges?'

[93] *J Barry Winsor & Associates Ltd v Belgo Canadian Manufacturing Co Ltd* (1975), 61 DLR (3d) 352 (BCSC), aff'd 76 DLR (3d) 685 (CA): non-compliance with law amounting to breach of implied obligation of title. Question of compliance with law and implied obligation of quiet possession was discussed but not definitively decided in *Meyknecht-Lischer Contractors Ltd v Stanford*, 2005 WL 4904857 (Ont Sup Ct), and in *Guillevin International Inc v Antique Building Supplies Ltd*, 1991 WL 1142203 (Ont Ct J (Gen Div)).

[94] E.g., there would be no implied warranty of quality or fitness for purpose in relation to a good sold that requires a certification or a repair for it to be operational and compliant with laws, if the lack of certification or repair is specifically brought to the attention of the consumer before the sale.

the purposes for which such good is normally used,[95] or if users can reasonably expect that copies of copyright works comply with laws,[96] depending on the jurisdiction in question. In the scenario currently being considered, copies of copyright works that restrict users from a fair dealing with the work, from copying the copyright work for private purposes, or from using the work to create a new work for non-commercial-purposes would still allow users to play the musical recording or film within the framework of the relevant copyright statute and any standard terms and conditions attached to the musical recording or film. As a result, the strength of a claim alleging that a copyright holder breached implied obligations of quality or fitness for purpose by depriving a user of the benefit of an exception to copyright infringement is low.

It is reasonably safe to predict that copyright holders would normally not notify users, either in restrictive terms of use or by the existence of TPMs, that they are not allowed (able) to exercise acts otherwise specifically authorized by copyright law.[97] Non-negotiated standard end-user agreements listing acts that are permitted and restricted would not necessarily amount to a notification that users are not allowed to perform acts that would be otherwise authorized by copyright law, such as through fair use or fair dealing exceptions to copyright infringement.[98]

While the non-compliance with copyright law may not be a breach of implied obligations of quality or fitness for purpose in the jurisdictions where the standard to meet is relatively low, such as the sale of goods standard of merchantable quality,[99] it may be a breach in jurisdictions that ground the application of copyright holders' or distributors' implied obligations on the reasonable expectations

[95] This is the case in most jurisdictions in Canada; see: Chapdelaine, 'Copyright Consumers' Bargain' (n 45) at 327–44.

[96] The jurisdictions applying the consumers' or person's reasonable expectation test to assess the scope of implied obligations of quality and fitness for purpose ['Jurisdictions applying reasonable expectation test'] include Saskatchewan: *SCPBPA* (n 69) ss 10(1)(a), 19(d)–(e); Quebec: *QCPA* (n 51) s 37. See also *Sale of Goods Act 1979* (UK), c 54, ss 14(2), (3) [*UKSGA*]; *Supply of Goods and Services Act 1982* (UK), c 29, ss 4(2), (4)–(5) [*UKSGSA*].

[97] Chapdelaine, 'Ambiguous Nature of Copyright Users' Rights' (n 56) at 26–28.

[98] It depends on the enforceability of the terms of use, in particular, how they were brought to the attention of the user under the doctrine of reasonable notice: Loos et al (n 5) at 65–66. See by analogy, treatment by courts of contract clauses stating that a product is sold 'as is' as not invalidating the application of implied obligations ['Courts' treatment of products sold "as is"']: *MacLeod v Ens*, [1982] 3 WWR 653, 15 Sask R 73, 135 DLR (3d) 365 (CA); *Radul v Daudrich*, [1983] 6 WWR 278, 1983 CarswellMan 135 (WL Can) (MCA) where the court held that a statement to the effect that a good was not of a merchantable quality and sold 'as is' did not fulfil the statement of quality that could limit the application of the statutory warranties under Manitoba's *Consumer Protection Act; Theriault v Roy* (1990), 109 NBR (2d) 75, 273 APR 75, 1990 CarswellNB 169 (WL Can) (QB) where the court held that a sale 'as is' did not remove the implied warranty of quality and durability; see also *Munro v Central Auto Sales Ltd 1994*, 1997 CarswellSask 798 (WL Can) (PC); *Parsons v Mont-Bleu Ford Inc*, 2002 CarswellQue 2932 (WL Can) (CQ); *Adams v J & D's Used Cars Ltd*, 1983 CarswellSask 311 (WL Can) (QB) which involved a case where the implied statutory warranty of fitness for a particular purpose applied, given that plaintiff had specifically brought that purpose of the car to the attention of the vendor. The reference to a sale 'as is' was of no legal effect in relation to the application of the warranty.

[99] See Chapdelaine, 'Copyright Consumers' Bargain' (n 45) at 327–44.

of the user. In the latter jurisdictions, the point of departure is whether users can reasonably expect that products are compliant with law,[100] whereas in the former jurisdictions the question is framed around whether the deficiency of legal compliance makes the product of non-merchantable quality or disables it so that it cannot perform at least one of the purposes for which copies of copyright works are supplied.[101]

There may be a stronger argument that copies of copyright works that do not comply with law breach the implied obligations of title and quiet possession. The jurisprudence on implied obligations of title and of quiet possession has interpreted the failure of goods to comply with laws or regulations as breaches of the sellers' implied obligations.[102] It depends on how courts are willing to interpret the effect of restrictions imposed by copyright holders on users' uses of copies of copyright works that would be otherwise permitted by law. Breach of the implied obligation of quiet possession occurs in a broad array of cases where the expectations of owners and possessors about their open-ended powers and privileges are compromised. The jurisprudence on quiet possession suggests that a constraint on how possessory or ownership rights can be exercised, even though the constraint does not entirely impair use, may amount to a breach of the implied obligation of quiet possession.[103] The public policy aspects and balancing act between competing interests that specific exceptions to copyright infringement embed could form the basis of an argument that, by unilaterally taking these permissions away, copyright holders breach their implied obligation of quiet possession.

In addition to claims based on breaches of implied obligations, users could invoke a breach of copyright holders' information disclosure requirements under consumer laws.[104] Typically, users are not explicitly notified when the restrictions imposed by copyright holders on the uses of copyright works restrict the users' ability to exercise fair dealing or other users rights that would otherwise not require the consent of copyright holders.[105] Consumer law imposes minimum disclosure information requirements for certain contracts on sellers and distributors.[106] Among the information disclosure requirements, any material term of the transaction needs to be disclosed to users.[107] Contract terms constraining acts that are otherwise specifically authorized without the permission of copyright holders could be regarded as a material term of any transaction involving copies of copyright works.[108] The French Cour de Cassation decided otherwise in *Mulholland*

[100] See 'Jurisdictions applying reasonable expectation test' (n 96).

[101] See Chapdelaine, 'Copyright Consumers' Bargain' (n 45) at 327–44.

[102] ibid at 345–51. [103] ibid. [104] ibid at 358–61.

[105] See Chapdelaine, 'Ambiguous Nature of Copyright Users' Rights' (n 56) at 26–28.

[106] Such as distance contracts and Internet agreements. See Chapdelaine, 'Copyright Consumers' Bargain' (n 45) at 358–61.

[107] ibid.

[108] Information disclosure requirements imposed for specific forms of agreements require that any term material to the conclusion of the contract be disclosed in writing prior to the conclusion of the agreement: ibid.

*Drive.*[109] Having held that the provisions allowing to make private copies could be invoked as a defence to copyright infringement and not as a right, the Cour de Cassation held that any restriction on private copying did not constitute material information under the *French Code de la Consommation.*[110] The fact that the private copying regime exception was held to be a non-mandatory defence and not a right, likely played an important role in the Court's judgment. Nevertheless, this should not preclude a restriction on the private copying exception from being material information. This is especially true given the underlying goal of consumer law to address asymmetry of information and bargaining power between sellers and users.[111] Given the complexity of copyright law, users should be informed of their basic rights (privileges) and how the commercial transaction alters those rights, and even more so in non-negotiated standard end-user agreements.

Finally, a non-negotiated agreement that deprives users of rights that law would otherwise give them could constitute an unfair practice.[112] In the US, the Federal Trade Commission (FTC) rejected a complaint filed by the Computer & Communications Industry Association (CCIA) that alleged that copyright warnings of a list of companies[113] constituted unfair and deceptive trade practices.[114] The CCIA alleged that the copyright warnings exaggerated the rights of the copyright holders by ignoring consumers' statutory fair use rights. The FTC responded that it did not have sufficient evidence to conclude that such warnings were unfair and deceptive practices and that 'consumers would be likely to refrain from engaging in lawful activities as a consequence of reading those warnings.'[115]

Users may generally not be aware of acts that they can perform without the authorization of copyright holders.[116] Yet those acts are permitted by copyright

[109] *Studio Canal* et al *v S Perquin and Union fédérale des consommateurs Que choisir*, CA, Paris, 4 April 2007, Gaz Pal 18/07/2007 No 199 at 23, confirmed by the Cour de Cassation, Cass civ 1re, 19 June 2008, (2008) Bull civ I, No 177. This case involved TPMs blocking users from making private copies.

[110] ibid. More particularly, *Code de la Consommation* art L 111-1.

[111] See Chapdelaine, 'Copyright Consumers' Bargain' (n 45) at 365–93, in particular at 365–68.

[112] In a European context, Loos et al (n 5) at 199, where the authors recommend that terms in digital content agreements that would limit uses that are otherwise authorized by copyright law should be added to the list of terms that are presumed to be unfair under the 'grey list' of unfair contract terms in European law; Lucie Guibault, 'Accommodating the Needs of iConsumers: Making Sure They Get Their Money's Worth of Digital Entertainment' (2008) 31 J Consumer Policy 409, more particularly at 416.

[113] The following companies were listed in the complaint filed by the CCIA to the FTC: National Football League, NFL Properties, Inc., NFL Enterprises LLC, Major League Baseball, Major League Baseball Properties, Inc., Major League Baseball Advanced Media, LP, NBC Universal, Inc., Universal Studios, Inc., Morgan Creek Productions, Inc., DreamWorks Animation SKG, Inc., DreamWorks LLC, Harcourt, Inc., and Penguin Group (USA), Inc.

[114] For a review of the complaint and the response by the FTC, see: Scott L Walker & Matthew Savare, 'Foul Use? FTC Declines to Take Action against Allegedly Overbroad and Misleading Copyright Warnings' (2008) 25 WTR Ent & Sports Law 1.

[115] FTC's letter in response to CCIA's complaint dated 6 December 2007, online: <http://www.google.ca/search?sourceid=navclient&ie=UTF-8&rlz=1T4ADBF_enCA275CA275&q=Computer+%26+Communications+Industry+Association+complaint+federal+trade+commission+2007> accessed 4 February 2017.

[116] See Chapdelaine, 'Ambiguous Nature of Copyright Users' Rights' (n 56) at 26–28.

law to preserve and promote important public policy interests.[117] The absence of notification of such restrictions (e.g., the presence of TPMs) could be an unfair practice.[118] An analogy can be made with consumer protection law provisions that forbid contract terms that deprive consumers of rights conferred by the law and limit their right of action before courts.[119] Similarly, a contract term that substantially deprives users from exercising their rights or privileges under copyright law would constitute an unfair practice.

### *The exceptions to copyright infringement are non-mandatory (may be waived by contract)*

In the present hypothesis, the exceptions to copyright infringement can be overridden by contract or TPMs.[120] If exceptions to copyright infringement may be waived by contract (are not mandatory), it follows that the commercial practice of overriding them by contract or by the application of TPMs is consistent with copyright law. It also means that users could not successfully allege a breach of contract on the basis of restrictions imposed on non-mandatory users' rights. If consumer law were to provide grounds to successfully challenge contractual restrictions that limit the exercise of exceptions to copyright infringement, it would allow users to strengthen their usage rights in a way that copyright law does not currently permit.

Claims made under sale of goods or consumer law to challenge restrictions of uses that preclude users the benefit of an exception to copyright infringement (such as the right to make copies for back-up purposes, or other computer software-related exceptions) are less likely to succeed if the said exception to copyright is non-mandatory than if it is.[121] The argument that restrictions that limit the exercise of mandatory exceptions to copyright infringement do not comply with law and breach various implied obligations would not be available here.[122] In this scenario, the copyright law framework gives the flexibility to right holders (and to users in negotiated contracts) to contract out of default rules put in place to benefit copyright users.

[117] See Chapter 2.

[118] In a European context, this is the argument made by Peter Rott, 'Download of Copyright-Protected Internet Content and the Role of (Consumer) Contract Law' (2008) 31 J Consumer Policy 441 at 447ff. Relying on the EC, *Council Directive 93/13/EEC of 5 April 1993 on unfair terms in consumer contracts*, [1993] OJ, L 095 at 29 [*Directive 93/13/EEC*] and particularly the article regarding as unfair any non-negotiated contracts 'if, contrary to the requirement of good faith, it causes a significant imbalance in the parties' rights and obligations arising under the contract, to the detriment of the consumer'; the author argues that the non-notification of TPMs that limits the exercise of private copying would be an unfair term. Once the limitation is specifically brought to the attention of consumers, it would no longer be an unfair term and such restriction would be in conformity with the contract.

[119] See *OCPA* (n 55) s 7; *QCPA* (n 66) s 11.1.

[120] See Chapter 2: 'May exceptions to copyright infringement be waived by contract?'

[121] See: 'The exceptions to copyright infringement are mandatory (may not be waived by contract).'

[122] ibid.

Even in those jurisdictions that are more auspicious to consumer claims by basing the application of implied obligations (such as quality, fitness for purpose, quiet possession) on users' reasonable expectations, the non-mandatory nature of exceptions to copyright infringement would make the success of such claims less likely.[123] The reasonable expectation of users' test requires consideration of a list of non-exhaustive factors.[124] Factors supporting users' claims would include the fact that the exception to copyright infringement overridden by the copyright holder is considered a user's right as opposed to a mere privilege or defence.[125] Industry practices allowing users to perform the permitted acts freely would be another factor. The absence of an explicit notification advising users that they are restricted to exercise acts that would otherwise be permitted by copyright law's default rules would be another factor.[126] However, copyright law's endorsement to override this right (privilege or defence) by not making it mandatory would weigh against users' reasonable expectations that they could exercise such rights (privileges or defences).

In addition to a potential breach of consumer implied obligations, copyright holders applying TPMs that restrict users' ability to perform acts that they would be otherwise authorized to do under copyright law, were it not for the TPMs, may be in breach of their information disclosure requirement obligations and copyright holders' restrictions could constitute an unfair commercial practice.[127] Once again these claims would have even less strength under the scenario that the benefit of the exception to copyright infringement that is restricted can be overridden by contract than if it is mandatory. The TPMs restriction of use operates *de facto* similarly to a contractual restriction (which copyright law allows in this scenario). And one would be hard pressed to find the commercial practice of restricting the benefit of exceptions to copyright infringement unfair when copyright law endorses such restrictions by not making exceptions to copyright infringement mandatory.

## Restricted uses outside the realm of the exclusive rights of copyright holders

This scenario examines how the law deals with usage restrictions that are not based on copyright holders' exclusive rights, either because of the nature of the product, in whole or in part, or because the restrictions of uses of the copyright work are beyond the ones that copyright holders can impose by relying on their exclusive rights. As such, any contravention to the use restriction would be a breach of contract that does not involve copyright infringement. And yet, in this scenario, there is some level of connection between the usage restrictions and copyright protection. Any successful claim in contract, sale of goods, or consumer law against these usage restrictions does not act as a property-limitation rule[128] as its effects would

[123] See 'Jurisdictions applying reasonable expectation test' (n 96). [124] ibid.
[125] See Chapter 2: 'User rights or privileges?'
[126] Chapdelaine, 'Copyright Consumers' Bargain' (n 45) at 327–51.
[127] See above: 'The exceptions to copyright infringement are mandatory (may not be waived by contract).'
[128] Harris (n 75) at 34: i.e., when the *prima facie* open-ended privileges of ownership are overridden.

not be to limit the exclusive property rights of copyright holders per se. Rather, such successful claims intervene in the contract sphere, outside the realm of copyright holders' exclusive rights.

This scenario pertains to two broad categories of usage restrictions. The first category concerns use restrictions that apply to works not protected by copyright, for example, works that are in the public domain, or that are supplied with works subject to copyright. The second category sets limits on acts that are not exclusively reserved to copyright holders.[129] There is controversy as to the types of restrictions of use that fall in the second category. As copyright is increasingly shaping itself as an access right, as the scope of copyright holders' distribution and communication rights with respect to online copyright works is unsettled,[130] it might be argued that at least some of the usage restrictions discussed here fall squarely within copyright holders' exclusive distribution or communication right and belong to the scenario examined earlier in this chapter.[131] For instance, does the distribution right or the right to authorize the first sale of a copy of a copyright work also entail the right to set time limits on the use of the work or any other restrictions that do not pertain to the exclusive right of reproduction, communication to, or performance in public reserved to copyright holders? For the purpose of the present analysis, the assumption is that the usage restrictions are not based on copyright holders' exclusive rights but that they are imposed through contract obligations restricting the usage of the work.

In the category of usage restrictions applying to works not protected by copyright, the application of TPMs restricting the use of a large portion of works not protected by copyright that are supplied with a significantly lesser portion of works protected by copyright could give rise to a breach of consumer implied obligations (quality, fitness for use, quiet possession).[132] The line of argument would apply to those works subject to TPMs that are not protected by copyright, on the basis that the restrictions of use of TPMs would go against their normal unconstrained uses and encroach upon powers and privileges that come with possession of such unprotected works.[133] The doctrine of copyright misuse[134] and of *abus de droit* in civil law jurisdictions,[135] could also apply here.[136] The application of TPMs

[129] For example, TPMs that would render the copy of a musical recording unusable after playing the song 30 times, as opposed to a time or territorial limitation that would restrict the performance of acts exclusively reserved to copyright holders.

[130] On the development of copyright as an access right, see e.g., Jane C Ginsburg, 'From Having Copies to Experiencing Works: The Development of an Access Right in U.S. Copyright Law' (2003) 50 J Copyright Society USA 113; Zohar Efroni, *Access-Right: The Future of Digital Copyright Law* (Oxford: Oxford University Press, 2010).

[131] See: 'Restricted uses fall within the exclusive rights of copyright holders.'

[132] Chapdelaine, 'Copyright Consumers' Bargain' (n 45) at 327–51.

[133] ibid.

[134] The doctrine of copyright misuse is a defence in US copyright law to copyright infringement under which the alleged infringer invokes the abusive use by the copyright holder of their exclusive rights, which may or may not involve antitrust considerations.

[135] See Pierre-Emmanuel Moyse, 'Kraft Canada c. Euro-Excellence: l'insoutenable légèreté du droit' (2008) 53 RD McGill 741.

[136] On the application of the doctrine of copyright misuse to other copyright holders' commercial practices, see Kristin Cobb, 'The Implications of Licensing Agreements and the First Sale Doctrine on U.S. and EU Secondary Markets for Digital Goods' (2014) 24 Duke J Comp & Intl L 529 at 545ff.

could also amount to unfair practices, such as when it leads users to believe that the works are protected by copyright, while all or a significant portion thereof are not.[137] Where all the works supplied are not protected by copyright and are subject to TPMs restricting access and use (such as literary works for which the copyright term has expired, or facts or data that do not qualify as copyright works) the legal regime protecting such TPMs would not apply on the basis that the TPM would not be considered 'effective' as not pertaining to a work protected by copyright.[138] On that basis, the circumvention of such TPMs would not amount to a contravention of the TPM provisions. This is not to minimize the obstacles that TPMs create on usage for most users not having the physical capabilities or other means to circumvent TPMs.

In the category of usage restrictions that limit acts that are not exclusively reserved to copyright holders, this includes copyright holders' widespread practice to restrict the user's right to transfer ownership in their commercial copies of copyright works when such practice would be in contravention to the first sale or exhaustion doctrine,[139] in particular, when users are led to believe that they own the copy they paid for.[140] Usage restrictions to commercial copies of copyright works owned by users that limit the number of times they can play the song, film, or read the book, or the devices on which they can play such works also fall into the present scenario. It is assumed here that the usage restrictions are limiting acts that are outside the exclusive rights of copyright holders: the restrictions do not seek to stop users from making a copy of the musical recording or film, telecommunicating it to the public or performing it in public, or distributing the copyright work.[141] The right to play the copy of the film or musical recording for an unlimited time, in unlimited territories[142] flows from users' *prima facie* open-ended powers and privileges as owners of the commercial copies of copyright works.[143]

Two French cases are illustrative of the interaction between consumer or sale of goods law implied obligations, and usage restrictions that limit acts that are not exclusively reserved to copyright holders under copyright law. The two cases involve the application of warranties of quality to the scope of use by consumers of musical recordings through the purchase of CDs.[144] In both cases, the

137 See Chapdelaine, 'Copyright Consumers' Bargain' (n 45) at 351–57.

138 In several jurisdictions, this would not be considered an 'effective' TPM which is what the *WIPO Internet treaties* (n 15) protect. See Chapter 6.

139 See Chapter 5.

140 Such commercial practice could amount to deceiving or unfair commercial practices. See Aaron Perzanowski & Jason Schultz, 'Reconciling Intellectual Property with Personal Property' (2014) 90 Notre Dame L Rev 1211 at 1235–36.

141 The most common acts reserved to copyright holders. See e.g., *Canada CA* (n 44) ss 3, 15, 18, 21, and 26.

142 This is subject to TPMs limiting the playing devices upon which work may be played, as a consequence of restrictions applied to control regional distributions, e.g., of films or music. This assumption is made on the basis that these restrictions are not allowed pursuant to copyright holders' exclusive rights including their distribution rights.

143 See Chapter 1: 'Copyright users and the ownership spectrum.'

144 Trib. gr. inst. 6e Nanterre, 2 September 2003, *Françoise M./EMI France, Auchan France*, online: <http://www.legalis.net/jurisprudence-decision> [*EMI France*]; Trib. gr. inst. 5$^{e}$ Paris, 10 January

adequacy (or lack thereof) of the permitted scope of use of the purchased CD was analysed under the latent defect rules of the French *Code Civil.*[145] In *EMI France*,[146] the Tribunal de Grande Instance de Nanterre held that a music CD functioning on some CD players but not on car CD players, as a result of technological protection measures restricting the use of the CD, constituted a latent defect that entitled the complainant to a rescission of the sale of the CD.[147] In arriving at this decision, the Tribunal took into consideration the fact that no such limitations existed on other CDs, as well as the fact that consumers were not notified of such restrictions.[148] In *Warner Music*,[149] the Tribunal of first instance ordered the rescission of the sale of CDs for digital music on the basis that the CD, which contained a technological measure, could not be used on a specific kind of laptop.[150] The CD contained a notification of the technological measure that stated that it could be read on most CD players and computers. The Tribunal held that this incompatibility with some computers constituted a latent defect under the French *Code Civil.*[151] The Court of Appeal reversed that order on the basis of a lack of evidence.[152]

Concerning restrictive uses that are outside the scope of acts reserved to copyright holders, the unfair practices that may potentially give rise to a claim[153] may be easily cured by simply notifying the consumer of the use restriction. Notification of the restriction may be sufficient to remedy the falsehood or misleading nature of the commercial transaction without impacting on the use restriction at a substantive level, unlike consumer protection implied obligations where notification would be one of the factors considered, in varying degrees based on the implied obligation (e.g., quality, fitness for purpose, or quiet possession) and the jurisdiction, in assessing whether a breach has occurred.

The operation of prohibitions against unfair practices is illustrated by two French cases. In *EMI Music France v Association CLCV*,[154] CLCV, an association representing the interests of consumers, alleged that EMI Music France was in contravention of several articles of the French *Code de la Consommation* and *Code*

2006, *Christophe R., UFC Que Choisir/Warner Music France, Fnac*, (2006) JurisData: 2006-292685 [*Warner Music*] reversed on appeal: Court of Appeal 4ᵉ A, Paris, 20 June 2007, *Fnac Paris/UFC Que Choisir et autres*, online: <http://www.legalis.net/jurisprudence-decision>; confirmed by Cour de cassation, civ. 1ère, 27 November 2008, *UFC Que Choisir/Fnac, Warner Music France*, online: <http://www.legalis.net/jurisprudence-decision>.

[145] Art 1641 C civ. [146] *EMI France* (n 144).

[147] ibid. In addition to a named consumer claimant, there was also a consumer association as claimant. The latter's claims against EMI France and Auchan were dismissed on procedural grounds.

[148] ibid. The CD had a notice to the effect that the CD contained a technological measure limiting the possibility to make copies.

[149] *Warner Music* (n 144). [150] ibid. [151] Article 1641 C civ.

[152] *Warner Music* (n 144). Confirmed by Cour de cassation 1ère chambre civile 27 November 2008, ibid.

[153] Such as 'a representation that the transaction involves or does not involve rights, remedies or obligations if the representation is false, misleading or deceptive', and other non-exhaustive listed practices in statutes: see e.g., *OCPA* (n 55) ss 14–15; *QCPA* (n 51) art. 8, 10,11 and 215ff.

[154] CA Versailles, 30 September 2004, *S.A. EMI Music France v Association CLCV*, online: <http://www.foruminternet.org/documents/jurisprudence/lire.phtml?id=809> [*EMI Music France, 2004*].

*Civil.*[155] The CDs could only be played on a limited number of CD players. CLCV alleged that the brief notice on the CDs, that is, that they were subject to technological measures and use restrictions was misleading consumers. The Court of Appeal confirmed the judgment by the Court of First Instance,[156] and held that EMI Music France had misled consumers on the fitness for use of its CDs, in contravention of article L213-1 of the French *Code de la Consommation.*[157] In doing so, the Court of Appeal confirmed the orders by the Court of First Instance that a specific notice that the CDs could not be played on all CD players be placed forthwith on the CDs, and of awarding damages to CLCV.[158]

In *Association UFC Que Choisir v Société Sony France, Société Sony United Kingdom Ltd,*[159] UFC Que Choisir, an association representing the interests of consumers, alleged that Sony France and Sony United Kingdom were misleading consumers in contravention of article L213-1 of the French *Code de la Consommation.* Sony United Kingdom operated the online music download site Connect. Sony France distributed digital MP3 players that were the only ones able to play the musical recordings downloaded from the Connect website. In other words, the technological protection measure applied to the musical recordings downloaded from the Connect website restricted the transfer, and those recordings could not be played on other digital MP3 players available on the market. Moreover, the MP3 players sold by Sony France could not play musical recordings downloaded from other platforms. Having reviewed the terms and conditions attached to the Connect platform and the MP3 players, the Court of First Instance found that Sony France and Sony United Kingdom contravened to their obligations under article L111-1 of the French *Code de la Consommation.*[160] The Court ordered Sony France to place forthwith on its MP3 players a notice that specifically mentioned the use restrictions of the MP3 players, and ordered Sony France and Sony United Kingdom to pay damages to UFC Que Choisir.[161]

In both *EMI Music France, 2004* and *Sony France and Sony UK,* the orders required that proper notices of the use restrictions be put in place, without impacting on the substance of the restrictive uses attached to the musical recordings and to the MP3 players per se.

In the US, the FTC rejected a complaint filed by the CCIA that alleged that copyright warnings of a list of companies[162] constituted unfair and deceptive trade practices.[163] The CCIA alleged that notices to the effect that descriptions and

[155] I.e., *Code de la Consommation.* art L 121-1, L 213-I, L 421-1; L421-2.1; L 421-9 and C civ. art 1382.

[156] Trib gr instance Nanterre, 24 June 2003, *Association CLCV/EMI Music France,* online: <www.legalis.net/cgi-iddn/french/affichejnet.cgi?droite= internet_dtauteur.htm>.

[157] ibid. [158] ibid.

[159] Trib gr instance Nanterre, 6th chamber, 15 December 2006, *Association UFC Que Choisir v Société Sony France, Société Sony United Kingdom Ltd,* online: <http://www.legalis.net/jurisprudence-decision.php3? id_article=1816> [*Sony France and Sony UK*].

[160] ibid. This case also involved the determination of the existence of 'tied selling' ('ventes liées').

[161] ibid. [162] See listed companies (n 113 above).

[163] For a review of the complaint and the response by the FTC, see: Walker & Savare (n 114 above).

accounts of sports games could not be disseminated were 'manifestly false' as the US *Copyright Act* does not protect facts and ideas, and that the warnings of possible harsh civil and criminal sanctions generally mislead the public.[164] The FTC responded that it did not have sufficient evidence to conclude that such warnings were unfair and deceptive practices and that 'consumers would be likely to refrain from engaging in lawful activities as a consequence of reading those warnings.'[165] The complaint by the CCIA to the FTC illustrates one avenue where prohibitions against unfair terms could target specific or more systemic practices by which copyright holders falsely depict consumers' rights to commercial copies of copyright works in a disparaging way.

Even with respect to restricted uses imposed by copyright holders that are outside the realm of their exclusive rights, the analysis presented here suggests that claims based on breach of contract, or statutory consumer law implied obligations, information disclosure requirements, or prohibitions against unfair practices offer limited prospect to consumers and may be easily dismissed in many cases if the said restrictions are notified to the consumer. Essentially, this allows copyright holders to expand the exclusive rights that copyright law confers with limited legal means to counter such expansion.

## User Claims Against Restricted Uses of Copyright Works for Breach of Obligation of Good Faith or in Tort

In addition to user-copy-owner claims based on common law or statutory implied obligations (of quality, fitness for purpose, quiet possession), information disclosure requirements, and unfair commercial practices, which have been the main focus of this chapter so far, in some instances users could assert claims based on the breach of the obligation of good faith, either in contract or in tort. These claims could potentially be made in relation to all scenarios examined here. However, they are more likely to arise in instances where copyright holders block users from making uses of works pursuant to exceptions to copyright infringement,[166] or block users from certain uses outside the exclusive domain of copyright holders.[167] In *Bragg v Linden Research*,[168] the claimant sued the virtual life website operator for blocking the claimant, a registered user of the website, access to the website, on the basis of the tortious breach of the covenant of good faith and fair dealing.[169] The

[164] See The Request for investigation and complaint for injunctive and other relief, dated 1 August 2007, filed by the CCIA with the FTC, online: <http://www.google.ca/search?sourceid=navclient&ie=UTF-8&rlz=1T4ADBF_enCA275CA275&q=Computer+%26+Communications+Industry+Association+complaint+federal+trade+commission+2007> accessed 4 February 2017.

[165] FTC's letter in response to CCIA's complaint dated 6 December 2007 (n 115).

[166] See above: 'Restricted uses fall within the exclusive rights of copyright holders and are allowed by law under certain conditions.'

[167] See above: 'Restricted uses outside the realm of the exclusive rights of copyright holders.'

[168] 487 F Supp (2d) 593 (2007).

[169] ibid, note 8.

user claimant had been ousted from the virtual world website where he had made significant monetary investments.[170] The case eventually settled out of court.

Copyright users could assert claims, founded upon various torts, against copyright holders. Blocking access to copyright works initially available to users, including access to improvements to those works, or new works of authorship that users have created, could give rise to claims based on intentional interference with contractual relations[171] or the tort of conversion.[172] These were among the claims made in *Bragg v Linden Research*[173] against the virtual life website operator having ousted the claimant registered user from its website, and in a case where a student sued and successfully settled with Amazon.com for losing his homework through annotations made on his e-book that were deleted.[174] The key elements of the tort of conversion have been defined as requiring the claimant to have a 'superior possessory right, a deprivation of the claimant's full benefit of that right, and an assumption by the defendant of that right.'[175] The tort of conversion would be available if the user can assert lawful possession (through a property right or otherwise) of the copyright work. Instances where the user experiences the copyright work through a service (e.g., content streaming) would likely not fulfil the requirements of a 'superior possessory right'.[176]

Copyright user claims founded in tort may also include a claim against mass-market standard non-negotiated terms restricting the user's ability to exercise permitted acts under copyright law (whether the exercise of the exception to copyright infringement can or cannot be waived by contract).[177] Finally, users may possibly assert a claim based on the tort of slander of title[178] when they are

170 ibid. 171 ibid.

172 The tort of conversion was invoked in two cases that were eventually settled out of court: *Bragg v Linden Research* (n 168); *Gorowski & Bruguier v Amazon.com*, Stipulation of settlement and [proposed] order of dismissal, 25 September 2009, online: <http://online.wsj.com/public/resources/documents/amazon20091001.pdf> accessed 8 September 2016. For an account of the *Bragg v Linden Research* case, see Juliet M Moringiello, 'What Virtual Worlds Can Do for Property Law' (2010) 62 Fla L Rev 159.

173 *Bragg v Linden Research* (n 168). The claimant Bragg had allegedly obtained virtual land at a rebate, contrary to the terms of use of the virtual world website operated by the defendant Linden Research which annulled transactions made by Bragg and froze Bragg's account.

174 See Geoffrey Fowler, 'Amazon Pays for Eating Student's Homework' (1 October 2009), *Wall Street Journal: Digits* (blog), online: <http://blogs.wsj.com/digits/2009/10/01/amazon-pays-for-eating-students-homework/?mod=rss_WSJBlog> accessed 4 February 2017. For the settlement, see: *Gorowski & Bruguier v Amazon.com* (n 172). See also Caitlin J Akins, 'Conversion of Digital Property: Protecting Consumers in the Age of Technology' (2010) 23 Loyola Consumer L Rev 215.

175 Sarah Green & John Randall, *The Tort of Conversion* (Oxford: Hart Publishing, 2009) at 75–80.

176 ibid.

177 Margaret Jane Radin, *Boilerplate: The Fine Print, Vanishing Rights, and the Rule of Law* (Princeton, NJ: Princeton University Press, 2014) at 209ff, proposes the introduction of a new tort of 'intentional deprivation of basic legal rights' to counter the potentially detrimental effects of mass-market right-deletion schemes in non-negotiated standard terms of use. The harm would be assessed on the basis of the nature of the rights deleted and on the effect of the deletion of rights on democratic degradation.

178 Defined as: 'a false statement, made orally or in writing, that casts doubt on another person's ownership of property and thereby causing damage or loss': *Black's Law Dictionary*, 10th ed, *sub verbo* 'slander of title' (WL).

restricted from making uses of copyright works that they should be entitled to make on the basis of their personal property rights in the copy. The basis of the claim would be that copyright holders partially deprived users of their ownership powers and privileges to the copy of the work.[179] Although such tortious claims have some merit, their chance of success with respect to copyright users remains speculative.[180]

## Goods and Services

While information disclosure requirements and prohibitions against unfair commercial practices generally apply equally to goods and services, in some jurisdictions, statutory implied obligations of quality, fitness for purpose, title, and quiet possession only apply to goods,[181] leaving any applicable claims and remedies against a defective service to the common law.[182] In others, a different statutory-implied obligation applies to services, requiring, for instance, that the services are deemed to be of a 'reasonably acceptable quality'.[183] Implied obligations applicable to goods impose a strict liability regime where users need to prove that goods are not meeting certain standards, for example, of quality or fitness for use, while implied obligations applicable to services apply a fault-based regime where users must prove that the supplier breached the duty of reasonable care, or similar obligation, in how the services were provided.[184] The difference between goods and services also affects the nature of remedies available[185] and involves evidentiary and statute of limitations considerations.[186]

Singling out services from the application of implied obligations (e.g., of quality or fitness for purpose) is more difficult to justify in an environment of automated services where processes are standardized. Consumers should be able to rely on minimum levels of protection similar to those that relate to goods, with necessary adaptations, as the case may be. Legislative proposals in the European Union (EU) will if implemented, level the playing field with respect to digital content, regardless of whether it is provided through services, downloaded, or

[179] The tort of slander of title has been invoked by copyright holders, see e.g., *SCO Group Inc v Novell Inc*, 721 F Supp (2d) 1050 (D Utah 2010).

[180] To the author's knowledge, there are no reported cases where the new tort of 'intentional deprivation of basic legal rights' proposed by Radin (n 177), has been invoked, or where the tort of slander of title has been invoked by users of copyright works.

[181] See Chapter 1: 'Sometimes a "good" ... and sometimes not.'

[182] ibid.

[183] Statutory implied warranties as adapted in the case of the provision of services have been introduced in some jurisdictions. E.g., under the *OCPA* (n 55) s 9(1), the implied warranty applicable to services is that the services are of a 'reasonably acceptable quality'; *UKSGSA* (n 96) s 13 provides that the 'supplier will carry out the service with reasonable care and skill.'

[184] Bradgate (n 5) at 28–29. See n 151.

[185] See the report analysing the laws of 11 states in relation to the regulation of digital content, mainly in Europe, including EU law, the UK, France, but also the US: Loos et al (n 5) at 125.

[186] Consumer protection laws tend to alleviate evidentiary requirements in favour of consumers. E.g., the parole evidence rule often does not apply to consumer contracts.

supported by a physical medium.[187] The EU proposal would impose requirements of conformity on digital content, for example, interoperability, quality, fitness for purpose,[188] and remedies for non-compliance.[189] In the UK, the *UKCRA*[190] provides a distinct regime for the supply to consumers of digital content, goods, and services. Digital content supplied without a supporting physical medium is subject to similar levels of protection than the ones that apply to the supply of goods, with some distinctions.[191] Absent similar legal reform as the EU proposal that would eliminate the distinction between goods and services with respect to digital products, or a *sui generis* regime for digital content such as in the UK, in most jurisdictions, the level of protection and nature of claims will vary based on whether the copyright work is experienced as a good or as a service.

The specific remedies users may have against copyright holders who block certain uses of copyright works with TPMs[192] would generally not be available when copyright works are accessed as on-demand services.[193] Users may be able to successfully invoke the tort of conversion against copyright holders blocking access to their work if users can establish superior possessory rights in the copy of the copyright work.[194] The tort of conversion would not be available to users enjoying a copyright work through a service.

Given the progressive shift from tangible copies of copyright works, to digital copies, and increasingly to on-demand services for such works, the changing nature of rights (and related remedies) copyright users have that result from that transformation needs closer attention. From the perspective of the permitted scope of uses of copyright works and possible claims and remedies, users are likely to have different expectations vis-à-vis a work that they experience through a service than in relation to a commercial copy that they acquire. For instance, the exceptions to copyright infringement become practically inaccessible to users experiencing works through services as opposed to through copies they possess. The ability to make multiple copies of the work for personal use or backup purposes, the ability to communicate the work to the public, and the ability to transfer the ownership in the commercial copy (and the application of the first sale or exhaustion doctrine) will not arise if users enjoy copyright works through services rather than through a commercial copy they own or possess.

Users who access copyright works through services are not empowered with the same degree of autonomy of usage as possession of a copy gives them.[195] In some cases, however, the line between accessing the work through a service or by

[187] EC, Commission, *Proposal for a Directive of the European Parliament and of the Council on certain aspects concerning contracts for the supply of digital content*, COM/2015/634, Preamble, recitals 11–12, art 2.

[188] ibid, art 6. [189] ibid, arts 11–18. [190] *UKCRA* (n 50).

[191] ibid, ss 17(1), (2)(c), 20: statutory warranties of right to transfer ownership and of quiet possession do not apply to supply of digital content, nor the remedy to reject goods.

[192] See above: 'User claims and remedies in copyright law.'

[193] *UKCDPA* (n 37) s 296ZE (9); see also *France CPI* (n 20) L 331-8.

[194] Green & Randall (n 146) at 75–80. [195] See Chapter 1.

possessing a copy will be blurred.[196] In many instances, the *prima facie* open-ended powers and privileges that flow from ownership in a resource and the underlying values that support them do not manifest themselves in the same manner, if at all, when users enjoy a work through services.[197] Questions remain on the extent to which users are notified or aware of the distinction between whether they are acquiring the copy of a work or accessing a service.[198] Chapter 8 looks more closely at the instances in which copyright-service-user rights should differ from the ones of user-copy-owners and the justifications therefor.[199]

Restrictive usages of copyright works can give rise to other issues of quality, fitness for purpose, and quiet possession (with the necessary adaptations) that are specific to service providers and how they make works available to users. A TV service provider offer whereby users can replay TV broadcasts at their leisure could potentially breach the minimum standards imposed by implied obligations if, for instance, TPMs restrain the replay of an important proportion of TV broadcasts. Other breaches of implied obligations of quality, fitness for purpose, title, and quiet possession (with necessary adjustments) could be invoked against service providers allowing access to copyright works (e.g., quality in how the signals, streaming, or other types of services are delivered). They are not of immediate concern to the present discussion because they are similar to breaches that can arise with other types of services that are unrelated to copyright works.

## Filling the Void of Copyright User Remedies

The oversight of the legal and normative value of possessing copies of copyright works, the inherent limits of exceptions to copyright infringement as a vehicle to so-called user rights, the prevailing silence of copyright laws on user remedies against copyright holders have a direct impact on the strength of the claims, if any, users have against restrictions of uses of copyright works. Given lawmakers' struggles to coherently define the legal nature of copies of copyright works with no physical embodiment, and as we are shifting away from possessing copies of works toward accessing copyright works as services, the remedies copyright users may have against copyright holders will also depend to some extent on how we define goods and services.[200] Table 3.1 User Claims/Remedies Against Restricted Use of

196 E.g., in the case of a streaming service, the line between the autonomous powers and privileges a user has through a service and those as the owner of a copy they lawfully download may be blurrier than when contrasting streaming services with watching the same movie in a theatre.

197 ibid.

198 See Chapdelaine, 'Ambiguous Nature of Copyright Users' Rights' (n 56) at 26–28, on a survey conducted on selected non-negotiated standard end-user agreements, and how certain terms refer to purchases of copies, but they then refer to licensing of copies and refer to services and purchases without making clear distinctions between the two.

199 See Chapter 8: 'The taxonomy and hierarchy of copyright user rights.'

200 See Chapter 1: 'Sometimes a "good" ... and sometimes not' and Chapter 4.

**Table 3.1** User Claims/Remedies Against Restricted Use of Copies of Copyright Works[a]

| Remedies / Restricted use | | Claim in copyright law order removal of obstacle to access or use[b] | Claim based on breach of contract/sale of goods consumer law implied obligations/information disclosure requirements (general remedies) | Claim based on breach of obligation of good faith/ tort (general remedies) |
|---|---|---|---|---|
| Within exclusive rights of copyright holder | | No | Unlikely | Less likely |
| Within exclusive right of copyright holder and permitted under certain conditions | Exception is mandatory | Yes | More likely | More likely |
| | Exception is non-mandatory | Yes | Somewhat likely | Likely |
| Outside exclusive rights of copyright holder | | Possible (on basis that obstacles may go against 'normal use of copy') | More likely | More likely |

[a] Table summarizes possible claims/remedies for users of individual copies of copyright works. For copyright works experienced exclusively as services, see above 'Goods and Services.'
[b] In limited jurisdictions only (see above 'User claims and remedies in copyright law').

Copies of Copyright Works, summarizes the various claims users may have against copyright holders and their likelihood of success.

The analysis that I presented in this chapter seriously puts in question the assumption that claims copyright users may have against restrictive uses of works are adequately addressed through contract, consumer, sale of goods and other laws. In the three scenarios explored in this chapter, claims to counter such restrictions on the basis of statutory warranties or implied obligations, unfair terms, or information disclosure requirements are in for an uphill battle. Laws extraneous to copyright laws interfere at the periphery of copyright law and largely defer to it. If, for instance, a breach of implied obligation, of quality, or an unfair practice is found, chances of successful claims are significantly lessened if the consumer is notified of such restrictions, without any legal tools to scrutinize at a substantive level the acceptability of the restriction. In other words, in spite of the attempts at balance sought in copyright law to address competing interests between copyright holders, users, and the public, carte blanche is given to copyright holders, if not by copyright law, then through other laws that lack the power to intervene efficaciously on behalf of copyright users where copyright law left off. A good example is the ripple effect of the uncertain legal nature of exceptions to copyright infringement (rights or privileges) and whether they are mandatory or can be overridden by contract. The likelihood of success of claims alleging breach of implied warranties of quality or quiet possession, against obstacles to making a fair use or fair dealing of the work will vary based on how copyright law defines exceptions to copyright infringement.[201]

A genuine commitment to the rights and interests of copyright users suggests taking another approach. User rights and interests may be best addressed within the confines of copyright law itself as it is the case in some jurisdictions (including France and Belgium) as seen earlier in this chapter.[202] Although this approach may have shortcomings from a legislative design standpoint, with the main fear being that copyright law will become a patchwork of eclectic rights and interests, this possible regulatory design shortcoming would be compensated by the provision of greater clarity to courts and of concrete tools to users to enforce their rights and interests.

Implementing user remedies is not without hurdles and a one-size-fits-all approach would most likely fail. For instance, while it would be relatively straightforward to put a remedy in place to allow users who are restricted to exercise their right to make copies of computer programs for backup purposes, the same could not be said of a remedy allowing users to make a fair dealing or fair use of the work. Fair dealing and fair use statutory provisions cover a broad range of uses elaborated by judge-made law.[203] Third-party intermediaries brokering legitimate fair dealing or fair use requests is one of the avenues proposed that I discuss in Chapter 6 and Chapter 8.

Putting user remedies in place would require a prior buy-in on the space that our laws are willing to give to copyright users; without that commitment the implementation of remedies is unthinkable. Chapter 8 addresses these questions in greater detail. Before that, the proper topography of copyright user rights requires a re-evaluation of the dichotomy between tangibility and intangibility, which is the common theme of the next three chapters.

[201] See above 'Restricted uses fall within the exclusive rights of copyright holders and are allowed by law under certain conditions.'

[202] See above 'User claims and remedies in copyright law.'

[203] See Chapter 2: 'The "mechanics" of exceptions to copyright infringement.'

# PART II

# RETHINKING TANGIBILITY AND INTANGIBILITY

# 4

# Redefining Goods, Services, Sales, and Licences

## Misconceptions About Tangibility and Intangibility in Defining Information Products

In an online environment, the absence of the hand-to-hand supply of a physical medium, compounded by the blurry line between 'goods' and 'services', is at the heart of the ambiguity on the nature of copies of copyright works. Chapter 1 introduced the determinacy of a physical object embodying the copy of a copyright work to categorize the copy as a good, and discussed why the requirement of a physical object created an artificial distinction leading to inconsistent outcomes.[1] Chapter 3 discussed the different levels of protection and remedies of copyright users depending on whether they access copyright works as goods they possess or as services, observing that user rights and remedies may decrease in the case of services as compared to goods.[2] By taking a closer look at the distinction between tangible and intangible property, this chapter challenges the requirement of a physical object to categorize copies of copyright works as goods.

The requirement of a physical object for copies of copyright works to qualify as goods needs to be put in context with how other areas of law deal with the immateriality of copies of copyright works. For instance, international classifications, in the area of trademarks, categorize software as goods regardless of the presence of a supporting tangible medium.[3] In the US, the *Copyright Act* defines 'copy' as: 'material objects ... from which the work can be perceived ... either directly

[1] See Chapter 1: 'Sometimes a "good" ... and sometimes not.'

[2] See Chapter 3: 'Goods and services.'

[3] Under the *Nice Agreement Concerning the International Classification of Goods and Services for the Purposes of the Registration of Marks*, 15 June 1957, as amended, online: <http://www.wipo.int/treaties/en/text.jsp?file_id=287532> accessed 4 February 2017, there are 45 registration classes, with 34 for goods and 11 for services. Class nine (goods) covers software. The explanatory notes to Class nine state that this class includes: 'All computer programs and software regardless of recording media or means of dissemination, that is, software recorded on magnetic media or downloaded from a remote computer network.' International classification of goods and services under the Nice Agreement, 10th edition, online: <http://web2.wipo.int/classifications/nice/nicepub/en/fr/edition-20160101/taxonomy/> accessed 4 February 2017. The trademark classification system fulfils different purposes: i.e., it allows trademark applicants to define for which types of goods and services they (intend to) use their trademark and claim exclusive rights.

or with the aid of a machine.'[4] If 'copy' was defined narrowly, that is, as requiring the form of a material object (book, CD, DVD), innumerable unauthorized copies would not be deemed as infringements of copyright. Pointing to the US *Copyright Act* definition of 'copy' as including 'immaterial' machine-readable copies, one commentator noted the double standard that results from not also treating copies of software as goods under sale of goods law: 'There is no good reason not to extend this version of tangibility, assuming tangibility is necessary, to the realm of Article 2 [referring to US *Uniform Commercial Code* art 2 (2002) regulating contracts of sales]. Software copies are perceivable by a machine and in that sense tangible, making them easily "things," which may not require tangibility.'[5]

When it comes to offering protection to copyright holders, lawmakers have no difficulty in defining a copy of copyright work as encompassing copies embodied within physical objects and those that are not. Other features of copies of copyright works should be more relevant when determining whether the works are goods under applicable laws than the presence of a physical object.[6]

In the case of copies of copyright works made available online with no supporting physical objects, one could be tempted to conclude that they are intangible property, if one were to rely on the ordinary meaning of tangible, that is, something capable of being perceived by the sense of touch.[7] As I discussed in Chapter 1, courts including the Court of Appeal of England and Wales in *St Albans City and District Council v International Computers Ltd*[8] have stated that a physical object needs to be present for copies of copyright works to qualify as goods.[9]

There is no requirement per se of tangibility in the definition of 'goods' under sale of goods laws, that is, as something that is perceptible by touch.[10] Choses in action (associated with intangible property) are often excluded from the application of sale of goods and consumer protection law,[11] which as I discuss further below in this part, may explain the alleged requirement of a physical object to

[4] The US *Copyright Act*, 17 USC § 101 [*USC*]. 'Copy' is not always defined in copyright statutes. See e.g., Canada's *Copyright Act*, RSC 1985, c C-42 [*Canada CA*]; *Copyright, Designs and Patents Act 1988* (UK), c 48 [*UKCDPA*].

[5] Jean Braucher, 'Contracting Out of Article 2 Using a "License" Label: A Strategy That Should Not Work for Software Products' (2007) 40 Loy LA L Rev 261 at 268.

[6] See below: 'The properties of information products' (p 101).

[7] *Canadian Oxford Dictionary*, 2nd ed, *sub verbo* 'tangible': 'perceptible by touch; having material form.' Tangible originates from the Latin *tangere*, which means *touch*: ibid [*Oxford Dictionary*].

[8] [1996] 4 All ER 481 (CA).

[9] See Chapter 1: 'Sometimes a "good" ... and sometimes not.'

[10] See UK, Department for Business, Innovation and Skills, *Consumer Rights in Digital Products*, by Robert Bradgate (2010), at 41–42, 50, online: <http://www.google.ca/search?sourceid=navclient&ie=UTF-8&rlz=1T4ADBF_enCA275CA275&q=Bradgate%2c+Consumer+rights+in+digital+products+2010> accessed 4 February 2017. However, the EU makes that distinction clearly: EC, *Council and Parliament Directive 2011/83/EU of 22 November 2011 on consumer rights, amending Council Directive 93/13/EEC and Directive 1999/44/EC of the European Parliament and of the Council and repealing Council Directive 85/577/EEC and Directive 97/7/EC of the European Parliament and of the Council*, [2011] OJ, L 304/64, Preamble, Recital 19 [*Directive 2011/83/EU*].

[11] Bradgate, *Consumer Rights in Digital Products* (n 10).

qualify a product as goods. The differential treatment between tangible and intangible property is stark in many other areas of the law: the tort of conversion and the common law possessory lien often have been held to apply solely in relation to tangible property (choses in possession),[12] but not always.[13] The lack of a physical object was a determinant factor for the Court of Appeal of England and Wales to qualify a database as intangible property and to hold that it could not be subject to a common law possessory lien.[14] In an increasingly immaterial world, the function of the distinction between tangible and intangible property may have become lost in translation.[15]

A closer look at how tangible property and intangible property have traditionally been defined at common law and the reason for the exclusion of choses in action (associated with intangible property) under sale of goods law indicate that the lack of a physical object should not be a relevant criterion per se to exclude copies of copyright works from being tangible property and, by extension goods. Personal property ('chattels personal') is subdivided between choses in possession and choses in action. Choses in possession are generally associated with tangible property, that is those 'unfixed movables perceptible by the senses and thus capable of actual physical possession,'[16] or 'corporeal things, tangible, movable and visible. They are always in the possession of someone.'[17] Choses in action originally referred to a tangible article that was in the possession of someone else than the owner—to recover it, the owner had to take an action at law—and later evolved to encompass 'intangible rights existing only in contemplation of the mind, ... all invisible and incorporeal rights.'[18]

Choses in action are generally associated with intangible property and are often negatively defined as 'embracing all forms of property not involving actual possession or right of possession as a necessary incident.'[19] Choses in action include debt,

[12] For the tort of conversion see: *OBG Ltd v Allan*, [2007] UKHL 21, [2008] 1 AC 1; *Telecom Vanuatu Ltd v Optus Networks Pty Ltd*, [2008] NSWSC 1209 at para 184; *UBS Wireless Services Inc v Inukshuk Wireless Partnership* (2008), 167 ACWS (3d) 223, [2008] OJ No 1704 (QL) (Ont. S. C. J.) at paras 35–39, 60, 67; *The Environment Agency v Churngold Recycling Ltd*, [2014] EWCA Civ 909 at paras 1, 15. For the common law lien, see *Your Response Ltd v Datateam Business Media Ltd*, [2014] EWCA Civ 281.

[13] US courts have applied the tort of conversion to intangible property. See: *Kremen v Cohen*, 337 F (3d) 1024 (9th Cir 2002) and *CRS Recovery Inc v Laxton*, 600 F (3d) 1138 (9th Cir 2010), applying the tort of conversion to domain names; *Thyroff v Nationwide Mutual Insurance Co*, 8 NY (3d) 283 at 292–93, 864 NE (2d) 1272, (NY Ct App 2007), applying the tort of conversion to intangible electronic records.

[14] *Your Response Ltd v Datateam Business Media Ltd* (n 12) paras 20–21.

[15] On the false categories that arise from the tangible versus intangible property dichotomy, see generally: Juliet M Moringiello, 'False Categories in Commercial Law: The (Ir)Relevance of (In) Tangibility' (2007) 35 Fla St UL Rev 119. See also Sarah Green & John Randall, *The Tort of Conversion* (Portland: Hart Publishing, 2009) at 131.

[16] WH Hastings Kelke, *An Epitome of Personal Property Law*, 3rd ed (London: Sweet & Maxwell, 1910) at 2.

[17] ELG Tyler & NE Palmer, *Crossley Vaines' Personal Property*, 5th ed (London: Butterworths, 1973) at 11.

[18] Frank Hall Childs, *Principles of the Law of Personal Property* (Chicago: Callaghan, 1914) at 54.

[19] Kelke (n 16) at 5. Tyler & Palmer (n 17) at 11 defines choses in action as 'all rights and incorporeal things not being chattels real or choses in possession.'

liquidated damages, promissory notes, shares, and various intellectual property rights.[20]

The key distinguishing factor between tangible and intangible property revolves around the ability of someone in physical possession to exercise power and control over the resource, which is possible in relation to tangible property (choses in possession). For intangible property (or choses in action), court intervention is generally necessary for the owner to exercise power and control over their resource.

Courts have been reluctant to recognize that one could exercise physical possession over an information product that was not embedded in a physical object. In *Your Response Ltd v Datateam Business Media Ltd*,[21] Moore-Bick LJ, for the Court of Appeal of England and Wales, held that the claimant data manager was barred from exercising a common law lien over a database owned by the defendant for unpaid services, because the data manager did not have physical possession of the database.[22] For the Court, 'possession is concerned with the physical control of tangible objects,' and although the data manager exercised 'practical control' over the database, he could not exercise physical possession over information because it is intangible.[23] The Court was not satisfied by the evidence relating to the actual physical control that the data manager exercised over the database.[24] It seems the Court of Appeal missed an opportunity to take a functional and substantive approach to apply 'possession' and 'physical control' to more recent forms of property interests such as an online database, an approach which I detail below and further in this chapter.[25]

Tangible property (choses in possession), in contrast with intangible property (choses in action), is perhaps better understood as actual, concrete versus conceptual or abstract. The copy of an information product downloaded to a computer (e.g., a musical recording, e-book, film) is not conceptual: it is perceivable, is concrete, physical, has defined boundaries,[26] and it is capable of physical possession,[27] and for those reasons, better fits the definition of tangible property (choses in possession) than intangible property (choses in action).

The exclusion of choses in action (associated with intangible property) from sale of goods law is understandable when looking at its purpose and scope, which is to regulate the trade between sellers and buyers, dealing with such concerns as methods of delivery and acceptance, perishable goods, implied warranties of quality, and fitness for purpose.[28] Many of these considerations are largely irrelevant to choses in action that are debts, liquidated damages, promissory notes, and copyright. By contrast, the preoccupations addressed in sale of goods law are highly relevant to copies of copyright works downloaded from the Internet. When was

[20] Kelke (n 16) at 5–6. [21] *Your Response Ltd v Datateam Business Media Ltd* (n 12).

[22] ibid paras 22–23. Davis LJ and Floyd LJ concurred with Moore-Bick LJ's judgment.

[23] ibid. [24] ibid. [25] See below: 'The properties of information products.'

[26] Green & Randall (n 15) at 118–19, discuss, in the context of the eligibility of digital assets to the tort of conversion, how the physicality of computer software is apparent from how it changes the hardware capacity once the computer software is stored on it.

[27] See below: 'The properties of information products.'

[28] See e.g., *Sale of Goods Act 1979* (UK), c 54 [*UKSGA*].

the information product delivered and accepted by the recipient? What implied warranties are attached to the information product? What are the remedies available to the recipient should there be a breach of contract? The rationale for the exclusion of choses in action (associated with intangible property) does not apply to these types of information products. Adopting a purposive approach to the US *Uniform Commercial Code* [US *UCC*] to assess the nature of computer software, one commentator observed that the concerns for excluding intangibles such as 'choses in action' from the definition of goods in the US *UCC* are not present in the context of computer software:[29] 'while the *UCC* does distinguish between goods and things in action, excluding the latter from coverage, software, no matter how it is classified, should not fall within this exclusion. ... It is unlike intangible legal rights, intangible laws and principles, and intangible assets.'[30] Looking more closely at how property law defines personal tangible property (choses in possession) and personal intangible property (choses in action), as well as the reasons underlying the exclusion of choses in action from sale of goods law, the requirement of a physical object to characterize an information product as good is unwarranted and unjustified.

## Tangible goods, intangible services, or *sui generis*

The tangible versus intangible property dichotomy is relevant to distinguish goods from services, through the ordinary meaning of the two words.[31] In contrast with 'goods', 'services' are rarely defined and when they are, not in a manner that elucidates their nature and scope.[32] Generally though, goods are more readily associated with tangibility, and services with intangibility.

[29] *Uniform Commercial Code* US [*US UCC*]; Bonna Lynn Horovitz, 'Computer Software as a Good under the Uniform Commercial Code: Taking a Byte out of the Intangibility Myth' (1985) 65 BUL Rev 129.

[30] Horovitz, 'Computer Software as a Good' (n 29), at 162, and at 151–52: 'The fact that a computer program cannot be seen or felt should not preclude UCC coverage, as the UCC does not make those qualities the test for exclusion. The type of intangibility meant to be excluded from Article 2, that of choses in action, is different from the type of intangibility characteristic of software. That program instructions are intangible does not rule out UCC applicability, as programs can be identified, moved, transferred, and sold in the same manner as other pieces of personal property classified as goods.' For a contrary view, e.g., that computer software does not fulfil the requirement of 'movability', see Lori Brennan, 'Why Article 2 Cannot Apply to Software Transactions' (2000) 38 Duq L Rev 459 at 535–37.

[31] Fiona Smith & Lorna Woods, 'A Distinction without a Difference: Exploring the Boundary between Goods and Services in the World Trade Organization and the European Union' (2005) 12 Colum J Eur L 1 at 40ff. As discussed by the authors, the distinction between tangible and intangible is dictated in part by the ordinary dictionary meaning attributed to 'goods' and 'services', which is the approach chosen by the authors when assessing the meaning of goods and services in an international trade context, e.g., at the World Trade Organization level.

[32] E.g., UK *Consumer Rights Act*, 2015 (UK), c15 [*UKCRA*], which regulates among others consumer service contracts does not define 'services'; British Columbia *Business Practices and Consumer Protection Act*, SBC 2004, c 2, s 1(1) [*BCBPCPA*], defines services as 'services, whether or not the services are together with or separate from goods, and includes a membership in a club or organization'; Alberta *Fair Trading Act*, RSA 2000, c F-2, s 1(1)(k) [*AFTA*], defines services as 'any service offered or provided primarily for personal, family or household purposes,' and

Court decisions that distinguish goods from services may not provide much more guidance on the nature of services.[33] Traditionally, the requirement of statutes of frauds that certain contracts be in writing to be enforceable, applied only to the sale of goods and not to the provision of services.[34] This has, at times, led courts to make artificial distinctions between goods and services.[35] In some cases, uncertainty about the difference between goods and services stems from the confusion about the difference between the labour involved to deliver the commercialized end result and the end result itself.[36] It also flows from the combination of goods and services in the same transaction, in which case courts tend to apply an essential character of the transaction test[37]

includes specific examples; Saskatchewan *Consumer Protection and Business Practices Act*, SS 2014, c C-30.2, ss 2(h) [*SCPBPA*] defines services as: 'Services ordinarily provided for personal, family or household purposes that have been or may be sold, leased or otherwise provided by a supplier to a consumer.'

[33] For a review of Canadian case law characterizing contracts as sale of goods or service agreements, or a combination of both, i.e., for 'work and material', see Gerald HL Fridman, *Sale of Goods in Canada*, 5th ed (Toronto: Thomson Carswell, 2004) at 16ff. See also, Jacob S Ziegel & Anthony J Duggan, *Commercial and Consumer Sales Transactions, Cases, Text and Materials*, 4th ed (Toronto: Edmond Montgomery Publications Limited, 2002) at 49–61. In a EU and World Trade Organization context, see Smith & Woods (n 31). In the context of the World Trade Organization, the treatment of digital products distributed online has not been settled and is the object of a work program on electronic commerce: online: <https://www.wto.org/english/tratop_e/ecom_e/wkprog_e.htm> accessed 4 February 2017. See also: Tania Voon, 'A New Approach to Audiovisual Products in the WTO: Rebalancing GATT and GATS' (2007) 14 UCLA Ent L Rev 1 at 8–9.

[34] In a sale of goods context, statutes of frauds require that contracts for the sale of goods above a certain amount be in writing if the contract is to be enforceable. E.g., the US Statute of Frauds requirements have been codified in the *US UCC* (n 29) § 2–201 which imposes a formal requirement for contracts of $500 or more to be in writing. This requirement was abolished in some provinces of Canada (e.g., British Columbia: *Statute Law Amendment Act*, SBC 1958, c 52, s 17); and in the UK by the repeal of s 4 of the *Sale of Goods Act of 1893* through the *Law Reform Enforcement of Contracts Act*, 1954 (UK), 2 & 3 Eliz II, c 34, s 21.

[35] E.g., see a leading case on the distinction between skill and labour and materials: *Robinson v Graves* [1935] 1 KB 579 (CA of England and Wales), where it was held that the commissioning of a painting by oral agreement, the order for which was later annulled by the defendant, was a contract for skill and labour and not material. Therefore the Statute of Frauds rule by which contracts of a certain value needed to be in writing to be enforceable was not applicable. It is debatable that this was not a contract for materials. See also generally, Michael Bridge, ed, *Benjamin's Sale of Goods*, 8th ed (London: Sweet & Maxwell, 2010) at para 1–041.

[36] E.g., see: *TK Power, Inc v Textron, Inc*, 3 F Supp (2d) 1058 (ND Cal 2006); *Systems America, Inc v Rockwell Software, Inc* 2007 WL 218242 (ND Cal 2007), where the court focused on the development aspect, e.g., of computer software, to determine that it was a contract for services, rather than focusing on the existence of an end product, the newly developed software. Horovitz (n 29) at 143 explains the need to make the distinction between the labour intensiveness of several information products and the end results. The distinction between services that are applied to perfect goods and other forms of services is a helpful distinction in that respect. See *Micro Data Base Systems, Inc v Dharma Systems Inc*, 148 F (3d) 649 (7th Cir 1998). The need to draw the distinction between the two forms of labour in a contract involving the supply of customized computer software was made in the leading case *Triangle Underwriters Inc v Honeywell Inc*, 457 F Supp 765 (EDNY 1978). See also *Propulsion Technologies, Inc v Attwood Corp*, 369 F (3d) 896 (5th Cir 2004) where the US Court of Appeals, 5th Circuit, characterized the sale of unfinished propeller castings as goods in spite of the contract contemplating substantial services from supplier.

[37] *Preload Co of Can Ltd v Regina (City)*, [1958] 23 WWR 433, 13 DLR (2d) 305 (Sask CA) at paras 51ff; aff'd [1959] SCR 801; *Keillian West Ltd v Sportspage Enterprises Ltd* (1982), 23 Alta LR (2d)

or similar tests[38] to determine on a case-by-case basis whether the commercial transaction is one for goods or services.

As services are typically involved in the online delivery of information products, there is a tendency to qualify the transaction as one involving services only, forgetting that the transfer of an information product to the recipient may also be involved, for instance when a digital copy is permanently downloaded by the recipient.[39] As discussed in Chapter 1, qualifying the transaction as one for the supply of services as opposed to the supply of goods limits the remedies the copyright user may have pursuant to sale of goods and consumer protection laws.[40] Another approach is to treat such digital products as neither good nor services but as *sui generis*, through more recent waves of regulation of 'digital content' both at the international and domestic levels.

The more recent wave of regulation treating digital content as neither goods nor services but as *sui generis* is an attempt to address the fluidity of transactions involving transfer of digital data that defy categorization, toward a functional tailored approach to the specific issues of supply of digital data such as ones of functionality and interoperability. Misconceptions about the divide between tangibility and intangibility persist, with the potential of engendering arbitrary results in the treatment of digital products that could be detrimental to information product users. To illustrate that point, I will briefly refer to *Directive 2011/83/EU*,[41] the *UKCRA*,[42] and a European Union (EU) proposal for a directive for the supply of digital content [*EU Directive Proposal for Digital Content*].[43] As a first remark,

199 (QB); *CIC Mining Corp v Saskatchewan Government Insurance*, [1994] 10 WWR 1, 123 Sask R 219 (CA); *Casden v Cooper Enterprises Ltd*, [1993] FCJ No 124, 151 NR 199 (FCA).

[38] In a US context, see e.g., *Advent Systems Ltd v Unisys Corp*, 925 F (2d) 670 (3rd Cir 1991); *Colonial Life Ins Co of America v Electronic Data Systems Corp*, 817 F Supp 235 (DNH 1993); In re *Mesa Business Equipment, Inc*, 931 F (2d) 60 (9th Cir 1991); *Micro Data Base Systems, Inc v Dharma Systems Inc*, 148 F (3d) 649 (7th Cir 1998); *Synergistic Dahlmann v Sulcus Hospitality Technologies Corp*, 63 F Supp (2d) 772 (ED Mich 1999); *Allstate Life Ins Co v Peoplesoft, Inc*, 2004 WL 1375383 (ND Ill 2004); *ePresence, Inc v Evolve Software, Inc*, 190 F Supp (2d) 159 (D Mass 2002); *Heidtman Steel Products, Inc v Compuware Corp*, 2000 WL 621144 (ND Ohio 2000); *Simulados Software Ltd v Photon Infotech Private Ltd*, 40 F Supp (3d) 1191 (ND Cal 2014).

[39] In the absence of a hand-to-hand physical medium the nature of digital content remains uncertain, which can result in the content being deemed as a service. In Trib gr inst 6e Nanterre, 15 December 2006, *Association UFC Que Choisir v Société Sony France, Société Sony United Kingdom Ltd*, online: <http://www.legalis.net/jurisprudence-decision.php3?id_article=1816> accessed 8 September 2016, the supply of downloadable musical recordings through an Internet platform was held by the court to be the supply of services under the French *Code de la consommation*. See Séverine Dusollier, *Droit d'auteur et protection des oeuvres dans l'univers numérique*, 2nd ed (Brussels: Larcier, 2007) at 382, 395–96, 399, who holds that copies of copyright works downloaded from the Internet cannot be the object of a sale but rather the provision of a service, conceding, however, that there is a product involved in the transaction but that the transmission of the product (the copy) characterizes the whole transaction as the provision of services. This is the case in the context of the World Trade Organization identification of such products as goods or services. Voon (n 33) at 17–18 proposes that in the context of the World Trade Organization agreements, such products should be treated as services. Braucher (n 5) at 269–70 notes the artificiality of the distinction between a copy of software that is preloaded in a physical medium from one that is downloaded.

[40] See Chapter 3: 'Goods and Services.'

[41] *Directive 2011/83/EU* (n 10) Preamble, Recital 19.

[42] *UKCRA* (n 32).

[43] EC, Commission, *Proposal for a Directive of the European Parliament and of the Council on certain aspects concerning contracts for the supply of digital content*, COM (2015) 634 final 2015/0287 (COD).

these three (proposed) legal instruments apply to consumer transactions only, creating a parallel regime from other commercial transactions for which the general regime of sale of good laws would continue to apply.

Starting with EU regulation, *Directive 2011/83/EU* harmonizes the laws of Member States with respect to traders' information disclosure requirements in consumer contracts, including distance or off-premises contracts, as well as with respect to formal requirements for these specific types of contracts.[44] *Directive 2011/83/EU* makes a distinction based on the presence of a supporting physical medium exchanged from hand-to-hand to determine whether the information products ('digital content') qualify as goods or not.[45] The Directive only refers to transfer of physical possession with respect to 'goods'. The consequences of this differential treatment may be beneficial by avoiding references to some aspects of goods (e.g., carriage of goods) irrelevant to digital content, and by adopting language that is tailored to the reality of digital content supplied with no physical embodiment. At the same time, *Directive 2011/83 EU* dismisses the possibility of a permanent transfer of possession of digital content in absence of a physical embodiment contrary to what may actually occur for some digital content transactions. While this distinction may bear no particular consequences given the specific scope of *Directive 2011/83 EU*,[46] it would if leading to a differential treatment on the scope of suppliers obligations such as quality and fitness for use. Prior to the adoption of *Directive 2011/83/EU*, the Green Paper on the Consumer Acquis[47] invited Member States to consider the expansion of the EU regime of consumer sale of goods to the supply of digital content.[48] This proposal met fierce resistance, especially with respect to the distribution of online software (among others for the fear that similar levels of warranties would apply to computer software as they apply to goods),[49] with the result that the proposal for reform did not expand the application of the general European consumer sales legal framework to the supply online of digital content.[50]

Unlike Directive *2011/83/EU*, the *EU Directive Proposal for Digital Content*[51] would do away with the distinction between goods and digital content based on the presence of a physical object, treating the obligations of suppliers of digital

[44] ibid. The classification of digital content as goods or services or *sui generis* is inconsistent across European domestic law: Natali Helberger et al, *Digital Consumers and the Law* (Alphen aan de Rijn: Kluwer Law International, 2013) 21–40.

[45] *Directive 2011/83/EU* (n 10) Preamble, Recital 19.

[46] ibid, which deals mainly with pre-contractual information requirements and the right of withdrawal.

[47] EC, Commission, *The Green Paper on the Review of the Consumer Acquis* (Brussels: EC, 2006) [Green Paper on the Consumer Acquis].

[48] ibid, at s 5.1.

[49] See Peter Rott, 'Download of Copyright-Protected Internet Content and the Role of (Consumer) Contract Law' (2008) 31 J Consumer Policy 441 at 452.

[50] EC, Commission, *Proposal for a Directive of the European Parliament and of the Council on consumer rights*, COM (2008) 614 final [Consumer Directive Proposal (2008)], art 2(4) defines 'goods', but leaves unchanged the definition of 'consumer goods' in *Directive 1999/44/EC* art 1 (2)b).

[51] *EU Directive Proposal for Digital Content* (n 43).

content and consumer remedies uniformly, including when the digital content is supplied through services.[52] *EU Directive Proposal for Digital Content* would supplement *Directive 2011/83/EU*[53] by clarifying digital content supplier obligations of conformity with the contract, which include obligations of quality and fitness for use that are mandatory.[54] To the extent that *EU Directive Proposal for Digital Content* will lead to a technologically neutral regulation of digital content and offer adequate levels of protection to digital content users that transcends physical objects, goods, and services, this would eliminate the arbitrariness of treating information products differently based on whether they are made accessible with a supporting physical medium or not.[55]

The *UKCRA*[56] is one among the other legal instruments that came into force in the UK to implement *Directive 2011/83/EU*.[57] The *UKCRA* regulates 'digital content' supplied to consumers distinctly from goods or services regimes through tailored statutory rights and remedies which take into account the distinct features of digital content, such as interoperability issues. At the same time, the *UKCRA* singles out digital content supplied through a physical medium by potentially broadening remedies available in such case to the ones available to goods, in addition to the ones available for digital content.[58] The *sui generis* treatment of digital content (supplied without a physical medium) evacuates the possibility of a transfer of possession and ownership and with it, the benefit of the traditional warranties related to title and quiet possession that are associated to goods.[59] The *UKCRA* does not adequately treat the cases where there is a transfer of possession and ownership of the digital content (supplied without a physical embodiment) and with that fails to give the proper level of protection befitting the transfer of ownership of goods.

The function of the division between tangible and intangible property and the impact it has on the definition of goods, and to some extent services, signals that commercial copies of copyright works distributed online should reside *prima facie* on the tangible property side of the divide and be regulated as such. The more recent wave of regulation that treats digital content as neither goods nor services but as *sui generis* perpetrates the impropriety of the tangible and intangible divide by assuming that digital content with no physical supporting medium is antithetical to tangible property and goods. This differential treatment may well by and large be beneficial from the view that it provides a more adapted protection to digital content, but at the same time it fails to acknowledge any property rights to users of digital content and the warranties that traditionally come with transfer of goods.

[52] ibid, Preamble, Recital 11.

[53] *Directive 2011/83/EU* (n 10) which deals with pre-contractual information requirements and the right of withdrawal.

[54] *EU Directive Proposal for Digital Content* (n 43) arts 6, 19.

[55] See Chapter 1: 'Sometimes a "good"… and sometimes not.'

[56] *UKCRA* (n 32).

[57] See UK, 'Explanatory Memorandum to the Consumer Contracts (Information, Cancellation and Additional Charges) Regulation 2013 No. 3134', online: http://www.legislation.gov.uk/uksi/2013/3134/memorandum/contents accessed 12 February 2017.

[58] *UKCRA* (n 32), s 16, ss 19ff.

[59] ibid, ss 42–46.

## Ripple Effects on Sales and Licences

The presence of a physical object influences how the commercial transaction of information products is viewed; more specifically, whether a sale or a licence took place. The absence of an embedding medium (e.g., a CD or a DVD) facilitates a growing commercial practice under which copyright holders dictate through their contract terms the absence of sale in the copy of the information product. The commercial practice of licensing rather than selling a copy of the copyright work has a long-standing tradition with computer programs.[60] The practice is far less common in the physical hand-to-hand exchange scenarios of books, music CDs, or film DVDs, which have long been considered as sales of goods.[61] At times, courts assimilate the licence granted to users on the exclusive intangible intellectual property rights of the copyright holder to the transaction as a whole, including the property rights that users should have to the individualized copy of the work that is transferred to them.[62] One can surmise that the confusion between the intellectual property rights of the copyright holder and the personal property rights to the copy of the information product will only increase when there is no physical object differentiating the two.[63] The struggles examined above to characterize information products as goods, services, or *sui generis* have ripple effects on the determination of whether the transaction is a sale or a licence, thereby leading to inconsistent outcomes.[64]

Replacing a sale by a licence of the copy of the information product has important consequences on the rights of users. First, the absence of a 'sale' will preclude the application of sale of goods and consumer protection statutes in some jurisdictions, leaving any protection to other statutes or to the application of similar implied obligations under the common law.[65] Second, licensing copies of copyright works rather than selling them to recipients enables copyright holders to circumvent the application of exceptions to copyright infringement that are dependent on ownership of the copy; the rationale for such licensing practices is

[60] See Chapter 5: 'The commercial practice not to sell copies.'

[61] ibid. The transfer of CDs, DVDs, and cassettes are commonly treated as sales of chattels movables, unless they are provided under a specific rental agreement.

[62] Pascale Chapdelaine, 'The Undue Reliance on Physical Objects in the Regulation of Information Products' (2015) 20 J Tech L & Pol'y 65 at 96–100.

[63] See below: 'Physical control and exclusivity.'

[64] For a review of the case law and how courts tend to be more lenient about enforcing a licence for software copies than copies of other types of copyright works, see Aaron Perzanowski & Jason Schultz, 'Reconciling Intellectual Property with Personal Property' (2014) 90 Notre Dame L Rev 1 at 32–36.

[65] In some jurisdictions, the requirement of the sale of a good is relevant to the application of implied obligations (e.g., quality, fitness for purpose, title, and quiet possession). It is generally not relevant for the application of information disclosure requirements or for the application of provisions prohibiting unfair terms: Pascale Chapdelaine, *Copyright Consumers' Bargain, Defining the Rights to Commercial Copies of Copyright Works* (Doctor of Philosophy Thesis, York University Graduate Program in Law, Osgoode Hall Law School Library, 2013) at 327–62.

well known and documented in relation to the first sale doctrine.[66] Whether an information product is sold or licensed determines recipients' benefit from certain exceptions to copyright infringement such as the first sale doctrine[67] or exceptions to copyright infringement related to computer programs.[68] In relation to these exceptions to or limitations on copyright infringement, recipients of copies of copyright works are allowed to perform acts without copyright holders' authorization on copies that they own, but not when the copies of copyright works are licensed.

In the context of determining whether the recipient of the information product should benefit from the relevant exception to copyright infringement (those exceptions requiring that a sale or transfer of the copy of the information product took place), courts have taken different approaches to decide whether a sale or a licence of the information product took place. The approaches vary between deferring in large part to how copyright holders characterize the transaction (i.e., it is a licence because right holder stated it as such in the agreement) to looking at the substance and economic characteristics of the transaction, regardless of how the transaction is designated by the right holder.[69] In the US, the Court of Appeals 9th Circuit judgment, *Vernor v Autodesk, Inc.*,[70] reflects the first approach. In that judgment, the Court gave more weight to the terms used by the software licensor than in previous judgments that focused more on the substance of the transaction.[71] The Court held that the applicable test to determine the nature of the transaction was: 'whether the copyright owner specifies that a user is granted a license. Second, we consider whether the copyright owner significantly restricts the user's ability to transfer the software. Finally, we consider whether the copyright owner imposes notable use restrictions.'[72] The test set by *Vernor v Autodesk* has been applied in subsequent 9th Circuit opinions, to enforce copyright holders' licence to copies of software and to

[66] Brian W Carver, 'Why License Agreements do not Control Copy Ownership: First Sales and Essential Copies' (2010) 25 BTLJ 1887. The practice is well recognized and prevails particularly in relation to copies of computer programs: see Perzanowski & Schultz (n 64) at 32–36.

[67] See Chapter 5.

[68] E.g., 17 USC § 117(a)(1); *Canada CA* (n 4) ss 30.6, 30.61; EC, *Directive 2009/24/EC of the European Parliament and of the Council of 23 April 2009 on the legal protection of computer programs*, [2009] OJ, L 111/16, arts 5–6 [*Directive 2009/24/EC*].

[69] On a case law analysis of how courts, predominantly in the US, take different approaches to determine the nature of the legal transaction as a sale or licence in cases involving software versus other cases, see Carver (n 66) at 1898–1925; Perzanowski & Schultz (n 64) at 19–27.

[70] *Vernor v Autodesk, Inc*, 621 F (3d) 1102, 2010 WL 3516435 (9th Cir 2008).

[71] A good illustration of how courts have characterized the transaction, regardless of whether suppliers have labelled the contract as a licence is *Softman Products Company, LLC v Adobe Systems Inc*, 171 F Supp (2d) 1075, 45 UCC Rep Serv 2d 945 at para 14 (CD Cal 2001): 'The following factors require a finding that distributing software under licenses transfers individual copy ownership: temporally unlimited possession, absence of time limits on copy possession, pricing and payment schemes that are unitary not serial, licenses under which subsequent transfer is neither prohibited nor conditioned on obtaining the licensor's prior approval (only subject to a prohibition against rental and a requirement that any transfer be of the entity), and licenses under which the use restrictions' principal purpose is to protect intangible copyrightable subject matter, and not to preserve property interests in individual program copies.'

[72] *Vernor v Autodesk, Inc* (n 70) at 8.

reject the application of the first sale doctrine.[73] In other cases, the 9th Circuit has refused to enforce the software licence of the copyright holder because of lack of evidence that the licence was brought to the attention of the user.[74] As a result, in these other cases the Court allowed the subsequent transfer of the copies of software, in accordance with the first sale doctrine.

In the EU, the judgment by the EU Court of Justice, *UsedSoft GmbH v Oracle International Corp*,[75] is illustrative of the second approach, focusing on the substance of the transaction. The Court had to assess whether a sale of the copies of Oracle International Corp's software to UsedSoft had taken place to decide whether the exclusive distribution right of Oracle International Corp on the copies of its computer programs had been exhausted.[76] The Court noted that the download of the copy of the computer program combined with the conclusion of a user licence constituted a whole for the purpose of their legal classification.[77] The Court relied on two components of the commercial transaction to conclude that there was a transfer of ownership of the copy downloaded from the Internet: the payment of a one-time fee and the fact that the user was allowed to use the copy for an indefinite period of time.[78] The Court reasoned that 'sale' needed to be given a broad interpretation and its presence assessed based on the substance of the transaction, otherwise the principle of exhaustion could be easily circumvented by suppliers.[79] In a recent judgment, the High Court of England and Wales took a similar functional approach to qualify a commercial transaction involving software as a sale.[80]

Questions on the nature and enforceability of the legal transaction in the commercialization of information products are not trivial: they determine the balance of power between supplier and recipient of the information product. They involve evaluating right holders' commercial practices (often through non-negotiated standard form agreements) in relation to the underlying objectives of copyright

[73] See *MDY Industries LLC v Blizzard Entertainment Inc*, 629 F (3d) 928 at 938–39 (9th Cir 2010); *Apple Inc v Psystar Corp*, 658 F (3d) 1150 (9th Cir 2011); *Adobe Systems Inc v Kornrumpf*, 577 Fed Appx 684 (9th Cir 2014).

[74] See *UMG Recordings Inc v Augusto*, 628 F (3d) 1175 (9th Cir 2011); *Adobe Systems Inc v Christenson*, 809 F (3d) 1071 (9th Cir 2015).

[75] *UsedSoft GmbH v Oracle International Corp*, C-128/11, [2012] OJ C 287 at 10.

[76] ibid. The court was seized with a reference to a preliminary ruling by the Bundesgerichtshof (Germany), which involved the question of whether exhaustion of the distribution right in art 4(2) of *Directive 2009/24/EC* (n 68) applied to a lawful acquirer who had made the copy by downloading the computer program from the Internet to a data carrier. See the discussion on the first sale or exhaustion doctrine in Chapter 5.

[77] ibid, at paras 44–49. [78] ibid at para 45.

[79] ibid at para 49, the court referring to the opinion of Advocate General Y. Bot: '[I]f the term "sale" within the meaning of Article 4(2) of Directive 2009/24 were not given a broad interpretation as encompassing all forms of product marketing characterised by the grant of a right to use a copy of a computer program, for an unlimited period, in return for payment of a fee designed to enable the copyright holder to obtain a remuneration corresponding to the economic value of the copy of the work of which he is the proprietor, the effectiveness of that provision would be undermined, since suppliers would merely have to call the contract a "licence" rather than a "sale" in order to circumvent the rule of exhaustion and divest it of all scope.'

[80] *The Software Incubator Ltd v Computer Associates UK Ltd* [2016] EWHC 1587 (QB) at paras 62–67.

and the delicate balance that copyright law needs to maintain between the competing interests of right holders, authors, users, and the public.[81] At a more obvious basic level, the sale versus licence of an information product ascertains whether the recipient owns the copy of the information product with all *prima facie* open-ended powers and privileges (including of transfer) that come with ownership, *against the world* (*in rem*), or if the recipient has a limited contractual right to use the information product (*in personam*) with no power of transfer, or if the recipient's entitlements to the information products lie somewhere in the middle.

Clarifying the criteria to define what constitutes goods in the absence of physical objects and, further, the criteria that allow goods to be distinguished from services, is likely to bring more consistency to how lawmakers apply concepts of sale or licence to copies of copyright works, in particular those not embedded in a physical object. Specifically, lawmakers may be more likely to characterize a transaction as a sale when the property of the recipient of the information product is identified as a good in the transaction. The inconsistencies noted above on the characterization of a sale or licence are attributable in part to a lack of attention to what users own, possess, or access in a commercial transaction. In Chapter 1, I discussed the anomaly of licensing rather than selling the copy of a copyright work.[82] Under this legal construct, neither the user nor the copyright holder seem to actually own the copy.[83] An increased readiness to recognize, when justified, commercial transactions as sales and not licences would have a significant impact on copyright user rights, in particular regarding those exceptions to copyright infringement that are entirely dependent on the user owning the copy of the work.[84]

## The Properties of Information Products

What I propose here is to distill the essential characteristics that should be present for an information product to be a good and the personal property possessed or owned by its recipient. This is in contrast to copyright works experienced through services with no control over an individualized copy. Drawing upon scholarly works that define the criteria that should prevail when applying traditional doctrines to an immaterial world, for example the tort of conversion, is helpful because of the similar issues and constraints that are involved.[85] A determination of the criteria

[81] See Lucie Guibault, *Copyright Limitations and Contracts, An Analysis of the Contractual Overridability of Limitations on Copyright* (The Hague: Kluwer Law International, 2002); Jacques De Werra, 'Moving Beyond the Conflict between Freedom of Contract and Copyright Policies: In Search of a New Global Policy for On-line Information Licensing Transactions' (2003) 25 Colum JL & Arts 239.

[82] See Chapter 1: 'If neither owned by the copyright user, nor a good, then what?'

[83] ibid. See also Carver (n 66) at 1934–1935, 1945, 1952, arguing against the commercial practice of licences to copies of copyright works under the US *Copyright Act*, on the basis that the act provides for limited forms of distribution of works.

[84] E.g., 17 USC § 117(a)(1); *Canada CA* (n 4) ss 30.6, 30.61; *Directive 2009/24/EC* (n 68) arts 5–6. See Chapter 8: 'Coming to terms with licence agreements.'

[85] E.g., Green & Randall (n 15) at 118–19.

necessary for the copy of a copyright work to qualify as a good or service of the recipient will bring a more refined understanding of tangible personal property beyond an object capable of being touched, and broaden the meaning of 'tangible' by encompassing its secondary meanings, that is: 'clearly intelligible; that can be grasped by the mind, not elusive or visionary' or 'substantial, definite; that may be clearly viewed, evaluated, tangible thing.'[86]

Because information products that have no supporting physical media tend to be fluid, with fewer dividing lines between the product, the method of delivery, the underlying code structure and operational services, possession and physical control help draw the line between goods and services, tangible and intangible property, choses in actions and choses in possession. Applying ownership 'as an organizing idea'[87] to copies of copyright works brings to the fore the distinction between a resource (a good) and a service, or a combination of the two. Ownership focuses on the relationship between the person and the resource,[88] and the following analysis will draw upon the application of the components of ownership to copies of copyright works discussed in Chapter 1.[89]

## Individuality and scarcity

The individuality or scarcity of a resource is necessary for the first requirement on the ownership spectrum to be met, that is, a juridical relation between a person and a resource, which implies, for example, a distinct user and a copy of a copyright work, and a separateness between the two.[90]

The individuality or scarcity of copies of copyright works available online with no supporting physical object may not be obvious. In fact, there is some confusion about the concept of scarcity when applied from the perspective of copyright users. Copyright law creates an artificial scarcity by prohibiting the unauthorized reproduction and other acts that could otherwise be performed freely in relation to a work of authorship.[91] Thus, copyright works are often associated with the absence of scarcity. From the perspective of copyright users, the artificial scarcity created by copyright enables the creation of rival, individually identifiable copies of copyright works. The copy of an information product downloaded lawfully from the Internet becomes the copy of the recipient to the exclusion of others, which sets it apart from all other copies of the same work.[92] The copy of the information product is

86 *Oxford Dictionary* (n 7).

87 James W Harris, *Property and Justice* (Oxford: Clarendon Press, 1996) at 63ff.

88 ibid at 67: 'Ownership powers of control and transmission all involve capacity to create relations with others by virtue of a person's ownership of something. Powers to control uses by others are as open-ended a class as are ownership use-privileges.'

89 See Chapter 1: 'Copyright users and the ownership spectrum.'

90 ibid.

91 ibid at 42–43; Mark A Lemley, 'Property, Intellectual Property and Free Riding' (2005) Tex L Rev 1031 at 1055.

92 On the discussion of rivalry and virtual property, see Joshua AT Fairfield, 'Virtual Property' (2005) 85 BUL Rev 1047 at 1053–55, who suggests that the perfect digital copies of copyright works do not embody the same rivalry aspects as virtual property developed in virtual worlds.

even more distinct when the recipient adapts or modifies it for their own personal uses, such as personal annotations to an e-book. When it comes to assessing the scarcity attributes of immaterial copies, this ability to personalize immaterial copies of copyright works largely compensates for the lack of distinct physical object boundaries.

Conceptualizing copies of copyright works in terms of individuality and scarcity, even in presence of identical digital commercial copies, is a helpful indicator of whether the user is in possession of a good or is accessing a service. When the user accesses the copyright work through a service, for example, by streaming the work online, there is some individuality; however, there is no specific copy dedicated to the user after the consumption of the work is complete: subsequently, the user will access the work through different streams each time the user logs on to the streaming site. The user would normally not be able (or allowed) to make any edits or modifications to the copyright work, in the same way they could with a dedicated copy that they control.

## Physical control and exclusivity

Physical control of a resource is another indicator of the presence of a good as opposed to a service. Physical control of an individualized concrete resource (as opposed to a conceptual resource, e.g., copyright) makes the second and third elements on the ownership spectrum possible: *prima facie* open-ended privileges and powers and that permit the owner's self-seekingness.[93] Storage, permanent access, and movability are three manifestations of physical control and exclusivity.

The ability to exercise open-ended privileges and powers implies some physical control of the resource. For instance, recipients of information products may exercise physical control over copies they download (e.g., ability to identify a copy as one's own, to the exclusion of others, and autonomously use it without resorting to a service provider). A musical recording or a copy of a film lawfully downloaded from the Internet gives recipients the open-ended privileges and powers to enjoy the work autonomously through physical control. By contrast, the streaming or broadcast of a film does not give the same autonomy to users, although with on-demand streaming and other services, the level of autonomy that consumers enjoy in relation to the service comes closer to the autonomy of an owner when compared to other service offerings involving copyright works.[94] However, recipients of streaming services do not exercise *prima facie* open-ended physical control over the copy they stream, to the extent that a large portion of the physical power remains in the hands of the service provider (i.e., the copy is stored on a server over which the recipient has no physical control, and each individual access to the information product is incumbent upon the service provider making streaming

[93] See Chapter 1: 'Copyright users and the ownership spectrum.'

[94] In comparison with streaming a movie online, viewing a film in a theatre offers an experience of the copyright work that is limited in space and in time.

available). Recipients may have a transferable interest in a subscription to the on-demand streaming services, which may share the attributes of a property interest. However, the power of control and transfer pertains to the subscription to the service, not to the information product per se.

The third element on the ownership spectrum, that the exercise of powers and privileges permits self-seekingness to the owner,[95] is helpful to distinguish the copies of copyright works that are goods from those that are accessed as services. An information product accessed through on-demand streaming services would allow some level of self-seekingness on the part of the recipient (i.e., no duty to account to anyone, e.g., the time of day, frequency, purpose of use, in what circles) while the recipient is still constrained to a large extent by the streaming service provider (the specific information product may only be available for a limited period of time, the service may be down from time to time, or the recipient may not have access to an Internet connection at any given time, the recipient may abandon the service provider if the fees increase, or the service supplier may be out of business; in all scenarios, the recipient would lose access to the information product). By contrast, when the recipient downloads the copy of an information product to their computer or their Internet storage space, the recipient is allowed a greater level of self-seekingness in that they can enjoy the information product independently, autonomously, and for an indefinite duration.

Here, the obstacles to ownership imposed by the supplier contract terms need to be distinguished from other conceptual or physical barriers to owning copies of copyright works (e.g., as would be the case where the copy is accessed through an on-demand streaming service). Copies of copyright works provided under a supplier contract denying any ownership rights to the recipient, but which for all intents and purposes gives the same level of self-seekingness as if the copies were legally owned by the recipient, is one factor that a court should consider to determine whether the sale of a good took place regardless of contract terms to the contrary.[96]

### *Storage and permanent access*

The ability to store a copy of a copyright work and to access it for an indefinite duration are indicators of physical control of a resource and that the copy is a good as opposed to the copyright work not being accessed as a service. In a position paper on the regulation of digital products prepared by BEUC,[97] a European

[95] See Chapter 1: 'Copyright users and the ownership spectrum.'

[96] See above: 'Ripple effects on licences.'

[97] BEUC, the European consumers' organization, is the umbrella organization for 42 independent national consumer organizations across Europe. Its main task is to represent the interests of these organizations and all consumers across Europe: see BEUC, The European Consumer Organization official website, online: <http://www.beuc.org/Content/Default.asp?PageID=591> accessed 4 February 2017.

consumers' organization, the ability to store and the ability to have permanent access to a copy have been highlighted as determining factors for assessing whether digital content could be deemed a good.[98] *Directive 2011/83/EU* opted for a different approach, treating digital content with no physical supporting medium exchanged hand-to-hand as neither goods nor services, but as *sui generis*.[99] When a user streams a copyright work, they lack the ability to store the work and have a time-limited access to the copyright work.

### *Movability*

Movability is one manifestation of physical control allowing movement from one location or device to another. Movability may be constrained by technological protection measures (TPMs). Where there are TPMs, suppliers may recreate movability by allowing users to have a certain number of copies of the computer software or musical recording on different devices. In the context of the US *UCC*, the movability requirement has been invoked as the predominant factor that has taken precedence over the divide between tangible and intangible, which were prominent in the earlier common law, to determine whether products are goods.[100] One commentator noted early on when categorizing computer software under the US *UCC*: 'A program is intangible in the sense that it cannot be touched or felt, but not in the sense that it cannot be moved and identified to a contract.'[101] Computer programs and other copies of copyright works are movable tradable objects regardless of their material form.[102] Movability takes place upon the transfer of ownership and may help distinguish a good from a service.[103]

## Power of transfer

The power to transfer title to a resource is among the prominent open-ended powers and privileges of ownership.[104] It exists whether or not physical control over a resource can be exercised.[105] The power to transfer title to a resource is also central to sale of goods and related consumer protection laws, as 'sale'

[98] BEUC, 'Digital Products, How to include them in the Proposal for a Consumer Rights Directive' (2010), Position Paper, Brussels, at 3: online: <http://www.beuc.org/Content/Default.asp?PageID=2135> accessed 4 February 2017.

[99] *Directive 2011/83/EU* (n 10) Preamble, at recital 19.

[100] See Horovitz (n 29) at 137–38.

[101] ibid at 162. For a contrary view, e.g., that computer software does not fulfill the requirement of 'movability', see Brennan (n 30) at 535–36.

[102] See Braucher (n 5) at 268: Software copies can be moved in various ways, including on computers and discs and by electronic download.

[103] See Smith & Woods (n 31) at 45.

[104] On the components of ownership, see Tony Honoré, 'Ownership' in Tony Honoré, ed, *Making Law Bind, Essays Legal and Philosophical* (Oxford: Clarendon Press, 1987) 161 at 165–79.

[105] Choses in action (which do not entail physical control) may be subject to ownership, which includes the power to transfer the resource.

traditionally embedded transfer of title.[106] The ability to transfer a resource to someone else is a determining factor in distinguishing goods from services. As noted in relation to the classification of goods and services under World Trade Organization and EU law:

> On one level, the notion of property transfer appears inherently bound up with goods and not services because the acquisition of ownership from the producer is predicated on the transfer of possession of the product. Such possession entails 'actual holding or having something as one's own,' implying either physical existence of the thing possessed or the right to exercise control over the product.[107]

Often, recipients' inability to transfer the copy of the information product is imposed by the supplier, either through a contractual restriction or through TPMs. As one seeks to determine which information products can be owned by recipients, barriers imposed by the supplier need to be distinguished from other physical or conceptual barriers to ownership (e.g., the information product is not under the physical control of the recipient and therefore the recipient has no power to transfer it). The distinction between barriers imposed by suppliers and other physical barriers focuses on suppliers' power to shape the nature of information products. When an information product fulfils, for all other intents and purposes, the requirements of ownership by its recipient, the restriction on transfer imposed by suppliers needs to pass the same level of scrutiny as any other restrictions on the alienation of property should.

## The Diminished Importance of the Physical Object

Users experience copyright works in myriad ways that continue to evolve. E-books did not eliminate hardcovers, music streaming services co-exist with individual music play lists, music CDs, and vinyl records, the last of which are even making a comeback. It is critical for traditional concepts of law to adapt to these various forms of user experiences so as to ensure coherence and predictability; proper adaptation also plays a determining role on copyright user rights.

The criteria that will help determine whether users experience copyright works as services or goods, and in the latter case, whether they own or possess the goods is summarized in Table 4.1.

Table 4.1 contrasts goods and services and how the physical object embodying the copyright work is always absent when users experience copyright works as services, but that the physical object's presence or absence should not determine whether an information product is a good. While either goods or services provide access to copyright works, only goods may be possessed or owned.

[106] For a discussion on the various potential meanings of 'property' and 'transfer of property' when employed in a sale of goods law framework, see Gerald HL Fridman (n 33) at 61ff; PS Atiyah & John N Adams, *The Sale of Goods*, 10th ed (Harlow: Pearson Education, 2001) at ch 19.

[107] Smith & Woods (n 31) at 45.

**Table 4.1** Properties of Information Products

| Relationship to the resource / Nature of resource | Access | Possession | Ownership |
|---|---|---|---|
| Good | | | |
| Physical object | Yes | • Individuality, scarcity<br>• Physical control, exclusivity (storage, permanent access, movability) | • Individuality, scarcity<br>• Physical control, exclusivity (storage, permanent access, movability)<br>• Power to transfer |
| No physical object | Yes | • Individuality, scarcity<br>• Physical control/exclusivity (storage, permanent access, movability) | • Individuality, scarcity<br>• Physical control/exclusivity (storage, permanent access, movability)<br>• Power of transfer |
| Service | | | |
| No physical object | Yes | No | No |

A clearer delineation between goods and services may bring more consistency to the distinction between sales of and licences to copies of copyright works. Once goods encompass copies of works with or without a physical embodiment, courts may be more willing to deem a legal transaction involving the copy of a copyright work as a sale than before.

# 5

# First Sale or Exhaustion Doctrine

## A Limitation to the Scope of Copyright

The exhaustion or first sale doctrine[1] is the rule by which once the first sale of physical objects embodying copyright works (such as a book, DVD, or a music CD) has occurred with the authorization of the copyright holder, they cannot dictate the fate of subsequent transfers of that object.[2] The first sale or exhaustion doctrine restricts copyright holders' exclusive distribution rights and does not apply to other exclusive rights, for example, the right to reproduce the work, the right to communicate the work to the public by telecommunication,[3] or the moral rights of the author with which the doctrine may conflict.[4] The doctrine can be invoked only by lawful owners of copies of copyright works and not by licensees, borrowers, or people who otherwise access copies of copyright works.[5] The geographic scope of exhaustion varies: in some jurisdictions or regions, copyright holders' distribution rights are exhausted once they authorize the sale in that jurisdiction or region only, and restrictions against importation of copyright works still apply (i.e., national or regional exhaustion).[6] In other jurisdictions, the copyright holders' exclusive

[1] The doctrine is known as the first sale doctrine in the US and as the principle of exhaustion in other jurisdictions.

[2] At the international law level, see: *WIPO Copyright Treaty*, 20 December 1996, WO033EN, art 6 [*WCT*]; *WIPO Performances and Phonograms Treaty*, 20 December 1996, WO034EN, art 8 [*WPPT*]. In the US, see 17 USC § 109(a) [*USC*]. See also US Copyright Office, *A Report of the Register of Copyrights Pursuant to Section 104 of the DMCA* (2001), online: <http://www.copyright.gov/reports/studies/dmca/dmca_study.html> accessed 4 February 2017 at 22–23 [*DMCA 2001 Report*]. In UK, see *Copyright, Designs and Patents Act 1988* (UK), c 48, ss 16(b), 18 [*UKCDPA*]. In France, see art L122-3-1 CPI [*France CPI*]. In Canada, see *Copyright Act*, RSC 1985, c C-42, ss 3(1)(j), 15(1.1)(e), 18(1.1)(b) [*Canada CA*] (the exclusive distribution right and its exhaustion were introduced in 2012 by the *Copyright Modernization Act*, SC 2012, c 20 [*Canada CMA*]).

[3] ibid. *DMCA 2001 Report* (n 2) at 79–80.

[4] Two judgments are particularly illustrative of the tension between the first sale or exhaustion doctrine and the moral rights of the author, see: *Théberge v Galerie d'art du petit Champlain Inc*, 2002 SCC 34; *Art & Allposters International BV v Stichting Pictoright*, C-419/13, [2015] (ECJ) online: <http://curia.europa.eu/juris/document/document.jsf?docid=161609&doclang=EN> accessed 4 February 2017.

[5] See international conventions and selected national copyright statutes (n 2).

[6] The EU applies regional exhaustion, i.e., within the EU territory: EC, *Directive 2001/29/EC of the European Parliament and of the Council of 22 May 2001 on the harmonization of certain aspects of copyright and related rights in the information society*, [2001] OJ, L 167/10, Preamble, recital 28, art 4(2) [*Directive 2001/29/EC*]; EC, *Parliament and Council Directive 2009/24/EC of 23 April 2009 on the legal protection of computer programs*, [2009] OJ, L 111 at 16, art 4(2) [*Directive 2009/24/EC*].

Copyright User Rights: Contracts and the Erosion of Property. First Edition. Pascale Chapdelaine.

distribution rights exhausts worldwide, once authorizing the sale of the copy of a copyright work anywhere in the world (i.e., international exhaustion).[7]

The distribution right gives copyright holders the exclusive power to authorize the transfer of ownership of the original or copies of a work, independently of any act of reproduction, communication to the public, or performance in public.[8] While the distribution right and the first sale doctrine have been well established in US copyright law with the codification of the early twentieth century Supreme Court judgment *Bobbs-Merrill Company v Isidor Straus*[9] [*Bobbs-Merrill*], until recently it was not part of the copyright legislation of several jurisdictions, including Canada.[10] It started to change when the exclusive right of distribution officially entered international copyright law with the adoption of the World Intellectual Property Organization (WIPO) Internet treaties [*WIPO Internet treaties*] in 1996.[11] Before that, copyright holders in many jurisdictions including Canada benefited from the exclusive right to authorize the first publication of the work, which has been described as a right of first distribution that did not extend to each subsequent copies put on the market for sale.[12] Incidentally, there was also a recognition that the doctrine of first sale applied in those jurisdictions including Canada.[13] The exclusive right of distribution has been implemented through European Union (EU) secondary legislation and is part of the national laws of its Member States, including the UK and France.[14]

The exhaustion or first sale doctrine acknowledges one of the basic powers and privileges of ownership that owners of copies of copyright works have to

[7] E.g., *USC* (n 2) s 109(a) is an example of international exhaustion, as recently confirmed by the US Supreme Court in *Kirtsaeng v John Wiley & Sons, Inc*, 133 S Ct 1351 (USSC, 2013); *Canada CA* (n 2) ss 3(1)(j), 15(1.1)(e), 18(1.1)(b), introduced in 2012, suggest the application of international exhaustion.

[8] *USC* (n 2) s 106(3); *Canada CA* (n 2) ss 3(1) (j), 15(1.1)(e), 18(1.1) (b); *UKCDPA* (n 2) s 16(b).

[9] *Bobbs-Merrill*, 210 US 339, 28 S Ct 722 (1908). First sale doctrine was codified in the year following this judgment [US codification of first sale doctrine]: 17 USC § 27 and was carried forward in s 109(a) of *An Act for the General Revision of the Copyright Law, Title 17 of the United States Code, and for Other Purposes*, Pub L No 94–553 (1976). It is now part of *USC* (n 2) §109(a). The distribution right was set out in 17 USC § 1(a) (1909 Act), s 106(3), and is now part of s 106(3) *USC* (n 2).

[10] *Canada CMA* (n 2). Paul Goldstein & Bernt Hugenholtz, *International Copyright Principles, Law, and Practice*, 2nd ed (Oxford: Oxford University Press, 2010) at 303–05. Herman Cohen Jehoram, 'Prohibition of Parallel Imports Through Intellectual Property Rights' (1999) 30 Intl Rev Intellectual Property & Competition L 495 at 498, on how the German scholar Joseph Kohler developed the principle of exhaustion at the end of the nineteenth century, a principle which was later followed by the German Supreme Court in relation to trademarks, patents, and copyright. For a comparative law analysis of the right of distribution see: Pierre-Emmanuel Moyse, *Le droit de distribution: Analyse historique et comparative en droit d'auteur* (Cowansville: Yvon Blais, 2007).

[11] *WCT* (n 2) art 6; *WPPT* (n 2) art 8.

[12] See e.g., *Canada CA* (n 2) s 3(1); David Vaver, *Intellectual Property Law Copyright, Patents, Trademarks*, 2nd ed (Toronto: Irwin Law, 2011) at 155–57.

[13] *Théberge* (n 4) at para 31, Binnie J for the majority: 'Once an authorized copy of a work is sold to a member of the public, it is generally for the purchaser, not the author, to determine what happens to it.' See Jeremy de Beer & Robert Tomkowicz, 'Exhaustion of Intellectual Property Rights in Canada' (2009) 25 CIPR 3.

[14] *Directive 2001/29/EC* (n 6) art 4; *Directive 2009/24/EC* (n 6) art 4(1)(c); see also: *UKCDPA* (n 2) s 18(3); *France CPI* (n 2) art L122-3-1.

transfer rights to the copies to another party.[15] This doctrine, commonly viewed as an 'exception' to copyright infringement, although 'limitation' is probably more accurate, confirms the boundaries where the distribution right no longer applies, as opposed to allowing an act that is normally prohibited (such as in the case of an exception, e.g., of fair dealing or fair use).[16] The first sale or exhaustion doctrine confirms how ownership of commercial copies of copyright works acts as a property-limitation rule on the exclusive rights of copyright holders.[17] As we will see below, the limitation is increasingly becoming an exception: the first sale or exhaustion is shrinking in its application and relevance.[18]

## Justifications Underlying the First Sale or Exhaustion Doctrine

The doctrine of first sale or exhaustion in copyright law is supported by three main theoretical justifications (with variations): (i) the idea of a just reward for copyright holders; (ii) the free circulation/free competition argument; and (iii) the property/aversion against restrictions on alienation of property theories. A brief overview of the various justifications will help ground the discussion that follows on the increasingly shrinking scope of application of the first sale or exhaustion doctrine.[19]

The idea of a just reward for copyright holders, also known as the remuneration theory, is frequently invoked to justify the existence of the exhaustion or first sale doctrine.[20] Under that theory, remunerating authors beyond the first sale of a copy protected by copyright would go above and beyond fair compensation.[21] In *UsedSoft GmbH v Oracle International Corp* [*UsedSoft*],[22] the EU Court of Justice applied a concept similar to the remuneration theory.[23] Relying on former judgments by the same Court, it justified the application in the EU of the exhaustion of the exclusive right of distribution as a means to balance two competing interests: the need to avoid the partitioning of the Common Market with the protection of copyright holders' exclusive rights 'to what is necessary to safeguard

[15] In *Kirtsaeng v John Wiley & Sons, Inc* (n 7) the US Supreme Court (majority opinion) reiterated the role of the first sale doctrine, setting an important limitation to copyright holders' exclusive rights.

[16] See Chapter 2: 'Exceptions to copyright infringement and limitations.'

[17] James W Harris, *Property and Justice* (Oxford: Clarendon Press, 1996) at 34. See Chapter 2: 'The "mechanics" of exceptions to copyright infringement.'

[18] See below: 'The (ir)relevance of the first sale or exhaustion doctrine.'

[19] ibid.

[20] André Lucas, 'International Exhaustion' in Lionel Bently, Uma Suthersanen, & Paul Torremans, eds, *Global Copyright: Three Hundred Years Since the Statute of Anne, From 1709 to Cyberspace* (Cheltenham: Edward Elgar Publishing, 2010) 304 at 306; Andreas Wiebe, 'The Economic Perspective: Exhaustion in the Digital Age' in Lionel Bently, Uma Suthersanen, & Paul Torremans, eds, *Global Copyright: Three Hundred Years Since the Statute of Anne, From 1709 to Cyberspace* (Cheltenham: Edward Elgar, 2010) 321 at 322; Moyse (n 10) at 432–35; Tomasz Targosz, 'Exhaustion in Digital Products and the "Accidental" Impact on the Balance of Interests in Copyright Law' in Lionel Bently, Uma Suthersanen, & Paul Torremans, eds, *Global Copyright: Three Hundred Years Since the Statute of Anne, From 1709 to Cyberspace* (Cheltenham: Edward Elgar, 2010) 337 at 341.

[21] ibid.

[22] *UsedSoft*, C-128/11, [2012] OJ C 287.

[23] ibid at para 62. See discussion of *UsedSoft* below: 'The requirement of a physical embodiment.'

the specific subject-matter of the intellectual property concerned', in this case, the online distribution of computer programs protected by copyright.[24]

It seems the remuneration theory fails to adequately justify the application of the exhaustion or first sale doctrine and is probably the least convincing of the theories examined here. To establish what is a fair reward for each commercial copy inevitably leads to some arbitrariness. Copyright holders can exploit commercially their exclusive rights through a multitude of offerings (e.g., sale involving a CD, DVD, book, online streaming services, online transfer of a commercial copy, rental of commercial copies for a limited duration), the majority of which do not involve the application of the exhaustion or first sale doctrine.[25] In *UsedSoft*, the Court referred to the need to compensate copyright holders to the degree that is necessary to safeguard their rights, as one rationale leading to the application of the exhaustion principle.[26] The Court did not rely on a market analysis to assess whether the licences to the computer programs offered by Oracle factored in the restriction on subsequent transfers of the copies or whether, on the contrary, Oracle had obtained a fair remuneration that would not justify retaining control over the subsequent transfer of copies by users. To have done so would have required market comparisons between different commercial offerings.[27] It is unclear whether such an exercise would determine that copyright holders obtained a fair remuneration for each of the copies of their works that they commercialized.

Given the limited application of the exhaustion or first sale doctrine to the exclusive distribution right of copyright holders and, consequently, the various means through which copyright holders can receive remuneration through the commercialization of their works that do not involve the application of exhaustion, the fair remuneration theory cannot on its own justify the application of the first sale doctrine. It seems to become even less plausible as a justification for the application of the exhaustion or first sale doctrine in an environment where the variety of ways through which copyright works are made available to consumers increases.[28] At a minimum, the fair remuneration theory cannot be applied without a case-by-case analysis of the actual reward received by copyright holders

[24] ibid (citing: *Metronome Musik*, C-200/96, [1998] ECR I-1953 at para 14; *Foreningen af danske Videogramdistributører v Laserdisken*, C-61/97, [1998] ECR I-5171 at para 13; and *Football Association Premier League Ltd and Others v QC Leisure and Others*, C-403/08 [2011] at para 106, online: <http://curia.europa.eu/juris/liste.jsf?num=C-403/08&language=en> accessed 4 February 2017). The Court concluded in *UsedSoft*, ibid, that to limit the exhaustion of the distribution right under Article 4(2) of *Directive 2009/EC/24* solely to copies of computer programs sold on a material medium would allow copyright holders to control subsequent sales and that such restriction 'would go beyond what is necessary to safeguard the specific subject-matter of the intellectual property concerned.' ibid, at para 63 (citing *Football Association Premier League and Others* paras 105–106).

[25] The exhaustion or first sale doctrine is limited to the exclusive distribution right and after the lawful transfer of ownership of the copy of the copyright work. See above: 'A limitation to the scope of copyright.'

[26] *UsedSoft* (n 22) at paras 62–63.

[27] The different commercial offerings to be compared would include factors such as whether the user has the right to transfer the copy and whether the use is for a fixed duration or a limited one.

[28] E.g., sale of copies of copyright works, rentals, services through which copyright works are accessed without involving a sale or a rental of the copy.

for the sale of copies of copyright works as compared to other offerings. The fair remuneration or just reward theory does, however, generally support the need to balance competing interests and, therefore, to set a limit on copyright holders' remuneration for the sale of copies of their works.[29]

The second frequently invoked justification for the exhaustion or first sale doctrine is the need to preserve the free circulation of commercial copies of copyright works.[30] This justification regroups the free competition arguments, that is, how the application of exhaustion or first sale doctrine favours the free movement of goods, which allows a secondary market that competes with the copyright holder's primary market in relation to the same goods.[31] In the EU, the promotion of a free market within all Member States underlies the application of the exhaustion principle as it applies to various forms of intellectual property rights, including copyright.[32]

The free circulation of copies argument used to justify the first sale or exhaustion doctrine includes public policy arguments for the ongoing free circulation of ideas, outside the control of copyright holders, allowing for a greater balance between the interests of copyright holders, copyright users, and the public.[33] Under that theory, the exhaustion or first sale doctrine protects the ideational interests of users beyond their economic interests in the commercial copies, and the flourishing of a 'second-hand market of ideas'.[34] It also ensures accessibility to works that might otherwise no longer be available.[35]

The justifications based on the free circulation of commercial copies underscore the benefits of the application of the exhaustion or first sale doctrine, but in my view, do not provide on their own a plausible justification for its existence. While it is true that the exhaustion or first sale doctrine favours secondary markets for commercial copies lawfully transferred that compete with the primary market of

[29] See discussion below in this section on the theoretical justification of the free circulation of copies of copyright works and the need to preserve a balance between the interests of copyright holders and the public interest.

[30] Moyse (n 10) at 427–32; Targosz (n 20) at 341, 344–45. The marketability theory, under which the primary purpose of the exhaustion principle is to avoid inappropriate hampering of trade in copies, also falls within the justification of the free circulation of commercial copies: Wiebe (n 20) at 322.

[31] ibid. The competition underpinnings of the first sale doctrine have been invoked as one justification for the doctrine in the US: *DMCA 2001 Report* (n 2) at 21, 86; Aaron Perzanowski & Jason Schultz, 'Digital Exhaustion' (2011) 58 UCLA L Rev 889 at 895ff. From an economic perspective, the distribution rights of copy owners enable price competition with copyright holders: Wiebe (n 20) at 323.

[32] EU, Opinion Advocate General Bot, *UsedSoft GmbH v Oracle International Corp*, Case C-128/11, 24 April 2012, at para 46 [Opinion Advocate General Bot, *UsedSoft*]. See also Targosz (n 20) at 341–42.

[33] Targosz (n 20) at 343. See also Moyse (n 10) at 435–42, who refers to the users' right justification of the exhaustion or first sale doctrine that falls under the broader argument of the need to balance competing interests within copyright law.

[34] Targosz (n 20) at 343.

[35] EC, Parliament, DG for Internal Policies, Policies Department: Citizens' Rights and Constitutional Affairs, *The Relations Between Copyright Law And Consumers' Rights From A European Perspective* by Séverine Dusollier (Brussels: European Parliament, 2010) at 26 [Dusollier 2010]; Perzanowski & Schultz (n 31) at 895.

copyright holders, exhaustion only applies to the exclusive right to control the distribution of copyright works.[36] It does not apply to all other exclusive copyrights, including rental rights, communication to the public by telecommunication, and other exclusive rights that allow copyright holders to control the market for their works with respect to a broad range of commercial offerings.[37] First sale or exhaustion only applies after a lawful transfer of ownership of the commercial copy.

The justifications based on the public policy arguments favouring free circulation of commercial copies underscore the benefits of the application of the exhaustion or first sale doctrine, but they do not provide on their own a plausible justification for its existence. Once again, first sale or exhaustion is limited in its application to lawful acquirers of commercial copies of copyright works. A broad category of users regularly access copyright works without ever becoming lawful owners of a copy. In such instances, the public interest would be safeguarded under other doctrines, including fair dealing, fair use, and non-commercial user-generated content.[38] The broader public interest arguments (and the need to balance competing interests within copyright law) justify, in the main, not first sale or exhaustion itself, but among other things, the need to maintain the integrity of copy owners' ownership rights by allowing them to freely transfer the commercial copies they own as part of their open-ended powers and privileges as owners of commercial copies.[39]

Last, another frequently invoked justification of the exhaustion or first sale doctrine is the property theory,[40] including the justification based on the English common law rule against restraints on alienation of property[41] and similar doctrines in civil law jurisdictions.[42] The property theory is centred on the reconciliation of copyright holders' exclusive copyrights and buyers' ownership rights in the commercial copy.[43]

Restrictions on alienation of property have always been treated with suspicion in property law, especially in the case of chattels.[44] The landmark US Supreme

[36] See above: 'A limitation to the scope of copyright.' [37] ibid.

[38] See Chapter 2: 'The mechanics of exceptions to copyright infringement.'

[39] See Chapter 7: 'The *prima facie* normative status of all ownership freedoms.'

[40] Herman Cohen Jehoram, 'Prohibition of Parallel Imports Through Intellectual Property Rights' (1999) 30 Intl Rev Intellectual Property & Competition L 495 at 497–500; Lucas (n 20) at 306; Wiebe (n 20) at 322; Targosz (n 20) at 340, 344; Moyse (n 10) at 426–27.

[41] See *Bobbs-Merrill* (n 9) at 349–350; *Kirtsaeng v John Wiley & Sons Inc*, 133 S Ct 1351 (USSC, 2013) at 1363 [*Kirtsaeng*]; *DMCA 2001 Report* (n 2) at 20, 86, referring to the English common law rule against restraints on the alienation of property as the historical and policy justification for the existence of the first sale doctrine.

[42] See Lucas (n 20) at 306; Wiebe (n 20) at 322 where the author refers to this justification as the 'marketability theory'.

[43] ibid. See also Perzanowski & Schultz (n 31) at 909–10; de Beer & Tomkowicz (n 13) at 18, who refer to a tool to calibrate copyright holders rights to the use of a physical object embodying the work.

[44] *Kirtsaeng* (n 7) at 1363 (citing Lord Coke). For a discussion on the law of servitudes and how it has been applied to chattels, and its relevance to the interpretation of current restrictive terms of copyright, see: Molly Shaffer Van Houweling, 'The New Servitudes' (2008) 96 Geo LJ 885 at 906ff. See also Molly Shaffer Van Houweling, 'Exhaustion and the Limits of Remote-Control Property' (2016) 93 Denv L Rev 951.

Court judgment *Bobbs-Merrill*[45] is one of the earlier articulations of the exhaustion or first sale doctrine that confirms that reticence. The copyright holder Bobbs-Merrill Company sued Isidor Straus for copyright infringement, claiming that its copyright in a book included the right to regulate the price of subsequent sales of books subject to its copyright by a notice affixed on the book. The Supreme Court referred to the rule against restraint of the alienation of property when applying a strict statutory interpretation of the rights that the US *Copyright Act* conferred on copyright holders.[46] Having found that the right to sell as defined by the statute was silent on granting such powers to copyright holders, the Court dismissed the copyright holder's claim and found that there had been no infringement of copyright.[47] The holding in *Bobbs-Merrill* was thereafter codified in the US *Copyright Act*,[48] and its rationale for supporting the first sale doctrine is still endorsed by the Supreme Court.[49]

Under the property theory, the exhaustion or first sale doctrine is justified by the ownership rights to the copy of the work imposing an outer limit on the competing exclusive rights of copyright holders in the same object, the copyright work. The exhaustion or first sale doctrine is one example of a property-limitation rule that is specific to the effects of copy ownership on copyright holders' exclusive rights. For the exhaustion or first sale doctrine to apply, a lawful transfer of ownership in the commercial copy is needed.[50] The doctrine recognizes and delineates the effects of the ownership rights of purchasers in the tangible embodiment of copyright works and sets those rights against the exclusive rights of copyright holders. The absence of the doctrine would lead to the strip of its bare essence the transaction through which the purchaser acquires the copy of the copyright work. It would amount to stripping off one of the fundamental attributes of full-blooded ownership, that is, the *prima facie* open-ended power and privilege to alienate the copy of the work without any duty to account to anyone.[51] The free circulation and free competition arguments justifying the first sale or exhaustion doctrine are made possible by the clear delineation of the property rights involved in a copyright work, which is at the centre of the property theory. In that sense, the free competition argument supports the need to entrust the right to transfer commercial copies with subsequent lawful owners of copies, in keeping with the broader imperative of free market competition.

In addition to the property theory, the free circulation of copies, free competition theories, and the remuneration theory, other justifications have been invoked in support of the exhaustion or first sale doctrine, including economic efficiency

[45] *Bobbs-Merrill* (n 9). [46] ibid at 349–51.

[47] ibid at 350–51. The Court was also able to arrive at that conclusion by distinctively separating the nature of the rights of the copyright holder from those of the copy owner and strictly confining them to a bundle of intangible rights, citing *Stephens v Cady*, 55 US (14 How) 528 at 530 (1852).

[48] See US codification of first sale doctrine (n 9).

[49] *Kirtsaeng* (n 7) at 1363, where the court delineated the instances where international exhaustion would apply in its interpretation of the *Copyright Act*'s restriction on parallel imports of copyright works.

[50] See above: 'A limitation to the scope of copyright.' [51] Harris (n 17) at 30.

arguments[52] and the need to ensure legal certainty.[53] The economic efficiency arguments support to some extent the property theory, and the free circulation of copies, free competition, and copyright policy arguments discussed above. The legal certainty argument supports the preservation of traditional powers and privilege associated with ownership, which include the ability by copyright users to transfer the copies they own. However, the legal certainty argument does not, in and of itself, provide a justification for the application of the exhaustion or first sale doctrine: it does not explain what the scope of exhaustion should be or the extent to which it should favour copyright users over copyright holders.[54]

Because the current scope of application of the exhaustion or first sale doctrine, that is, the fact that it applies only to the exclusive distribution right and only to copies of copyright works that have been lawfully transferred to users, the more plausible justification for its application is the property rights in the copies that are vested in lawful copy owners. From this perspective, the ownership in the copy creates a property-limitation rule on the exclusive rights of copyright holders. The free circulation of copies theories (i.e., centred around competition considerations or on the need to balance copyright holders' rights with public interest issues) and, to some extent, the fair remuneration theory and the legal certainty theory support the property theory even further but fall short of justifying on their own the existence of the exhaustion or first sale doctrine.

## The Shrinking Application of the First Sale or Exhaustion Doctrine

The application of the first sale or exhaustion doctrine, narrow in scope to begin with, is progressively shrinking and risks becoming obsolete in the predominant digital and standard form contracts environment. The prevailing view is that the exclusive distribution right of copyright holders is not exhausted when copies of copyright works are distributed online with no physical object embodiment. Even if it would be accepted that the exclusive distribution right and its exhaustion apply to digital copies of copyright works with no physical object embodiment, the resale of copies of copyright works often requires the performance of other reserved acts, such as the exclusive right of reproduction. This means that the exhaustion or first sale doctrine needs to be adjusted to be effective in the digital environment, which necessitates the authorization of copyright holders. Second, copyright holders

[52] Perzanowski & Schultz (n 31) at 895ff, discuss other advantages of the first sale doctrine. See in particular, Perzanowski & Schultz at 897–98 where they refer to the protection of consumer privacy, the promotion of market efficiency and transaction clarity, the promotion of innovation (i.e., 'innovation by copyright owners to compete with secondary markets, innovation by secondary market providers, and user innovation'), and platform competition (i.e., the reduction of 'consumer lock-ins' who remain tied to a platform because of the high costs of switching to another provider even if the latter is more competitive and offers a superior product). The first sale doctrine allows consumers to recoup their investment through resale and the doctrine stimulates lower prices of competing platforms.

[53] Targosz (n 20) at 341.

[54] ibid.

resort to the widespread commercial practice of 'licensing' rather than 'selling' copies of their works, making the first sale or exhaustion doctrine inapplicable.[55] Looking as we do here at the various arguments supporting or against the shrinking application of the first sale doctrine, with possible solutions, will situate where copyright users stand regarding the basic privilege and power to transfer their copies of information products.

## The thorny question of digital exhaustion

### *The requirement of a physical embodiment*

The application of the first sale or exhaustion doctrine to copies of copyright works distributed online with no physical object embodiment is an unsettled area of law.[56] The prevailing view is that the exclusive right of distribution and its exhaustion only apply with respect to copyright works embodied in physical tangible objects and that it does not apply to digital copies of information products made available to recipients with no supporting physical medium exchanged hand-to-hand.[57]

At the international level, article 6 of the *WIPO Copyright Treaty* [*WCT*] and article 8 of the *WIPO Performances and Phonograms Treaty* [*WPPT*] impose on their member states the substantive minima needed to confer an exclusive distribution right to copyright holders for their literary and artistic works (or of their performances fixed in phonograms, in the case of *WPPT*), that is, to authorize 'the making available to the public of the original and copies of their works through sale or other transfer of ownership.'[58] Each treaty leaves it up to member states to determine the application of exhaustion (including the geographic breadth of its application) 'after the first sale or other transfer of ownership of the original or a copy of the work with the authorization of the author.'[59] The agreed statements concerning these articles specify that the copies that are subject to the right of distribution refer exclusively to 'fixed copies that can be put into circulation as tangible objects.'[60] The *Trans-Pacific Partnership* signed in 2016 takes the same approach as the one adopted in the *WCT* and *WPPT*, regarding the mandatory nature of the distribution right, that it applies only to copies put in circulation as tangible objects, and by leaving the application of exhaustion of intellectual property rights covered by the partnership to the discretion of its member states.[61] On that basis, commentators argue that the effect of *WCT* and

[55] See Chapter 1: 'If neither owned by the copyright user nor a good, then what?', and Chapter 4: 'Ripple effects on sales and licences.'

[56] See AIPPI, Thierry Calame et al, 'Summary Report, Question 240, Exhaustion Issues in Copyright Law' (2014), question 7, online: <http://aippi.org/wp-content/uploads/committees/240/SR240English.pdf> accessed 4 February 2017, gathering responses from expert groups representing 40 countries and regional organizations.

[57] ibid.

[58] *WCT* (n 2) art 6. See also *WPPT* (n 2) art 8.

[59] *WCT* (n 2) art 6.

[60] ibid, Agreed statement concerning arts 6 and 7.

[61] *Trans-Pacific Partnership*, 4 February 2016, online: <http://www.international.gc.ca/trade-agreements-accords-commerciaux/agr-acc/tpp-ptp/text-texte/toc-tdm.aspx?lang=eng>, art 18.60, 18.11.

*WPPT* is to exclude the application of the exhaustion of the distribution right to digital copies of information products distributed online.[62] The distribution right in article 6 of *WCT* and article 8 of *WPPT* was adopted with little resistance.[63] Leaving the thorny question of its exhaustion open to the discretion of each member state most likely facilitated this outcome.[64] The *Trans-Pacific Partnership* (2016)[65] takes a similar approach by leaving it up to each member state to determine whether, or under what conditions, exhaustion will apply to intellectual property rights.[66]

Various interpretations of the distribution right and its exhaustion in the laws of member states to the *WIPO Internet treaties*, including the US,[67] the EU,[68] and Canada, [69] tend to confirm the view that it does not apply to copies made available online with no supporting physical media,[70] although the jurisprudence is still relatively limited on the issue.[71] In the US, legislative reform attempts to adapt the application of the first sale doctrine in the digital environment have failed.[72]

Two widely commented upon judgments have dealt with the question of copyright digital exhaustion: *UsedSoft*[73] by the EU Court of Justice, and *Capitol*

[62] See Lucas (n 20) at 309ff. The author argues that *WCT* (n 2) art 6, read in conjunction with art 8, closed the path to the application of an immaterial exhaustion principle. See also Moyse (n 10) at 559–62.

[63] Zohar Efroni, *Access-Right: The Future of Digital Copyright Law* (Oxford: Oxford University Press, 2010) at 266–69.

[64] *Agreement on Trade-Related Aspects of Intellectual Property Rights, Marrakesh Agreement Establishing the World Trade Organization, Annex 1C*, 15 April 1994, 1869 UNTS 29, 33 ILM 1197 (1994), art 6, leaves out the question of exhaustion of intellectual property rights from the dispute settlement mechanism applicable to the agreement.

[65] 4 February 2016, online: <http://www.international.gc.ca/trade-agreements-accords-commerciaux/agr-acc/tpp-ptp/text-texte/toc-tdm.aspx?lang=eng> accessed 4 February 2017.

[66] ibid, art 18.11.

[67] Marybeth Peters, 'The Legal Perspective on Exhaustion in the Borderless Era: Consideration of a Digital First Sale Doctrine for Online Transmissions of Digital Works in the United States' in Lionel Bently, Uma Suthersanen, & Paul Torremans, eds, *Global Copyright: Three Hundred Years Since the Statute of Anne, From 1709 to Cyberspace* (Cheltenham: Edward Elgar Publishing, 2010) 329 at 331, citing the *DMCA 2001 Report* (n 2) at 80, 97. See also *Capitol Records LLC v ReDigi Inc*, 934 F Supp (2d) 640 at 651 (USDC, 2013) (on appeal) [*ReDigi*].

[68] See discussion below on *Directive 2001/29/EC* (n 6). See, however, the discussion below on *Directive 2009/24/EC* (n 6) and *UsedSoft* (n 22).

[69] *Canada CA* (n 2) ss 3(1)(j), 15(1.1)(e), 18(1.1)(b) refer to work (or other subject matter of copyright) 'that is in the form of a tangible object'.

[70] In particular, the implementation of the *WIPO Internet treaties* by the EU goes one step further than *WCT* (n 2) and *WPPT* (n 2) in that it emphasizes the need for the transfer of a tangible object embedding the copyright work for the rule of exhaustion to apply: *Directive 2001/29/EC* (n 6) Preamble, recital 28, art 4(2).

[71] See discussion below in this section.

[72] US, Bill S 1621, *Consumers, Schools, and Libraries Digital Rights Management Awareness Act of 2003*, 108th Cong, 2003, s 2(8); US, Bill HR 1066, *Benefit Authors without Limiting Advancement or Net Consumer Expectations (BALANCE) Act of 2003*, 108th Cong, 2003, s 4. See also proposal by Representative Rick Boucher, US, Bill HR 3048, *Digital Era Copyright Enhancement Act*, 105th Cong, 1997, s 4 to amend *USC* (n 2) s 109 and which was not incorporated in the *Digital Millennium Copyright Act*, Pub L No 105-304, 112 Stat 2860 (1998) [*DMCA*].

[73] *UsedSoft* (n 22), where the Court had to determine whether the transfer of ownership (sale) of the copy of the computer program had taken place, the transfer of ownership being a requirement for the application of exhaustion.

*Records, LLC v ReDigi Inc* [*ReDigi*][74] by the South District Court of New York. In *UsedSoft*, the EU Court of Justice ruled that the exhaustion of the distribution right in article 4(2) of *Directive 2009/24/EC*[75] applied to a lawful acquirer who had made the copy of a computer program by downloading it from the Internet to a data carrier, that is, regardless of whether the right holder put the copies of computer programs in circulation with a physical supporting medium exchanged from hand-to-hand.[76]

Although significant for affirming that digital exhaustion may apply to computer programs under EU law, the *UsedSoft* judgment may not have ramifications beyond computer programs, given that they are regulated separately from other copyright works in the EU through *Directive 2009/24/EC*.[77] The Court emphasized the *lex specialis* character of *Directive 2009/24/EC* regulating computer programs in relation to the broader framework of copyright protection in *Directive 2001/29/EC*.[78] The language of the distribution right and its exhaustion spelled out in *Directive 2001/29/EC* varies from the language of computer programs' *Directive 2009/24/EC*, and has been interpreted as not applying to the copies of copyright works made available online with no physical supporting media.[79] Subsequent to *UsedSoft*, in *Art & Allposters International BV v Stichting Pictoright*[80] [*Allposters*], the EU Court of Justice did not have to address the question of digital exhaustion; however, it placed the 'tangible object' embodying the copyright work at the centre of the exclusive distribution right.[81] That digital exhaustion would apply to computer programs and not to other types of copyright works is not supported by a cogent rationale; if anything, the contrary might be more defensible.[82]

In *ReDigi*, Capitol Records, an established record label company, alleged that ReDigi's platform and services, in particular its users' resale of digital music files, amounted to copyright infringement.[83] The Court held that the resale services involved unauthorized distributions and reproductions of music files and that the latter were not covered by the first sale doctrine which does not exhaust any other rights than the distribution right.[84] Therefore, ReDigi infringed the copyright of

[74] *ReDigi* (n 67). [75] *Directive 2009/24/EC* (n 6).

[76] *UsedSoft* (n 22) at paras 53ff. The Court pointed to various possible interpretations of art 4(2) of Directive 2009/24/EC: ibid at para 32. The possible interpretations are based on different applications of art 4(2) of *Directive 2009/24/EC* (n 6) and *Directive 2001/29/EC* (n 6) Preamble, recitals 28 and 29, art 4, read in conjunction with art 8 of *WCT* (n 2) and the agreed statement concerning arts 6 and 7 of *WCT*, the implementation of is one of the objectives of *Directive 2001/29/EC*.

[77] *Directive 2009/24/EC* (n 6). [78] *UsedSoft* (n 22) at para 56.

[79] *Directive 2001/29/EC* (n 6): interpretation is based on the application of the exclusive distribution right (art 4(2)) read in conjunction with recitals 28 (referring to the distribution right as applying to the work incorporated in a ' tangible Article') and Preamble, recital 29. See Lucas (n 20) at 309ff; Targosz (n 20) at 337; Dusollier 2010 (n 35) at 26–27. However, see Opinion Advocate General Bot, *UsedSoft* (n 22) at paras 75–76, where the Advocate General raises doubts as to whether *Directive 2001/29/EC* (n 6) limits the distribution right and its exhaustion to copyright works embodied in physical objects.

[80] *Allposters* (n 4). [81] ibid at paras 29–40.

[82] I.e., that computer programs might require more ongoing maintenance and support which might justify greater legal and physical control remaining with copyright holders.

[83] *ReDigi* (n 67). [84] ibid at 655.

Capitol Records. The Court rejected ReDigi's argument that at the end of each migration of the music files the system ensured that there was only one copy of the relevant music files remaining.[85] The Court recognized that the online transfer of digital music files could trigger the exclusive distribution right, in other words, that distribution of a copyright work does not necessarily require a tangible object embodiment.[86] The Court fell short of recognizing that the first sale doctrine could apply, holding that the distribution right of Capitol Records was infringed on the basis that no affirmative defence was available to ReDigi.[87] It seems that the Court may have adopted this position by relying on its opinion that ReDigi infringed the exclusive reproduction rights of Capitol Records, which in and of itself is a separate infringement that does not support a finding of infringement of the exclusive distribution right of the copyright holder, or of the non-application of the first sale doctrine as a limitation thereto.

### *Assessing the legal and normative arguments for the requirement of a physical embodiment*

Just as we saw that the requirement of a physical embodiment is to a large extent unjustified and somewhat arbitrary in regulating information products as goods or services,[88] a similar conclusion can be drawn from the limited scope of application of the first sale or exhaustion doctrine. The *WIPO Internet treaties* and national copyright laws unequivocally refer to a 'tangible object' vehicle to trigger the application of the exclusive right of distribution and its exhaustion.[89] Narrowing the exclusive distribution right and its exhaustion to transfer of ownership of copyright works embedded in physical objects may have resulted in part from the confusion around the various components involved in the digital distribution of copyright works.[90] In that view, the absence of a physical embodying object would necessarily implicate exclusive rights other than the exclusive right to distribute a product to a copyright user.[91] By way of example, EU regulations reflect a dichotomy between the distribution of physical objects embedding information products and the delivery of downloadable information products online, as if it necessarily implied that online information products could only involve services.[92] By doing so, the EU regulations bury the delivery component of the distinct copy of an

[85] ibid at 650. See the discussion below in this section on the possible involvement of other exclusive rights in the context of digital distribution of copyright works.

[86] ibid at 13. [87] ibid. [88] See Chapter 4.

[89] See above: 'The requirement of a physical embodiment.'

[90] See Chapter 4: 'Misconceptions about tangibility and intangibility in defining information products.'

[91] E.g., the exclusive right to communicate to the public by telecommunication or the 'make available right' under *WCT* (n 2) art 8, and *WPPT* (n 2) arts 10, 14.

[92] Eric Tjong Tjin Tai, 'Exhaustion and Online Delivery of Digital Works' (2003) 25 Eur IP Rev 207 at 208, referring to the authoritative commentary by J Gaster on the EU Database Directive, who was closely involved with the drafting of various EU directives pertinent to copyright exhaustion. In relation to the assumption made that works made available online necessarily only implicate services, see e.g., *Directive 2001/29/EC* (n 6) Preamble, recital 29.

information product in the services, which are generally viewed as intangibles.[93] A closer look leads to a more nuanced view: copyright works are made available online in myriad ways and some of them should account for the exclusive distribution right and its exhaustion.

Based on the arguments developed in Chapter 4, some products made available online with no physical object embodiment should fulfil the requirement of the 'tangible object' more broadly defined than an object that can be touched.[94] If the copy of a copyright work bears for its recipient the characteristics of individuality and scarcity, physical control, and exclusivity (i.e., storage, permanent access, movability) and is capable of being transferred, it is the functional equivalent to an information product with a physical embodiment (a disc, DVD, CD, etc.).[95] Subject to addressing the specificities of digital copies of copyright works, the first sale or exhaustion doctrine should apply to functional equivalents to copies of copyright works embedded in physical embodiments.[96]

The legal and normative arguments against the application of the exhaustion or first sale doctrine to digital copies of information products distributed online reflect a copyright-holder-centric view of copyright that favours copyright holders increased control powers with little attention to the rights of information product recipients.[97] These arguments focus on the general functioning of the market, from the point of view of copyright holders,[98] with little or no attention to the rights and the reasonable expectations of recipients of copyright works.[99] The opinion of the New York South District Court in *ReDigi* reflects that approach.[100]

A narrow application of the exhaustion or first sale doctrine that excludes digital copies distributed online with no physical embodiment seems to be less concerned by substantive considerations guided by a principled approach than it is with securing stronger control for copyright holders over their work. Opponents to the application of the exhaustion or first sale doctrine to digital copies with no physical supporting media invoke the distinct features of digital copies: they can be reproduced with the exact same quality with no possibility of differentiating between the two.[101] Moreover, reproduction and dissemination capabilities are

[93] ibid. [94] See Chapter 4: 'The properties of information products.' [95] ibid.

[96] For a general discussion on the merits of a standards-based approach versus a ruled-based approach to enabling digital exhaustion, see: Aaron Perzanowski & Jason Schultz, 'Legislating Digital Exhaustion' (2014) 29 BTLJ 1535 at 1546ff.

[97] Peters (n 67) as former US Register of Copyrights at the US Copyright Office, referencing the *DMCA 2001 Report* (n 2) at 82–83, 89, recalls: 'The Copyright Office recommendation was based on interrelated economic and practical considerations. One concern was the impact of a digital first sale doctrine on the ability of right holders to exploit their works. Works in digital format can be reproduced without any degradation in quality and transmitted rapidly with little cost. Thus digital transmissions, and the ease of pirating perfect copies, are likely to affect adversely the market for copies of a work to a greater degree than transfers of physical copies.' The *DMCA 2001 Report* (n 2) at 100–101 considered briefly the reasonable expectations of consumers with respect to digital copies as an argument to support the application of the first sale doctrine to digital copies of copyright works distributed online but dismissed it expeditiously, giving way to the threat that its application would represent to the exclusive rights of copyright holders.

[98] ibid. [99] *DMCA 2001 Report* (n 2) at 100–101. [100] *ReDigi* (n 67).

[101] Wiebe (n 20) at 323, 324; Peters (n 67) at 334.

much greater than for copies embodied in a physical object. These attributes of digital copies would likely have more adverse effects on copyright holders' ability to exploit their work than is the case with the transfer of tangible copies.[102] Given that view, copyright holders should be entitled to deprive recipients of digital copies of copyright works of the right to exercise one of the basic powers and privileges of ownership, that is, to subsequently transfer their copy to another person.

The perfect copy phenomenon—with no deterioration—and the facility of reproduction and dissemination arguments that are used against the application of exhaustion to digital copies of copyright works distributed online are attributes of digital copies, not of the fact that there is no supporting physical object.[103] Following this argument, exhaustion should not apply to the sale of music CDs and film DVDs, which is presently not the case and points to the arbitrary reliance on a physical object as the criterion guiding the application of the first sale or exhaustion doctrine. Moreover, the perfect copy phenomenon and the claim that secondary market copies would directly compete with initial market copies may be unfounded; digital copies with no supporting physical objects go through a similar deterioration to copies embodied in a physical object and lose appeal over time after the initial launch of the relevant copyright work.[104] There would be little if any interest in immediately reselling at a lower price digital copies paid for at the full price, unless after their use the recipient wants to part with them at a lower price, having extracted sufficient value from the initial use.

Requirements can be imposed on the application of the first sale or exhaustion doctrine to address the functional differences between digital copies and copies in the analog world.[105] Among those, the adaptation of first sale or exhaustion to digital copies distributed online could include the requirement that the recipient destroy any remaining copies when they transfer their copy to a subsequent purchaser.[106] Similar requirements not to retain any copies upon transfer of the

[102] ibid. See Peters (n 67) comments as former Register of Copyrights, US (n 97).

[103] CDs and DVDs of digital works can be replicated in perfect copies unless protected by technological protection measures, which can also be applied to copies distributed online.

[104] Dan L Burk, 'Copyright and the New Materialism' in Jessica C. Lai & Antoinette Maget, eds, *Intellectual Property And Access To Im/Material Goods* (Cheltenham: Edward Elgar Publishing, 2016) 44 at 46–47, 50.

[105] See comments by 12th Register of Copyrights and director of the US Copyright Office, Maria A Pallante, 'The Next Great Copyright Act' (2013) 36 Colum JL & Arts 315 at 331–32, setting out the choices of Congress, one of which is to rely on technological advances, monitoring, and other capabilities, enabling the replication of the first sale doctrine from the analogue world to the digital environment.

[106] Dusollier 2010 (n 35) at 26–27. In the US, see Peters (n 67) at 335, who, as former Register of Copyright US Copyright Office, notes that there were concerns around forward-and-delete types of technologies in that they did not correspond to typical uses users would make of digital copies of copyright works. Consumers would not readily delete the copy upon transfer and there was concern that it would be difficult to monitor whether deletion had taken place. See also: Evan Hess, 'Code-ifying Copyright: An Architectural Solution to Digitally Expanding the First Sale Doctrine' (2013) 81 Fordham L Rev 1965 at 2007–10, recommending the application of technologies allowing the degradation of digital copies over time, to replicate the condition of physical (paper) copies.

original copy already exist for other exceptions to copyright infringement.[107] In *UsedSoft*, the EU Court of Justice referred to the necessity of such a condition for copyright exhaustion to apply to computer programs distributed online.[108] The improved capabilities of technologies mimicking transfers similar to the analogue world should attenuate concerns that previously prevailed regarding the application of digital exhaustion, leading the way for a principled approach that acknowledges the functional equivalent of digital copies with no physical embodiment.[109]

Other solutions, including a digital market controlling resale,[110] a compulsory licensing regime applying to the resale of digital copies,[111] and a cap on subsequent sales of the original digital copy,[112] are a compromise to address the concerns of copyright holders, while enabling copyright users to exercise a basic right to transfer their copies to subsequent purchasers.

Solutions to facilitate some form of digital exhaustion fall short of fully acknowledging the first sale or exhaustion role in mediating between competing property rights embedded in the commercial copy of a copyright work. The proposed solutions cave in, perhaps too easily, to copyright holders' fears of relinquishing control of digital copies of their works, and drift away from a principled approach giving due weight to the property rights of copyright holders and users.

### *Reserved acts to be performed in the context of digital distribution*

Another wrinkle in the application of digital exhaustion is that unlike the analog world, the resale of copies of copyright works will almost inevitably require the reseller to perform other acts reserved to copyright holders, such as the exclusive right to reproduce copies of the work, to complete the transfer of the copy to another party. The first sale doctrine only exhausts the exclusive distribution right.[113] The need to perform reserved acts creates an obstacle to the reseller's ability to benefit from the first sale or exhaustion doctrine: the unauthorized

[107] See e.g., *Canada CA* (n 2) s 29.22(4) (the right to make reproductions for private purposes includes the requirement to destroy any copies made upon transfer of the original copy).

[108] *UsedSoft* (n 22) at paras 69–70.

[109] Peters (n 67) at 334, as former Register of Copyrights, US Copyright Office, referencing the *DMCA 2001 Report* (n 2) at 98–99: 'It was also not clear at the time that reliable technology existed to delete automatically the sender's copy in a forward-and-delete system.' New commercial offerings, including those of ReDigi, create a market place for the resale of pre-owned digital copies of musical recordings purchased online and provide a mechanism for erasing the seller's original copy when they transfer it to the buyer.

[110] Sarah Reiss, 'Toward a Digital Transfer Doctrine? The First Sale Doctrine in the Digital Era' (2014) 109 Nw UL Rev 173 at 204–05.

[111] Theodore Serra, 'Rebalancing at Resale, ReDigi, Royalties, and the Digital Secondary Market' (2013) 93 BUL Rev 1753 at 1791–98; see also Nicholas Costanza, 'Digital Music Garage Sale: An Analysis of Capitol Records, LLC v ReDigi Inc., and a Proposal for Legislative Reform in Copyright Enabling a Secondary Market For Digital' (2015) 37 Hastings Comm & Ent LJ 135 at 157–60.

[112] See also Hess (n 106) suggesting the simulation of the degradation of copies.

[113] *UsedSoft* (n 22) at para 70, where the EU Court of Justice emphasized that for the doctrine of exhaustion to apply, the original acquirer reselling their copy of the computer software must make their own copy unusable, otherwise the reseller would infringe the exclusive reproduction right of the computer software copyright holder.

performance may constitute copyright infringement unless it benefits from an exception or is authorized by the copyright holder. In *ReDigi*, even though the digital music platform reseller ReDigi had taken all steps to ensure that the original copy was destroyed after the digital music file was transferred to another party, the South District Court of New York held that ReDigi infringed the copyright of Capitol Records.[114] The Court rejected ReDigi's argument that at the end of each migration of the music files the system ensured that there was only one copy of the relevant music files remaining.[115]

There are various ways to dispense with the obstacles that other reserved acts present to the application of digital first sale. One would be for the judiciary to apply a purposive approach to the exclusive acts required for the distribution and to the first sale doctrine. The Court's finding in ReDigi that ReDigi infringed the exclusive right of reproduction of Capitol Records leads to a narrow application of the first sale doctrine, based on a literal meaning and technical application of the act of reproduction rather than taking a functional and purposive approach to the *Copyright Act*.[116] After the transfer, there was only one copy remaining and this fact should have been sufficient for the Court to hold that there was no infringement of the exclusive reproduction right.

As an alternative, legislative reform allowing the performance of reserved acts necessary to enable copyright users to transfer the rights to their copies of copyright works would be a solution to address the issue, similar in spirit to exceptions such as ephemeral recordings for broadcasters[117] and making copies of computer programs for backup purposes.[118] Forbidding copyright users from transferring their copies on the basis of reserved acts that are merely incidental to enabling the transfer with no actual encroachment on the interests of copyright holders defies logic and shows signs of a law headed toward obsolescence. Alternatively, recognizing a principle of exhaustion for copyright users beyond the exclusive right of distribution would go a long way to alleviating the current obstacles to the application of the first sale or exhaustion doctrine.[119]

## The commercial practice not to sell copies

The application of the exhaustion or first sale doctrine to commercial copies of copyright works is limited by another important factor that applies to copies, whether embodied in physical objects or not. As the first sale or exhaustion doctrine only

[114] *ReDigi* (n 67). [115] ibid.

[116] ibid at 13: 'Simply put, it is the creation of a new material object and not an additional material object that defines the reproduction right. The dictionary defines "reproduction" to mean, inter alia, "to produce again" or "to cause to exist again or anew." See *Merriam-Webster Collegiate Edition*, 10th ed. Significantly, it is not defined as "to produce again while the original exists." Thus, the right "to reproduce the copyrighted work in ... phonorecords" is implicated whenever a sound recording is fixed in a new material object, regardless of whether the sound recording remains fixed in the original material object.'

[117] See e.g. *Canada CA* (n 2) s 30.8. [118] ibid s 30.6.

[119] See discussion below: 'The (Ir)relevance of the first sale or exhaustion doctrine.'

applies to owned copies of copyright works, there is a well-documented practice by which copyright holders have circumvented and continue to circumvent the application of the doctrine by licensing the copy of the work and not selling it.[120] This practice has been established for some time in relation to copies of computer programs[121] and is increasingly used for copies of copyright works that are made available online with no supporting physical object, including music, e-books, and student course materials.[122] Therefore, courts' enforcement of (or reluctance to enforce)[123] copyright holders' licences of copies of copyright works is critical to determine the actual scope of the first sale or exhaustion doctrine.

Licences are the vehicle used by intellectual property right holders to grant authorizations, by contract or otherwise, to perform certain acts that would otherwise not be permitted by the application of the property regime created by copyright or other intellectual property statutes.[124] Licences are not required and have not traditionally been present in a multitude of commercial transactions involving copyright holders' exclusive rights, for example, the sale of a book, film DVD, or music CD. In those cases, copyright holders rely primarily on the default property regime of copyright law to protect their rights in the work.

One question that courts face when interpreting and enforcing licences to copies of copyright works is whether such commercial practices effectively preclude the application of the first sale doctrine as dictated by the relevant copyright statute. In the US, where courts are increasingly enforcing licences to copies of copyright works,[125] my short answer, and the answer of other commentators to this question is that it should not. Here is why.

[120] Jean Braucher, 'Contracting out of Article 2 Using a "License" Label: A Strategy that Should Not Work for Software Products' (2007) 40 Loy LA L Rev 261 at 271–72; Glen O Robinson, 'Personal Property Servitudes' (2004) 71 U Chicago L Rev 1449 at 1473–74; Brian W Carver, 'Why License Agreements do not Control Copy Ownership: First Sales and Essential Copies' (2010) 25 BTLJ 1887 at 1931–34.

[121] *Step-Saver Data Systems, Inc v Wyse Technology*, 939 F (2d) 91 (3d Cir 1991) and *Softman Products Co v Adobe Systems Inc*, 171 F Supp (2d) 1075, 45 UCC Rep Serv (2d) 945 (CD Cal 2001), each case referring to the historical background of computer software licensing practices in the US; Robinson (n 120) at 1473–74, discusses the history of software licensing commercial practices going back to the 1960s.

[122] Pascale Chapdelaine, 'The Ambiguous Nature of Copyright Users' Rights' (2013) 26 IPJ 1 at 26–28. See Juliet M Moringiello, 'What Virtual Worlds can do for Property Law' (2010) 62 Fla L Rev 159 at 191–96, who questions the increasing practice to license copies rather than selling them in the context of virtual worlds, noting that traditionally in property law, licences have not granted a possessory interest but have been used to grant a permission (e.g., to certain uses of reserved intellectual property rights, or to limited access to land). C Todd Mosley, 'Mourning the Loss of Copyright's Unsung Hero: Destruction of the First Sale Doctrine' (2014) 14 Chicago-Kent J Intellectual Property 235, referring to Aspen Pay-to-see business model: see Josh Blackman, 'Aspen Casebook Connect Textbooks Must Be Returned At End Of Class, Cannot Be Resold' (5 May 2014), *Josh Blackman's Blog*, online: <http:// joshblackman.com/blog/ 2014/05/05/aspen-casebook-connect-textbooks-must-be-returned-at-end-of-class-cannot-be-resold/> accessed 4 February 2017.

[123] See Chapter 4: 'Ripple effects on sales and licences.'

[124] See e.g., *Patent Act*, RSC, 1985, c P-4; *Trademarks Act*, RSC, 1985, c T-13; or *Industrial Design Act*, RSC, 1985, c I-9.

[125] A leading case in the US is *Vernor v Autodesk, Inc*, 621 F (3d) 1102, 2010 WL 3516435 (9th Cir 2008). See Chapter 4: 'Ripple effects on sales and licences.'

Copyright statutes spell out the exclusive rights conferred by the state on copyright holders and the limitations of those rights, and in doing so those statutes rely to a large extent on traditional concepts of private law, especially in relation to how copyright holders exploit their rights. Copyright statutes refer to concepts such as 'ownership', 'sale', 'rental', and 'bequests' without defining those terms. The uniformity with which courts will apply these traditional concepts of private law will inevitably impact the consistency and coherence of copyright law. As discussed in Chapter 4, uniformity in applying concepts of private law was a preoccupation that guided the EU Court of Justice's approach in *UsedSoft*,[126] bringing the contract of sale to its essence, that is, as the transfer of possession for an indefinite duration, in exchange for a one-time payment, regardless of how the copyright holder characterized the transaction.[127] While considerations specific to the politico-economic constitution of the EU explain to some extent the approach taken by the EU Court of Justice in *UsedSoft*,[128] other grounds justify other jurisdictions similarly interpreting[129] what constitutes a sale for the purpose of the application of the first sale or exhaustion doctrine. As one US commentator astutely pointed out,[130] the US *Copyright Act* lists the transactions under which copyright holders may exercise their exclusive distribution right, that is, 'by sale or other transfer of ownership, or by rental, lease, or lending,'[131] which does not include the 'licence to the copy'.[132] The licence to the copy is often a sale in disguise that entails a permanent transfer of possession (or for an indefinite duration) in exchange for a one-time payment. In those instances, copyright holders do not retain control of the copy in the same manner as would a party renting a copy to a user. Thus, unless the licence to the copy is a sale or other transfer of ownership, of a rental, lease or lending (which normally implicate a temporary transfer of possession), the copyright holder does not exercise their exclusive distribution right, with the somewhat surprising result (certainly for copyright holders) of shielding subsequent distributions from copyright infringement.[133] This interpretation of the actual nature of licence to copies as often amounting to sales (unless they implicate a temporary transfer of possession) is consistent with the first sale or exhaustion doctrine. The doctrine singles out transfers of ownership (i.e., sales, gifts, bequests) to bar any restraints on alienation of property,[134] from rentals, leases, or lending, where exhaustion does not apply.[135]

Viewed with that lens, the distribution right would restrain methods of distribution to sale, rental, lease, or lending. The widespread commercial practice to license the copy while transferring possession indefinitely, and relinquishing physical control of the copy, is a practice similar to the one that the US Supreme Court sought to constrain in the landmark judgment *Bobbs-Merrill*.[136] This commercial

[126] *UsedSoft* (n 22). [127] ibid. See Chapter 4: 'Ripple effects on sales and licences.'
[128] *UsedSoft* (n 22). [129] ibid. [130] Carver (n 120) 1945–48.
[131] *USC* (n 2) § 106(3). [132] Carver (n 120) 1945–48. [133] ibid.
[134] See above: 'Justifications underlying the first sale or exhaustion doctrine.'
[135] *USC* (n 2) § 109. [136] *Bobbs-Merrill* (n 9).

practice is a sale in disguise that may even amount to copyright misuse,[137] and the doctrine of first sale should apply.

Proponents of the enforcement of the licence to the copy may oppose the streamlined approach that categorizes the licence to copy either as sales (gifts and bequests) or lease (rental, lending), and that rejects indefinite or perpetual licences to copies as another category. Such proponents would argue that this streamlining would go against copyright holders' freedom to exploit their exclusive rights as they please, which is an important power and privilege of their exclusive property rights.

The (non-)enforcement of 'licensing copies' involves determining the scope of application of the exclusive distribution right and its exhaustion; freedom of contract is beside the point here. Arguments supporting a clear categorization of copyright holders' commercial practice for the purpose of the application of first sale between transfer of ownership and rentals (leases, lending) include avoiding the creation of idiosyncratic rights for the benefit of economic efficiency.[138] As the US Supreme Court recently opined in *Kirtsaeng* on the purpose of the first sale doctrine, it 'frees courts from the administrative burden of trying to enforce restrictions upon difficult-to-trace, readily movable goods. And it avoids the selective enforcement inherent in any such effort.'[139] Another benefit would be to promote ownership among copyright users,[140] one of the objectives US Copyright Register Maria Pallante invited US Congress to consider in copyright reform.[141]

## The (Ir)relevance of First Sale or Exhaustion Doctrine

The future of digital first sale or exhaustion is uncertain.[142] There is an increasingly widespread practice to license (not sell) copies of copyright works, which some courts have been willing to enforce, bypassing the application of the first sale or exhaustion doctrine.[143] Increasingly, copyright users access copyright works through services, with no personal property of their own in the equation, which altogether sets aside the application of the first sale or exhaustion doctrine. Is the first sale or exhaustion doctrine becoming increasingly irrelevant?[144] Judging by

[137] See Kristin Cobb, 'The Implications of Licensing Agreements and the First Sale Doctrine on U.S. and EU Secondary Markets for Digital Goods' (2014) 24 Duke J Comp. & Intl L 529 at 545ff, on the application of the doctrine of copyright misuse to certain licensing agreement practices and their effect on the application of the first sale doctrine.

[138] Aaron Perzanowski & Jason Schultz, 'Reconciling Intellectual Property with Personal Property' (2014) 90 Notre Dame L Rev 1 at 54.

[139] *Kirtsaeng* (n 7) at 1363.

[140] See Chapter 1.

[141] Maria A Pallante, 'The Next Great Copyright Act' (2013) 36 Colum JL & Arts 315 at 331–32.

[142] See above: 'The thorny question of digital exhaustion.'

[143] See above: 'The commercial practice not to sell copies.'

[144] See US, The Department of Commerce Internet Policy Task Force, *Copyright Policy, Creativity, and Innovation in the Digital Economy* (2013), at 37, online: <http://www.uspto.gov/sites/default/files/news/publications/copyrightgreenpaper.pdf> accessed 4 February 2017, suggesting legislative reform or revised interpretation of copyright licences, and pointing to the first sale or exhaustion doctrine becoming increasingly irrelevant.

the increased access to copyright works through services and digital means, the answer is probably yes. The doctrine would remain relevant in the world of physical objects, but even then, the contract pertaining to physical objects embodying copyright works may preclude recipients' rights of resale to the extent that the commercial practice to license (not sell) copies would continue to prevail and be enforced by courts.[145]

Understood as a limitation on the exclusive right to distribute copies of copyright works, the first sale or exhaustion doctrine, while enabling the basic privilege of copyright users to freely dispose of the copies they own, is relatively limited in its application. Other exceptions to or limitations on copyright, such as fair dealing, fair use, or the non-commercial-user-generated content exception, may be more suitable for the fulfilment of other important aspirations of users than the freedom to transfer their copy. This said, envisaging the doctrine of exhaustion as limiting other exclusive copyrights for copy owners beyond the distribution right would radically change the discussion on the future relevance of the doctrine.[146]

A doctrine that would exhaust exclusive rights beyond the distribution right to give fuller recognition to the normative value of the personal property rights of copyright users would also set aside one of the major obstacles to the application of digital exhaustion. It would do so by recognizing the exhaustion of other exclusive rights, such as reproduction, involved in the digital distribution of copyright works. A broader doctrine of exhaustion would be one legal tool of choice among other regulatory design options. Unlike the model of specific statutory lists of exceptions to copyright infringement, a broader doctrine of exhaustion evolved through judicial interpretation, would fill a gap in copyright law by affirming what copy owners should always be legitimately entitled to do, and constrain copyright's propensity to expansion.[147] Therefore, a broader doctrine of exhaustion for copy owners would elevate their status vis-à-vis other users, and recognize the normative implications of owning a copy of the work with which they interact.[148]

[145] E.g., enforcing licence to copies and precluding the application of first sale doctrine on computer software embedded in CDs. See above: 'The commercial practice not to sell copies.'

[146] See Chapter 8: 'Exhaustion of copyright beyond the exclusive distribution right.'

[147] ibid. [148] ibid.

# 6

# Digital Locks, Physical Objects, and Immaterial Works

## A Paradigm Shift for Digital Copyright Users

One of the greatest controversies in contemporary copyright law is the legal protection afforded to digital locks, those technological measures that restrain users' powers and privileges in e-books, musical recordings, films, computer software, and, increasingly, other objects the main purpose of which is not to embody copyright works, for example, cars, and farming equipment.[1] The controversy concerns the introduction of technological protection measures (TPMs) by the *WIPO Internet treaties* of 1996,[2] their necessity, and the required level of implementation by member states.[3] As quickly as TPMs solidified copyright holders' rights to digital works, their introduction undermined arguments for the existence of copyright user rights in general and digital copyright user rights in particular.[4] By creating a separate parallel regime for digital copyright works, TPMs shifted the paradigm by redefining the rules of engagement as to how users would increasingly access and experience copyright works.

Technological measures and their protection through TPMs impact copyright holders' intangible property rights by augmenting them, as much as they constrain the scope of copyright users' tangible personal property powers and privileges in the copies they protect.[5] Copyright holders apply technological measures to copies

[1] Branislav Hazucha, Hsiao-Chien Liu, & Toshihide Watabe, 'Copyright, Technological Protection Measures and Their Acceptance by Consumers in Japan' (2013), SERCI, at 6–10, online: <http://www.serci.org/2013/Hazucha-SERCI-2013.pdf> accessed 4 February 2017, providing an overview of various technological measures applied to different types of copyright works.

[2] *WIPO Copyright Treaty*, 20 December 1996, WO033EN, art 11, online: <http://www.wipo.int/treaties/en/ip/wct/trtdocs_wo033.html#P8_189> accessed 4 February 2017 [*WCT*]; *WIPO Performances and Phonograms Treaty, 20 December 1996*, WO034EN, art 18, online: <http://www.wipo.int/treaties/en/ip/wppt/trtdocs_wo034.html> accessed 4 February 2017 [*WPPT*].

[3] For a Canadian perspective on the digital agenda of the *WIPO Internet treaties*, and particularly the TPM provisions, see Michael Geist, ed, *From 'Radical Extremism' to 'Balanced Copyright': Canadian Copyright and the Digital Agenda* (Toronto: Irwin Law, 2010), in particular ch 7: Carys Craig, 'Locking Out Lawful Users: Fair Dealing and Anti-Circumvention in Bill C-32' and ch 8: Michael Geist, 'The Case for Flexibility in Implementing the *WIPO Internet Treaties*: An Examination of the Anti-Circumvention Requirements.' [Geist, 'The Case for Flexibility'].

[4] See Chapter 2: 'User rights or privileges?'

[5] See below: 'Technological protection measures and the search for balance in copyright law.'

of copyright works, whether embodied in a physical object, whether distributed online,[6] and whether users experience the copyright work through an individual copy they control or as a service.[7] The legal protection of copyright holders' technological measures through TPMs is arguably the sharpest illustration of the trivialization of copyright users' property rights in copies of copyright works,[8] and of exceptions to copyright infringement.[9] In the case of TPMs, courts and legislators' struggles toward the coherent treatment of copies of copyright works with and without a physical embodiment, identified in Chapters 4 and 5 are still present,[10] while there is another layer of complexity added to the difficulty to deal with the tangible and intangible dichotomy. The increased presence of digital locks in physical objects, the primary function of which is not to embody copyright works (e.g., cars, coffee makers), magnifies the regulatory design shortcomings that were identified at the outset of the introduction of TPMs more than two decades ago.

This chapter delves further into the tangible and intangible divide by looking at the effect of TPMs on a larger pool of users than traditional copyright users: that is, those *inadvertent copyright users* who buy a car or a tractor without suspecting that it embeds copyright works (e.g., software), let alone digital locks blocking access and use to important components of the physical object. In parallel, this chapter explores the changing role of TPMs in light of the shift from accessing copyright works through individualized digital copies to experiencing works through services.

## Technological Protection Measures and the Search for Balance in Copyright Law

### International obligations

The controversy around TPMs forms part of the broader debate about the proper balance that needs to subsist between the exclusive rights of copyright holders, the rights of copyright users, and the broader public interest.[11] The *WIPO Internet treaties'* obligation to protect technological measures is one of the outcomes of the *digital agenda* put forward by the World Intellectual Property Organization (WIPO) that sought to address 'the profound impact of the development and convergence of information and communication technologies on the creation and use of literary and artistic works.'[12]

6 ibid. 7 ibid. 8 See Chapter 1.

9 See Chapter 2: 'User rights or privileges?'; see below: 'Technological protection measures and the search for balance in copyright law.'

10 See below: 'Technological protection measures and the search for balance in copyright law.'

11 For an overview of the policy and legal debate around TPMs from the perspective of copyright holders and copyright users and the public interest, and about where the proper balance should be struck, see Peter K Yu, 'Anticircumvention and Anti-Anticircumvention' (2006) 84 Denv UL Rev 13, in particular at 17–19.

12 *WCT* (n 2) Preamble. For a discussion of the new international obligations brought on by the *WIPO Internet treaties* in relation to TPMs and digital rights management, and of the drafting process

The *WIPO Internet treaties* require member states to provide 'adequate legal protection and effective legal remedies against the circumvention of effective technological measures' used by copyright holders in relation to digital works.[13] Questions about the minimum level of protection of technological measures that needs to be put in place to comply with the *WIPO Internet treaties* remain controversial and pertinent more than 20 years after the signature of the treaties as evidenced by national jurisdictions' efforts to implement the treaties in their domestic sphere.[14] For instance, is there an obligation to prohibit the trafficking of circumventing devices or services, of technological measures (the *WIPO Internet treaties* being silent on that question), or should the prohibition be limited to the circumvention of technological measures?[15] Does the copyright doctrine of contributory infringement or authorization, or general legal regimes of tort, contracts, criminal law provide *adequate legal protection and effective legal remedies* under the *WIPO Internet treaties* or is there a need to implement specific TPM provisions?[16]

Regional treaties implementing the *WIPO Internet treaties* and subsequent international agreements have been more explicit (and arguably have gone further) than the *WIPO Internet treaties* on the scope of obligations of TPMs.[17] Independently of the required level of protection of technological measures under the *WIPO Internet treaties*, other factors, including bilateral and regional trade agreements and political pressures by influential trading partners, have

leading up to their adoption, see Mihaly Ficsor, *The Law of Copyright and the Internet, The 1996 WIPO Treaties, Their Interpretation and Implementation* (Oxford: Oxford University Press, 2002) Part III; Sam Ricketson & Jane C Ginsburg, *International Copyright and Neighbouring Rights, The Berne Convention and Beyond*, 2nd ed (Oxford: Oxford University Press, 2006) at 964ff.

13 *WCT* (n 2) art 11; *WPPT* (n 2) art 18.

14 This is illustrated by Canada's various attempts at copyright legislative reform that finally led to the entry into force of the *Copyright Modernization Act*, SC 2012, c 20 in 2012. TPMs occupied the larger part of the debates throughout this copyright legislative reform. For earlier critiques of TPMs, see Pamela Samuelson, 'Intellectual Property and the Digital Economy: Why the Anti-Circumvention Regulations Need to Be Revised' (1999) 14 BTLJ 519 at 534–43; David Nimmer, 'A Riff on Fair Use in the Digital Millennium Copyright Act' (2000) 148 U Pa L Rev 673; P Bernt Hugenholtz, 'Why the Copyright Directive is Unimportant, and Possibly Invalid' (2000) 22 Eur IP Rev 499 at 499–501.

15 For different views on that question, see: Geist, 'The Case for Flexibility' (n 3), and Mihaly Ficsor, 'TPMs and Flexibility ("The Ability of Bending without Breaking")—Why Should the TPM Provisions of Bill C-32 Protect Access Controls and Prohibit "Preparatory Acts"', online: Osgoode Intellectual Property Law & Technology Program <http://www.iposgoode.ca/2010/11/digital-locks-circumvention-and-the-copyright-reforms-proposed-by-bill-c-32/> accessed 4 February 2017.

16 Samuelson (n 14) at 530–34; Séverine Dusollier, 'Situating Legal Protections for Copyright-Related Technological Measures in the Broader Legal Landscape: Anti-Circumvention Protection Outside Copyright' in JC Ginsburg & JM Besek, eds, *Adjuncts and Alternatives to Copyright: Proceedings of the ALAI Congress, June 13–17, 2001, New York, U.S.A.* (New York: ALAI-USA, 2002) at 123.

17 EC, *Directive 2001/29/EC of the European Parliament and of the Council of 22 May 2001 on the harmonisation of certain aspects of copyright and related rights in the information society*, [2001] OJ, L 167/10 [*Directive 2001/29/EC*]: art 6.2 requires its Member States to put in place an anti-trafficking prohibition against TPM circumvention devices. *Trans-Pacific Partnership*, 4 February 2016, online: <http://www.international.gc.ca/trade-agreements-accords-commerciaux/agr-acc/tpp-ptp/text-texte/toc-tdm.aspx?lang=eng> accessed 4 February 2017 [*TPP*]: art 18.68(1)(b) imposes obligations similar to those in *Directive 2001/29/EC*, and uses similar language.

played a role in the level of protection of technological measures adopted by some member states.[18]

The *WIPO Internet treaties* in their purpose and design seek to secure greater protection for copyright holders. As special agreements of the *Berne Convention for the Protection of Literary and Artistic Works* [*Berne Convention*],[19] the *WIPO Internet treaties* must increase the legal protection conferred on copyright holders or, at a minimum, contain no provisions that are contrary to the *Berne Convention*.[20] It may come as no surprise that the *WIPO Internet treaties'* TPM provisions impose no counterbalancing obligation on member states to preserve users' exercise of permitted acts on copyright works without the permission of the copyright holders, such as through fair use, fair dealing, and other long-established exceptions to copyright infringement.[21] Member states may enact provisions to preserve exceptions to or limitations on copyright in the digital age, as long as they are not inconsistent with their obligations under the *WIPO Internet treaties*.[22]

The absence in the *WIPO Internet treaties* of obligations to copyright holders who benefit from TPMs, that is, to allow users to perform acts not requiring their authorization, did not preclude some jurisdictions from imposing counterbalancing obligations on copyright holders who benefit from TPMs. EU *Directive 2001/29/EC*[23] imposes obligations on its Member States to require copyright holders to make available to beneficiaries of certain exceptions or limitations to copyright (including reprographic copying and quotations used for teaching or scientific research purposes),[24] the means of benefiting from those exceptions and limitations.[25] However, the Member States' obligations apply to certain exceptions only,[26] and are subject to an important caveat. The obligations do not apply to 'works and other subject matter of copyright made available by contract under which members of the public may access them from a place and at a time individually chosen by them.'[27] Excluding copyright holders from having to accommodate

[18] See e.g., Canada *Copyright Modernization Act* (n 14) Preamble, which specifically refers to the need for Canada to coordinate its approach with other countries through the adoption of internationally recognized copyright norms. For many years, the US placed Canada and other countries on its Special 301 'Watch List' of countries that allegedly fail to enforce intellectual property rights (including copyright) at the proper level. See Office of the United States Trade Representative (USTR) government's Special 301 'Watch List', online: <https://ustr.gov/issue-areas/intellectual-property/Special-301> accessed 4 February 2017.

[19] 9 September 1886, 828 UNTS 221, art 20.

[20] ibid.

[21] On how this void does not allow a balance between copyright holders and users, see David Vaver, 'Copyright and the Internet: From Owner Rights and User Duties to User Rights and Owner Duties?' (2007) Case W Res L Rev 731.

[22] See *WCT* (n 2) art 10, under which exceptions to copyright exclusive rights must meet three requirements (the 'three-step test'); agreed statement to art 10, ibid. See Chapter 2: 'Exceptions to copyright infringement and international obligations.'

[23] EC, *Directive 2001/29/EC of the European Parliament and of the Council of 22 May 2001 on the harmonisation of certain aspects of copyright and related rights in the information society*, [2001] OJ, L 167/10 [*Directive 2001/29/EC*].

[24] ibid, art 6.4. The exceptions are: reprographic copying, quotations used for teaching or scientific research purposes, uses benefiting people with a disability and, at the option of Member States, private copying: ibid.

[25] ibid.

[26] ibid.

[27] ibid, art 6.4 para 4.

exceptions to copyright infringement, when their works are made available online, with no further distinction on how the works are made available, reflects the confusion between copyright works accessed through services (such as streaming), and copies of copyright works made available online and downloaded by users, as identified in Chapter 4.[28] When users download a copy from the Internet, that copy allows them to exercise a level of autonomy similar to, if not greater than, the one they exercise with copies they obtain in the offline world. It should allow users to benefit from the same protection that *Directive 2001/29/EC* offers to copies of copyright works not made available 'on demand'.[29] Overall, the copyright holders' obligations to accommodate users pursuant to *Directive 2001/29/EC*, as a counterbalance to the additional protection of TPMs conferred by the Directive, are limited.[30]

More than 20 years after the adoption of the *WIPO Internet treaties*, developments at the international level signal greater attention to the effects of TPMs on users' legitimate uses. The *Marrakesh Treaty to Facilitate Access to Published Works for Persons Who Are Blind, Visually Impaired, or Otherwise Print Disabled* [*Marrakesh Treaty 2013*][31] departs from the copyright-holder-centric approach of the *WIPO Internet treaties* by mandating each member state to ensure that TPMs implemented in its jurisdiction do not prevent beneficiaries from enjoying the exceptions to copyright infringement set out in the treaty.[32] The *Trans-Pacific Partnership* [*TPP*] does not impose obligations on member states to ensure that users maintain the benefit of non-infringing uses of copyright works, but it sets parameters under which member states *may* provide limitations on and exceptions to TPMs.[33]

## Implementation of technological protection measures at national level

The *WIPO Internet treaties* of 1996 gave rise to the implementation of different levels of legal protection by member states.[34] With the entry into force of the *Digital Millennium Copyright Act* [*DMCA*][35] in 1998, the US adopted one of the strongest TPM regimes. Preparatory works leading to the adoption of the

[28] See Chapter 4: 'Misconceptions about tangibility and intangibility in defining information products.'

[29] I.e., the level of protection offered by *Directive 2001/29/EC* (n 23) art 6.4, para 1.

[30] Zohar Efroni, *Access-Right: The Future of Digital Copyright Law* (New York: Oxford University Press, 2011) at 367–80, analysing the TPM regime of *Directive 2001/29/EC* and how limited is the Member State obligation to accommodate the exercise of exceptions to copyright infringement.

[31] 27 June 2013, online: <http://www.wipo.int/treaties/en/text.jsp?file_id=301016> accessed 4 February 2017.

[32] ibid art 7.

[33] *TPP* (n 17) art 18.68(4).

[34] Giuseppe Mazziotti, *EU Digital Copyright and the End-User* (Berlin: Springer-Verlag, 2008) at 179–229, comparing the EU, selected Member States, and US implementation of TPMs pursuant to the *WIPO Internet treaties* (n 2); see also Efroni (n 30) at 348–80; see generally Geist, 'The Case for Flexibility' (n 3).

[35] *Digital Millennium Copyright Act*, Pub L No 105-304, 112 Stat 2860 (1998), amending 17 USC, including the introduction of §§ 1201–1205 [*DMCA*].

*DMCA* acknowledged that the *DMCA* went beyond the minimum requirements of the *WIPO Internet treaties*,[36] but that the threat posed by the digital environment to the relevant creative industries and electronic commerce required a strong level of protection.[37] *Directive 2001/29/EC*[38] imposed on EU Member States the implementation of a strong level of protection for TPMs,[39] tempered by a limited obligation to require copyright holders to make available to beneficiaries of certain exceptions to copyright infringement the means to benefit from those exceptions.[40] A closer look at *Directive 2001/29/EC* reveals that the obligations imposed on Member States to accommodate exceptions to copyright infringement are limited,[41] situating the EU among other regimes of TPMs that impose a high level of protection.[42] Countries including Canada and Australia have enacted a high level of protection for technological measures comparable to the US.[43] Countries offering a lower level of protection of technological measures include Japan, Switzerland, and New Zealand.[44]

The following overview highlights the detrimental effects that stronger regimes of TPMs have on copyright user rights, in particular in the US and the EU, given the political and economic importance of these jurisdictions, the size of their cultural and innovation industries, and their ability to influence the adoption of similar regimes of protection through bilateral, regional, or multilateral trade agreements.

Stronger regimes of TPMs typically comprise two forms of prohibition. The first prohibits the trafficking of products or provision of services that allow the circumvention of a technological measure that *controls access* to a protected copyright work

[36] US, House Judiciary Committee, *WIPO Copyright Treaties Implementation and on-line Copyright Infringement Liability Limitation* (HR Rep No 105-551) (1998) at 5, online: <http://www.gpo.gov/fdsys/pkg/CRPT-105hrpt551/html/CRPT-105hrpt551-pt2.htm> accessed 4 February 2017 [US House Judiciary Committee].

[37] ibid.

[38] *Directive 2001/29/EC* (n 23). The Directive does not apply to the legal protection of computer programs: ibid Preamble, recital (50), art 1. The legal protection of computer programs is covered by EC, *Parliament and Council Directive 2009/24/EC of 23 April 2009 on the legal protection of computer programs*, [2009] OJ, L 111[*Directive 2009/29/EC*].

[39] *Directive 2001/29/EC* (n 23), art 6.

[40] See above in this section the discussion on the EU TPM regime imposing limited obligations on copyright holders to ensure users have the benefit of certain exceptions to copyright infringement.

[41] ibid.

[42] *Directive 2001/29/EC* (n 23) art 6. See Mazziotti (n 34) at 184; Efroni (n 30) at 367–80.

[43] *Canada Copyright Act*, RSC 1985, c C-42, s 41 [*Canada CA*]; Australia *Copyright Act 1968* (Cth), ss 116AK–116AQ [*Austl CA*].

[44] *Federal Act on Copyright and Related Rights* (SWITZ), of 9 October 1992 art 39a; *Copyright Act* (JP), (Act No 48 of 6 May 1970, as amended up to Act No 35, of 14 May 2014) art 2(1); *Copyright Act 1994* (NZ), 1994/143, ss 226ff, in particular s 226(D) (prior to amendments made by *Trans-Pacific Partnership Agreement Amendment Act* 2016 (NZ)). For a summary of the main features of the national implementation of TPMs in Japan, Switzerland, and New Zealand, see Geist, 'The Case for Flexibility' (n 3) at 233–36. See also: WIPO Standing Committee on Copyright and Related Rights, 'Study on Copyright Limitations and Exceptions for Libraries and Archives: Updated and Revised' by Kenneth D Crews (10 June 2015) at 287–88, 396, online: <http://www.wipo.int/edocs/mdocs/copyright/en/sccr_30/sccr_30_3.pdf> accessed 4 February 2017 ['IPO Study on Copyright Limitations and Exceptions'].

('access controls')[45] or that *protects a right* in a work ('copy controls').[46] The second prohibits the circumvention of effective access-control technological measures,[47] and in some jurisdictions (e.g., EU), the prohibition extends to the circumvention of copy-control technological measures.[48] The prohibitions apply to *effective technological measures*.[49] The anti-trafficking prohibition often requires certain thresholds to be met to trigger infringement, for example, the degree to which the device or service is used to circumvent a technological measure relative to other non-infringing uses.[50] In jurisdictions including the US and Canada, exemptions to the prohibition of the circumvention of access controls may apply from time to time to a certain class of persons or type of works if there is a likelihood of adverse effects on the ability to make non-infringing uses of a particular class of works.[51] Various exceptions apply to the TPM prohibitions to address among others, law enforcement and interoperability issues.[52]

Beyond the online distribution of copyright works where copyright holders protect their works with various forms of technological measures, digital locks are also increasingly present in the world of physical objects, which primary purpose is not to embody the copy of the copyright work (e.g., a DVD, a CD) but to serve broader functions, such as in the case of a game console, a car, or a tractor. Courts have enforced anti-trafficking prohibitions against chips that circumvent protections in game consoles,[53] against software ('bot') to help video game users to advance game levels,[54] against mechanisms allowing users to circumvent content-scrambling system (CSS) technology in DVDs and make copies

[45] 17 USC § 1201(a)(2) (2010) [*USC*]; *Canada CA* (n 43) s 41.1(b); *Austl CA* (n 43) ss 116AO–116AP.

[46] *USC* (n 45) § 1201(b)(1); *Directive 2001/29/EC* (n 23) art 6.2; *Canada CA* (n 43) s 41.1(b); *Austl CA* (n 43) ss 116AO–116AP.

[47] USC (n 45) § 1201(a)(1)(A); *Directive 2001/29/EC* (n 23) art 6.2; *Canada CA* (n 43) s 41.1(1)(a); *Austl CA* (n 43) s 116AN.

[48] *Directive 2001/29/EC* (n 23) art 6.1.

[49] USC (n 45) §§ 1201(a)(1)(A), 1201(b)(1) 1201(a)(2); *Directive 2001/29/EC* (n 23) art 6.3; *Canada CA* (n 43) s 41 'technological protection measure.'

[50] *USC* (n 45) §§ 1201(a)(2), 1201(b)(1); *Directive 2001/29/EC* (n 23) art 6.2; *Canada CA* (n 43) s 41.1(1); *Austl CA* (n 43) s 116AN(1). In the EU, see *Nintendo Co Ltd v PC Box SRL*, C-355/12, [2014] (ECJ) at para 30, online: <http://curia.europa.eu/juris/document/document.jsf?docid=146686&doclang=EN> accessed 4 February 2017 [*Nintendo*], the EU Court of Justice (fourth Chamber) applying *Directive 2001/29/EC* (n 23) art 6.2, in light of recital 48 as imposing a requirement of proportionality on the legal protection of technological measures which 'should not prohibit devices or activities which have a commercially significant purpose or use other than to circumvent the technical protection.'

[51] *USC* (n 45) § 1201(a)(1)(c). See also *Canada CA* (n 43) s 41.21(2)(a).

[52] *USC* (n 45) §§ 1201(d)–(j); *Canada CA* (n 43) ss 41.11–41.18; *Austl CA* (n 43) ss 116AN(2)–(9).

[53] *US v Reichert*, 747 F (3d) 445 (6th Cir 2014), violation of *USC* (n 45) § 1201(a)(2)(A); *Kabushiki Kaisha Sony Computer Entertainment Inc and Others v Ball and Others*, [2004] EWHC 1738, [2005] ECC 24; *R v Gilham (Christopher Paul)*, [2009] EWCA Crim 2293, [2010] ECDR 5; see also *Nintendo* (n 50) at para 28, where the EU Court of Justice held that microchips in game consoles constituted technological measures that could be protected under *Directive 2001/29/EC* (n 23) art 6, even if the technological measures were not applied to the copies of the work or other subject matter of copyright per se, such as the DVD of a videogame.

[54] *MDY Industries v Blizzard Entertainment and Vivendi Games et al*, 629 F (3d) 928 (9th Cir 2011) (upholding finding of violation of USC (n 45) § 1201(a)(2)).

of DVDs,[55] against the link to a software that facilitated the circumvention of technological measures,[56] and against cable filters and other devices that gain access to television signals.[57] Courts have enforced prohibitions against the circumvention of access-control technological measures, for example, access controls on servers hosting videogames (only made available to authorized users),[58] against circumvention technologies permitting the decryption of software securing video distribution on the Internet[59] (to protect access-control software preventing streaming technology from being copied),[60] as well as against the use of decryption software to gain access to the operating system of a major computer software and hardware provider.[61]

## Link between copyright infringement and contravention to technological protection measures

Two of the most striking features of stronger TPM regimes are, first, the absence of a link between copyright infringement and the anti-circumvention prohibitions.[62] Liability for circumventing access-control technological measures may arise independently of an infringement of copyright.[63] As one commentator notes, the legal protection of technological measures is blind to the lawfulness of the use.[64] TPMs do not parallel the existing exclusive rights of copyright holders, but rather endorse an indiscriminate lockout approach.[65] The second striking feature of strong TPM

[55] *Realnetworks, Inc v DVD Copy Control Association*, 641 F Supp (2d) 913 (ND Cal 2009), preliminary injunction granted based on likelihood of contravention of § 1201(a)(2) and § 1201(b).

[56] See *Universal City Studios, Inc v Corley*, 273 F (3d) 429 at 435 (2d Cir 2001), where defendant found to be in violation of *USC* (n 45) § 1201(a)(2)(A).

[57] *CoxCom Inc v Chaffee*, 536 F (3d) 101 (1st Cir 2008); *Directv Inc v Carrillo*, 227 Fed Appx 588 (9th Cir 2007).

[58] *Evony v Holland* 2011 US Lexis 34700 (WD Pa) violation of *USC* (n 45) § 1201(a)(1)(a).

[59] *Eyepartner Inc v Kor Media Group*, 2013 US Lexis 98370 (SD Fla Dist Ct, interlocutory injunction granted for violation of *USC* (n 45) § 1201(a)(1)(a).

[60] *Stockwire Research Group Inc v Lebed*, 577 F Supp (2d) 1262 (SD Fla 2008).

[61] *Apple Inc v Psystar Corp*, 673 F Supp (2d) 931 (ND Cal 2009), preliminary judgment pursuant to which Psystar was found to be in contravention of *USC* (n 45) §§ 1201(a)(1), 1201(a)(2), and 1201(b)(1); permanent injunction granted against defendant: *Apple Inc v Psystar Corp*, 673 F Supp (2d) 943 (ND Cal 2009); permanent injunction, summary judgment finding of absence of copyright misuse affirmed on appeal: *Apple Inc v Psystar Corp*, 658 F (3d) 1150 (9th Cir 2011).

[62] *USC* (n 45) § 1201(a)(1)(A); *Directive 2001/29/EC* (n 23) art 6.1; *Canada CA* (n 43) s 41.1(1)(a); *Austl CA* (n 43) s 116AN. See, however, *Chamberlain Group, Inc v Skylink Techs, Inc*, 381 F (3d) 1178 (Fed Cir 2004) [*Chamberlain*] establishing a test linking the application of the TPM provisions to copyright infringement; see also *Storage Technology Corp v Custom Hardware Engineering and Consulting Inc*, 431 F (3d) 1374 (Fed Cir 2005); see however *MDY Industries v Blizzard Entertainment and Vivendi Games et al* (n 54) not linking TPM provisions to copyright infringement as was done in *Chamberlain*.

[63] *USC* (n 45) § 1201(a)(1)(A); *Directive 2001/29/EC* (n 23) art 6.1; *Canada CA* (n 43) s 41.1(1)(a); *Austl CA* (n 43) s 116AN.

[64] Craig (n 3) at 192. On a review of the effects of TPMs blocking lawful uses of copyright works, including research, fair use, see Electronic Frontier Foundation, 'Unintended Consequences: Fifteen Years Under the DMCA' (March 2013), online: <https://www.eff.org/document/unintended-consequences-fifteen-years-under-dmca>.

[65] Craig (n 3) at 192.

regimes is that exceptions to copyright infringement are no defence against alleged violations of the TPM prohibitions.[66] TPMs created a parallel universe with their own rules and exceptions, adding another layer of protection or 'para-copyright' to copyright holders' exclusive rights.[67]

In the EU, the statement that in stronger TPM regimes there is typically no link between the copyright infringement and the anti-circumvention provisions may need to be tempered in light of recent jurisprudential developments. In *Nintendo Co Ltd v PC Box SRL* [*Nintendo*],[68] the EU Court of Justice interpreted the legal protection offered by *Directive 2001/29/EC*[69] as applying 'only in the light of protecting that right holder against acts which require his authorisation.'[70] While *Nintendo* makes clear that the role of technological measures must be to prevent and block copyright infringement in order for them to be protected by law (therefore making a link between copyright infringement and the legal protection of technological measures), it is uncertain whether *Nintendo* could be interpreted as allowing users to circumvent a technological measure by self-help methods for the purpose of an act for which the users would not normally require authorization from the copyright holder.[71] The Court stated that 'legal protection is granted only with regard to technological measures *which pursue the objective of preventing or eliminating*, as regards works, acts not authorised by the right holder of copyright,'[72] adding a proportionality requirement that the measures 'must not go beyond what is necessary for this purpose.'[73] It is one thing to say that the technological measure must be linked to preventing or eliminating non-authorized acts to receive legal protection. It is quite another to say that a technological measure that fully achieves that goal can be circumvented as self-help for the purpose of an act that does not require the authorization of the right holder. *Nintendo* needs to be interpreted in the context of the EU legal framework of TPMs as set out in *Directive 2001/29/EC*.[74] Unlike other jurisdictions including the US and Canada, *Directive 2001/29/EC* prohibits the circumvention of copy controls, and not only the circumvention of access controls.

Countries granting a lower level of protection to technological measures (e.g., Japan, New Zealand, and Switzerland) typically link the liability for circumvention to an infringement of copyright.[75] In doing so, jurisdictions linking liability

[66] See *Universal City Studios, Inc v Corley* (n 56); *Universal City Studios, Inc v Reimerdes*, 111 F Supp (2d) 294 (SDNY 2000); *Apple Inc v Psystar Corporation*, 673 F Supp (2d) 931 (ND Cal 2009), on appeal: *Apple Inc v Psystar Corporation* 658 F (3d) 1150 (9th Cir 2011); *Realnetworks, Inc v DVD Copy Control Association*, 641 F Supp (2d) 913 (ND Cal 2009). Users are, however, allowed to perform acts covered by exceptions to copyright infringement because the circumvention prohibitions do not ban the circumvention of 'copy controls': *USC* (n 45) § 1201(a)(1)(A); *Canada CA* (n 43) s 41.1(1)(a); see discussion below in this section.

[67] Glynn S Lunney, Jr, 'The Death of Copyright: Digital Technology, Private Copying and the Digital Millennium Copyright Act' (2001) 87 Va L Rev 813 at 839–40; see Efroni (n 30) at 348–67.

[68] *Nintendo* (n 50). [69] *Directive 2001/29/EC* (n 23) art 6.

[70] *Nintendo* (n 50) at para 25. [71] ibid. See also para 31. [72] ibid at para 31.

[73] ibid. [74] *Directive 2001/29/EC* (n 23).

[75] See 'WIPO Study on Copyright Limitations and Exceptions' (n 44); see Geist, 'The Case for Flexibility' (n 3).

for circumvention to an infringement of copyright seek to offer greater protection for digital copyright works while promoting access to and lawful uses of copyright works.

The missing link in strong TPM regimes, that is, between circumvention and an infringement of copyright to trigger the application of the anti-circumvention provisions, combined with anti-trafficking provisions, shifted the paradigm in copyright law. Access controls and use controls are now merged under the helm of copyright holders, and included in copyright holder's ability to control and constrain the exercise of basic user property rights to the work and exceptions to copyright infringement.[76]

For supporters of strong TPM regimes, copyright has come of age with the aid of new technologies optimizing the protection of works.[77] Strong TPM regimes are the confirmation that copyright holders have the right to control access to their copyright works.[78] The proper balance lies in providing a sufficient level of protection that will promote the future creation of digital copyright works to be disseminated for the benefit of users and the public.[79]

Critics of strong TPM regimes argue that copyright underwent an important transformation from what it had been since the Statute of Anne: a limited exclusive right qualified by strong public interest underpinnings limiting the monopoly consequences of overly broad protection.[80] For some commentators, TPMs brought on 'The Death of Copyright',[81] or were a 'A Riff on Fair Use'.[82] Access controls were never part of the exclusive rights of copyright holders.[83] Critics raise concerns about the effect of the legal protection of technological measures on access to copies of copyright works (which may include materials that are in the public domain),[84] as well as the power the protection gives copyright holders to control uses of copyright works (amount of reading, viewing, and listening) that are traditionally outside the scope of copyright holders' exclusive rights.[85]

[76] On the progressive transformation of copyright toward an access right, see generally Efroni (n 30).

[77] Jane C Ginsburg, 'From Having Copies to Experiencing Works: The Development of an Access Right in U.S. Copyright Law' (2003) 50 J Copyright Society USA 113 [Ginsburg, 'From Having Copies to Experiencing Works'].

[78] Jane C Ginsburg, 'Can Copyright become User-Friendly? Review: Jessica Litman, Digital Copyright' (2001) 25 Colum JL & Arts 71 at 75–76; Ginsburg, 'From Having Copies to Experiencing Works' (n 77) at 123. Ginsburg acknowledges troubling aspects of the implementation of the *WIPO Internet treaties* in the US through the *DMCA*: Jane Ginsburg, 'Copyright Legislation for the Digital Millennium' (1999) 23 Colum JL & Arts 137 at 152–53.

[79] For a copyright-holder-centric account of the goals of the *DMCA* (n 35) as primarily implemented to protect copyright holders against online piracy, see *US v Reichert* (n 53) at 448.

[80] Lunney (n 67) at 818. [81] ibid at 818–19. [82] Nimmer (n 14).

[83] David Vaver, *Intellectual Property Law Copyright, Patents, Trademarks*, 2nd ed (Toronto: Irwin Law, 2011) at 199 [Vaver, *Intellectual Property Law*]; Craig (n 3) at 197; Séverine Dusollier, *Droit d'auteur et protection des oeuvres dans l'univers numérique*, 2nd ed (Brussels: Larcier, 2007) at 384–85, 394–95.

[84] Craig (n 3) in particular at 195.

[85] Jessica Litman, 'Lawful Personal Use' (2007) 85 Tex L Rev 1871 at 1872; Niva Elkin-Koren, 'Making Room for Consumers Under the DMCA' (2007) 22 BTLJ 1119 at 1143–44.

In Canada, where the Supreme Court held in 2004 in *CCH Canadian Ltd v Law Society of Upper Canada*[86] that exceptions to copyright infringement are user rights,[87] the introduction thereafter of a strong TPM regime has cast doubt on the exact nature and scope of user rights in a digital environment.[88] As discussed in Chapter 2, TPMs weaken arguments that exceptions to copyright infringement are rights and that they are mandatory. [89] This weakening effect arguably extends beyond rights to digital works into other types of works.[90] The cloud of uncertainty over the nature of exceptions to copyright infringement brought on by strong TPM regimes has rippling effects outside copyright law: it weakens even further the chance that users may build successful claims in contracts or consumer protection law against copyright holders who constrain their uses of copyright works.[91]

In the landmark US judgment *Chamberlain Group, Inc v Skylink Techs* [*Chamberlain*],[92] the Court of Appeals, Federal Circuit, bridged the act of circumvention or trafficking to copyright infringement by the requirement of a 'reasonable relationship' between the two:

> A copyright owner seeking to impose liability on an accused circumventor must demonstrate a reasonable relationship between the circumvention at issue and a use relating to a property right for which the Copyright Act permits the copyright owner to withhold authorization—as well as notice that authorization was withheld. A copyright owner seeking to impose liability on an accused trafficker must demonstrate that the trafficker's device enables either copyright infringement or a prohibited circumvention.[93]

The Court in *Chamberlain* arrived at these conclusions by contrasting the nature of TPM provisions, that is a liability regime, to copyright, that is creating property rights,[94] making the scope of application of TPMs necessarily dependent on the transgression of the property rights of copyright holders.[95] The judicial interpretation in *Chamberlain* of the US *Copyright Act*, which led to a 'reasonable relationship' requirement between the circumvention and copyright infringement, and enablement of copyright infringement or prohibited circumvention for attracting liability under the trafficking prohibitions, has not been consistently applied in subsequent judgments.[96] A more literal interpretation of TPMs supports the creation of a para-copyright regime of protection strongly denounced in *Chamberlain*.[97]

86 2004 SCC 13.

87 See Chapter 2.

88 See Chapter 2: 'User rights or privileges?'

89 ibid. Pascale Chapdelaine, 'The Ambiguous Nature of Copyright Users' Rights' (2013) 26 IPJ 1 at 37–43; see Chapter 2: 'May exceptions to copyright infringement be waived by contract?'

90 Pascale Chapdelaine, 'The Ambiguous Nature of Copyright Users' Rights' (2013) 26 IPJ 1 at 37–43; see Chapter 2: 'May exceptions to copyright infringement be waived by contract?'

91 See Chapter 3.

92 *Chamberlain* (n 62).

93 ibid at 1204.

94 ibid at 1192.

95 ibid at 1204.

96 See *MDY Industries v Blizzard Entertainment and Vivendi Games et al* (n 54).

97 *Chamberlain* (n 62) at 1999–2001.

## Prohibition against circumvention of access controls and not copy controls

For some courts and commentators, and as evidenced in preparatory works leading to the enactment of TPM provisions under the US *DMCA*, the prohibition against the circumvention of access controls and not copy controls (unlike the anti-trafficking provisions which apply to access controls and copy controls) reflects a balance between the competing interests of copyright holders on the one hand, and those of copyright users and the public domain on the other.[98] The premise behind punishing circumvention of access controls but not copy controls is that copyright holders should legitimately control the lawful access to their works. Once this lawful access is granted, users should be able to make any lawful use of the copyright work, including uses that do not require the consent of copyright holders (such as fair use, fair dealing, or non-commercial user-generated content). Users should not be liable for infringement if they circumvent copy controls to achieve that goal.

At first sight, the prohibition of the circumvention of access controls, but not copy controls, seems to strike a balance between the interests of copyright holders and those of copyright users by allowing users to circumvent copy controls for lawful uses of the copyright work.[99] While copyright law may not have granted access controls to copyright holders in the past, the law did not allow users to access copies unlawfully either. Unlawful access to copies was addressed in another legal sphere: the theft of a chattel (e.g., copy of a book, music CD), bypassing library loan privileges, etc. Following that line of reasoning, the prohibition of circumvention of access controls was justified given the perceived lack of adequate legal protection against such acts: circumventions can take place without any taking or stealing, hence the lack of an actionable wrong.[100]

The appeal of the balance that TPMs seek to strike between diverging interests by distinguishing circumvention of access controls from that of copy controls for the purpose of infringement may be short lived.[101] In those jurisdictions prohibiting the circumvention of access controls, but not copy controls, while there is no infringement for circumventing copy controls for lawful uses, the onus is entirely placed on the users' ability to circumvent the technological measures with no counterpart obligation on the part of copyright holders to facilitate such uses. Makers of circumventing devices, distributors, service providers, and others are

[98] US, House Judiciary Committee (n 36) 'fair use in the digital environment'; *Universal City Studios, Inc v Reimerdes* (n 66); *United States of America v Elcom Ltd*, 203 F Supp (2d) 1111 at 1138–1141 (ND Cal 2002).

[99] See e.g., *Canada CA* (n 43) s 41.1(1).

[100] Vaver, *Intellectual Property Law* (n 83) at 197–98; Jeremy F de Beer, 'Locks & Levies' (2006) 84 Denv UL Rev 143 at 152–55.

[101] Efroni (n 30) at 355–56, discussing how the distinction between access controls and copy-control technological measures is murky and how it might collapse.

also liable for infringement,[102] which diminishes even further consumers' and other users' ability to circumvent copy controls, in spite of the lawfulness of their intended uses.

While advocates of TPMs will argue that this is the only effective means to counterbalance the scourge of digital piracy, a legal framework that allows the combination of unfettered powers of access controls with exclusive copyright, and that does not place the onus on copyright holders to allow lawful uses of their works by 'lifting' copy controls, tilts the balance toward copyright holders even further and imposes the burden of countering piracy on lawful copyright users, by constraining their uses of copyright works. Courts have acknowledged that a strong TPM regime effectively favours copyright holders to the detriment of users and the public domain.[103]

Even lower levels of protection of technological measures linking liability for circumvention to copyright infringement do not on their own adequately balance the interests of copyright holders with the legitimate interests of users. The onus remains on users to find adequate circumvention tools to make lawful uses of protected copyright works. Something more is required than linking liability for circumvention to copyright infringement, if one is to take digital copyright user rights seriously.

## Setting requirements for technological protection measures

The biggest flaw with strong TPM regimes is that they give almost carte blanche as to how copyright holders may protect their copyright works. Without carefully mapping TPMs with the purpose, function, scope of copyright, its limitations and exceptions, technological measures protected by such strong TPM regimes effectively allow copyright holders to 'write their own intellectual property statute in computer code.'[104] How courts have enforced stronger regimes of TPMs in conjunction with contract terms, allowing the latter to effectively waive fair use or other exceptions to copyright infringement,[105] confirms that view. In jurisdictions with stronger TPM regimes, there is little hope that judicial interpretation alone could properly balance competing interests.[106] A natural inclination of courts seems to be to view TPMs as embedding the required balance between competing interests, even in jurisdictions with stronger TPM regimes.[107]

[102] See e.g., *USC* (n 45) §§ 1201(a)(2), 1201(b)(1); *Directive 2001/29/EC* (n 23) arts 6(2)–(3), 8(2); *Canada CA* (n 43) s 41.1(1)(b)–(c); *Austl CA* (n 43) ss 116(AO), 116(AP).

[103] See e.g., *Realnetworks, Inc v DVD Copy Control Association* 641 F Supp 2d 913 (USDC ND Cal., 2009) 943–44.

[104] Dan L Burk & Julie E Cohen, 'Fair Use Infrastructure for Rights Management Systems' (2001) 15 Harv JL & Tech 41 at 51. See also: Giuseppe Mazziotti (n 34) at 227.

[105] See e.g., *Davidson & Associates Inc, et al v Internet Gateway*, 334 F Supp (2d) 1164 at 1180–81 (ED Mo 2004); *Eyepartner Inc v Kor Media Group LLC et al*, 2013 US Lexis 98370 at 10–11 (SD Fla).

[106] See discussion above on *Chamberlain* (n 62) and how the court's interpretation of the *DMCA* (n 35) as linking the prohibition of circumvention to infringement has not been consistently followed.

[107] See e.g., *Universal City Studios, Inc v Reimerdes* (n 66); *US v Elcom* (n 98). See, however, *Chamberlain* (n 62).

There is generally no requirement that to receive legal protection, technological measures need to embed a mechanism that facilitates the exercise of fair dealing, fair use, or other exceptions to copyright infringement. Without such a requirement, the view that TPMs properly balance the competing interests of right holders, users, and the public domain is not convincing at best. Imposing requirements on technological measures that accord with the main objectives of copyright law (including exceptions to copyright infringement) ties in to the broader discussion on the extent to which contracts may or should alter the exercise of exceptions to copyright infringement.[108] As part of that discussion, arguing that the benefit of exceptions to copyright infringement may not be compromised through private ordering is generally based on the idea that (some) exceptions fulfil an important public interest function.[109]

By setting requirements on the design of technological measures to allow the exercise of user rights or exceptions to copyright infringement, the law would aim to recalibrate the effects of TPMs toward a greater recognition of the public and user interests embedded within copyright law.[110] As required by *Directive 2001/29/EC*,[111] European jurisdictions, including France and Belgium, impose a requirement on right holders protecting their works with TPMs to take adequate measures to allow users to benefit from certain exceptions to copyright infringement.[112] Daniel Burk and Julie Cohen proposed a 'mixed fair use infrastructure' that could help achieve that goal.[113] The law could require that the architecture of technological measures embed a minimum automatic level of fair use or fair dealing of copyright works, based on customary norms and practice.[114] For instance, a music provider could allow a limited number of copies of a musical recording for non-commercial use. The US *Copyright Act* already imposes similar requirements on the structure of some technological measures.[115] For uses beyond a pre-set allowance of exercises of fair use, a trusted third-party intermediary would be put in place to manage access keys.[116] Copyright holders failing to make the necessary key deposits would not benefit from the legal protection of their technological measures, thereby effectively giving way to a 'right to hack' as a substitute for access through

[108] See Chapter 2: 'User rights or privileges?' and 'May exceptions to copyright infringement be waived by contract?'

[109] ibid. See also Chapter 8: 'Adjusting the balance.'

[110] Burk & Cohen (n 104) discussing various legal and technological designs that can be put in place; Stephan Bechtold, 'The Present and Future of Digital Rights Management' in E Becker et al, eds, *Digital Rights Management* (Berlin: Springer-Verlag, 2003) at 597–654, discussing the flexibility of digital rights management including technological measures; Mazziotti (n 34) at 215ff, on how such requirements are feasible in light of ongoing digital rights management technology developments.

[111] *Directive 2001/29/EC* (n 23) art 6.4.

[112] Art L 331-7 CPI (France). See also *Wetboek van Economische Recht/Code de Droit Economique (Belgium)*, art X 291 § 2. See Chapter 3: 'User claims and remedies in copyright law.'

[113] Burk & Cohen (n 104) at 65ff.

[114] ibid at 65.

[115] ibid at 58, citing the *Audio Home Recording Act*, 17 USC § 1002 (2001) regarding digital audio tape recordings and allowing the production of only one generation of perfect copies, and 17 USC § 1201(k)(2) (2001), imposing certain requirement on copy-control technologies for videocassette recorders to allow time-shifting of broadcasts and cable television programming.

[116] ibid at 65–67.

the escrowed access keys.[117] Prohibitions on the manufacture and distribution of circumvention technologies would need to be adapted accordingly.[118]

Proposals to introduce an exception of fair circumvention of technological measures are another way to rectify the imbalance TPMs brought in favour of right holders.[119] A requirement that technological measures facilitate the exercise of exceptions to copyright infringement, such as the 'mixed fair use infrastructure' proposed by Burk and Cohen, would incorporate the fair circumvention exception,[120] and would be even more beneficial to copyright users as it would place the onus on copyright holders to facilitate users' fair dealing, fair use, or other exceptions to copyright infringement.

## The constitutionality of technological protection measures

TPMs raise issues of balance of powers outside the confines of copyright law. In some jurisdictions including the US, the constitutionality of TPMs is questioned.[121] The constitutionality of TPMs has three main themes. First, TPMs may exceed the legislative power and jurisdiction of the constitutional clause that vests in the relevant legislative authority (e.g., Parliament, Congress) the power to confer exclusive rights to copyright holders for their works.[122] Based on that line of argument, TPMs are either unconstitutional because (i) they are unrelated to the purpose for which copyright was created[123] or (ii) they spill over powers that the relevant constitution confers to other jurisdictions (e.g., province or state), such as regulating the sphere of traditional property rights, contracts, or consumer protection.[124] In other words, merging the sphere of access control and use control over the physical copy of works with the sphere of control over the intangible intellectual property in the work would transgress the separation of powers conferred by the relevant constitution. Second, TPMs, in particular anti-trafficking provisions, may violate free speech or freedom of expression by limiting the expression embedded in the prohibited software code.[125] Anti-circumvention provisions may also

[117] ibid at 66. See also Mazziotti (n 34) at 220, proposing that TPMs that fail to allow the exercise of exceptions to copyright infringement should not receive legal protection.

[118] Burk & Cohen (n 104) at 66; Mazziotti (n 34) at 220.

[119] Samuelson (n 14) at 543–46; Mazziotti (n 34) at 220–24.

[120] I.e., limiting the protection of technological measures that are user friendly implies that users can circumvent technological measures that do not comply with user-friendly requirements.

[121] On the constitutionality of TPMs in the US, see generally Julie E Cohen, 'Copyright and the Jurisprudence of Self-Help' (1998) 13 BTLJ 1089 at 1140–42. In Canada, see Jeremy G de Beer, 'Constitutional Jurisdiction over Paracopyright Laws' in M Geist, ed, *In the Public Interest: The Future of Canadian Copyright Law* (Toronto: Irwin Law, 2005) 89 [de Beer, 'Constitutional Jurisdiction'].

[122] See e.g., US *Constitution*, Art I, s 8; Canada *Constitution Act, 1867* (UK), 30 & 31 Vict, c 3, s 91, para 23.

[123] See e.g., *US v Elcom* (n 98) at 1137–42, where the court assessed the constitutionality of TPMs by determining whether TPMs are 'not fundamentally inconsistent' with the purpose of copyright. In Canada, the test is whether TPMs fall, 'in pith and substance' within the copyright clause conferring power to Parliament: see de Beer (n 121) at 92–112.

[124] See de Beer (n 121) at 99–100.

[125] See *Universal City Studios, Inc v Corley* (n 56): finding that the TPMs under the US *Copyright Act* were not unconstitutional on the ground that the effect of the prohibition was content neutral on

violate free speech by blocking access to protected and unprotected works and by restricting the exercise of fair use, on the basis that fair use should be conferred constitutional status as a vehicle enabling free speech through the limits it sets on the scope of copyright.[126] Third, TPMs may violate constitutional protections of due process by being too broad or vague.[127] On several occasions in the US, courts have rejected arguments challenging the constitutionality of TPMs.[128]

A closer look at stronger TPM regimes in various countries reveals the weakness of arguments that they allow an adequate balance between various competing interests. TPM regimes have been implemented predominantly with the interests of copyright holders in mind. By now, more than two decades following the signature of *WIPO Internet treaties*, stronger TPM regimes ought to be recalibrated, benefiting from a more refined understanding of the effects of the digital environment on the creation and dissemination of copyright works, as well as the effects of digital locks' infrastructures which espouse rather than disturb copyright law's public interest underpinnings.

## From Immaterial Works to Physical Objects

Initially, the focus of attention leading up to the adoption of the TPM provisions at international and national levels was on copyright works made available online. The TPM provisions in the *WIPO Internet treaties* of 1996 incorporate one of the main objectives of the *digital agenda*, which was to provide adequate legal safeguards to encourage authors and copyright holders to make their works available online.[129] In the US, preparatory works leading to the entry into force of the *DMCA* TPM provisions in 1998 refer mainly if not exclusively to the promotion of electronic commerce and the online distribution of copies of copyright works.[130]

owners' speech and did not burden substantially more speech than necessary to further government's interest. See also Efroni (n 30) at 359.

[126] *Universal City Studios, Inc v Corley* (n 56) at 458–59: the court not having to decide on the constitutionality of TPMs restraining fair use, but nevertheless rejecting the argument that fair use enjoyed constitutional status. See Neil Weinstock Netanel, 'First Amendment Constraints on Copyright After Golan v. Holder' (2013) 60 UCLA L Rev 1082 at 1113–20.

[127] See *US v Elcom* (n 98) at 1122–25, the US district court (ND Cal) rejecting the argument that *USC* (n 45) § 1201(b) was unconstitutional and against the fifth amendment because '[t]he law, as written, allows a person to conform his or her conduct to a comprehensible standard and is thus not unconstitutionally vague.' ibid at 1125.

[128] See *Universal City Studios, Inc v Corley* (n 56); *US v Elcom Ltd* (n 98); *Universal City Studios, Inc v Reimerdes* (n 66); *321 Studios v Metro Goldwyn Mayer Studios, Inc*, 307 F Supp (2d) 1085 (ND Cal 2004).

[129] See above: 'International obligations.'

[130] See Senate Judiciary Committee, S Rep No 105-190 (1998) at 1–2, online: <http://digital-law-online.info/misc/SRep105-190.pdf> accessed 4 February 2017: 'The Digital Millennium Copyright Act of 1998 is designed to facilitate the robust development and world-wide expansion of electronic commerce, communications, research, development, and education in the digital age.' See HR Rep No 105-551 (1998), online: http://www.gpo.gov/fdsys/pkg/CRPT-105hrpt551/html/

While the enactment of TPMs led to intense debate in several jurisdictions,[131] focusing the attention on online immaterial copyright works likely facilitated their adoption. As discussed in previous chapters, the property rights of users in copies of copyright works are more easily overshadowed in the online world by the application of the exclusive rights of copyright holders.[132] At the same time, the minimization of underlying property rights of users and of exceptions to copyright infringement through the adoption of TPMs reflects a phenomenon similar to the difficulty of defining online copies of copyright works as goods[133] or to declaring that copyright exhaustion cannot apply to digital copies.[134] In all of these cases, the threats of the online world, with its pirates and instantaneous worldwide dissemination of works, provided a fertile ground for downplaying the significance of copyright users' rights and broader public policy interests in the equation.[135]

Technological measures are now reaching far beyond the online world of copyright works and are frequently used and applied to physical objects not readily associated with copyright works: game consoles,[136] cellphones,[137] coffee machines, garage door locks,[138] printer toner cartridges,[139] coupons,[140] cars, and farming equipment all form a disparate ensemble of chattels subject to TPMs. Although there might have been early indicators that courts might be more reluctant to enforce TPMs when they relate to digital locks embedded in chattels than when they relate to copyright works distributed online,[141] recent developments show that courts are willing to enforce digital locks in chattels the function of which is not solely to embody a copyright work, as witnessed by cases in the EU and in the US applying TPM provisions to digital locks embedded in game consoles.[142]

CRPT-105hrpt551-pt2.htm accessed 4 February 2017: 'Purpose and summary,' 'Promoting electronic commerce,' and 'Understanding the nexus between electronic commerce and intellectual property.'

131 See above: 'Implementation of technological protection measures at the national level.'

132 See Chapters 1, 4, and 5. 133 See Chapter 4. 134 See Chapter 5.

135 On the rhetoric and metaphors utilized to secure greater copyright protection, see William Patry, *Moral Panic and the Copyright Wars* (New York: Oxford University Press, 2009) at 139–70. See *US v Reichert* (n 53) at 448, interpreting more than 15 years after its adoption the main purpose of the US *DMCA* TPM provisions to be the strengthening of copyright holders' rights against online piracy.

136 Courts have recognized that TPMs protect technological measures in game consoles. See: *Sony Computer Entertainment America, Inc v Divineo, Inc*, 457 F Supp (2d) 957 (ND Cal 2006); *Sony Computer Entertainment America v Hotz*, 2011 WL 347137 (ND Cal); *US v Reichert* (n 53); *Sony Computer Entm't Am, Inc v Gamemasters*, 87 F Supp (2d) 976 at 987 (ND Cal 1999); *Nintendo* (n 50).

137 See *TracFone Wireless, Inc v GSM Group, Inc*, 555 F Supp (2d) 1331 (SD Fla 2008): the court finding no violation of US copyright TPM provisions.

138 *Chamberlain* (n 62) involved a technological measure inserted in an electronic garage door. The Court held that the defendant had not breached the *USC* (n 45) TPM provisions.

139 *Lexmark Int'l, Inc v Static Control Components, Inc*, 387 F (3d) 522 (6th Cir 2003) [*Lexmark*] dealt with microchips in toner cartridges. The Court denied the plaintiff's claims under *USC* (n 45) TPM provisions.

140 *Coupons Inc v Stottlemire*, 588 F Supp (2d) 1069 (ND Cal 2008) where the court held that registry keys downloaded to computers to limit the number of coupons issued to the public were technological measures protected under *USC* (n 45).

141 Elkin-Koren (n 85) at 1132–37, citing *Chamberlain* (n 62) and *Lexmark* (n 139) as examples.

142 See e.g., *US v Reichert* (n 53); *Kabushiki Kaisha Sony Computer Entertainment Inc and Others v Ball and Others* (n 53); *R v Gilham (Christopher Paul)* (n 53); see also *Nintendo* (n 50).

The enforcement of TPM provisions in relation to digital locks embedded in physical objects magnifies the regulatory design deficiencies denounced when TPMs were initially adopted and enacted in various jurisdictions.[143] First, a violation for circumventing access controls (independently of copyright infringement), where the technological measure is ancillary to a physical object, the primary function of which is not to embody a copyright work (e.g., a car or tractor), is strikingly beyond the scope and objectives of copyright protection, even more so than when the digital lock applies solely to a copyright work (e.g., an e-book or a film).[144] Here the user would seek to circumvent a technological measure (protecting a software embedded in the chattel) to perform acts completely unrelated to a copyright work: repair a car, reset safety controls in the garage door, etc. The interaction with the copyright work (i.e., the software to which the digital lock applies) would be ancillary to the main underlying goal behind the circumvention. In that scenario, one might argue that the circumvention would be lawful because the technological measure would fail to be an 'effective technological measure' as required to merit the protection of TPM provisions. To be 'effective' a technological measure must pertain to a protected work and hence a technological measure controlling access beyond the copyright work would not receive protection under the TPM provisions.[145] The counterargument is that the technological measure does protect a copyright work (i.e., the software) and is therefore an 'effective technological measure', making any practical access constraints beyond that irrelevant. The statutory language found in strong TPM regimes would support the far-reaching effects of technological measures beyond protecting the use of copyright works per se, as evidenced by recent case law on game consoles.[146] The disproportionate encroachment of digital locks as enforced through TPMs on the *prima facie* open-ended privileges and powers of personal property owners is even more striking with a chattel where the copyright work it embodies is an ancillary portion of the chattel (e.g., a software chip in a tractor) than with a chattel the essential function of which is to embody the copyright work (e.g., a CD).

Second, arguments that TPMs are unconstitutional based on the legislative authority exceeding conferred powers and jurisdiction[147] may be even stronger when digital locks, protected by TPM provisions, are embedded in chattels such as cars, farming equipment, and other objects not even remotely associated with copyright. In such cases, arguments that TPMs regulate traditional property and civil rights or extend beyond the jurisdiction of copyright protection become even more cogent when the TPM provisions impact the use and enjoyment of chattels

[143] See discussion above: 'Implementation of technological protection measures at the national level.'

[144] ibid.

[145] ibid. See *Lexmark* (n 139) where the Court applied a similar reasoning, holding that a technological measure was not effective and therefore did not mandate protection under the *DMCA* (n 35), because it restrained access to computer code that was not protected under the *USC* (n 45).

[146] See e.g., *US v Reichert* (n 53); *Kabushiki Kaisha Sony Computer Entertainment Inc and Others v Ball and Others* (n 53); *R v Gilham (Christopher Paul)* (n 53); see also *Nintendo* (n 50).

[147] See discussion above: 'The constitutionality of technological protection measures.'

where the main function is not to embody copyright works, for example, tractors, refrigerators, and printer cartridges, than when the TPMs seek to protect the online distribution of musical recordings or e-books.

Third, the use of digital locks with copyright works (software) ancillary to chattels where the main function is not to embody a copyright work may raise anti-competition issues; for example, tied selling and control of the end-to-end distribution chain of related products. Anti-competition issues are even more likely in such situations than with technological measures that apply solely to copies of copyright works. In *Chamberlain*, the US Court of Appeals for the Federal Circuit discussed how a literal interpretation of TPMs would favour anti-competitive behaviour.[148] Arguments that the use of digital locks amount to anti-competitive behaviour or copyright misuse have been made, often unsuccessfully.[149] Given the explicit powers and privileges that TPMs confer on copyright holders, proving that their use leads to anti-competitive practices or copyright misuse is an uphill battle.[150] The argument that the deployment of digital locks amounts to a misuse of rights is difficult to support when TPM regimes endorse the far-reaching effects of digital locks.

Fourth, the lack of notification of digital locks in products and the lack of a clear legal obligation to do so are even more problematic when digital locks protect a copyright work (software) ancillary to a chattel. In other words, the case for the users' right to be notified of the presence of digital locks is even stronger when users are less likely to expect the presence of digital locks in the personal property they own or possess.[151]

Last, the increasingly pervasive intrusion of digital locks in the world of chattels unrelated to copyright works may, in some jurisdictions, encourage review mechanisms that lead to exempting specific works, objects, and uses from the application of TPMs.[152] More than half of the current exemptions to circumvention prohibitions under the US *Copyright Act* concern physical objects that are not commonly associated with copyright works.[153] An ever-growing list of exemptions to the application of TPMs is less than desirable from a regulatory design perspective. It may signal too broad protection of TPMs. A long list of exemptions to TPM prohibitions would make their application increasingly complex and uncertain, adding to the already convoluted regulatory design layers of TPMs. A growing list of exemptions may also provide compelling evidence

[148] See *Chamberlain* (n 62) at 1201.

[149] See e.g., *Apple Inc v Psystar Corp*, 658 F (3d) 1150 (9th Cir 2011); *Davidson & Associates Inc v Internet Gateway Inc*, 334 F Supp (2d) 1164 (ED Mo 2004). See Mazziotti (n 34) at 190–93, discussing anti-competitive claims against Apple's digital rights management (DRM) system and the interaction between TPMs and competition law.

[150] ibid.

[151] See Chapter 3: 'Restricted uses that fall within the exclusive rights of copyright holders and are permitted by law under certain conditions.'

[152] See e.g., *USC* (n 45) § 1201(a)(1)(c). See also *Canada CA* (n 43) s 41.21(2)(a).

[153] *Exemption to Prohibition on Circumvention of Copyright Protection Systems for Access Control Technologies*, 80:208 Fed Reg 65944 (2015).

of the need for legislative reform or may trigger jurisprudential developments that could limit the scope of TPMs, as calls for consultation by the US Copyright Office suggest.[154]

## The Shift from Possessing Copyright Works to Experiencing Them Through Services

Parallel to the increased presence of TPMs in the world of physical objects beyond traditional copyright works (e.g., literary works, musical recordings, films) and their physical embodiments (e.g., books, music CDs, film DVDs), the shift from possessing individualized copies of copyright works to experiencing works through online services is a further manifestation of the prominent role of technological measures in digital copyright works. In an online service environment, technological measures are the backbone that defines the service offering and without which it could not exist.[155] Digital copyright work service offerings, enabled through technological measures and TPMs, further distance users from the copyright work. In a service environment, the remoteness of the user from the copyright work changes their interaction with technological measures. Users of digital copyright services have lower expectations vis-à-vis how they can use the work and, as a consequence, are less likely to view the technological measure as interfering with how they experience the copyright work. In a service environment, the abdication of *prima facie* unlimited powers and privileges of copyright users to copies of copyright works for the benefit and control of copyright holders is now complete, and technological measures, as enforced by TPMs, are responsible for that to a great degree.

Some jurisdictions explicitly regulate technological measures applying to online copyright services differently from other technological measures. In relation to such services, EU *Directive 2001/29/EC* does not require Member States to take adequate legal measures for the regulation of TPMs to allow users to exercise the exceptions to copyright infringement specified in the Directive, as it does with respect to other technological measures that are not applied to online services.[156] The exclusion in EU *Directive 2001/29/EC* is particularly problematic as it fails to distinguish online copyright services from copies of copyright works downloaded

[154] *Section 1201 Study: Notice and Request for Public Comment*, 80:249 Fed Reg 81369 (2015). Areas the study hopes to address include the current permanent exemptions to the application of TPMs under the US *Copyright Act*, i.e., questioning the raison d'être of existing categories and whether other permanent categories of exemption should be established.

[155] See e.g., the technological measures considered in: *Evony v Holland* (n 58); *Stockwire Research Group Inc v Lebed* (n 60).

[156] EU *Directive 2001/29/EC* (n 23) art 6(4) para 4: 'The provisions of the first and second subparagraphs shall not apply to works or other subject-matter made available to the public on agreed contractual terms in such a way that members of the public may access them from a place and at a time individually chosen by them.' See also Efroni (n 30) at 377–78.

online.[157] The indiscriminate and unfettered application of TPMs makes the abnegation of copyright users' rights in the environment of online on-demand services unequivocal.

## A Silver Lining for Copyright Users?

The progressive intrusion and enforcement of digital locks in the world of physical objects will either provide a silver lining to users by triggering favourable legal reform, or will trivialize their rights even further.

While the disregard for copyright user property rights may have started when the application of TPMs focused on the online distribution of copyright works, the increased presence of digital locks and enforcement of TPMs on physical objects make the disproportionality between the protection of the property rights of copyright holders and disregard for the property rights of users even more striking.

The application of TPMs to digital locks embedded in chattels that serve a broader function than to embody the copy of a copyright work (e.g., cars, tractors, printer cartridges) is receiving public attention.[158] As the application of TPMs to such chattels magnifies the defects of stronger regimes of TPM protection identified in the early days of TPMs,[159] the application of TPMs to objects not typically associated with copyright works may be the silver lining for the future of copyright user rights. Such application may create the impetus for legal reform that will impose further limitations on the application of TPMs. Maintaining the status quo would confirm the strength of copyright holders' rights. Paradoxically however, adding more exceptions of the application of TPMs in the world of physical objects not typically associated with copyright works would further reinforce the legitimacy of the application of TPMs to traditional forms of embodiment of digital copyright works (CDs, DVDs, etc.).

[157] EU *Directive 2001/29/EC* (n 23) art 6(4) para 4. See discussion in Chapter 4: 'The trouble with the requirement of a physical object to distinguish goods from services: misconceptions about tangibility and intangibility.'

[158] Kyle Wiens, 'Forget the Cellphone Fight—We Should be Allowed to Unlock Everything We Own,' *Wired.com* (18 March 2013), online: <http://www.wired.com/2013/03/you-dont-own-your-cellphones-or-your-cars/> accessed 4 February 2017; Dayna J Sondervan, 'Can Farmers Hack Tractor Software? Copyright Office Will Decide', *Growing Georgia* (5 May 2015), online: <http://growing-georgia.com/features/2015/05/can-farmers-hack-tractor-software-copyright-office-will-decide/> accessed 4 February 2017.

[159] See above: 'From immaterial works to physical objects.'

# PART III

# RETHINKING USER RIGHTS THROUGH PROPERTY, RIGHTS, AND PRIVILEGES

# 7
# Why User Rights?

## The Contributions of Property and Other Theories

A vast body of literature questions the existence and justifications of intellectual property and copyright, often by resorting to various theories about property.[1] Through this exercise, commentators often analyse the broader effects of copyright on users and on the public domain. The theoretical justifications of copyright user rights, however, are much less explored.[2]

The purpose of this chapter is to open new lines of inquiry to develop a framework to justify user rights. Because justifying copyright often necessitates looking at the broader interests of users, intermediaries, and the public domain, and as user rights are heavily interdependent with copyright subject matter, a natural

[1] See e.g., Edwin C Hettinger, 'Justifying Intellectual Property' (1989) 18 Philosophy & Public Affairs 31, reprinted in David Vaver, ed, *Intellectual Property Rights, Critical Concepts in Law* (London: Routledge, 2006) vol 1 at 97; William W Fisher, 'Theories of Intellectual Property' in Stephen R Munzer, ed, *New Essays in the Legal and Political Theory of Property* (Cambridge: Cambridge University Press, 2001) at 168; Peter Drahos, *A Philosophy of Intellectual Property* (Aldershot: Ashgate, 1996); Wendy J Gordon, 'A Property Right in Self-Expression: Equality and Individualism in the Natural Law of Intellectual Property' (1993) 102 Yale LJ 1533; Sunny Handa, *Copyright Law in Canada* (Markham, ON: Butterworths Canada, 2002) at 59–134; Carys J Craig, 'Locke, Labour and Limiting the Author's Right: A Warning Against a Lockean Approach to Copyright Law' (2002) 28 Queen's LJ 1; Abraham Drassinower, 'A Rights-Based View of the Idea/Expression Dichotomy in Copyright Law' (2003) 16 Can JL & Juris 3; William M Landes & Richard A Posner, *The Economic Structure of Intellectual Property Law* (Cambridge, MA: Belknap Press, 2003); Richard A Posner, 'The Law and Economics of Intellectual Property' (2002) Daedalus 5; Richard Polk Wagner, 'Information Wants to be Free, Intellectual Property and the Mythologies of Control' (2003) 103 Colum L Rev 995; David Lametti, 'Coming to Terms with Copyright' in Michael Geist, ed, *In the Public Interest: The Future of Canadian Copyright Law* (Toronto: Irwin Law, 2005) at 480; Mark A Lemley, 'Property, Intellectual Property and Free Riding' (2005) Tex L Rev 1031; Giuseppina D'Agostino, *Copyright, Contracts, Creators: New Media, New Rules* (Cheltenham: Edward Elgar, 2010) at 201–59.

[2] There are exceptions. See e.g., L Ray Patterson & Stanley W Lindberg, *The Nature of Copyright: a Law of Users Rights* (Athens, GA: University of Georgia Press, 1991); Jeremy Waldron, 'From Authors to Copiers: Individual Rights & Social Values in Intellectual Property' (1993) 69 Chicago-Kent L Rev 841, reprinted in David Vaver, ed, *Intellectual Property Rights, Critical Concepts in Law* (London: Routledge, 2006) vol 1 at 114 [Waldron, 'From Authors to Copiers'], looking at copyright from the perspective of the limitations it imposes on users and copyright infringers; Joseph P Liu, 'Owning Digital Copies: Copyright Law and the Incidents of Copy Ownership' (2001) Wm & Mary L Rev 1245; Joseph P Liu, 'Copyright Law's Theory of the Consumer' (2003) 44 Boston College L Rev 39.

inclination, which I follow here, is to rely to some extent on copyright theory as the starting point from which to develop a theory on copyright user rights.

The task of a unified theory of copyright user rights is more ambitious than it might first appear, given what we have discovered so far on the heteroclite nature of user rights, encompassing personal property rights in copies of works, exceptions to copyright infringement, and from the standpoint that users experience works as goods, *sui generis* products, services, or as a combination thereof. Users' relationship with copyright works does not always occur (and in fact less so) through property in the copy of the copyright work. Thus, while property theory offers a starting point from which to substantiate copyright user rights, for instance, when we look at the normative status of all ownership freedoms,[3] it cannot fully account for the significance and role of users within copyright law. The instrumental theories that we explore here support a broader spectrum of human experiences than the one between a person and a resource, and offer more flexibility to justify a wide range of copyright user rights, from the rights of user-copy-owners to those of service users.[4]

The theoretical approach in relation to users that I take here is more closely related to concepts of private law than public law, that is, to the extent that a divide effectively subsists between the two.[5] This is consistent with the deliberate choice in this book to look at copyright user rights predominantly through property, contracts, and copyright, for reasons I discussed in the Introduction to this book. The choice of looking at user rights from property and copyright theory does not ignore the fact that human rights law (associated with the public law sphere) provides important justifications for specific user rights. A significant body of literature looks at intellectual property and copyright user rights from the perspective of human rights, in particular, how exceptions and limitations to copyright are justified by freedom of expression and freedom of speech.[6] Although this chapter does not discuss the human rights law justifications of copyright user rights, Chapter 8 looks at the practical difficulties of ensuring that copyright and user rights are consistent with human rights and at the most

[3] See below: 'The *prima facie* status of all ownership freedoms.'

[4] See below: 'Instrumental justifications of (intellectual) property.'

[5] See Michel Rosenfeld, 'Rethinking the Boundaries between Public Law and Private Law for the Twenty-First Century: An Introduction' (2013) 11 Intl J Constitutional L 125; Alain Supiot, 'The Public-Private Relation in the Context of Today's Refeudalization' (2013) 11 Intl J Constitutional L 129.

[6] See e.g., Human Rights Council, *Report of the Special Rapporteur in the field of cultural rights, Farida Shaheed—Copyright policy and the right to science and culture*, UNGAOR, 28th Sess, Agenda Item 3, UN Doc A/HRC/28/57 (2014); P Bernt Hugenholtz, 'Copyright and Freedom of Expression in Europe' in RC Dreyfuss, DL Zimmerman, & H First, eds, *Expanding the Boundaries of Intellectual Property: Innovation Policy for the Knowledge Society* (Oxford: Oxford University Press, 2001); Elena Izyumenko, 'The Freedom of Expression Contours of Copyright in the Digital Era: A European Perspective' (2016) 30 J World Intellectual Property 1; Neil Weinstock Netanel, 'First Amendment Constraints on Copyright after *Golan v. Holder*' (2013) 60 UCLA L. Rev. 1082; Julie E Cohen, 'A Right to Read Anonymously: A Closer Look at "Copyright Management" in Cyberspace' (1997) 28 Conn L Rev 981 at 1014ff, making an argument in favour of protecting users' rights to read without intrusion from copyright holders that is based on the US Constitution First Amendment.

efficient manner to ensure compliance with human rights values and law to support user rights.[7]

It is beyond the scope and purpose of this chapter to provide a detailed review of all theoretical justifications of copyright, many of which are grounded in property theory. Among the several justificatory theories for property and copyright that are not discussed here,[8] personhood-constituting theories are among them.[9] Personality-based theories are frequently invoked to justify the creation of private property rights through copyright, based on notions of freedom and autonomy,[10] and, particularly, to justify the exclusive right of the author to authorize the first publication of their work.[11] Once the work is published, personhood arguments to justify copyright exclusive rights are arguably less persuasive.[12] Because this book focuses on copyright user access to copyright works after their first publication, theories justifying copyright once the copyright work is published are more relevant, and hence the lesser interest in theories that serve predominantly to justify authors' rights to their works before publication.

Personhood-constituting theories may be well suited to justifying copyright user rights in specific cases. For instance, personality-based theories may help delineate the rights of tattoo-bearers of artistic works as those rights are in direct competition with the exclusive copyrights of tattoo artists.[13] The (re)production of tattoos, as forms of artistic works on human bodies, the intimate rapport that tattoo-user-bearers may have with the tattoos they wear, and how it may tie to their identity, and the personality-based expressive elements that tattoos may exhibit are considerations that may call for different theoretical justifications of user rights than in other scenarios, requiring as a consequence to adjust the scope of copyright.[14]

Starting with the normative status of *prima facie* open-ended freedoms reflected in the concept of ownership and the ramifications of these freedoms that justify the scope of ownership in commercial copies of copyright works, this chapter then

[7] See Chapter 8: 'Cohesion between copyright law, private law, and public law.'

[8] These property theories include the 'first occupancy theory' and sovereignty theories.

[9] See e.g., Margaret Jane Radin, 'Property and Personhood' (1982) 34 Stan LR 957.

[10] For a survey of theoretical justifications of intellectual property, in particular personality-based theories, see Fisher (n 1) at 171–72, 174 and 189–92. Personality-based theories also come to mind, to justify moral rights to copyright works, given the inalienability of moral rights and the intimate relationship between the author and their work that moral rights seek to protect. Utilitarian theories may also justify moral rights: see Handa (n 1) at 128–30.

[11] There are distinct theoretical justifications to support the right of an author (not) to authorize the first publication of a work, which are not explored here. See e.g., Handa (n 1) at 125–26, suggesting copyright be approached in two phases to apply coherent theoretical justifications. The first right to publish would be justified on the basis of privacy, while the exploitation right after publication has occurred would be justified on the basis of a social utility model.

[12] See e.g., Waldron, 'From Authors to Copiers' (n 2) at 137, with the author concluding that it is a mistake to generalize beyond the first right to publish that a copier's actions compromise the liberty of the author whose work they are using. For a contrary view, see Abraham Drassinower, *What's Wrong with Copying?* (Cambridge, MA: Harvard University Press, 2015) at 14, 115–20 [Drassinower, *What's Wrong with Copying?*].

[13] See Yolanda M King, 'The Enforcement Challenges for Tattoo Copyrights' (2014) 22 J Intell Prop L 29, discussing cases opposing the rights of the tattoo owners and of the tattoo artists.

[14] ibid.

looks at how other prevailing underlying theories of property and copyright may justify, or better inform, user rights. Among them, I focus more particularly on instrumental theories as they relate to copyright, commercial copies of copyright works, and user rights more generally. Instrumental theories are the most influential justifications for the existence of private property in general, and copyright in particular.[15] This chapter also looks at the fruits of one's labour theory—another influential natural law theoretical justification of property and of copyright—and how it might affect our conceptions of ownership in commercial copies of copyright works and, more generally, user rights.

## The *Prima Facie* Normative Status of All Ownership Freedoms

Our inquiry into the theoretical justifications of copyright user rights begins with James W Harris's theory, in *Property and Justice*,[16] on the normative status of all ownership freedoms. Theories about ownership help us understand and support the instances where users have rights in commercial copies of copyright work and the scope thereof.[17] Other theoretical justifications examined below justify copyright user rights more generally, independently of ownership in the copy of a copyright work.[18]

Central to James Harris's theory of property is the notion that property is the incarnation of freedom and autonomous choice. This idea is further reflected by the ubiquitous manifestation in society of a wide spectrum of ownership interests. Ownership is an 'organizing idea' in which all of these interests share, to various degrees, open-ended privileges, powers, and self-seekingness.[19] To invoke freedom as a moral justification for maintaining a property institution, one needs to ask 'whether inherent property freedoms are a necessary feature of the just society.'[20] The proposition is that, quite apart from instrumental reasons, 'property institutions by their very nature confer freedoms (ranges for autonomous choice) which would not exist without them; and for this reason no citizen is treated justly by his community unless it institutes or maintains a property institution.'[21] Hence, open-ended uses and privileges nurture freedoms that contribute to autonomous choice and *prima facie* justify property institutions.[22] Harris arrives at this conclusion as he finds no convincing argument that

[15] See below: 'Instrumental justifications of (intellectual) property.' [16] Harris (n 22).

[17] I.e., to understand the copyright user rights that pertain to their personal property in copies of copyright works: see Chapter 1.

[18] See below: 'Instrumental justifications of (intellectual) property.'

[19] Harris (n 22) at 63ff. [20] ibid at 231.

[21] ibid at 230. James O Grunebaum, *Private Ownership* (London: Routledge & Kegan Paul, 1987) at 183, bases the moral justification of ownership on autonomy and develops a theory of 'autonomous ownership'. Within that framework, Grunebaum acknowledges how use controls of consumer goods violate autonomy: 'Community control over consumer goods, either in the form of what goods are produced or control in the form of what uses consumer products may be put to, would violate autonomy.'

[22] James W Harris, *Property and Justice* (Oxford: Clarendon Press, 1996) at 231.

any of the powers and privileges on the ownership spectrum should be *a priori* excluded from the concept of ownership: 'the spectrum has evolved in human history and is available within property institutions as a means of conferring ranges of autonomous choice on individuals or groups.'[23] *A contrario*, if there were no property-specific justice reasons to support those freedoms, 'countless day-to-day unquestioned assumptions about people being free to do what they like with their own things and their own money would turn out to be morally suspect.'[24] Autonomy is a value frequently invoked to justify property and, more particularly, personal property.[25]

Based on the premise that there is no natural right to full-blooded ownership, none of these freedoms is sacrosanct, and they all may be overridden by justifiable property-limitation and expropriation rules, which are also widely observed and accepted in modern societies.[26] Although Harris's theory of a right to property based on freedoms—which is derived from Hegel's theory of property[27]—unequivocally rejects a natural right to full-blooded ownership, it may rejoin what Jeremy Waldron would call a 'general right-based argument' to property (as opposed to a 'special right-based argument').[28]

The *prima facie* normative status of ownership freedoms is central to the justification of copyright user rights in at least two respects. First, it is central to understanding the dynamics behind the prevailing commercial practice of copyright holders to license rather than transfer ownership in copies of copyright works (blocking subsequent users' power to transfer title to the copy).[29] Second, where users own the copy of a copyright work, the *prima facie* normative status of ownership freedoms provides a baseline to analyse what the proper scope of copy ownership freedoms should be.

[23] ibid at 275. [24] ibid at 65. See also Grunebaum (n 21).

[25] E.g., see Grunebaum (n 21) at 183: 'The idea that autonomy requires a wide range of rights of title over consumer goods implies that so-called consumer sovereignty is a moral as well as the economic requirement to maintain the value of income and to achieve or measure efficiency. That consumers legitimately exercise a wide range of rights of title over goods for personal consumption applies not only to what they actually purchase but to what is available for their purchase. Not only should individuals be able to exercise a broad range of rights of title over their living quarters, for example, but they should also have a wide range of options about the kinds of living quarters made available.'

[26] Harris (n 22) at 275.

[27] ibid at 230ff. Harris develops his property justification based on freedom mainly from the analysis of Hegel's theory.

[28] Jeremy Waldron, *The Right to Private Property* (Oxford: Clarendon Press, 1988) at 116 [Waldron, *Private Property*], defines the two concepts as follows: 'A special-right-based argument ... is an argument which takes an interest to have this importance not in itself but on account of the occurrence of some contingent event or transaction. A general-right-based argument ... is one which does not take the importance of such an interest to depend on the occurrence of some contingent event or transaction, but attributes that importance to the interest itself, in virtue of its qualitative character.' Waldron's theory, based on Hegel, supports a general right-based argument for property. As an example of a special right-based argument he uses John Locke's natural right theory of property that is based on labour-desert type of arguments. See also David Lametti, 'Concept of Property: Relations through Objects of Social Wealth' (2003) 53 UTLJ 325 at 356ff, who discusses Harris's 'right-based' theory.

[29] See Chapter 5: 'The commercial practice not to sell copies.'

In relation to copyright holders' commercial practice to license and not sell copies of copyright works, as enforced by courts,[30] leaving users with indefinite rights (short of ownership) in the copy,[31] the questions to ask are: how can the property institution of copyright serve as a justification to *a priori* exclude the powers and privileges that relate to the ownership in commercial copies of copyright works? Is it just to allow a shift to take place from day-to-day unquestioned freedoms (albeit limited) of users as copy owners of a copyright work to suspicion, monitoring, and control by copyright holders of the fate of their copyright works? Given the ubiquity and centrality of ownership as a vehicle for infinite and repetitive minuscule exercises of freedom in all spheres of consumption and modern life, allowing such a shift to take place through copyright holders' changes of business practices requires closer examination.

Copyright holders justify their increased control over commercial copies, particularly by restricting users' rights to assign and transfer commercial copies that they lawfully acquired, based on the need to combat piracy, which is a matter of legitimate concern. However, how much burden can copyright holders reasonably ask users to bear and how far can they impede users' legitimate freedom on that basis? Commentators invoke autonomy as one of the aspirations of users of copyright works, for example, 'freedom in choosing when, how, and under what circumstances to consume a copyright work,'[32] and in that context 'the sale of a copy represents a fixed bundle of entitlements giving the purchaser the ability to exercise a good deal of autonomy in consumption.'[33] For its part, the institution of intellectual property, as created by various statutes, is not self-justifying.[34] As Jeremy Waldron puts it: 'whether or not we speak of a burden of proof, an institution like intellectual property is not self-justifying; we owe a justification to anyone who finds that he can move less freely than he would in the absence of the institution.'[35] Given the lack of recognition of the personal property rights of user-copy-owners in copyright law,[36] and the general legal uncertainty that results therefrom, copyright holders are able to create material changes about the ownership of commercial copies of copyright works and to effectively broaden the scope of their exclusive rights.[37]

In those instances where ownership in the copy of the copyright work subsists, what is the normative force of these increasingly open-ended capabilities of users as new technologies empower them more than ever before in how they access and experience copyright works? The *prima facie* normative status of ownership freedoms brings a substantive argument to support and understand ownership in commercial copies of copyright works, both for its scope and its subsistence, and

[30] ibid.

[31] ibid. See also Chapter 1: 'If not owned by the copyright user, nor a good, then what?'

[32] Liu, 'Copyright Law's Theory of the Consumer' (n 2) at 406. More generally, on the fact that autonomy requires a wide range of rights of title over consumer goods, see Grunebaum (n 21) at 183.

[33] Liu, 'Copyright Law's Theory of the Consumer' (n 2) at 408.

[34] Waldron, 'From Authors to Copiers' (n 2) at 146.

[35] ibid.

[36] See Chapter 1.

[37] See Chapter 5: 'The commercial practice not to sell copies.'

to situate copy ownership vis-à-vis the private property regime that is created by copyright.[38] Various forms of property including personal property predate the existence of copyright and, therefore, it is one of the underlying assumptions upon which copyright laws were created.[39]

The *prima facie* normative status of ownership freedoms justifies and helps substantiate users' claims to *prima facie* open-ended privileges and powers to commercial copies of copyright works. The *prima facie* open-ended privileges and powers evolve in the environment in which the commercial copies are being supplied. The technological environment in which commercial copies can be experienced changes users' expectations of their open-ended powers and privileges to commercial copies of copyright works and should be taken into account. The *prima facie* normative status of ownership freedoms can also provide a framework to respond to and constrain copyright holders' substantial transformation of copy ownership through copyright holders' commercial practice of restraining users' rights to assign and transfer the commercial copies they lawfully acquire.

## The Right to Privacy

The right to privacy is somewhat connected to the normative value of ownership freedom as a justification informing the scope of powers and privileges deriving from ownership of copies of copyright works.[40] Privacy is also relevant in the broader debate about copyright holders' possible controls over uses of copyright works and about user rights beyond copy ownership. In relation to the reasons that justify private property, Waldron arrives at a similar conclusion, as does Harris, about the *prima facie* normative force of all ownership freedoms, but does so by emphasizing the need to preserve privacy.[41] For Waldron, if every resource was publicly controlled, every use of that resource by an individual would be an 'other-regarding' action; we would be accountable to all and this would be untenable.[42] This makes him conclude that: 'there must be a realm of private freedom somewhere for each individual—an area where he can make decisions about what to do and how to do it, justifying these decisions if at all only to himself.'[43] As to Harris's theory of the *prima facie* normative force of all ownership freedom, the

[38] Liu, 'Owning Digital Copies' (n 2) at 1301, reflects on the place of the incidents of copy ownership within the copyright regime as follows: 'Copyright law, then, does not so much expressly build in such incidents of copy ownership, as it accepts and assumes such incidents as given. That is, under this view, understandings about physical copy ownership antedate the relatively more recent development of copyright law.' On a related idea—the interaction between intellectual property and tangible property—see Jeremy de Beer & Robert Tomkowicz, 'Exhaustion of Intellectual Property Rights in Canada' (2009) 25 CIPR 3 at 20–24.

[39] Liu, 'Owning Digital Copies' (n 2) at 1301.

[40] See above: 'The *prima facie* normative status of all ownership freedoms.'

[41] Waldron, *Private Property* (n 28) at 295 and at 343ff, where the author develops a general right to property derived from Hegel's theory of freedom and property.

[42] ibid at 295. [43] ibid.

right of privacy derives from values of autonomy and freedom. Privacy is a specific expectation, in certain circumstances, of a secure space where these values can optimally flourish. Yet, for Harris, privacy plays a role distinct from freedom when it comes to justifying private property. For Harris, privacy can be the 'shell' of a natural right to private property[44] in very limited circumstances, when the intimate relationship that arises between a person and a thing is such that a just treatment would entail recognition of an ownership right in the resource.[45] An example of such natural right to property based on privacy would be the exclusive rights of an author to their work before it is published, including the right to authorize the first publication of their work or to keep it private, which stems from the sphere that we ought to preserve around an author and their work before it is (if ever) made available to the public.[46]

Privacy considerations (just like freedom and autonomous choice) have applications that go above and beyond justifying the existence of private property rights in a resource (here the copy of a copyright work). It is one thing to say that, on the basis on privacy, the state will not enter the home of users or install cameras in public spaces to monitor their uses of copyright works. For instance, privacy has been invoked as one of the possible justifications for the private copy exception to copyright infringement in several European jurisdictions.[47] Those privacy considerations are something separate from privacy seen as the constitutive and justificatory theory of the nature of the scope of exclusive rights and powers that users have in commercial copies of copyright works that they own. Although privacy is relevant to users as it preserves their right to non-intrusion in a general context, it does not necessarily support the scope of their ownership rights in commercial copies of copyright works, although it is not implausible that it might do so.[48] If this were to be the case, users ought to be granted privileges and powers in relation to commercial copies of copyright works through

[44] By 'shell', Harris means that the extent of the natural right cannot be determined until 'the problematic balance between the requirement of a range of specially protected autonomous choice and necessary intervention by the community to prevent abuse' has been exercised: Harris (n 22) at 227–28.

[45] ibid at 224.

[46] ibid at 225; *Millar v Taylor* (1769), 4 Burr 2303 at 2379; Samuel D Warren & Louis D Brandeis, 'The Right to Privacy' (1890) 4 Harv LR 193 at 199–201, where the authors argue that the nature of the claim in that case is the enforcement of the right of privacy or 'the right to be let alone' (not a property right) with exclusive reproduction rights (a property right). See also Handa (n 1) at 125–26. For a critique that an author's exclusive right to authorize first publication is based on the right to privacy, see Drassinower, *What's Wrong with Copying?* (n 12) 14, 115–20.

[47] See Natali Helberger & P Bernt Hugenholtz, 'No Place Like Home for Making a Copy, Private Copying in European Copyright Law and Consumer Law' (2007) 22 BTLJ 1061 at 1068–72; Christophe Geiger, 'The Answer to the Machine Should Not be the Machine: Safeguarding the Private Copy Exception in the Digital Environment' (2009) 30 Eur IP Rev 121 at 122, although the author questions whether privacy is still a justification of the private copy exception in a digital environment where copy controls can be effected remotely and outside the private sphere of individuals.

[48] However, see in a US context, Julie E Cohen, 'Overcoming Property: Does Copyright Trump Privacy?' (2002) U Ill JL Tech & Pol'y 375 at 377–78, where the author links the first sale doctrine, which gives copy owners the right to resell copies of copyright works without copyright holders' consent, and is therefore one of their freedoms as owners, to user privacy.

ownership because not to do so would violate the intimate relationship that users have with copyright works.[49]

Given that commercial copies of copyright works are not creations of the users, and are often by nature, although not necessarily, works that are communicated and shared with others, at first sight, privacy, as a specific subset of freedoms and autonomous choice, may not be the most persuasive justification for the existence of ownership in commercial copies of copyright works. However, as copyright access and user controls become more and more refined, and as the scope of ownership users have in copies of copyright works become increasingly malleable,[50] privacy could justify opposition to any obstacle to the amount of reading or listening that a copy owner could do with the copy of a work they own, or recognize the tinkering or any other act that a user may do with a work in a private sphere as a power and privilege of copy ownership. Privacy could also be a justification for ownership in the 'mini' or more substantive derivative works or compilations of works that users may create from commercial copies of copyright works, certainly in relation to the right to authorize or restrict the disclosure and publication of such mini acts of authorship.[51] Although in that case we are dealing with a new work—not the copy of the copyright work—and how privacy may illuminate what the proper scope of powers and privileges of ownership in that copy should entail.

A different way to characterize the relationship between privacy and ownership in commercial copies of copyright works, and user rights more generally, could be that the right of privacy acts in certain circumstances as an 'independent property-prohibition rule'[52] that would set limits on the exclusionary powers (and related enforcement rights) of copyright holders that are imposed on users.[53] One illustration of the application of privacy rights to limit the exclusionary powers conferred by copyright is *BMG Canada Inc v John Doe*.[54] In that case, the plaintiffs, various music providers in Canada, sought an order to compel various Internet service providers to disclose the names of the customers who used specific IP addresses at times that were material to the proceedings.[55] The Federal Court dismissed the order on the basis that the plaintiffs did not meet the 'equitable bill of discovery requirements.' On appeal, the resolution of the issue centred on the proper test to balance the

[49] See Harris (n 22) at 224 on the relationship between privacy and moral justifications for private property.

[50] See Chapter 1: 'Copyright users and the ownership spectrum.'

[51] I.e., through the exclusive right to authorize first publication of a work: Harris (n 22) at 224–25; *Millar v Taylor* (n 46); Warren & Brandeis (n 46) at 199–200; Handa (n 1) at 125–26.

[52] Harris (n 22) at 32–33: independent-property-prohibition rules are prohibitions that effectively limit the open-ended-use privileges of an owned resource, but that do so regardless of the status of ownership. They vary in time and in space. Safety regulation could fall into that category, as well as criminal law prohibitions: e.g., owning or possessing a book does not entitle you to hit someone with it.

[53] ibid.

[54] *BMG Canada Inc v John Doe*, 2004 FC 488, aff'd *BMG Canada Inc v John Doe*, 2005 FCA 193.

[55] *BMG Canada Inc v John Doe* (FC) (n 54) at para 9.

personal property rights of the plaintiffs as copyright holders and the privacy of Internet service providers' users, a balance that the Federal Court of Appeal described as follows:

> Thus, in my view, in cases where plaintiffs show that they have a *bona fide* claim that unknown persons are infringing their copyright, they have a right to have the identity revealed for the purpose of bringing action. However, caution must be exercised by the courts in ordering such disclosure, to make sure that privacy rights are invaded in the most minimal way.[56]

The Federal Court of Appeal dismissed the appeal, but without prejudice to the plaintiffs' right to commence a further application for disclosure of the identity of the 'users', taking into account the reasons given by the Federal Court of Appeal.[57] The plaintiffs decided not to pursue their claims.

The right to privacy serves different functions for copyright users. It may justify, to some extent, the scope of ownership powers and privileges in copies of copyright works. Privacy may justify certain exceptions to copyright infringement, independently of the user owning a copy of the work they access, and beyond that scenario, act more generally as an 'independent property-prohibition rule' on the exclusive rights of copyright holders. The instrumental justifications of property and copyright, which we explore next, justify and explain copyright user rights beyond copy ownership.

## Instrumental Justifications of (Intellectual) Property

Instrumentalist theories, whereby law is a means to achieve goals that are geared toward increasing net social welfare, are among the most influential justifications for the existence of private property in general,[58] and copyright in particular. International treaties and regional instruments often reflect an instrumentalist view of copyright.[59] Instrumentalist theories centred around the need to incent and reward creation and innovation are often invoked to justify copyright and other intellectual property rights in jurisdictions where copyright law derives from the Anglo-American tradition.[60] In civil law jurisdictions of continental Europe, a rights-based view is often invoked to justify the protection of works of art and of the intellect as extensions of the personality of the author. The scope of protection of moral rights, among others, illustrates an author rights-based justification

[56] *BMG Canada Inc v John Doe* (FCA) (n 54) at para 42.

[57] ibid at para 55.

[58] Waldron, *Private Property* (n 28) at 3.

[59] E.g., *Agreement on Trade-Related Aspects of Intellectual Property Rights, Marrakesh Agreement Establishing the World Trade Organization, Annex 1C*, 15 April 1994, 1869 UNTS 29, 33 ILM 1197, art 7; *WIPO Copyright Treaty*, 20 December 1996, WO033EN, Preamble, recital 4–5; EC, *Parliament and Council Directive 2001/29/EC of 22 May 2001 on the harmonisation of certain aspects of copyright and related rights in the information society*, [2001] OJ, L167/10, Preamble, recital 4 [*Directive 2001/29/EC*].

[60] Fisher (n 1) at 169, 173; Handa (n 1) at 75.

of copyright in these jurisdictions.[61] The extent of the divide between the Anglo-American and the continental civil law theoretical justifications of copyright is questionable,[62] and in light of various international treaties that seek to harmonize copyright law at a substantive and procedural level, the divide between these two traditions lessens. Above all, the lack of one single unifying theoretical justification of copyright in any given jurisdiction probably explains to a large extent the presence of resemblance as much as dissemblance between these two legal traditions.

Two instrumentalist justifications of copyright are particularly relevant to the discussion about copyright user rights, including justifications informing what the proper scope of copy ownership of copyright works should entail. The first justification is the incentive for the creation and dissemination of works, that is, the extent to which this widely invoked justification for the existence of copyright also justifies user rights (including a determination of the proper scope of copy ownership in copyright works). Concepts of freedom and autonomy are being explored in the context of this creator-incentive justification, here from an instrumental perspective, that is, certain behaviours that ought to be promoted within the framework of copyright laws. The second justification is an economic efficiency argument that is generally invoked to support ownership in chattels and that is applied here more specifically to user ownership of commercial copies of copyright works.

## Incentive for the creation and dissemination of works

Under Harris's theory of property, the creator-incentives instrument is the sole plausible justification for creating private property through copyright.[63] Under the US Constitution, Congress's power in relation to copyright (and patents) is 'to promote the progress of science and useful arts, by securing for limited times to authors and inventors the exclusive right to their respective writings and discoveries.'[64] In Canada, instrumental justifications support the existence of copyright to a large extent.[65] As stated by the leading majority decision of the Supreme Court

[61] On the legal regime applicable to freelance authors in civil law jurisdictions, see D'Agostino (n 1) at 121–29.

[62] See Jane C Ginsburg, 'A Tale of Two Copyrights: Literary Property in Revolutionary France and America' (1990) 64 Tul L Rev 991.

[63] Harris (n 22) at 296ff. [64] US Const art I, § 8.

[65] Canadian copyright policy reports often reflect an instrumentalist view of copyright. See e.g., Economic Council of Canada, *Report on Intellectual and Industrial Property*, Information Canada, by BV Hindley (Ottawa: Economic Council of Canada, 1971) at 37, which states that 'the institution of the copyright system implies ... that the additional titles produced as a result of copyright are worth more to the community than the loss resulting from any reduction in the number of copies titles that would have been distributed in the absence of copyright'; Canada, Departments of Consumer and Corporate Affairs and Communications, *From Gutenberg to Telidon: A White Paper on Copyright: Proposals for the Revision of the Canadian Copyright Act* (Ottawa: Supply and Services Canada, 1984) at 1, where copyright justification is said to be to 'reinforce the general principle of protecting the results of creative effort in the social and technological context in which it must be applied.' Instrumentalism (in particular, utilitarianism) is the most frequently invoked theoretical justification for Western copyright law: Handa (n 1) at 75. For a review of Supreme Court of Canada

in *Théberge v Galerie d'Art du Petit Champlain Inc* [*Théberge*]:[66] 'The Copyright Act is usually presented as a balance between promoting the public interest in the encouragement and dissemination of works of the arts and intellect and obtaining a just reward for the creator (or, more accurately, to prevent someone other than the creator from appropriating whatever benefits may be generated).'[67] The reference by the Supreme Court in *Théberge* to a need to reward authors also leans toward natural property rights in the fruits of one's labour justificatory arguments.[68] In the EU, *Directive 2001/29/EC*,[69] with its objective being the harmonization of certain aspects of copyright law, reflects a pluralistic approach to copyright, pointing to utilitarian justifications,[70] alongside fruits of one's labour theory[71] and personality-based theories.[72]

The biggest flaws in the instrumental justification of copyright to incent creators and the dissemination of works reside in its inconsistency, lack of persuasiveness,[73] and difficulty of application.[74] What scope of property rights needs to be conferred on copyright holders for them to be incented to create? Is property the *sine qua non* condition of encouraging creativity or are there other means to reach the same objectives?[75] Is there not sufficient evidence of creative processes taking place independently of an immediate motive of financial gain[76] or in areas where no intellectual property rights are conferred?[77] What type of creativity and innovation should

copyright cases confirming an instrumentalist approach to copyright law, see Daniel Gervais, 'The Purpose of Copyright Law in Canada' (2005) 2 U Ottawa L & Technology J 315.

[66] *Théberge*, 2002 SCC 34.

[67] ibid, at para 30. The Supreme Court of Canada has frequently referred to the objectives of copyright law as stated in *Théberge* (n 66) in subsequent judgments: e.g., *CCH Canadian Ltd v Law Society of Upper Canada* 2004 SCC 13 at para 10 [*CCH*]; *Society of Composers, Authors and Music Publishers of Canada v Canadian Assn of Internet Providers*, 2004 SCC 45 at para 40; *Entertainment Software Association v Society of Composers, Authors and Music Publishers of Canada*, 2012 SCC 34 at para 7; *Society of Composers, Authors and Music Publishers of Canada v Bell Canada*, 2012 SCC 36 at paras 8ff; *Rogers Communications Inc v Society of Composers, Authors and Music Publishers of Canada*, 2012 SCC 35 at para 40. See also *BMG Canada v John Doe* (FCA) (n 54) at para 40.

[68] See below: 'Natural property rights in the fruits of one's labour.'

[69] *Directive 2001/29/EC* (n 59).

[70] ibid Preamble, recital 4.

[71] ibid Preamble, recital 10.

[72] ibid Preamble, recital 11.

[73] See e.g., Ruth Towse, 'Creativity, Copyright and the Creative Industries Paradigm' (2010) 63 KYKLOS 461, where the author evaluates studies on economics of creativity to see the correlation between copyright as an economic incentive for individuals to create and actual individual creativity, concluding that much work remains to be done to assess the effectiveness of economic incentives to individual creativity. See David Vaver, 'Intellectual Property Today: Of Myths and Paradoxes' (1990) 69 Can Bar Rev 98 at 102–13 where the author reviews utilitarian justifications of copyright through three myths: the myth that copyright law is designed to protect authors, the myth that copyright law encourages art and literature, and the myth that copyright law encourages dissemination of works.

[74] For a review and critique of instrumental and utilitarian theories as they relate to intellectual property, see e.g., Hettinger (n 1) at 107–10; Fisher (n 1) at 169, 173–74, and 177–84.

[75] See Hettinger (n 1) at 109.

[76] E.g., the various forms of works that fall within the scope of copyright law and are freely shared and communicated through the Internet by individual authors are among the many manifestations of creative processes taking place independently of financial or other reward. See also: Julie E Cohen, 'Copyright as Property in the Post-Industrial Economy: A Research Agenda' (2011) Wis L Rev 141 at 143 [Cohen, 'Copyright as Property'].

[77] E.g., the high-end cuisine industry is one area where innovation and creativity take place in spite of very little intellectual property rights protection. On the theme of innovation in areas where

be promoted to maximize net social welfare and is copyright law preoccupied at all by this question?[78] Who are we incenting to invest in the production and distribution of copyright works: authors or firms?[79]

The declared instrumentalist justifications of copyright to provide incentives to create and disseminate works while rewarding creators fairly may have failed to fulfil their promise in an important way. The embedded balance within these justifications calls for as much attention to be paid to the level of access and enjoyment that should be afforded to the recipients or intended beneficiaries of copyright works as to be paid to the scope of the rights of copyright holders. In their book devoted to users of copyright works, Ray Patterson and Stanley Lindberg attributed this imbalance, detrimental (to copyright users) to the focus of copyright's function on creation rather than on distribution, and the abstractedness of users' interests:

> By treating copyright's function as encouraging the creation (rather than the distribution) of works, courts have increased the difficulty of equating the user's interest in having access to the work for learning with the copyright owner's interest in protecting the right to profit. The difficulty is compounded because the claim of profit is a concrete right with an equitable basis (creation and distribution of the work), whereas learning is only an abstract right with no equitable basis. Yet the fallacy that copyright is intended to encourage the creation of works has been a prime cause of the copyright-is-the-ownership-of-the-work fallacy. And given this latter fallacy, it takes judges with vision to balance the right of learning with the right to profit, as did the framers of the copyright clause.[80]

Other commentators make a similar argument to that of Patterson and Lindberg and point to the need to centre the instrumentalist justifications of copyright on

there is little intellectual property protection, see Kal Raustiala & Jonathan Springman, *The Knockoff Economy: How Imitation Sparks Innovation* (New York: Oxford University Press, 2012), where the authors explore highly creative industries where copying is generally legal, such as fashion, food, finance, and professional sports.

[78] Copyright protects 'original' works in the sense of artistic, dramatic, literary, or musical works 'originating' from, or independently created by, their authors, with a relatively low threshold required for protection. Copyright law is not concerned with the artistic quality or novelty or contribution of the work to society. In the US, see *Feist Publications, Inc v Rural Tel Service Co*, 499 US 340 at 345ff (1991); in Canada see *CCH* (n 67) at paras 14–16.

[79] In the EU, *Directive 2001/29/EC* (n 59) Preamble, 10th recital, emphasizes the need to encourage investment in cultural industries to justify strong intellectual property rights: 'If authors or performers are to continue their creative and artistic work, they have to receive an appropriate reward for the use of their work, as must producers in order to be able to finance this work. The investment required to produce products such as phonograms, films or multimedia products, and services such as on-demand services, is considerable. Adequate legal protection of intellectual property rights is necessary in order to guarantee the availability of such a reward and provide the opportunity for satisfactory returns on this investment.' See Fiona Macmillan, 'Copyright and Corporate Power' in Ruth Towse, ed, *Copyright and the Cultural Industries* (Cheltenham: Edward Elgar, 2002) at 99–118, where the author argues how copyright law is structured to promote power hegemony of a few leading firms in the cultural industry; Cohen, 'Copyright as Property' (n 76) invites us to reframe the justifications of copyright from an author-incentive-based theory to a capital-investment incentive in creative industries as the more accurate account of the objectives of copyright.

[80] L Ray Patterson & Stanley W Lindberg, *The Nature of Copyright: a Law of Users' Rights* (Athens, GA: University of Georgia Press, 1991) at 208–09.

the work–public rather than on the current author–work relationship upon which the framework of copyright is based.[81]

Another difficulty resides in the implementation of the instrumental objective of copyright to incent the creation and dissemination of works. An assumption is often made that the progress of science and the promotion of creation are to serve primarily as justifications for the property rights of copyright holders. In international and regional copyright conventions and other instruments, reference to the creativity-incentive policy objective behind stronger copyright protection often posits users as necessarily benefiting from this creativity as passive recipients, but not as participants in this process.[82] Such assumption explains in part the expansion of copyright to a point where it can become counterproductive to its initially stated goals of incenting creations and the dissemination of works.[83] Too strong protections of copyright may impede the proper dissemination and access to works and the role they play in incenting creation of future works.[84]

Modern societies generally value and encourage innovation and creativity as important engines for growth and prosperity.[85] Recent technological developments allow users to experience copyright works in ways that were, not so long ago, unthinkable, and in volumes that are unprecedented. The digital revolution, the explosion of communication networks, and the access to information technologies, including reproduction tools, have led to unprecedented dissemination and sharing of works protected by copyright.

[81] See e.g., Craig (n 1) at 5–6: '[the] public interest approach justifies copyright in light of its public purpose of encouraging intellectual creativity. Rights are granted to authors in the belief that intellectual works will be under produced unless there is sufficient opportunity to exploit them for financial return. Only if we appreciate the relationship between society and intellectual works can we recognize this underproduction as a danger that public policy should seek to avert,' adding that 'if we understand copyright as based upon some conception of the author-work link, we fail to see the relationship between the public and the work as anything other than the consequence of the author-work relationship. Conversely, an effective and justifiable copyright system requires that the copyright interest (the link between author and work) be structured with deference to the public-work link.'

[82] Regarding the framework of international copyright law, e.g., see *WIPO Copyright Treaty*, 20 December 1996, WO033EN, Preamble, online: <http://www.wipo.int/treaties/en/ip/wct/> accessed 4 February 2017 [*WCT*]; and the *WIPO Performances and Phonograms Treaty*, 20 December 1996, WO034EN, Preamble, online: <http://www.wipo.int/treaties/en/ip/wppt/> accessed 4 February 2017 [*WPPT*]. In a European context, see *Directive 2001/29/EC* (n 59) Preamble, Recital 9–10.

[83] Michael Heller refers to overprotection of intellectual property leading to the 'tragedy of the anti-commons': see Michael Heller, *The Gridlock Economy: How Too Much Ownership Wrecks Markets, Stops Innovation, and Costs Lives* (New York: Basic Books, 2008); Peter S Menell, 'The Property Rights Movement's Embrace of Intellectual Property: True Love or Doomed Relationship?' (2007) 34 Ecology LQ 713 at 744, arguing that treating intellectual property too much like tangible real property can lead to an underutilization of intellectual property, while exclusionary powers associated with tangible real property are meant to avoid an overutilization of the resources (i.e., the 'tragedy of the commons').

[84] ibid. For a critique of an instrumentalist view of copyright and how it is detrimental to the public domain see: Drassinower, *What's Wrong with Copying?* (n 12) at 147–53.

[85] See Handa (n 1) at 118, for whom the reason why utilitarian theories have been more prevalent in Anglo-American traditions of copyright than creator-natural-right-based theories is consistent with emphasis on knowledge and progress in jurisdictions sharing this copyright tradition.

International intellectual property treaties adopted in recent years, and which set legal requirements for copyright reform at the domestic level, responded to one perspective of the technological revolution by strengthening copyright holders' rights as part of the digital agenda.[86] The agenda was led chiefly by the fear of the ravages of piracy on copyright works and by the fear that copyright holders would be reluctant to make their works available through the Internet.[87] In the digital agenda there was no regard for the other perspective on the technological revolution and how this could empower users in ways that could support and promote the declared creator-incentive objectives of copyright. Now, many years into the digital revolution, while we are slowly seeing a greater recognition of user rights and interests at the international level,[88] we are still waiting for a legal and normative even-handed treatment that includes looking at the beneficial impacts and legitimate expectations that technological evolution has created for copyright users.

Alongside the place that is given to copyright holders, there is a need to make room for copyright users by recognizing their integral role in the 'incent to create and disseminate work' instrumental justification of copyright.[89] Why stimulate creations if it is not for the benefit of those who will access them?[90] As Niva Elkin-Koren argues, in a US context:

> to promote creativity it is insufficient to provide incentives to authors by empowering them to exclude second-comers. It is also inappropriate to exempt only transformative uses of copyright works. Promoting creativity requires expanding access to creative works. Copyright law must therefore expand the balance it strikes between authors and users to cover not only subsequent authors but also simply consumers of cultural goods who might become authors in the future.[91]

[86] See Chapter 2: 'Exceptions to copyright infringement and international obligations.'

[87] ibid.

[88] ibid. The first international treaty focused on copyright user rights and interests was signed in 2013: *Marrakesh Treaty to Facilitate Access to Published Works for Persons Who Are Blind, Visually Impaired, or Otherwise Print Disabled*, 27 June 2013, online: <http://www.wipo.int/treaties/en/text.jsp?file_id=301016> accessed 4 February 2017.

[89] Niva Elkin-Koren, 'Making Room for Consumers Under the DMCA' (2007) 22 BTLJ 1119 at 1141, argues: 'What we call "consumption" of informational works is never a passive behavior—it is a conversation, or a social activity of interaction. When a reader engages with an artistic expression, she contributes to its meaning. Thus, consumption of informational works, even for one's sole benefit, promotes copyright goals ... This reality of exchange and interaction suggests that in order to promote creativity it is insufficient to simply provide incentives to authors to produce. It is also necessary to expand access to creative works. Access, in this sense, becomes a central means for promoting production, creation, and progress'; see also Liu, 'Owning Digital Copies' (n 2) at 1309ff. For a discussion on the alignment between copy ownership and the copyright incentives, see Aaron Perzanowski & Jason Schultz, 'Copyright Exhaustion and the Personal Use Dilemma' (2012) 96 Minn L Rev 2067 at 2110–12.

[90] Jessica Litman, 'Lawful Personal Use' (2007) 85 Tex L Rev 1871 at 1879 ['Lawful Personal Use'], refers to 'copyright liberties': i.e., the fact that 'copyright law was designed to maximize the opportunities for non-exploitative enjoyment of copyright works in order to encourage reading, listening, watching, and their cousins.' The author argues that they are 'both deeply embedded in copyright's design and crucial to its promotion of the "Progress of Science."'

[91] Elkin-Koren (n 89) at 1141.

For Elkin-Koren, users are means of production as much as authors.[92] From that perspective, the justification of copyright based on the incentive to create and to disseminate works also needs to consider the optimal access to users that can further support that goal at a broader level and on a longer-term basis.[93] In that light, the information age offers an unprecedented opportunity to reconsider the role of user rights, including competing property rights in commercial copies of copyright works, as part of the overall property design of copyright. Balancing the incentive to create and to disseminate works while fairly rewarding the creator also means balancing those interests in the immediate term—that is, through the property rights conferred on the creator—and on a longer-term basis—that is, by incenting users to be culturally engaged and innovative. Without this balancing act, there is a risk of taking copyright out of its instrumental justification orbit.[94]

One means to incent users to be culturally engaged and promote innovation in relation to commercial copies of copyright works that they access is to protect a certain level of freedom and autonomy in how they experience the works.[95] Ownership is one important vehicle for the exercise of freedom and autonomy, which includes, for instance, the ability to choose how and when and with whom a user will enjoy the copyright work. In that sense, freedom and autonomy allow communication and self-expression in relation to the copyright work.[96] Here, freedom and autonomy are promoted to perfect the overarching goal of copyright as instruments. Niva Elkin-Koren argues that the consumption of copyright works may require even greater protection than other consumptive goods to preserve essential autonomy and freedoms:

> Cultural artifacts are not simply useful commodities. While they often have an entertainment value that could be quantified, they also possess a communicative value and a symbolic significance. They engage our minds in a more direct and intimate way than do mundane commodities and, therefore, expose consumers to a higher risk of deeper and

[92] ibid. See also Litman, 'Lawful Personal Use' (n 90) at 1880.

[93] See Geiger (n 47) at 123, who argues in favour of maintaining the private copy exception to copyright infringement as a means to ensure future creations by future authors: 'If the idea that copyright is intended to be the instrument for cultural and social progress is taken seriously, it is appropriate to favour the uses of works already created that serve the creation of future works ("creative" uses), to an extent going beyond the cases provided for teaching and research. The freedom of expression and information of the creator could impose such a solution.'

[94] See Jessica Litman, 'Creative Reading' (2007) 70 Law & Contemp Probs 175 at 187 [Litman, 'Creative Reading'], on how to support a 'cultural environmentalism': 'We need to do this by developing much more robust language, theories, and stories about the rights of readers, listeners, and viewers. We need to gather a more compelling collection of justifications for the borders between controlled and uncontrolled uses of copyright works.'

[95] Liu, 'Copyright Law's Theory of the Consumer' (n 2) at 406–20; Elkin-Koren (n 89) at 1143, refers to a 'breathing space' that may include 'the freedom to choose the work one wishes to consume or any part of it (and, likewise, the freedom to ignore or refuse other parts); the freedom to choose where to experience the work and how; the freedom to experience the work in privacy without the fear of surveillance; and the freedom to make one's own reading of the work, to experiment with it, and to share that reading.'

[96] Liu, 'Copyright Law's Theory of the Consumer' (n 2) at 406–11; Elkin-Koren (n 89) at 1143; Litman, 'Lawful Personal Uses' (n 90) at 1879.

more intrusive restrictions of freedom. This particular vulnerability of information consumers is often overlooked.[97]

Our failure to better acknowledge the place and role of user rights (including users' personal property in copies of copyright works) in the copyright design departs from the instrumental justifications of copyright to incent the creation and dissemination of works. The failure may effectively weaken expectations in relation to copyright users' participation in a modern, cultural, and innovative society.[98] In that view, a creator-work dissemination-incentive instrumental justification of copyright, which takes into account copyright users' interests, leads to the need to preserve a certain level of freedom and autonomy of user-copy-owners and other users.

## Economic efficiency and copy ownership

Parallel to how the objective of incenting to create and to disseminate copyright works may also support stronger copyright user rights, there is a widespread economic efficiency argument that can be made in favour of copyright users, and more particularly user-copy-owners. An economic efficiency instrumental argument generally supports maintaining a property institution in relation to chattels and real property. By supporting property institutions, the state delegates 'use-channelling and use-policing functions' to individual owners and removes the burden from the community for such functions.[99] Conversely, a society that does not support property institutions would offer access to resources in a communal, controlled, monitored, and policed use environment.[100] In their work pleading for a greater recognition of the place and role of copyright users within copyright law, Patterson and Lindberg invoked a similar market efficiency argument:

> The law of users' rights, in other words serves a socially desirable purpose in that it promotes market discipline by allowing market forces to determine prices. To deny the right of individual use would be to employ copyright to control the conduct of countless citizens for the alleged financial benefit of a few. But contrary to the claims of the industry, copyright was never intended to create and guarantee profit, only to protect the work in the market place. Users also have rights.[101]

Efficiency may not on its own be an objective of copyright design or justification for the existence or limitation of copy ownership that exists in isolation of other substantive values or instrumental goals.[102] Nevertheless, efficiency is often an important indicator that can lend support to substantive values or point to important difficulties in the promotion and implementation of those values. In the context of copyright and user rights and copy ownership, an efficiency analysis

[97] Elkin-Koren (n 89) at 1136–37. [98] ibid at 1143. [99] Harris (n 22) at 242.
[100] ibid. [101] Patterson & Lindberg (n 2) at 193.
[102] A contrary view may be provided by law and economics theories, which tend to focus on how copyright law can promote economic efficiency as an end goal. See e.g., William M Landes & Richard A Posner, 'An Economic Analysis of Copyright Law' (1989) 18 J Leg Stud 325.

of the interests at stake can signal the proper scope of property rights that should be maintained to incent creations on the one hand, and to value and allow *prima facie* open-ended freedom powers and privileges of user-copy-owners and other users on the other.[103] In relation to copyright works embedded in tangible objects, for example, books, CDs, and DVDs, users are generally aware of their privileges and powers as owners of the copies of the copyright works and look after their own interests in putting their ownership rights to the most efficient and productive use (e.g., unlimited reading, listening, viewing, sharing, lending, donating, second-hand sale, etc.).

The economic efficiency argument supports the *prima facie* normative status of ownership freedoms as a justification to define the scope of ownership in commercial copies of copyright works discussed above in this chapter.[104] It is the widespread and well-established concept of ownership that creates the efficiency: as copy-owners, users generally know what they can do with their copyright works embedded in physical objects without the need to resort to elaborate lists of terms and conditions of use.[105] However, in the case of digital copies, either distributed online or with a physical medium, and supplied with a non-negotiated standard end-user agreement, at least two factors compromise economic efficiency materializing through copy ownership. First, the potential freedoms of use by users of digital works are growing exponentially with new network, access, copying, and sharing capabilities,[106] with the result that users' understanding about ownership in commercial copies of copyright works will evolve with the changes in their environment that impact how they interact with copyright works. Copyright law and the contractual terms dictated by copyright holders do not necessarily corroborate users' understanding and expectations of what they are allowed to do with digital copies of copyright works. The gap between users' expectations and the law, and the unpredictability that results therefrom, lead to significant information costs for users.[107] Second, the traditional economic efficiency justification for maintaining ownership in chattels has failed to counter the growing commercial practice of copyright holders, enforced by courts, to license rather than sell copies of copyright works, thereby restricting users' ability to transfer and assign the

[103] In several European jurisdictions, economic arguments such as the realization of a market failure have been invoked to justify exceptions to copyright infringement such as the private copying regime, together with other justifications, such as privacy, consumers' freedom of expression, justice to authors through the automatic levy remuneration system. See Helberger & Hugenholtz (n 47) at 1068–72.

[104] See above: 'The *prima facie* normative status of all ownership freedoms.'

[105] Michael Seringhaus, 'E-Book Transactions: Amazon "Kindles" The Copy Ownership Debate' (2009) 12 Yale JL & Technology 147 at 171, arguing that copy ownership of copyright works needs to be maintained on that basis.

[106] This includes all capabilities made available through the digitization of works and the accessibility that the Internet provides: MP3 devices, Facebook, and YouTube are examples of widespread reproduction tools and network-sharing capabilities.

[107] Eduardo M Penalver & Sonia K Katyal, *Property Outlaws* (New Haven: Yale University Press, 2010) at 40, refer generally to intellectual property's 'unpredictability', engendering huge information costs for consumers, and pointing generally to inefficiency and counterproductivity of intellectual property's private property regime.

commercial copies they lawfully acquired.[108] By licensing rather than selling copies of works, copyright holders are creating an environment whereby every act is subject to potential scrutiny and varies according to the terms and conditions that copyright holders dictate, as opposed to being subject to the efficiencies that come with copy ownership.

Over time, it is possible, although somewhat speculative, that efficiency would be increased—and even brought to a similar level as traditional common understandings of copy ownership—by users becoming accustomed to new access rights to commercial copies of copyright works and to the fact that they no longer own the commercial copies. This would require *inter alia* that all copyright holders' terms and conditions be substantially similar. In the meantime, and generally, the implementation and enforcement costs of an environment of non-negotiated standard end-user agreements with possible variable terms for each agreement tend to be underestimated.[109]

The cost of use-channelling and use-policing functions is not to be borne by private copyright holders alone; it also becomes a societal burden, through other private intermediaries,[110] the court system, and involvement of police authorities, to enforce copyright holders' trespassory powers. The efficiency argument to support the subsistence of copy ownership of copyright works only has value to the extent that we can address the first issue adequately, namely the modified understanding that consumers have about owning digital commercial copies of copyright works. Until we are willing to consider the implications of the shift that has taken place in the basic understanding of copy ownership in a digital environment,[111] and make the proper adjustments, the confusion that prevails about the meaning of ownership of commercial copies of copyright works will remain an important obstacle to transaction efficiency.

The instrumental creator-incentive justification to support the creation of property interests through the copyright regime also supports the interests of copyright users as full participants in the creative process. As one of the most influential justifications of copyright, the instrumental creator-incentive rationale also justifies a scope of ownership of *prima facie* open-ended powers and privileges in commercial copies of copyright works that recognizes that the incentive to create should also apply to consumers. Another influential theoretical justification of copyright, based on natural property rights in the fruits of one's labour, merits a closer look. In particular, the impact that the fruits of one's labour theory, and similar theories may have on copyright user rights.

108 See Chapter 5: 'The commercial practice not to sell copies.'

109 Liu, 'Owning Digital Copies' (n 2) at 1321.

110 Such as the resources that need to be deployed by Internet service providers to comply with their legal obligations in case of (alleged) copyright infringements.

111 Penalver & Katyal (n 107), on the idea of paying attention to certain manifestations of 'property outlaws'; the authors' main thesis being to look at the effect that property disobedience has had in recent history on the evolution of the concept of property. The authors argue that movements or property disobedience are an essential component to property's dynamism, evolution, and longevity.

## Natural Property Rights in the Fruits of One's Labour

Natural right property theories on the fruits of one's labour are invoked to justify the existence of copyright and focus on the rewards that should come with something being created. Property theories that justify natural rights in the fruits of one's labour offer little direct support to the advancement of copyright user rights, including the determination of the proper scope of ownership in commercial copies of copyright works.[112] The consumption of copyright works by users does not necessarily or effectively entail the immediate creation of anything ideational or corporeal, and yet paying attention to the relation that develops between a user and a copyright work is central to any meaningful enunciation of user rights.[113] The implications of natural rights property theories on the fruits of one's labour require a closer look because of their lasting influence on copyright law and theory[114] and, in turn, on copyright user rights.

Views diverge on the appropriateness of resorting to the fruits of one's labour theory, in particular, Locke's labour-desert theory of property to justify and support the legitimacy of copyright.[115] Invoking the fruits of one's labour to justify the creation of property rights in general and copyright in particular has given rise to strong criticism. The question of whether a person can claim a natural right to property boils down to whether they have a moral claim to a resource, independent of social convention or positive legal provisions, so that others must confer or be subject to ownership use-privileges and control powers over that resource.[116] The applicability of the fruits of one's labour theory to intangible property has been questioned,[117] as has been the ability of applying proportionality between the labour contribution and the exclusive rights conferred by copyright.[118] Other criticisms include the argument that exclusive property rights do not 'naturally' flow as the sole reward or recognition for one's labour[119] and that the right to use and possess one's labour and the right to profit from it by selling it in the marketplace derive from distinct justifications.[120] At a more fundamental level, the natural property rights in the fruits of one's labour theory becomes problematic when it

[112] Liu, 'Owning Digital Copies' (n 2) at 1326, arrives at the same conclusion by looking at various justificatory theories that can support the ownership in copies of copyright works.

[113] See above: 'Incentive for the creation and dissemination of works.'

[114] See e.g., Hettinger (n 1) at 100, referring to the entitlement to the fruits of one's labour as perhaps the 'most powerful intuition supporting property rights', including in relation to products of the mind.

[115] For a review and critique of the arguments that Lockean fruits of one's labour property theory can effectively ensure a robust public domain, see Craig (n 1) in particular at 51–57.

[116] Harris (n 22) at 182.

[117] Fisher (n 1) at 184–89.

[118] Hettinger (n 1) at 101, 104.

[119] One of the mistakes is to conflate the issue of deserving a reward with what the reward should be: Hettinger (n 1) at 103. The type of reward is in fact dictated by social convention and is not as such a natural right: Harris (n 22) at 207.

[120] E.g., Hettinger (n 1) at 100–03, argues that while there may be a natural right to possess and use one's labour, there is no natural right to sell it and make a profit from it in the marketplace, which is largely a socially created phenomenon.

leads to the over-propertization of copyright, or when it is interpreted as inferring that copyright holders *own their work*, a fallacy that I have denounced elsewhere.[121] In the same vein, critics of natural property in the fruits of one's labour as a theory to justify copyright will argue that it inevitably leads to copyright-holder-centric regimes as it fails to account for other rights and interests beyond the ones of copyright holders.[122] For other commentators, a more nuanced application of the natural property to the fruits of one's labour theory may not lead to such expansionist tendencies of copyright.[123] For instance, the application of John Locke's natural law justification of property to intellectual property, that fully accounts for Locke's provisos or limitations to property rights,[124] may on the contrary enable the flourishing of a robust public domain.[125]

Even if one were to concede that fruits of one's labour justifications of copyright embed limitations that may contain the expansion of copyright, it is not clear how such theories could go as far as supporting user rights. For instance, regarding the creation by users of mini acts of authorship or works derived from another copyright work, the entitlements of the user-creator would run against the entitlements of the creator in the underlying work as a result of their labour. It is not clear how fruits of one's labour theories would mediate between competing acts of labour relating to the same work. In instances when there is no immediate creation resulting from uses of a copyright work, it is unclear to what extent limitations to the natural property in the fruits of one's labour would do more than tolerate such uses as opposed to actively promoting them.

Constitutions[126] and the reasoning of the highest courts in some countries[127] on the nature and purpose of copyright, which should have put to rest arguments

[121] Pascale Chapdelaine, 'The Property Attributes of Copyright' (2014) 10 Buffalo Intellectual Property LJ 34.

[122] See Craig (n 1) in particular at 51–57.

[123] Gordon (n 1) in particular at 1555–72.

[124] John Locke, 'Second Treatise of Civil Government,' ch 5, §§ 27, 31, online: <http://www.constitution.org/jl/2ndtreat.htm> accessed 4 February 2017: John Locke's provisos are commonly referred to as the 'enough, and as good left in common for others' and 'no spoilage' provisos: 'for this labour being the unquestionable property of the labourer, no man but he can have a right to what that is once joined to, *at least where there is enough, and as good, left in common for others*' (emphasis added) (ibid, § 27). 'As much as any one can make use of to any advantage of life before it spoils, so much he may by his labour fix a property in: whatever is beyond this, is more than his share, and belongs to others' (ibid § 31). See Gordon (n 1) at 1560–72; for a review and critique of the application of Locke's provisos as a means to limit the scope of copyright, see Craig (n 1) in particular at 22ff and at 48ff.

[125] See e.g., Christopher M Newman, 'Transformation in Property and Copyright' (2011) 56 Vill L Rev 251 at 297–98. On the application of Locke's natural law theory to copyright freelancers and publishers, see D'Agostino (n 1) at 205–19.

[126] US Const, art I, § 8, stipulates that Congress's power in the area of copyright (and patents) is to promote the progress of science and useful arts, by securing for limited times to authors and inventors the exclusive right to their respective writings and discoveries.

[127] The Supreme Court of Canada declaration in *Compo Co v Blue Crest Music Inc*, [1980] 1 SCR 357 at para 23, considerably weakens the strength of any argument that copyright derives from natural law: 'copyright law is neither tort law nor property law in classification, but is statutory law. It neither cuts across existing rights in property or conduct nor falls between rights and obligations heretofore existing in the common law. Copyright legislation simply creates rights and obligations upon the terms and in the circumstances set out in the statute.' (Subsequently applied in numerous Supreme Court judgments: see *Society of Composers, Authors and Music Publishers of Canada v Canadian Assn of Internet Providers*, [2004] 2 SCR 427 at para 82.)

that copyright derives from a natural right to the fruits of one's labour, have not deterred other courts and lawmakers in the relevant jurisdictions from linking copyright raison d'être to the fruits of one's labour. Copyright case law abounds with legal analyses based on natural property rights in the fruits of one's labour to clarify the scope of copyright and in some cases with the effect of expanding that scope.[128] Foundational components of copyright law, such as the low threshold of originality required for a work to be protected by copyright, seem to fit better with the fruits of one's labour theory than other justifications of copyright.[129] For instance, the instrumental justification to incent creation and dissemination of works would arguably lead to greater scrutiny and selection in the types of works that society wants to incent to create and disseminate, and hence a higher threshold for the types of works that would deserve copyright protection.[130]

There is an undeniable appeal to applying the fruits of one's labour natural law theory to copyright, one of the elements of which is a disconcerting facility of conceptualization and of application: everything that emanates from an author is a copyright work that they own. Copyright confers the trespassory powers that concretize that ownership. This is a much simpler proposition than trying to establish the optimal scope of copyright insofar as it incents creations and dissemination of works under the instrumental justification of copyright.[131] Commentators attribute the tendency to rely on the fruits of one's labour theories to justify copyright on the centrality that is placed on the author–work relationship in copyright law.[132] This relationship embeds a reliance on a romantic vision of authorship and a conception of the requirement of originality as implying the notion of 'independent work'.[133] As a result, '[t]he individuality and originality of authorship establishes a simple route towards individual ownership and the propertization of creative achievement.'[134]

The way in which the fruits of one's labour theory has been applied to copyright is harmful to the assertion of clearer user rights (including property rights in commercial copies of copyright works) in at least two respects. First, under that theory, the competing claims are unequivocally framed as labourers (i.e., copyright holders) versus idlers and free riders (i.e., consumers and other users).[135] The users cannot reap where they have not sown is the premise. The copyright holder labourers are deemed to be *a priori* meritorious (even if copyright law does not impose any requirement of artistic quality or novelty for a work to be protected). The use

[128] For a Canadian perspective, see Craig (n 1). For a US perspective, see Fisher (n 1) at 174, where the author cites examples from law reform debates, US Supreme Court decisions, and lower court decisions. In *Théberge* (n 66) the Supreme Court of Canada also seems to invoke the fruits of one's labour theory as a justification for copyright.

[129] See *CCH* (n 67) at para 15, where the Supreme Court of Canada refers to how the various existing legal traditions on the applicable threshold of originality in copyright law derive from natural law concepts based on the fruits of one's labour.

[130] See above: 'Instrumental justifications of (intellectual) property.'

[131] ibid.

[132] See Craig (n 1) at 7.

[133] ibid.

[134] ibid.

[135] On the emphasis that law and policymakers place on the concept of 'free riding' and its harmful effects, see Lemley (n 1) in particular at 1044.

of the fruits of one's labour theory to justify copyright places copyright holders on a pedestal.[136] Any claim of unauthorized use of the copyright-holder labourers' work is, from that standpoint, *a priori* suspicious. Second, the fruits of one's labour natural law theories can be harmful to copyright users if, in spite of their own internal limitations, for instance by Locke's famous provisos,[137] the theories effectively lead to an over-propertization of copyright. The inflation of copyright holders' exclusive rights then acts as an ever-expanding limitation on the assertion of user rights, including through ownership of commercial copies of copyright works, to the point that the property interests in copies of copyright works are hollowed out of any meaningful substance.[138]

## A Pluralistic Account of Copyright User Rights

Different, and sometimes seemingly contradictory, justificatory theories play a central role in how legislatures, courts,[139] lawmakers, scholars,[140] and interest groups shape and define the exclusive rights conferred on copyright holders. Different aspects of copyright, as laid out in statutes and international instruments, point toward different justificatory theories.[141] Personhood-constituting theories may justify the legal protection of moral rights better than instrumentalist theories.[142] Fruits of one's labour theories may explain the low threshold of originality required for works to be protected by copyright law better than an instrumentalist account of copyright.[143] This suggests that it may be a difficult task to justify copyright by one unified theory alone. Rather, a pluralistic approach to copyright may provide a better account of what copyright is than any unified theory may ever be able to

[136] See also, Craig (n 1) at 58, on how with a labour-desert derived analysis to copyright law the reasoning begins from the copyright holder standpoint, and how this directly impacts on the outcome.

[137] See Locke (n 124); for a review and critique of the application of Locke's provisos as a mean to limit the scope of copyright, see Craig (n 1) in particular at 22ff and at 48ff.

[138] See Chapter 1.

[139] See below discussion on *Théberge* (n 66). In *BMG Canada* (FCA) (n 54) at para 40, the Federal Court of Appeal adopts a utilitarian approach to copyright while resorting to Lockean fruits of one's labour theory language.

[140] For a US perspective, see an analysis of the justificatory theories reflected in American copyright and intellectual property case law in Fisher (n 1) at 168; see also Adam Mossoff, 'Is Copyright Property?' (2005) 42 San Diego L Rev 29 at 36.

[141] E.g., the various theoretical justifications seem to co-exist in the European Union efforts to harmonize copyright. See e.g., EC, *Directive 2001/29/EC* (n 59) Preamble, which points to utilitarian justifications (recital 4), fruits of one's labour theory (e.g., recital 10), and personality-based theories (e.g., recital 11); see Canada's *Copyright Act*, RSC 1985, c C-42 [*Canada CA*], which generally exemplifies an instrumentalist approach to copyright (e.g., section 13(3), which states that the first owner of copyright is the employer of the author who created the work in the course of their employment) but also includes rights that can be justified by personality-based theories (e.g., moral rights: ss 14.1–14.2) and provisions that illustrate both justifications (s 83, which provides for the reversion of copyright to the author in case of bankruptcy, which can be justified by instrumentalist theories as well as personality-based theories).

[142] See above: 'The contributions of property and other theories.'

[143] See above: 'Natural property rights in the fruits of one's labour.'

achieve, no matter how unattractive and 'patchwork-like' this proposition may appear to be.

In *Théberge*,[144] the leading case of the Supreme Court of Canada on the objectives of *Canada Copyright Act*, three of the four theoretical justifications of property and copyright discussed in this chapter are present to some extent in the reasons by the majority: the underlying normative value of copy ownership, the instrumentalist goal to incent creation and dissemination of works,[145] efficiency, and arguably fruits of one's labour justifications of copyright (i.e., the need to give a just reward to the author).[146]

In *Théberge*, Binnie J for the majority drew the line between the rights of the owner in the physical copy of a copyright work and the rights of the copyright holder. Having decided that the transposition of lawfully purchased posters of artist Claude Théberge's paintings on a canvas was not a 'reproduction' of the copyright work as per the exclusive rights conferred to Théberge under *Canada CA*, the Court decided that such transposition did not fall within the economic rights of the artist (while it may have fallen under his moral rights). One of the reasons given by the majority was:

> The proper balance among these [i.e., the creator's rights] and other public policy objectives lies not only in recognizing the creator's rights but in giving due weight to their limited nature. In crassly economic terms it would be as inefficient to overcompensate artists and authors for the right of reproduction as it would be self-defeating to undercompensate them. Once an authorized copy of a work is sold to a member of the public, it is generally for the purchaser, not the author, to determine what happens to it. Excessive control by holders of copyrights and other forms of intellectual property may unduly limit the ability of the public domain to incorporate and embellish creative innovation in the long-term interests of society as a whole, or create practical obstacles to proper utilization.[147]

This passage from *Théberge* articulates the balancing act between various competing interests that needs to take place in copyright law, with a particular emphasis on owners of commercial copies of copyright works. While the Court refers to the need to incent the creation of works and to offer a just reward to creators, it emphasizes the freedoms that are intrinsic to the property rights in the posters of Claude Théberge's paintings that had been lawfully sold, the need to set limits to copyright holders' ownership rights to encourage future creations, as well as the instrumental efficiency that results from such freedoms and proper limitations. *Théberge* illustrates a pluralistic approach both to explaining the objectives of copyright as well as in relation to the place and role of user-copy-owners within the copyright framework.

The variety of identities and interests of copyright users, from individual personal users to institutional users (e.g., libraries and archives) to intermediaries

[144] *Théberge* (n 66).

[145] With long-term interests in mind, to avoid that copyright protection creates undue hindrances to the incorporation and embellishment of future creative works, or that it does not create 'practical obstacles to proper utilization': ibid, at para 32.

[146] ibid. [147] ibid at paras 31–32.

(e.g., Google),[148] as well as the different means by which users experience copyright works—through their property in the copy of the work, as service users, or as public-space-users[149]—call for a pluralistic approach to justify the existence and scope of user rights.

Perhaps the least explored justification for user rights is the *prima facie* normative status of all ownership freedoms.[150] It is a strong point of departure from which to promote and solidify users' place and rights, and level the playing field of competing property rights in copyright. Too often has the personal property that some users have in the copy of a work been neglected or ignored. The personal property rights of users in the copy should remain the base line and copyright, as a bundle of exclusive rights imposing restrictions on the free movement and enjoyment of goods, should be treated as the exception. As with other forms of property, the scope of the rights of personal property copy owners is contextual and in constant evolution, subject to its environment and how it internalizes (technological) change, and subject to various forms of limitations. At the same time, property is a vehicle of rights opposable to all and that secures *prima facie* open-ended powers and privileges based on autonomy and freedom.

The right to privacy serves as a justification of the existence and scope of copy ownership in relation to specific types of users and in limited instances where there is a need to preserve a secure space where values of autonomy and freedom can optimally flourish.[151] With copyright holders applying increased access and copy controls to copies of their works, privacy can serve as a justification for user rights or privileges more generally to limit copyright holders' rights, without privacy having to be tied to ownership in the copies of the works.[152] Instrumentalist theories of economic efficiency can also help to clarify what the proper scope of ownership in copies of copyright works should be, or how to contain copyright holders' exclusive rights and commercial practices that undermine the personal property of copy owners.

As users experience copyright works increasingly through services, or as public-space-users, without owning the copy of a work, other justificatory theories are more inclusive of the broader spectrum of user experiences. Instrumental theories that justify copyright on the basis of the need to incent the creation and dissemination of works are an attractive base for user rights, given their widely influential impact on copyright doctrine, perhaps more than for the strength of these theories per se. From a user perspective the exercise consists of deconstructing the widely accepted objective of copyright to incent the creation and dissemination of works by applying this objective to user rights. Just as in the case of confronting copyright exclusive rights with the personal property rights of copy owners, applying the most commonly accepted justification of copyright

148 See Introduction. 149 See Chapter 8: 'Public-space-users.'
150 See above: 'The *prima facie* normative status of all ownership freedoms.'
151 See above: 'The right to privacy.' 152 ibid.

to copyright user rights offers a solid ground upon which to level the playing field between copyright holders and copyright users.

Justifying copyright user rights through distinct and complementary theoretical approaches, with the identity of the user and the way they experience copyright works in mind, does more justice to copyright user rights than the broad public policy, public interest, and public domain considerations that are brought to the fore in support of users in copyright theory. The normative status of all ownership freedoms, the right to privacy, and instrumental theories explored in this chapter lay foundations that help better substantiate and define copyright user rights and their role in copyright law.

# 8

# User Property, User Rights, and User Privileges

## The Dysfunction of Copyright User Rights

Copyright user rights operate on two planes that interact with each other. When they own an individualized copy, copyright users have rights that derive from the personal property in the copy of the work (Chapter 1). Copyright users also benefit from various exceptions to copyright infringement (Chapter 2), which often operate independently of their ownership of the copy. Personal property rights in the copy have been largely overlooked and overshadowed by the copyright intangible property in the work, with the result that they fare rather poorly on the ownership spectrum.[1] Exceptions to copyright infringement do not typically form the base of legal claims against copyright holders, and reference to exceptions as 'user rights' is misleading. Exceptions are more properly referred to as defences or privileges, and the prevailing view is that unless the copyright statute provides otherwise, exceptions to copyright infringement are not mandatory, that is, they can be waived or set aside by contracts, such as may often be the case in non-negotiated standard terms of use.[2] As a result, copyright user remedies in relation to restricted uses of copyright works remain sparse or uncertain, if not non-existent.[3]

The struggle by courts and legislatures with immateriality, as it relates to online copies of copyright works disembodied from a physical object, or in relation to copyright as a form of intangible property, has led to inconsistent and somewhat arbitrary results on the legal application of the concepts of goods, services, sales, and licences.[4] The same observation can be made in relation to the application of the first sale or exhaustion doctrine.[5] Finally, the introduction of technological protection measure legal regimes (TPMs), often existing in parallel with regimes of copyright infringement, shifted the paradigm in the regulation of copyright, with the potential of significantly weakening the rights and interests of users in the digital sphere.[6]

[1] See Chapter 1: 'A peculiar form of personal property.' [2] See Chapter 2.
[3] See Chapter 3.
[4] See Chapter 1: 'Sometimes a 'good' ... and sometimes not' and 'Do users own the copies of copyright works they buy?' Also see Chapter 4.
[5] See Chapter 5. [6] See Chapter 6.

Copyright User Rights: Contracts and the Erosion of Property. First Edition. Pascale Chapdelaine.

Building on the structural and substantive analysis of copyright and user rights presented in Part I and Part II of this book, and on the theoretical justifications supporting copyright user rights developed in Chapter 7, this chapter proposes two guiding tools and principles that will be critical to assist law-makers in the future development of copyright user rights, and presents a taxonomy and hierarchy of copyright user rights that is based on those tools and guiding principles.

## Shaping the Contours of Copyright User Rights

Based on the main deficiencies identified throughout this book about copyright and user rights, two broad principles and tools emerge as possible guides to shape copyright user rights in the future. The first principle calls for a greater cohesion and harmony between copyright law and traditional concepts of private and public law. The second principle or tool calls for important structural change to how copyright law currently addresses the balance between competing interests. Moving toward a greater equilibrium between competing interests in copyright law will require the explicit recognition of copyright user rights and interests, and incentives to respect those rights in the regulatory frameworks inherited in part from the World Intellectual Property Organization (WIPO) digital agenda[7] and *WIPO Internet treaties*.[8]

### Cohesion between copyright law, private law, and public law

User rights and interests comprise property rights and derive from copyright statutes (through the exclusive rights of copyright holders and exceptions to copyright infringement) and are further shaped by contracts, or through implied licences. The commercial transactions between users and copyright holders are subject to myriad other laws and regulations, including consumer law, competition law, and criminal law.

The sustainability of copyright as a credible body of law designed to encourage the creation and dissemination of works[9] will rest in part on a more explicit formulation of the rights and interests of copyright users. A better articulation of copyright user rights and interests requires greater cohesion between how copyright law interacts with other bodies of law and, in particular, property and contract law.

Many of the deficiencies identified in Part I and Part II of this book and relating to the regulation of copyright users could be attenuated by giving due weight

[7] See Chapter 6, 'International Obligations.'

[8] *WIPO Copyright Treaty*, 20 December 1996, WO033EN, online: <http://www.wipo.int/treaties/en/ip/wct/> [*WCT*] accessed 4 February 2017 and *WIPO Performances and Phonograms Treaty*, 20 December 1996, WO034EN, online: <http://www.wipo.int/treaties/en/ip/wppt/> [*WPPT*] accessed 4 February 2017.

[9] See Chapter 7: 'Instrumental justifications of (intellectual) property.'

to copyright's *sui generis* nature, without falling into the possible trap of exceptionalism. More often than not, the tendency to treat copyright as exceptional has conveniently avoided the need to pay attention to the rights that users properly deserved, either by downplaying their personal property rights or by failing to adequately apply familiar concepts in private law to users of copyright works, for example, goods, services, sales, licence, and *prima facie* bars on restraints of trade. The reluctance to apply the first sale or exhaustion doctrine to digital copies of copyright works not embodied in a physical object comes to mind.[10] The unique nature of digital copies of copyright works and the ease with which they can be reproduced have led courts to set aside the application of the first sale or exhaustion doctrine and to fail to acknowledge that the user could still have personal property in the copy regardless of the presence of a physical embodiment. Similarly, the endorsement of copyright holders' commercial practice to license and not sell the copy of the work seems to have become possible only by confusing the personal property rights in the copy with the intangible property of copyright in the work, and by failing to recognize that in many instances a sale of the copy is what effectively took place.[11]

In the realm of public law, copyright users stand a better chance that copyright law will comply with human rights law if the conflicts that may exist between the two are explicitly addressed in the relevant copyright statutes, by setting the proper limitations to copyright holders' exclusive rights. One example is the specific inclusion of the purpose of parody or satire as an exception to copyright infringement.[12] Allowing the use of a substantial part of a copyright work to parody it for the purpose of satire is justified, based on, among other things, freedom of speech or expression, and it encourages the creation of new copyright works. Trusting that courts will be able to safeguard copyright users' human rights by interpreting copyright law in accordance with the higher order of human rights and constitutional law may not be the safest way to ensure that copyright user (human) rights will be adequately protected.

The Canadian judgment *Cie Générale des établissements Michelin v CAW-Canada*[13] is an example that illustrates the challenges of successfully invoking constitutional human rights arguments to defend the use of a copyright work. The plaintiff Michelin sought an injunction against defendants Canadian Auto Workers (CAW) Union and others (CAW Union) based on trademark and copyright infringement for the use of the Bibendum (Michelin man) logo owned by Michelin. In an attempt to unionize the employees of Michelin Canada, CAW Union distributed various leaflets depicting the Bibendum logo in humorous

[10] See Chapter 5: 'The thorny question of digital exhaustion.'

[11] See Chapter 4: 'Ripple effects on sales and licences.' See also Chapter 5: 'The commercial practice not to sell copies.'

[12] *Copyright Act*, RSC 1985, c C-42, s 29 [*Canada CA*]; art L122-5 4° CPI [*France CPI*]; in the US, parody can be invoked as an exception to copyright infringement and is assessed under the fair use doctrine (17 USC § 107): *Campbell v Acuff-Rose Music, Inc*, 510 US 569 (1994).

[13] (1996) 71 CPR (3d) 348 (FCTD) [*Michelin*].

or satirical ways. CAW Union was unsuccessful in arguing that its use of the Bibendum logo was permissible as a parody or satire. Until the amendments to the Canada *Copyright Act* in 2012,[14] the Act did not provide an exception to copyright infringement based on parody or satire.

One of CAW Union's defences in *Michelin* was based on the *Canadian Charter of Rights and Freedoms* [*Charter*] [15] and argued that their posters and leaflets depicting the Bibendum logo were forms of expression protected by section 2(b) of the *Charter* and that Canada's *Copyright Act* was unconstitutional to the extent that it forbade such use.[16] Teitelbaum J for the Federal Court (trial division) rejected that argument: 'The *Charter* does not confer the right to use private property—the Plaintiff's copyright—in the service of freedom of expression.'[17] It granted injunctive relief to Michelin, ordering CAW Union to stop using the Bibendum logo on its leaflets. Although Teitelbaum J was willing to entertain an argument based on the scope of interpretation of copyright in accordance with the *Charter* without having to declare the whole *Copyright Act* unconstitutional, the transposition and application of the jurisprudence of freedom of expression under the *Charter* to support the Union's defence to use Michelin's protected Bibendum proved to be arduous and sinuous.[18] The difficulty of making constitutional arguments to constrain the scope of copyright law in favour of users is also apparent in the numerous unsuccessful attempts by alleged copyright infringers to have TPM provisions declared unconstitutional in the US.[19]

The call for greater coherence between copyright and other bodies of law serves the greater purpose of maintaining copyright law's relevance and legitimacy. Ideally, law would be in constant movement, keeping abreast with the technological and other changes, and evolution of values and social norms. Users' reasonable expectations with or without an existing commercial relationship with copyright holders or their distributors derive in part from social norms, as much as they shape them. Legislatures, the judiciary, and policy-makers need to stay attuned to social norms and be receptive to 'the information value of disobedience.'[20] Otherwise, they run the risk of making the laws they enact or

[14] *Copyright Modernization Act*, SC 2012, c 20, s 21 [*Canada CMA*].

[15] Part I of the *Constitution Act, 1982*, being Schedule B to the *Canada Act 1982* (UK), 1982, c 11.

[16] *Michelin* (n 13) at paras 82–86. [17] ibid at para 85.

[18] For a discussion of the *Michelin* judgment and on the interaction between copyright and freedom of expression, see Carys Craig, 'Putting the Community in Communication: Dissolving the Conflict between Freedom of Expression and Copyright' (2006) 56 UTLJ 75; see also Jane Bailey, 'Deflating the Michelin Man: Protecting Users' Rights in the Canadian Copyright Reform Process' in Michael Geist, ed, *In the Public Interest: The Future of Canadian Copyright Law* (Toronto: Irwin Law, 2005) 125.

[19] See Chapter 6: 'The constitutionality of technological protection measures.'

[20] Eduardo Moises Penalver & Sonia K Katyal, *Property Outlaws* (New Haven: Yale University Press, 2010) at 172–82; at page 174, the authors note: 'Particularly in cases of protracted and pervasive acquisitive free riding, these transgressions may demonstrate the need for responsible legal shift to update and ossified regime of entitlements or to address the presence of high transaction costs that precluded efficient transfers.'

enforce obsolete quickly, leading to those laws increasingly lacking credibility and legitimacy.[21]

A movement away from copyright exceptionalism and toward a more standardized application of traditional concepts of law to copyright and to users, while paying attention to changing (technological) environments and social norms, will go a long way toward the greater recognition and development of copyright user rights. The effort would be in vain without establishing the proper regulatory framework to explicitly recognize user rights and provide the right level of incentives to ensure compliance with those rights.

## Adjusting the balance

The objective of ensuring a proper balance between copyright holders, users, intermediaries, and the public interest occupies centre stage in copyright law and theory.[22] The goal of achieving a balance between competing interests works hand in hand, it seems, with the plea for a greater cohesion between copyright law and private and public law discussed above.[23] Paying closer attention to the rights and interests of users, including where applicable their personal property rights in copies of copyright works, involves balancing the rights of users with the statutory rights of copyright holders and invites to more cohesion between copyright and other bodies of private law and public law. In spite of the inherent difficulties of balancing competing interests,[24] it is a common and legitimate goal to pursue in many areas of law (e.g., copyright law, property law, criminal law, human rights law). Balancing competing interests and finding a compromise somewhere is a somewhat ineluctable exercise.

Courts' application of the objective of balance has played an important role, in some jurisdictions more than others, in supporting the advancement of the rights and interests of copyright users.[25] When balancing interests courts often apply the principle of technological neutrality.[26] *Adjusting the balance* is an invitation to go one step further, with a more robust and necessary intervention. Positive legal obligations of copyright holders toward users need to be laid out, and concrete remedies need to be available. In some cases, the legal foundations upon which user rights and interests rely will need to take precedence over freedom of contract.

[21] ibid. Jessica Litman, *Digital Copyright* (Amherst: Prometheus Books, 2001) at 85–86, discussing the complete disconnect in people's minds about what may constitute copyright infringement, and at 115–16, about how it is generally bad policy to maintain laws that people don't believe in.

[22] See Chapter 2: 'Exceptions to copyright infringement and international obligations.' See Chapter 7: 'Instrumental justifications of (intellectual) property.' See Chapter 6: 'Technological protection measures and the search for balance in copyright law.' In Canada, see *Théberge v Galerie d'Art du Petit Champlain Inc*, 2002 SCC 34 at para 30.

[23] See above: 'Cohesion between copyright law, private law, and public law.'

[24] *Inter alia*, because of the disagreements on where the balance should lie or how it should be implemented.

[25] See *Sony Corp v Universal City Studios, Inc*, 464 US 417 (1984). See Chapter 2: '"User rights" as a rule of interpretation.'

[26] See below: 'The role of technological neutrality.'

*The role of technological neutrality*

Technological neutrality has been defined in the context of copyright law as the principle that the law should 'apply equally between traditional and more technologically advanced forms of the same media,'[27] allowing the relevant copyright statute to operate 'consistently, regardless of the form of media involved, or its technological sophistication.'[28] The principle is often embedded in copyright legislation[29] and as a stated objective in legislative reform.[30]

The application of technological neutrality calls for a purposive interpretation of copyright law, rather than applying a literal interpretation of the law to a novel technology, which may lead to results that are unfair or contrary to the broader objectives of the relevant statute.[31] Thus, the application of technological neutrality is interdependent with the objective that the law pursues. It is, therefore, no surprise that courts will invoke and apply the principle of technological neutrality as a means to maintain the balance between competing interests, which is a central objective of copyright law in many jurisdictions, including Canada.[32]

The appeal of technological neutrality is to act as a self-adjusting interpretation tool that allows the law to evolve and to retain its legitimacy and relevancy in the face of ongoing technological change. The flexibility that technological neutrality enables and its proximity to the objective of balancing competing interests support the plea made here for a greater cohesion among copyright law, private and public law.[33] The difficulty with technological neutrality, as with any other principle of interpretation, resides in how and when it will be applied.

In recent applications of the principle of technological neutrality, courts have given a particular attention to the rights and interests of copyright users. In *Entertainment Software Association*,[34] the Supreme Court of Canada had to decide whether downloading video games through the Internet amounts to a communication to the public of the musical works that the games contain, which communication to the public would be the object of a separate tariff.[35] In a

[27] *Entertainment Software Association v Society of Composers, Authors and Music Publishers of Canada*, 2012 SCC 34 at para 5 [*Entertainment Software Association*], citing *Robertson v Thomson Corp*, [2006] 2 SCR 363 at para 49.

[28] *Society of Composers, Authors and Music Publishers of Canada v Bell Canada*, 2012 SCC 36 at para 43 [*Bell Canada*].

[29] E.g., *Canada CA* (n 12) s 3(1)c describing a right to produce or reproduce a work 'in any material form whatever.'

[30] See e.g., Canada *CMA* (n 14) Summary at para (g); EC, Commission, *Proposal for a Directive of the European Parliament and of the Council on certain aspects concerning contracts for the supply of digital content*, COM (2015) 634 final 2015/0287 (COD), [*EU Directive Proposal*] applying a technologically neutral approach to the definition of 'digital content'.

[31] *Canadian Broadcasting Corp v SODRAC 2003 Inc*, 2015 SCC 57 at para 170, Abella J, dissenting [*Sodrac*].

[32] ibid at paras 146–48.

[33] See generally this part: 'Cohesion and harmonious co-existence of copyright law with private and public law.'

[34] *Entertainment Software Association* (n 27).

[35] ibid. In that case, the tariff in question had been submitted by the Society of Composers, Authors and Music Publishers of Canada (SOCAN) to the Canadian Copyright Board for approval.

five-to-four decision, the Court held that downloading video games involved no act of communication to the public and could not trigger the application of a separate tariff.[36] The Court majority invoked the principle of technological neutrality, leading it to treat the various forms of copies of copyright works and methods of delivery as one and the same phenomenon in relation to copyright infringement. The Court found a functional equivalent between the online delivery of the copy of a copyright work and the supply of a material medium.[37] The Court applied technological neutrality to interpret the purpose of the *Copyright Act* 'in a way that avoids imposing an additional layer of protections and fees based solely on the *method of delivery* of the work to the end user. To do otherwise would effectively impose a gratuitous cost for the use of more efficient, Internet-based technologies.'[38] The Court concluded that the objective of copyright law was not to attract additional infringement and liability for the method of delivery simply because it occurred on the Internet, noting that delivery offline did not amount to copyright infringement.[39] In *Society of Composers, Authors and Music Publishers of Canada v Bell Canada* [*Bell Canada*],[40] the Supreme Court of Canada, in a unanimous judgment, applied the principle of technological neutrality to support its argument that the fairness of the dealing of the online preview of musical recordings had to be assessed from the perspective of individual users and not by looking at the practice in the aggregate.[41] In light of the volume of digital works that are made available on the Internet, the Court found that taking an aggregate approach 'could well lead to disproportionate findings of unfairness when compared with non-digital works.'[42]

In other cases, courts' failure to apply the principle of technological neutrality has led to a broader application of copyright holders' rights in light of the new technological environment, at the expense of user rights and interests. In Chapter 5, I discussed how in *Capitol Records, LLC v ReDigi Inc*,[43] the New York South District Court's literal and mechanical application of the copyright holders' exclusive reproduction right led the Court to hold that ReDigi, a company offering a platform for the resale of digital music, had infringed the exclusive reproduction right of music label copyright holders.[44] In that case the reproduction was ephemeral and incidental to the delivery of digital music from seller to buyer.[45] This led the Court to not apply the first sale or exhaustion doctrine to copies distributed online with no physical embodiment.[46]

In *Canadian Broadcasting Corp v SODRAC 2003 Inc* [*Sodrac*],[47] the Supreme Court of Canada majority held that broadcast-incidental copies made by the Canadian Broadcasting Corporation to ensure greater quality of its broadcasts engaged copyright holders' reproduction rights in musical recordings, remitting

[36] ibid at para 5. [37] ibid at paras 5–9. [38] ibid at para 9. [39] ibid.
[40] *Bell Canada* (n 28). [41] ibid at para 43. [42] ibid.
[43] 934 F Supp (2d) 640 (USDC, 2013) (on appeal). [44] ibid.
[45] ibid. See Chapter 5: 'The requirement of a physical embodiment' and 'Reserved acts to be performed in the context of digital distribution.'
[46] ibid. [47] *Sodrac* (n 31).

the finalization of the terms of the licence between the two parties to the Copyright Board.[48] According to the Court's majority, nothing in the text, context, and legislative history of the *Copyright Act* [*Canada CA*][49] suggested that broadcast-incidental copies did not amount to reproductions that required the authorization of the relevant copyright holders.[50] In his reasons for judgment, Rohstein J took issue with Abella J's application of technological neutrality in her dissenting reasons,[51] positing that technological neutrality does not allow to override what in the majority of the courts' view were express statutory terms.[52] In her dissenting reasons, Abella J argued that through the application of technological neutrality and the purpose of the *Canada CA*, broadcast-incidental copies did not engage the exclusive reproduction right:[53]

> It is, in fact, difficult to see how the creation of broadcast-incidental copies implicates the legitimate reproduction interests of the creators of the works in any way. These copies are, to borrow the language of *Entertainment Software Association*, merely technological taxis required for the delivery of the digital broadcast process. They are not recordings which fix a particular embodiment of the protected works, they are not delivered as durable copies to the viewer or listener, and they do not alter the degree of control that the composer once had over how the work will be presented to the public.[54]

Abella J linked technological neutrality to the objective of seeking a balance in copyright law, as affirmed by the same court in *Théberge v Galerie d'Art du Petit Champlain Inc* [*Théberge*][55] and noted how the majority reasons for judgment departed from those objectives.[56] Abella J also noted that the function of the application of media neutrality, as a subset of technological neutrality, was to protect the rights of copyright holders as much as the rights of users.[57]

The extent to which technological neutrality, as a principle of statutory interpretation, can effectively adjust the balance in copyright law to optimize the competing interests of its constituents, including copyright users, is unclear. The biggest obstacle that the principle of technological neutrality faces lies in courts shying away from it. The temptation may be high to apply a more literal interpretation of the law that appears to provide the more obvious answer, rather than applying a functional equivalence between the old and the new, or applying the law to a drastically new technological environment. The tension as to of how far courts should go in interpreting legislative intent—from judicial restraint to a more active role that seeks to solve the puzzles that technological evolution bring on—is at the heart of the application of technological neutrality.

It may be that technological neutrality, as a principle of statutory interpretation or as a norm of legislative or judicial governance, holds more promises than it is capable of fulfilling. The concept is intuitively appealing[58] but the principle of

[48] ibid at paras 1–116. [49] *Canada CA* (n 12). [50] *Sodrac* (n 31) at paras 1–116.
[51] ibid at paras 117–92. [52] ibid at para 47.
[53] ibid at paras 144, 164, 166, 168, 170. [54] ibid at para 168.
[55] *Théberge* (n 22) at para 30; *Sodrac* (n 31) at paras 145–46.
[56] *Sodrac* (n 31) at para 179. [57] ibid at para 151.
[58] See e.g., *EU Directive Proposal* (n 30).

technological neutrality suffers from inescapable limitations. There are instances where the technological development is so disruptive that courts will be reluctant to apply the principle of technological neutrality and instead call on the relevant legislative body to clarify its response to the technological disruption through legislative amendment.

To the extent that it enables flexibility and seeks to promote and preserve an adequate balance between competing interests in ever-changing technological environments, technological neutrality remains an important principle of interpretation that should be promoted, as the scope of copyright and of user rights continue to be defined.

### *The obligations of copyright holders*

*Copyright user rights* need to rely on positive obligations of copyright holders and others, to be properly so called. The regulatory model that led to the adoption of the *WIPO Internet treaties* and their domestic implementations worldwide does not impose, with some exceptions, any obligations on copyright holders that could form the basis of a claim by copyright users against obstacles to lawful uses of a copyright work.[59] The response to the opportunity and also to the threat of the digitization of copyright works and new means of dissemination was to bolster copyright holders' rights by imposing obligations and further restrictions on users and the public. The most dramatic regulatory design outcome of the *WIPO Internet treaties* for copyright users was arguably the introduction of TPMs.[60] Outside copyright law, sale of goods, claims based on breach of consumer and contract law, and the doctrine of copyright misuse or *abus de droit* are often an uphill battle, offering copyright users a weak legal base for successful claims or limited remedies.[61]

To take user rights seriously, it will be necessary to impose explicit obligations on copyright holders for the benefit of copyright users. Initial fears about the viability of creative industries in a post-digitization era have led the way to new methods of dissemination, new platforms and means of protection, and new ways of generating revenues from the commercialization of copyright works. The next generation of copyright laws will require a re-engineered balance that makes greater room for the rights of users.

[59] See Chapter 2. See however EC, *Parliament and Council Directive 2001/29/EC of 22 May 2001 on the harmonisation of certain aspects of copyright and related rights in the information society*, [2001] OJ, L167/10, which invites Member States to put the proper mechanisms in place to ensure that copyright users can benefit from certain exceptions to copyright infringement when copyright works are supplied with TPMs. Provisions imposing obligations on copyright holders applying TPMs to their work to make their works accessible have been put in place in some jurisdictions, including France and Belgium: see Chapter 3: 'User claims and remedies in copyright law.'

[60] See Chapter 6.

[61] See Chapter 3: 'User claims and remedies against restricted uses of copyright works based on breach of contract, sale of goods, or consumer law'; Chapter 6: 'From immaterial works to physical objects.'

Various mechanisms creating positive obligations on copyright holders to remove obstacles that block access to copyright works to users have started to emerge in some jurisdictions.[62] The positive obligations imposed on copyright holders will need to factor in users' personal property rights in the copy when users have such rights in the copies. In those instances, a re-engineered balance needs to address how users' copy ownership acts as a property-limitation rule of copyright, just as copyright acts as a property-limitation rule of copy ownership.[63]

To the extent that certain uses of existing copyright works are justified by human rights (e.g., freedom of expression or the public interest, e.g., relating to the integrity and security of individuals and the public), a re-engineered balance of copyright that is attentive to users will allow such possible uses under the relevant copyright statute by setting limits on copyright exclusive rights that may be in conflict with human rights, and will not rely solely on judicial interpretation of copyright legislation in accordance with constitutional or human rights law.[64]

### *Steering freedom of contract toward the objectives of copyright law*

When the vehicles of private law (e.g., contracts) allow the balance to tilt too far in favour of copyright holders, legislators and courts need to consider regulatory designs that will reconcile freedom of contract with the public law and policy aspects of copyright law and take into account interests that compete with those of copyright holders. Making exceptions to copyright infringement mandatory, or presumptively non-waivable, is one regulatory design that may reconcile freedom of contract with the objectives of copyright law when necessary.[65]

The argument that is frequently invoked against making exceptions to copyright infringement mandatory or non-waivable is that it would impede freedom of contract and constrain the flexibility of how copyright holders exploit their exclusive rights.[66] The arguments used to support the mandatory nature of exceptions to copyright infringement include the need to extend to the private contractual sphere the balance between competing interests through statutory exceptions to copyright infringement. If a legislative body enacts constraints to the exclusive rights it confers on copyright holders, the scope of copyright holders' proprietary

[62] See Chapter 3: 'User claims and remedies in copyright law.'

[63] James W Harris, *Property and Justice* (Oxford: Clarendon Press, 1996) at 34: Property limitation rules occur when *prima facie* normative claims founded on the prevailing ownership conception (here of copyright) are overridden. But for the limitation they contain (personal property of users in the copy of the work), the (copyright) owner would be free to do as they please, e.g., apply trespassory protection powers or ask remuneration for the use permitted under the exception. See below: 'The taxonomy and hierarchy of copyright user rights.' See Chapter 2: 'A peculiar form of personal property.'

[64] See discussion above under 'Cohesion and harmonious co-existence of copyright law with private and public law.'

[65] See Chapter 2: 'May exceptions to copyright infringement be waived by contract?' on the interaction between exceptions to copyright infringement and contracts, in particular in the context of non-negotiated standard form agreements.

[66] See e.g., Barry Sookman, 'Copyright Reform for Canada: What Should We Do? A Submission to the Copyright Consultation' (2009) 22 IPJ 1 at 12ff.

rights should not be extended by contracts at the copyright holder's own discretion, in particular in the case of non-negotiated standard end-user agreements. Commentators, including Ian Hargreaves, recommend that exceptions to copyright infringement in the UK *Copyright, Designs and Patents Act*[67] be made mandatory to ensure greater legal certainty.[68] The argument for legal certainty could also be used to support statutes that would explicitly state that exceptions to copyright infringement are not mandatory, that is, that they may be waived by contract. In such cases, however, the legal certainty would be incumbent upon the terms of the contract and how clear the intention of the parties was to set aside the application of exceptions to copyright infringement. As a result, a statute that explicitly states that exceptions to copyright infringement are mandatory (are non-waivable) is likely to bring more legal certainty on that particular point than a statute that is silent on the subject or leaves it up to contracting parties to decide whether exceptions to copyright infringement will apply to their contractual relationship. However, making exceptions to copyright infringement mandatory in all situations, even if it would bring more legal certainty, may not be the ideal regulatory model, for reasons that I discuss further below.

There are at least three difficulties with the proposition that freedom of contract and copyright holders' flexibility in how they exploit their exclusive rights justify overriding the application of exceptions to copyright infringement. First, freedom of contract is, for the greater part, non-existent in non-negotiated standard end-user agreements, which are increasingly used in the commercialization of copyright works in consumer markets.

Second, the flexibility to commercialize copyright works needs to be understood in the context of the rights that are conferred on copyright holders by statute. Exceptions are by definition outside the scope of those exclusive rights.[69] Exceptions to copyright infringement serve a specific purpose for the benefit of designated users or broader public policy and public interest goals.[70] To agree that copyright holders may override the application of exceptions to copyright infringement, is to concede that copyright holders are allowed to expand the scope of their exclusive rights carefully delineated by the state, and in some cases on a large scale.

Third, exceptions to copyright infringement are in essence defences to copyright infringement. The ability to waive in advance one's defence against a claim before a court of law raises issues of validity based on public policy, particularly in the case of consumer mass markets. Are legal defences tradable commodities?[71] Also,

[67] 1988, c 48 (UK).

[68] Ian Hargreaves, 'Digital Opportunity, a Review of Intellectual Property and Growth' 2011 at 51 online: www.ipo.gov.uk/ipreview-finalreport.pdf (The Hargreaves Report was commissioned by the UK Prime Minister in 2010); see also Lucie Guibault, 'Accommodating the Needs of iConsumers: Making Sure They Get Their Money's Worth of Digital Entertainment' (2008) 31 J Consumer Policy 409 at 421ff.

[69] See Chapter 2: 'The "mechanics" of exceptions to copyright infringement.'

[70] ibid.

[71] See Margaret Jane Radin, *Boilerplate: The Fine Print, Vanishing Rights, and the Rule of Law* (Princeton: Princeton University Press, 2013) at 168–70, arguing that intellectual property user rights should not be fully alienable in the context where a standard term agreement can 'achieve widespread cancellation of user rights' which 'contributes to democratic degradations.'

to treat the benefit of exceptions to copyright infringement as something that can be bargained assumes that users would (or could) be aware that they had a right or benefit that they gave up when they agreed to the standard terms and conditions of their agreement with the copyright holder, an assumption one would be hard pressed to make for non-negotiated agreements. In reality, it is unlikely that copyright holders would adequately notify users of their rights and/or about the overriding effect of the standard form agreement.[72]

Compelling arguments support the mandatory nature of exceptions to copyright infringement: the need to preserve the fragile balance sought by a legislature so that competing interests are reconciled against private ordering undermining the balance sought, the protection of weaker parties based on asymmetries of information and bargaining power; and the greater legal certainty and economic efficiency resulting from the explicit mandatory nature of exceptions. To the extent that these concerns are not present, and that there are legitimate reasons that may secure other important objectives, the beneficiary of an exception should be allowed to waive its application. A rebuttable presumption that exceptions to copyright infringement cannot be waived (as opposed to an unfettered mandatory clause) would address those instances where freedom of contract should prevail over exceptions to copyright infringement. The presumption could be non-rebuttable in relation to non-negotiated standard terms, when the user is a consumer, and when the exception is justified by strong public policy objectives. Although it may provide a more refined calibration between freedom of contract and the public policy objectives of copyright, the downside of a rebuttable presumption (as opposed to an unfettered mandatory clause) is that it adds a layer of legal uncertainty; however, that may be contained by clear terms setting out the conditions under which the presumption can be rebutted.

On the need to steer freedom of contracts toward the objectives of copyright law as a means to adjust the balance for a greater recognition of copyright user rights, the *numerus clausus* principle or standardization of property is a norm of judicial governance that restricts the forms of property interests and sets limits on freedom of contract.[73] It reinforces the 'opposability to all' distinctive feature of property and promotes efficiency by reducing information costs.[74] *Numerus clausus* promotes cohesion by setting bright line rules on the interaction between property and contracts. The standardization of property could be one way to address commercial practices that undermine user rights and interests, such as the practice of some copyright holders not to sell copies of copyright works to avoid the application of the first sale or exhaustion doctrine.[75] The

[72] See Pascale Chapdelaine, 'The Ambiguous Nature of Copyright Users' Rights' (2013) 26 IPJ 1 at 26–28, on the discussion based on a sample of non-negotiated standard terms of use for online copies.

[73] See Chapter 1: 'Commercial copies of copyright works and the standardization of property.'

[74] ibid.

[75] ibid. See Chapter 5: 'The commercial practice not to sell copies.' See also Molly Shaffer Van Houweling, 'Exhaustion and the Limits of Remote-Control Property' (2016) 93 Denv L Rev 951, applying an economic analysis to 'remote-control' restrictions imposed by right holders on copies of their works.

existence of *numerus clausus* is controversial in both the civil law and common law systems,[76] making it a less appealing tool in the regulatory design of copyright and user rights.

## The Taxonomy and Hierarchy of Copyright User Rights

This part illustrates how more cohesion amongst concepts of private, public law, and copyright law, steering away from copyright exceptionalism, would help shape and define the rights of copyright users differently than they currently are. The taxonomy of copyright user rights that I present here underscores differences that matter in how we regulate the rights of copyright users, while recognizing the role of user rights in promoting the core objectives of copyright. The legal relationship (e.g., copy owner or service user) that users have with the copyright work (or absence thereof) should guide the scope of their entitlements to a large extent. Owning a copy of a work should bear a different weight and significance than accessing a copyright work with no formal legal relationship with the copyright holder or distributor.

### User-copy-owners

The property of the copy of a copyright work confers distinct rights on copyright users, and those rights call for greater recognition than at present.[77] This is one of the consequences of the more cohesive approach between copyright law and other areas of private and public law proposed here. The property rights in the copy of a copyright work carry a different weight than, for instance, if the same work is accessed through a service. Ownership of a copy of a work should guide the interpretation of any contract that seeks to limit the personal property rights of the copyright user. The same principle applies to the interpretation of statutes conferring exclusive rights on copyright holders when those statutes constrain the exclusive property rights of copy owners.

Just as copyright has undergone significant changes over time to adapt to technological developments and to reflect social values about greater protection and promotion of creators and their works, so should our understanding of the property rights in the copy of those works. The scope of rights attached to ownership of copies of copyright works needs to evolve with technological changes and social norms. The scope of ownership of copies of copyright works needs to remain in sync with the objective to promote the dissemination of works and the creation of future works through the use of pre-existing works and the dialogue that it stimulates between users and authors, and proper access to pre-existing works to that end. At the same time, the scope of copy ownership as a vehicle to safeguard

[76] See Chapter 1: 'Commercial copies of copyright works and the standardization of property.'
[77] See discussion in Chapter 1.

proper dissemination and access to works, needs to be balanced with the copyright holders' right acting as a property-limitation rule on copy ownership.[78]

Copyright user-owners of one copy among a multitude of copies (e.g., of a book, musical work, cinematographic work, computer program) should benefit from the strongest rights on the copyright user spectrum regardless of whether the copy has a physical embodiment or not. The inadvertent copyright users identified in Chapter 6 also fall in this category.[79] The criteria developed in Chapter 4 provide tools to distinguish online copies of works with no physical embodiments that are owned from the ones that are accessed through a service.

Owners of unique (or limited) copies of artistic works, for example, paintings, sculptures, tattoos, buildings comprising an architectural work, also fall in the category of users with the strongest rights on the copyright user spectrum: they entail *a priori* open-ended powers and privileges and that includes the power to transfer title of the copy. At the same time, physical constraints inherently limit the exercise of certain powers and privileges of owners of such copies, for example when compared to a user owning a digital copy of a copyright work, whose reproduction powers are broader.

A more harmonious integration of copyright law with principles of property and contract law is not without obstacles, not the least of which are the diverging views on what the consequences of property rights (should) entail. Property is by no means monolithic, and opinions on the extent to which contracts can alter property rights vary greatly.[80] I take by no means an absolutist view of property, but advocate for a greater recognition of the property rights of copyright users when determining what the scope of the exclusive rights of copyright holders is (or should be). International organizations, legislatures, and the judiciary have for the most part and for too long failed to address the complex interaction of the competing property rights that are involved in the commercialization of copyright works. A more harmonious integration of copyright law with basic principles of property and contract law begins with acknowledging the property rights of copyright users as fully as lawmakers have endorsed the proprietary rights of copyright holders. A more rigorous attention to the property rights of users in copies should implicate the following legal reforms, by way of illustration.

### *Coming to terms with licence agreements*

A licence agreement setting the terms of access to the proprietary intellectual property rights of copyright holders, does not equate to a licence to the copy of the work. If the user obtains indefinite access to the work with no form of control retained by the copyright holder on the manner of its use, etc., the user is the

[78] See above: 'Adjusting the balance.'

[79] I.e., those users who buy a car, a tractor, or any other object with a copyright work integrated in the physical object (e.g., software) that is incidental to the main object in which it is embedded. See Chapter 6: 'From immaterial works to physical objects.'

[80] See Chapter 1: 'Commercial copies of copyright works and the standardization of property.'

owner of that copy, and not a licensee. That is, irrespective of the copyright holder characterization of the transaction as a licence to the copy in the contract (including standard form contracts). The widespread commercial practice, endorsed by courts, to license the copy is for all intents and purposes an unfortunate anomaly in the law and needs to be left behind. Only in instances of copyright holders retaining control over the copy, usually under an arrangement for a limited term, with legal control over the use of the copy and restrictions on its disposition (similar to a rental agreement) does the licence in the copy have its place. Otherwise, we are left in a situation where neither the user nor the copyright holder is the owner—a sort of legal no man's land.[81]

Several consequences flow from setting a bright line that distinguishes a licence to copies from ownership of copies. First, the distinction recognizes the property of copyright users in its own right and counters the erosion of property that has progressively taken place through the commercial practice of licensing rather than selling the copy. As owners of the copy of the work, copyright users will benefit from long-established conditions and warranties in sale of goods and consumer protection law. As owners, copyright users can freely transfer their title to the copy of the work without any duty to account to anyone, regardless of the presence of a physical embodiment, and do away with the false tangible and intangible dichotomy discussed in Chapter 4. By transferring title, users exercise the basic property power and privilege to transfer title to the copy of the work, long recognized in copyright law through the exhaustion or first sale doctrine. In the same vein, copyright statutes referring to the exhaustion or first sale doctrine need to be interpreted or amended to reflect the bright line that distinguishes a licence to the copy from ownership. This outcome would by no means bring an expansive extension of copyright user rights. It would merely illustrate a proper mediation between the property rights of users and those of copyright holders. As limited forms of monopolies, copyright and other intellectual property rights are exceptions to long-established principles of property, free movement, use and transfer of goods, free movement of ideas and knowledge, etc. Recognizing the property rights of users in copies is the acknowledgement and application of copyright's limited scope.[82]

### *Exhaustion of copyright beyond the exclusive distribution right*

A more rigorous attention to the property rights users have in their copies of copyright works would give due consideration to the *prima facie* open-ended powers and privileges that those rights entail as distinct from those of other copyright user rights. The *prima facie* normative status of all ownership freedoms, the instrumental objective to incent the creation and dissemination of works, and economic

[81] See Chapter 5: 'The commercial practice not to sell copies'; Chapter 1: 'If neither owned by the copyright user, nor a good, then what?'
[82] *Théberge* (n 22) at para 31.

efficiency arguments justify conferring more rights to user-copy-owners than current copyright laws allow.[83] The ongoing confusion over the distinction between the rights in the copy and the copyright in the work discussed in Chapters 1 and 4, and the current copyright statutes framing copyright as the rule and user interests as the exceptions to the rule favour an explicit statutory recognition of the personal property rights of copy owners. This explicit statutory recognition would permit a further articulation of the principles that the Supreme Court of Canada majority laid out in *Théberge*:[84]

> Once an authorized copy of a work is sold to a member of the public, it is generally for the purchaser, not the author, to determine what happens to it. Excessive control by holders of copyrights and other forms of intellectual property may unduly limit the ability of the public domain to incorporate and embellish creative innovation in the long-term interests of society as a whole, or create practical obstacles to proper utilization.[85]

The articulation of the property rights of users could take different forms, including the expansion of the doctrine of copyright exhaustion, which is currently restricted to the exclusive distribution right of copyright holders.[86] Perzanowski and Schultz point to the implicit powers and privileges of personal uses embedded in copy ownership of copyright works, in contrast with the US copyright framework under which users need permission from copyright holders, or need to fall under the four fair use factors (or other exceptions to copyright infringement):

> Copy ownership offers a much more intuitive basis for embracing incidental copying by consumers than either the fickle permission of copyright holders or the four fair use factors. The exhaustion principle teaches that the ability to make personal use of a copy is implicit in its purchase. For digital works, use and copying are deeply intertwined. Owners of lawful copies are best positioned to assert a privilege to reproduce copies in the course of personal use.[87]

What I propose here is that the exclusive rights of copyright holders should be exhausted vis-à-vis personal property owners of lawful copies, so long as it does not have a substantial adverse effect on the exploitation or potential exploitation of the copyright work or, where applicable, the moral rights of the author. A reference to the source, unless impractical to do so, would be required as a means to provide an adequate balance between the personal property right in the copy and

[83] See Chapter 7: 'The *prima facie* status of all ownership freedoms,' and 'The instrumental justifications of (intellectual) property.'

[84] *Théberge* (n 22).

[85] ibid at paras 31–32, Binnie J for the majority: 'Once an authorized copy of a work is sold to a member of the public, it is generally for the purchaser, not the author, to determine what happens to it. Excessive control by holders of copyrights and other forms of intellectual property may unduly limit the ability of the public domain to incorporate and embellish creative innovation in the long-term interests of society as a whole, or create practical obstacles to proper utilization.'

[86] See Aaron Perzanowski & Jason Schultz, 'Digital Exhaustion' (2011) 58 UCLA L Rev 889, in particular at 913ff, who rely on earlier copyright case law that recognized lawful copy owners with privileges, e.g., rights of repair and renewal, adaptation and modification, display, and performance, to argue in favour of a copyright exhaustion doctrine to be applied to digital copies of copyright works.

[87] ibid at 943.

the exclusive rights in the copyright work. Reference to the source would address some of the moral right concerns attached to the use of the work.[88] Just as personal property in the copy acts as a property-limitation rule on copyright holders' exclusive rights, the constraints set by copyright and moral rights act as legitimate property-limitation rules on the personal property rights of the copy owner. The uses of the personal property right in the copy could be made in a commercial or non-commercial context, the criteria being how the use may affect the exclusive rights of copyright holders as opposed to whether the use falls within a commercial activity or not.[89]

Unlike the other user scenarios explored below,[90] here the copyright holder exercises their distribution right, which creates separateness between the copyright holder and the copy of their work in favour of the user-copy-owner. From then on, any encroachment on the personal property of the user-copy-owner would give them the rights to make uses of the work as proposed here, not mere privileges.[91]

By way of illustration, making multiple copies and marking and editing the copies for personal use and convenience with no performance in public or communication to the public would fall within the personal property rights of the user-copy-owner. The user-copy-owner would be entitled to transfer title to one copy of the work (i.e., not more than was received).

Communicating the work to the public by telecommunication or distributing the exact same copy to the public would not fall under that personal property right, unless those acts were to be done through a platform providing a lawful mechanism of proper remuneration to copyright holders. Otherwise, those acts would interfere with the (potential) exploitation of the copyright work. Communicating to the public or performing in public substantial parts of the work may be allowed, within the limits set above for user-copy-owners.

The fair use doctrine may cover to a large extent the user-copy-owner right outlined here.[92] The fair dealing framework, delineated by a list of specific purposes (e.g., private study, news reporting, education, parody) would not.[93] The important distinction, however, is that under the user-copy-owner rights that I propose here, the personal property in the copy is the legal foundation of their user-copy-owner's rights, unlike in a fair use or fair dealing analysis, where the personal property in the copy of the work is not a relevant factor.

One criticism on the user-copy-owner rights that I propose here might be: how to determine that a contemplated use will have a substantial adverse effect on the exploitation or potential exploitation of the copyright work? Given diametrically

[88] More specifically, the right of attribution of the author. Other moral rights include the right to the integrity of the work. See e.g., *Canada CA* (n 12) s 14.1.

[89] ibid s 29.21. Non-commercial user-generated content exception to copyright infringement, sets similar parameters, with the important distinction that it requires the acts to be done solely for non-commercial purposes.

[90] See below: 'Services users' and 'Public-space-users'. In the majority of cases, copyright holders do not exercise their exclusive distribution right as they make their works available to users.

[91] See discussion below in this part.

[92] 17 USC § 107.

[93] See e.g., *Canada CA* (n 12) ss 29–29.2.

opposed views on what copyright holder entitlements should be, and the relative elasticity of what 'substantial adverse effect' would mean as a result thereof,[94] we may be back to square one in relation to our search for a greater recognition and substantiation of copyright user rights. The short answer to this legitimate criticism is that a substantial adverse effect analysis that gives more weight to the personal property of users will also need to break with the tendency to set users' interests against copyright holders' interests, and see more commonality between the two.[95] We can no longer afford a knee-jerk reaction that uses of a work should fall *a priori* within the exclusive domain and control of copyright holders when it does not support or worse runs against the core objectives and function of copyright.[96]

Recognizing the effects of copy ownership through the broader application of the doctrine of copyright exhaustion presented here has many advantages. It would allow copyright user rights to evolve with technological developments and social norms, in keeping with the changes to the scope of copyright holders' exclusive rights. It would constrain (although not completely) the unsatisfactory piecemeal regulatory trend of continually adding exceptions to copyright infringement analyzed in Chapter 2. Last, the rights of the user-copy-owners proposed here would calibrate copyright vis-à-vis the competing personal property of copy owners, and weaken arguments that TPM regimes are unconstitutional as *ultra vires* of the relevant legislative powers regulating copyright (in some federated states, on the basis that TPMs would encroach upon the powers of another level of legislative power).[97]

Preferably, the right of user-copy-owners proposed here should be explicitly spelled out in the relevant copyright legislation, and be accompanied by a presumption that the right cannot be waived either through contract or by the *de facto* application of TPMs. User-copy-owners would have the right to enforce this right against copyright holders that block its exercise (e.g., through TPMs), taking into account the physical limitations of the embodiment of the work and the normal usage that users can reasonably expect from certain works as opposed to others. Here, various regulatory models would be available, including a combination of the following: a direct remedy against the copyright holder, an administrative body facilitating the exercise of those user rights, or the non-enforceability of TPMs that do not comply with the user-copy-owner right.[98]

In the alternative, limiting the user-copy-owner to a privilege, for example, by a presumption that contractual restrictions or technological protection measures that go against user-copy-owners' privilege are unenforceable (as opposed to imposing a positive obligation on copyright holders to remove the obstacle impeaching the

[94] See Chapter 2: 'Exceptions to copyright infringement and international obligations' and a similar critique of the three-step test in international intellectual property law.

[95] See Chapter 7: 'Incentive for the creation and dissemination of works' and 'Natural property rights in the fruits of one's labour.'

[96] ibid.

[97] See Chapter 6: 'The constitutionality of technological protection measures.'

[98] See Chapter 3: 'User claims and remedies in copyright law.'

lawful use) would be a partial solution for user-copy-owners. It would make the personal property rights of legitimate copy owners weaker by leaving the burden on user-copy-owners to free the work of any obstacles limiting its lawful use.

User-copy-owners should be entitled to the strongest form of copyright user rights, compared to any other right or mechanism in place for any other copyright users. This is a consequence of the exercise of the exclusive distribution right that takes place when users become owners of copies of works, and of the application of the guiding principle of a greater cohesion between copyright law and private and public law, coupled with the need to adjust the balance in copyright law.[99]

Stronger personal property rights for user-copy-owners are no panacea for the shortcomings of the law of copyright users. As copyright works are increasingly experienced through services, and less as individualized copies enjoyed autonomously by users, the proper articulation of copyright user rights necessitates paying close attention to service users.

## Service users

Users experience copyright works increasingly through services that, in many instances, will engender different expectations than those in relation to the copy of a copyright work they own. There is a wide range of service users and scenarios that raise distinct user issues. For example, free content-sharing web platforms[100] operate under different rules than services allowing the streaming of books, films, or music, recording for later viewing of broadcasts, such services providing a substitute to individualized copies of copyright works acquired with or without a physical embodiment. And then there are service users who engage with physical embodiments of copyright works, for example, as visitors at a museum looking at sculptures or paintings. For the purposes of our discussion, there will be a particular emphasis on those services that provide an alternative to the physical distribution of copyright works (such as streaming platforms), to contrast such service offerings with the situation of user-copy-owners,[101] hopefully not at the expense of keeping sight of a broader landscape of service users.

Unlike in the case of user-copy-owners, in most cases involving service users, copyright holders do not exercise their exclusive distribution right,[102] but rather their exclusive right to display, perform, or communicate to the public by telecommunication. In contrast to public-space-users discussed below,[103] service users

[99] See above: 'Cohesion between copyright law, private law, and public law' and 'Adjusting the balance.'

[100] E.g., Instagram, described on its website as 'a community of more than 500 million who capture and share the world's moments on the service,' online: <https://www.instagram.com/about/us/> accessed 4 February 2017.

[101] See above 'user-copy-owners'.

[102] In some jurisdictions, rental of a copy of a copyright works falls under the exclusive distribution right (see e.g., 17 USC § 106(3)) and to the extent that a rental is predominantly a service agreement, lessees would fall under the present category of 'service users'.

[103] See below: 'Public-space-users'.

have a contractual relationship with the copyright holder or provider that grants them access to copyright works (e.g., an Internet streaming service, a content-sharing web platform, a library loan, a museum with works of art) and that may subject users to terms of use.

Watching a movie in a theatre, viewing art in a museum, or streaming a film or music online usually occurs through the provision of a service (as opposed to the provision of goods). There is no autonomous control over a copy of the copyright work. In those scenarios, the user expectations generally differ from the ones they have in relation to a book or musical recording they own (with or without a physical embodiment), with some exceptions where the line may be blurrier.[104] The physical distance between the user and the work, either real (the space between the seat at the theatre and the screen) or artificially created (TPMs applied to online streaming services), limits the user's choices and capacity to perform certain acts (copying, uploading, sharing, modifying). Also, absent autonomous powers and privileges on an individualized copy of the work, the service users should not expect to have powers to transfer title to the copy of the work they are experiencing. This settles issues on the application of the first sale or exhaustion doctrine. Of course, a service user may have the ability to assign their streaming services agreement to another party, which is a different matter than transferring title to the copy of a copyright work.

Technological environments surrounding works accessed through a service will confer different powers to users and hence create different expectations. Users watching a movie in a theatre have different expectations than those of users watching the same movie via a broadcast or through a streaming service provider. In the case of a movie that is broadcast, time- and place-shifting technologies allow users to make a copy for later viewing. In the case of a streaming service, the line between the autonomous powers and privileges the user has as a service user and as the owner of a copy they lawfully download may be blurrier than when contrasting streaming services with watching the same movie in a theatre.

How should the law factor in the different property, contract, and user expectations between service users and copy owners, when mapping copyright user rights? Is a stark distinction between the rights of user-copy-owners and service users, on the basis of the personal property rights of copy owners, justified? As users increasingly experience works through services, would conferring greater rights to user-copy-owners than to service users accelerate the trend of service offerings by creating an incentive for copyright holders to move away from the sale of individualized copies of their works? Would a clear differentiation between user-copy-owners and service users tilt the balance too far in favour of copyright holders and weaken the regulatory design for copyright user rights proposed here?

Giving the attention to the property rights that copy owners deserve necessarily leads to distinguishing between user-copy-owners and service users. The broader application of copyright exhaustion proposed above for user-copy-owners, that is,

[104] See discussion further below in this section.

beyond the exclusive distribution right, would not be applicable to service users, and similarly in relation to the power to transfer title to the copy. On a practical level, service users will often experience copyright works with physical limitations different from the ones of user-copy-owners. This said, there will be instances where the line will be finer and the expectations similar between user-copy-owners and service users, for example, user-copy-owners downloading a playlist of music versus service users having an on-demand streaming access to musical recordings. An attentive redesign of copyright user rights will need to factor in these different expectations, as the rights will often dictate different social norms.

Because of the differences between user-copy-owners and service users, the legal and normative bases for articulating service user rights or privileges will need to be adapted accordingly. In the absence of personal property rights to the copy of the work, the instrumental justification of copyright law to promote the creation and dissemination of works,[105] together with arguments based on fair commercial practices (especially in standard terms of use environments),[106] would provide foundations on which to build the contours of service-user rights.

Conferring service users a privilege to perform any acts that do not have a substantial adverse effect on the (potential) exploitation of the copyright work, and with the moral rights of the author, with reference to the source where applicable,[107] accompanied by a presumption that such privilege cannot be waived, would take into account the inherent distance that prevails between the service user and the copy of the work. Unlike the rights proposed above for user-copy-owners, the privilege conferred on service users would not impose a blanket positive obligation on copyright holders to grant access beyond the practical limits and expectations of the service through which users experience the work, while at the same time it would allow users to perform acts that do not have substantial adverse effects on the exploitation of the work or with moral rights. To this presumptively non-waivable privilege, a procedure mediated by an administrative body to facilitate the access by service users to exceptions to copyright infringement relevant to the service they use[108] would calibrate the effects of near absolute control that copyright holders or their distributors may have when works are accessed through the service they provide. Copyright holders' obligation to facilitate service users' access to the benefit of exceptions to copyright infringement would take into account the physical limitations of the service and the normal usage that users can reasonably expect from the service.

The presumptively non-waivable service-user privilege proposed here to perform any acts that do not have substantial adverse consequences on the exploitation of

[105] See Chapter 7: 'Incentive for the creation and dissemination of works.'

[106] See Chapter 3: 'User claims and remedies against restricted uses of copyright works as a breach of contract, sale of goods, or consumer law' and 'User claims against restricted uses of copyright works for breach of obligation of good faith or in tort.'

[107] Similar to the limitations proposed in relation to the rights of user-copy-owners: see above 'User-copy-owners'.

[108] See Chapter 3: 'User claims and remedies in copyright law.'

the copyright work and with moral rights would bring the respective rights of copyright holders and service users in closer alignment with the instrumental objective of copyright to encourage the creation and dissemination of works.[109] Failing the implementation of the service-user privilege proposed here, there should, at a minimum, be a presumption that exceptions to copyright infringement available to service users cannot be waived.[110] The presumption of non-waiver would provide some legal certainty to an obscure area of law,[111] but would fall short of recognizing the interests that service users deserve in accordance with the objectives of copyright.[112]

The broader horizon of service users subject to contractual terms of use includes users of content-sharing platforms. The difference from the other service users contemplated so far is that the copyright works are created by and made available in large part from other individual users (as opposed to copyright work publishers or distributors commercializing their works) and often with no immediate intent of commercial gain. Here, the platform providers (e.g., Facebook, YouTube, Instagram) typically require users to comply with copyright laws, and the providers distance themselves from possible copyright infringements by their platform users.[113] At the same time, content-sharing-platform providers design and control the architecture of the service, which will dictate to a large extent how users access each other's works.[114]

Service users are able to share, comment on, and create derivative works from the works of others through new web applications and platforms.[115] Such activities are at the core of copyright instrumentalist raison d'être to encourage the creation and dissemination of works and to enable a dialogue between creators and users that stimulates the creation of other works.[116] While some may raise an eyebrow at the view that content-sharing web platforms promote the core objectives of copyright law, given the high volume of works with a low level of originality that are shared on these platforms[117] (hence a lower level of copyright protection afforded to these works), the widespread appeal of content-sharing platforms for users and their level of engagement with the copyright works of others are undeniable.[118]

[109] See Chapter 7: 'Incentive for the creation and dissemination of works.'

[110] See above: 'Steering freedom of contract toward the objectives of copyright law.'

[111] See Chapter 2: 'May exceptions to copyright infringement be waived by contract?'

[112] See Chapter 7: 'Incentive for the creation and dissemination of works.'

[113] See e.g., Instagram, 'Terms of use,' online: <https://www.instagram.com> accessed 4 February 2017.

[114] ibid.

[115] Examples of hugely popular platforms in recent years: Facebook, online: <www.facebook.com> accessed 4 February 2017; Instagram, online: <https://www.instagram.com/?hl=en> accessed 4 February 2017; Snapchat, online: <https://www.snapchat.com/> accessed 4 February 2017.

[116] See Chapter 7: 'Instrumental justifications of (intellectual) property.'

[117] E.g., the innumerable selfies and other photos of the mundanities of everyday life.

[118] YouTube has over 1 billion users: YouTube, Statistics, online <https://www.youtube.com/press.html> accessed 4 February 2017; as of August 2016, Instagram had over 500 million users: Instagram, News room, online: <https://www.instagram.com/press/?hl=en> accessed 8 September 2016; as of June 2016, daily average users of Facebook was 1.13 billion: Facebook, company info, online: <http://newsroom.fb.com/company-info/> accessed 4 February 2017.

The copyright and moral rights issues that service users of content-sharing platforms face, may have less to do with restricted uses of copyright works and more to do with unwarranted uses of the photos, literary works, and music samples that service users as authors, make available to other platform users. By agreeing to use the platform, users typically grant to platform providers a licence to perform a broad range of uses worldwide of the works users make available.[119] As between platform users, the famous US appropriation artist Prince's exhibition of enlarged screenshots of photos posted on Instagram by other users without their knowledge or consent, and sold to the public at a high price, created a stir on social media.[120] While Prince's use of the Instagram photos was possibly contrary to the terms of use of the Instagram platform, the use would comply with copyright law if the use was fair (a defence that Prince has successfully invoked in previous cases of appropriation art),[121] and raises the question whether users of the Instagram platform should have the benefit of exceptions to copyright infringement such as fair use, regardless of the terms of use.[122] I argued above that there should be a presumption that exceptions to copyright infringement cannot be waived.[123] Service users of content-sharing platforms face other important issues that go above and beyond copyright and the scope of this chapter: privacy, possible misappropriation of personality,[124] and lack of transparency regarding the (commercial) uses by the platform operators of the copyright works or data that service users make available on the content-sharing platform, are among the other legal issues that service users of content-sharing platforms may face.

The presumptively non-waivable service-user privilege proposed here, coupled with an administrative body facilitating access to the benefit of applicable exceptions to copyright infringement would clarify the rules of engagement between content-sharing platform users and provide them a level of access that supports the core objective of copyright law to encourage the creation and dissemination of works.

## Public-space-users

Users experience copyright works in public spaces in myriad ways. For the purposes of our discussion, I refer here to copyright works that are not in the public domain and that are freely accessible through the Internet (e.g., blog posts, photographs) or in public spaces (e.g., architectural works, sculptures, Banksy's public art) and not subject to a commercial transaction between the user and the copyright holder

[119] Instagram terms of use (n 113).

[120] See Jessica Contrera, 'A Reminder that your Instagram Photos aren't Really Yours: Someone Else Can Sell Them for $90,000,' *The Washington Post*, 25 May 2015, online: <https://www.washingtonpost.com/news/arts-and-entertainment/wp/2015/05/25/a-reminder-that-your-instagram-photos-arent-really-yours-someone-else-can-sell-them-for-90000/> accessed 4 February 2017.

[121] *Cariou v Prince*, 714 F (3d) 694 (2d Cir 2013).

[122] See Chapter 2: 'May exceptions to copyright infringement be waived by contract?'

[123] See above: 'Steering freedom of contract toward the objectives of copyright law.'

[124] See e.g., *Fraley v Facebook Inc*, 830 F Supp (2d) 785 (ND Cal 2011).

or distributor. We are working under the assumption (qualified by a rebuttable presumption as discussed further below) that the copyright holder has authorized making their work available to the public. Similarly to service-users, but unlike user-copy-owners, copyright holders do not exercise their exclusive distribution right, the trigger that would otherwise separate the copyright holder from the copy of their work in favour of the user-copy-owner.

There is no user property right conflicting with the exclusive rights of copyright holders in this scenario. This could be an *a priori* signal to give carte blanche to copyright holders. A re-engineered balance of copyright attuned to social norms needs to take this category of users seriously: public-space-users are natural stewards in the pollination of core objectives of copyright law to encourage the creation and dissemination of works. Making works available to the public creates expectations for users. Respect for social norms, legal certainty, and the promotion of economic efficiency involves taking these expectations into consideration.

The rebuttable presumption of an implied licence to use the work in any manner that does not conflict with the commercial exploitation of the copyright work and that does not infringe moral rights would respect the legitimate interests of copyright holders, while taking into account reasonable user expectations. Here, it may be pointed out that the limit of not interfering with the commercial exploitation of the work would be at odds with the fact that innumerable copyright works are made available to the public (and that are the subject of the public-space-user interests discussed here), with no commercial exploitation in mind or in sight. At the same time, the ability to choose whether, how, and when to commercialize a copyright work is one of the defining characteristics of the exclusive rights conferred by copyright. The decision not to operate in the commercial sphere at any given moment in time should not mean relinquishing the ability to do so, or letting anyone other than the copyright holder take free advantage of that unoccupied field. Hence, the non-interference with the commercial exploitation of the work would set a proper limit to the implied licence.

The public-space-user could benefit from the presumption of an implied licence subject to making reference to the source of the work, unless impractical to do so. The presumption would be rebuttable by a notice to the contrary, by the presence of TPMs, or by indications that the copyright work was not lawfully made available to the public.

Through the presumption of an implied licence, the public-space-user would not have a positive user right of access that could form the basis of a legal claim. Given the conditions of free and open access under which the copyright work is made accessible to users, it would seem that imposing a positive obligation to grant access to copyright holders might tilt the balance too far in favour of users. The presumption of an implied licence proposed here would give public-space-users the privilege of performing all such uses, provided that they fall within the limits of the implied licence set out here, and would serve as the basis of a defence to a copyright infringement claim.

## From User Property to User Privileges

From goods to services, from physical objects to immaterial works, from user-copy-owners to public-space-users, from personal property to copyright exceptions and to contracts, and from private law to public law, copyright users simultaneously access copyright works through these different planes, which shape their rights to a large extent. Defining what copyright user rights are and should be means paying close attention to the context in which those rights arise, whether grounded in property or contracts or whether there is an implied licence, and by demonstrating how they further the core objectives of copyright.

# One Last Word

Motion pictures have not displaced live theatre performances. Television did not displace the radio. Podcasts have not replaced broadcasts. E-shopping has not replaced brick and mortar stores. E-books have not eliminated hard cover and soft cover books and bookshops. Online music and films have not yet completely displaced CDs and DVDs. Even vinyl records are making a comeback after a prolonged absence. These literary, dramatic, musical, and artistic expressions and their various means of dissemination will, in varying proportions and for indefinite periods of time, continue to co-exist side by side.

As much as an increasingly digitized world has revolutionized the way copyright holders make their works available, and how users experience them, immaterial copyright works run alongside architectural works, visual arts embodied in sculptures, canvas, and other physical objects, and tattoo art adorning human flesh. New technologies have not wiped out traditional methods and mediums. They serve different functions, engage our senses, mind, and intellect differently, and attract different publics.

The challenge for copyright and other areas of law has been, and will continue to be, how to adequately regulate the old alongside new forms of expression and their vehicles as they continue to evolve. How is the law to adapt to this constant state of flux and retain its relevancy and legitimacy? How is it to continually address the competing interests of copyright holders, users, and the public?

Maintaining cohesion between copyright law and private and public law, away from exceptionalism, is, it seems, critical in light of the eclectic type of works, shapes, and vehicles of dissemination that copyright law regulates, some more traditional, and some emanating from constant technological advancement.

An approach that transcends the (non)shape of things, that rethinks preconceived notions of tangibility and intangibility and their effects, that applies technological neutrality as a principle of statutory interpretation, is what I proposed in this book. This avenue favours an ontological and purposed-based approach to law in the face of ever-changing technological environments and embraces the old and the new.

Some things change, but do they really? And some things stay the same.

The analytical framework that I presented in this book to define the contours of the law of copyright users' private rights, will find application in other areas of law. The proposed framework promotes a de-compartmentalization between various bodies of law including copyright law—a relatively recent area of law compared to property and contract law. The possible application 'in silo' of newer bodies of law, at the expense of a more integrated approach with other areas of law, is not a phenomenon unique to copyright law. The success of newer regulatory fields of law (or models to address technological changes, e.g., the introduction of technological protection measures in copyright law) depends in part on ensuring greater cohesion of those newer fields of law with private law and public law.

The dematerialization of e-products and, generally, of how information is transmitted and shared obscures the application of concepts of private law, for example, goods, ownership, and sales, in areas including cloud computing, state surveillance, taxation, and privacy law, to name only a few. The analytical framework to distinguish ownership of immaterial goods from the provision of a service is one example among others of a possible application of the concepts developed in this book to these other fields of law.

# *Bibliography*


Akerlof, George K. 'The Market for "Lemons": Quality Uncertainty and the Market Mechanism' (1970) 84 The Quarterly Journal of Economics 488.

Akins, Caitlin J. 'Conversion of Digital Property: Protecting Consumers in the Age of Technology' (2010) 23 Loy Consumer L Rev 215.

Alexander, Gregory S. 'The Social-Obligation Norm in American Property Law' (2008–2009) 94 Cornell L Rev 745.

Alexander, Gregory S et al. 'A Statement of Progressive Property' (2008–2009) 94 Cornell L Rev 743.

Amir, On & Orly Lobel. 'Stumble, Predict, Nudge: How Behavioural Economics Informs Law and Policy', 108 Colum L Rev 2098, book review of Richard H Thaler & Cass R Sunstein, *Nudge: Improving Decisions About Health, Wealth, and Happiness* (New Haven, CT: Yale University Press, 2008), and of Dane Ariely, *Predictably Irrational: The Hidden Forces That Shape Our Decisions* (NY: HarperCollins, 2008).

Ariely, Dan, *Predictably Irrational, The Hidden Forces That Shape Our Decisions* (New York: Harper Collins, 2009).

Auferderheide, Patricia & Peter Jaszi, *Reclaiming Fair Use* (Chicago: Chicago University Press, 2013).

Austin, Lisa. 'Person, Place, or Thing? Property and the Structuring of Social Relations' (2010) 60 UTLJ 445.

Bailey, Jane. 'Deflating the Michelin Man: Protecting Users' Rights in the Canadian Copyright Reform Process' in Michael Geist, ed, *In the Public Interest: The Future of Canadian Copyright Law* (Toronto: Irwin Law, 2005) 125.

Bakardjieva Engelbrekt, Antonina. 'Accommodating the Interests of the Copyright Consumer: New Institutional Dynamics in the Wake of the Infosoc Directive' in Antonina Bakardjieva Engelbrekt et al, eds, *Särtryck ur Festskrift till Marianne Levin* (Norstedts Juridik, 2008) 65.

Bar-Gill, Oren. 'Seduction by Plastic' (2004) 98 Nw U L Rev 1373.

Bar-Gill, Oren & Franco Ferrari. 'Informing Consumers About Themselves' (2010) 3 Erasmus Law Review 93.

Bechtold, Stefan. 'The Present and Future of Digital Rights Management' in E Becker et al, eds, *Digital Rights Management* (Berlin: Springer-Verlag, 2003) 597.

Bell, Abraham & Gideon Parchomovsky. 'A Theory of Property' (2005) 90 Cornell L Rev 531.

Bell, Tom W. 'Fair use vs. Fared use: The Impact of Automated Rights Management on Copyright's Fair Use Doctrine' (1998) 76 NCL Rev 557.

Benabou, Valeri-Laure. 'Pourquoi une œuvre est immatérielle' (2005) n° 1 Lamy Droit de l'immatériel 53.

Benkler, Yochai. 'From Consumers to Users: Shifting the Deeper Structures of Regulation Toward Sustainable Commons and User Access' (2000) 52 Fed Comm LJ 561.

Borghi, Maurizio & Stravoula Karapapa, *Copyright and Mass Digitization* (Oxford: Oxford University Press, 2013).

Bourgoignie, Tierry. 'Characteristics of Consumer Law' (1992) 14 J Consum Policy 293.

Braucher, Jean. '12 Principles for Fair Commerce in Mass-Market Software and Other Digital Products' in Jane K Winn, ed, *Consumer Protection in the Age of the 'Information Economy'* (Aldershot, UK: Ashgate, 2006) 177.

Braucher, Jean. 'Contracting Out of Article 2 Using a "License" Label: A Strategy that Should not Work for Software Products' (2007) 40 Loy LA L Rev 261.

Brennan, Lori. 'Why Article 2 Cannot Apply to Software Transactions' (2000) 38 Duq L Rev 459.

Bridge, Michael, ed, *Benjamin's Sale of Goods*, 8th ed (London: Sweet & Maxwell, 2010).

Brownsword, Roger. 'Regulating Transactions: Good Faith and Fair Dealing' in Geraint Howells & Reiner Schulze, eds, *Modernising and Harmonising Consumer Contract Law* (Munich: Sellier European Law, 2009).

Burk, Dan L. 'Copyright and the New Materialism' in Jessica C. Lai & Antoinette Maget, eds, *Intellectual Property and Access to Im/Material Goods* (Cheltenham, UK: Edward Elgar, 2016) 44.

Burk, Dan L. & Julie, E. Cohen, 'Fair Use Infrastructure for Rights Management Systems' (2001) 15 Harv JL & Tech 41.

Burrell, Robert & Allison Coleman, *Copyright Exceptions: The Digital Impact* (Cambridge, UK: Cambridge University Press, 2005).

Cameron, Alex & Robert Tomkowicz. 'Competition Policy and Canada's New Breed of Copyright Law' (2007) 52 McGill LJ 291.

Carver, Brian W. 'Why License Agreements do not Control Copy Ownership: First Sales and Essential Copies' (2010) 25 BTLJ 1887.

Chandra, Rashree, *Knowledge as Property* (New Delhi: Oxford University Press, 2010).

Chapdelaine, Pascale. 'Living in the Shadow of the Intangible, the Nature of the Copy of a Copyrighted Work' Part One (2010) 23 IPJ 83.

Chapdelaine, Pascale. 'Living in the Shadow of the Intangible, the Nature of the Copy of a Copyrighted Work' Part Two (2011) 23 IPJ 205.

Chapdelaine, Pascale. 'The Ambiguous Nature of Copyright Users' Rights' (2013) 26 IPJ 1.

Chapdelaine, Pascale, *Copyright Consumers' Bargain, Defining the Rights to Commercial Copies of Copyright Works* (Doctor of Philosophy Thesis, York University Graduate Program in Law: Osgoode Hall Law School Library, 2013).

Chapdelaine, Pascale. 'The Property Attributes of Copyright' (2014) 10 Buff Intell Prop LJ 34.

Chapdelaine, Pascale. 'The Undue Reliance on Physical Objects in the Regulation of Information Products' (2015) 20 J Tech L & Pol'y 65.

Childs, Frank Hall, *Principles of the Law of Personal Property* (Chicago: Callaghan, 1914).

Christie, Andrew F. 'Maximising Permissible Exceptions to Intellectual Property Rights' in Annette Kur & Vytautas Mizaras, eds, *The Structure of Intellectual Property Law: Can One Size Fit All?* (Cheltenham, UK: Edward Elgar, 2011) 121.

Christou, Richard, *International Agency, Distribution & Licensing Agreements*, 6th ed (London: Sweet & Maxwell, 2011).

Cobb, Kristin. 'The Implications of Licensing Agreements and the First Sale Doctrine on US and EU Secondary Markets for Digital Goods' (2014) 24 Duke J Comp & Intl L 529.

Cohen Jehoram, Herman. 'Prohibition of Parallel Imports Through Intellectual Property Rights' (1999) 30 Intl Rev of Intellectual Property and Competition L 495.

Cohen, Julie E. 'A Right to Read Anonymously: A Closer Look at "Copyright Management" in Cyberspace' (1997) 28 Conn L Rev 981.

Cohen, Julie E. 'Copyright and the Jurisprudence of Self-Help' (1998) 13 BTLJ 1089.

Cohen, Julie E. 'Overcoming Property: Does Copyright Trump Privacy?' (2002) U Ill JL Tech & Pol'y 375.

Cohen, Julie E. 'The Place of the User in Copyright Law' (2005) 74 Fordham L R 347.

Cohen, Julie E. 'Copyright as Property in the Post-Industrial Economy: A Research Agenda' (2011) Wis L Rev 141.

Collins, Hugh, *Regulating Contracts* (Oxford: Oxford University Press, 1999).

Costanza, Nicholas. 'Digital Music Garage Sale: An Analysis of Capitol Records LLC v ReDigi Inc and a Proposal for Legislative Reform in Copyright Enabling a Secondary Market for Digital Music' (2015) 37 Hastings Comm & Ent LJ 135.

Craig, Carys J. 'Locke, Labour and Limiting the Author's Right: A Warning Against a Lockean Approach to Copyright Law' (2002) 28 Queen's LJ 1.

Craig, Carys J. 'The Changing Face of Fair Dealing in Canadian Copyright Law: A Proposal for Legislative Reform' in Michael Geist, ed, *In the Public Interest: The Future of Canadian Copyright Law* (Toronto: Irwin Law, 2005) 437.

Craig, Carys J. 'Putting the Community in Communication: Dissolving the Conflict between Freedom of Expression and Copyright' (2006) 56 UTLJ 75.

Craig, Carys J. 'Locking Out Lawful Users: Fair Dealing and Anti-Circumvention in Bill C-32' in Michael Geist, ed, *From Radical Extremism to Balanced Copyright: Canadian Copyright and the Digital Agenda* (Irwin Law: Toronto, 2010) 177.

Craig, Carys J, *Copyright, Communication and Culture, Towards a Relational Theory of Copyright Law* (Cheltenham, UK: Edward Elgar, 2011).

Cseres, Katlin Judith, *Competition Law and Consumer Protection* (The Hague: Kluwer Law International, 2005).

Dagan, Hanoch. 'Property and the Public Domain' (2006) 18 Yale JL & Human 84.

Dagan, Hanoch, *Property Values and Institutions* (Oxford: Oxford University Press, 2011).

D'Agostino, Giuseppina. 'Fair Dealing After CCH' (study funded by Canadian Heritage, Copyright Policy Branch, 2007), online: <http://www.pch.gc.ca/pc-ch/org/sectr/ac-ca/pda-cpb/publctn/cch-2007/index-eng.cfm>.

D'Agostino, Giuseppina. 'Healing Fair Dealing? A Comparative Copyright Analysis of Canadian Fair Dealing to UK Fair Dealing and US Fair Use' (2008) 53 McGill LJ 309, online: <http://papers.ssrn.com/sol3/cf_dev/AbsByAuth.cfm?per_id=688965>.

D'Agostino, Giuseppina, *Copyright, Contracts, Creators, New Media, New Rules* (Cheltenham, UK: Edward Elgar, 2010).

D'Agostino, Giuseppina. 'Copyright Exceptions and Limitations and Copyright Board of Canada' in ALAI Canada, ed, *The Copyright Board of Canada: Bridging Law and Economics for Twenty Years* (Cowansville, Que: Yvon Blais, 2011) 195.

de Beer, Jeremy F. 'Locks & Levies' (2006) 84 Denv UL Rev 143.

de Beer, Jeremy F. 'Copyrights, Federalism, and the Constitutionality of Canada's Private Copying Levy' (2006) 51 McGill LJ 735.

de Beer, Jeremy F & Robert Tomkowicz. 'Exhaustion of Intellectual Property Rights in Canada' (2009) 25 CIPR 3.

Derclaye, Estelle. 'Copyright Contracts, Public Policy and Antitrust' in Christopher Heath & Kung-Chung Liu, eds, *Copyright Law and the Information Society in Asia*, IIC Studies (Oxford: Hart Publishing, 2006) 167.

De Werra, Jacques. 'Moving Beyond the Conflict between Freedom of Contract and Copyright Policies: In Search of a New Global Policy for On-line Information Licensing Transactions' (2003) 25 Colum JL & Arts 239.

Dinwoodie, Graeme B. 'The International Intellectual Property System: Treaties, Norms, National Courts and Private Ordering' in Daniel Gervais, ed, *Intellectual Property, Trade and Development: Strategies to Optimize Economic Development in a TRIPS Plus Era* (Oxford: Oxford University Press, 2007) 61.

Dinwoodie, Graeme B & Rochelle C Dreyfuss. 'Designing a Global Intellectual Property System Responsive to Change: the WTO, WIPO, and Beyond' (2009) 46 Hous L Rev 1187.

Dinwoodie, Graeme B & Rochelle C Dreyfuss, *A Neofederalist Vision of TRIPS: The Resilience of the International Intellectual Property Regime* (Oxford: Oxford University Press, 2012).

Doern, G Bruce & Markus Sharaput, *Canadian Intellectual Property, The Politics of Innovating Institutions and Interests* (Toronto: University of Toronto Press, 2000).

Drahos, Peter, *A Philosophy of Intellectual Property* (Aldershot, UK: Ashgate, 1996).

Drassinower, Abraham. 'A Rights-Based View of the Idea/Expression Dichotomy in Copyright Law' (2003) 16 Can JL & Jur 3.

Drassinower, Abraham. 'Taking User Rights Seriously' in Michael Geist, ed, *In the Public Interest: The Future of Canadian Copyright Law* (Toronto: Irwin Law, 2005) 462.

Drassinower, Abraham. 'From Distribution to Dialogue: Remarks on the Concept of Balance in Copyright Law' (2009) 34 J Corp L 991.

Drassinower, Abraham. 'Exceptions Properly So-called' in Ysolde Gendreau & Abraham Drassinower, eds, *Langues et droit d'auteur/Language and Copyright* (Cowansville, Quebec: Yvon Blais, 2009) 217.

Drassinower, Abraham, *What's Wrong with Copying?* (Cambridge, MA: Harvard University Press 2015).

Dreier, Thomas. 'Balancing Proprietary and Public Domain Interests: Inside or Outside of Proprietary Rights?' in Rochelle Cooper Dreyfuss, Diane Leenheer Zimmerman, & Harry First, eds, *Expanding the Boundaries of Intellectual Property: Innovation Policy for the Knowledge Society* (Oxford: Oxford University Press, 2001) 295.

Duggan, Anthony. 'Consumer Credit Redux' (2010) 60 UTLJ 687.

Dusollier, Séverine. 'Les nouvelles dispositions belges en matière de protection technique des œuvres' (2005) *Auteurs & Médias* 532.

Dusollier, Séverine, *Droit d'auteur et protection des oeuvres dans l'univers numérique*, 2nd ed (Bruxelles: Larcier, 2007).

Easterbrook, Frank H. 'Intellectual Property is Still Property' (1990) 13 Harv JL & Pub Pol'y 108.

Edwards, Jeffrey, *La garantie de qualité du vendeur en droit québécois* (Montreal: Wilson et Lafleur, 1998).

Efroni, Zohar, *Access-Right: The Future of Digital Copyright Law* (Oxford: Oxford University Press, 2010).

Elkin-Koren, Niva. 'A Public-Regarding Approach to Contracting over Copyrights' in R Cooper Dreyfuss, D Leenheer Zimmerman, & H First, eds, *Expanding the Boundaries of Intellectual Property: Innovation Policy for the Knowledge Society* (Oxford: Oxford University Press, 2001) 191.

Elkin-Koren, Niva. 'Making Room for Consumers under the DMCA' (2007) 22 BTLJ 1119.

Endicott, Timothy & Michael Spence. 'Vagueness in the Scope of Copyright' (2005) 121 Law Q Rev 657.

Epstein, Richard A. 'Liberty versus Property? Cracks in the Foundations of Copyright Law' (2005) 42 San Diego L Rev 1.

Epstein, Richard A. 'Behavioral Economics: Human Errors and Market Corrections' (2006) 73 U Chicago L Rev 111.

Epstein, Richard A. 'Contract, Not Regulation: UCITA and High-Tech Consumers Meet Their Consumer Protection Critics' in Jane K Winn, ed, *Consumer Protection in the Age of the 'Information Economy'* (Aldershot, UK: Ashgate, 2006) 205.

Epstein, Richard A. 'Exchange, The Neoclassical Economics of Consumer Contracts' (2008) 92 Minn L Rev 803.

Epstein, Richard A. 'The Disintegration of Intellectual Property? A Classical Liberal Response to a Premature Obituary' (2010) 62 Stan L Rev 455.

Epstein, Richard A. 'What is So Special about Intangible Property? The Case for Intelligent Carryovers' (2010). New York University Law and Economics Working Papers. Paper 243, online: <http://lsr.nellco.org/nyu_lewp/243>.

Evans, Gail E. 'Opportunity Costs of Globalizing Information Licenses: Embedding Consumer Rights within the Legislative Framework for Information Contracts' (1999) 10 Fordham IP Media & Ent LJ 267.

Fagundes, David. 'Property Rhetoric and the Public Domain' (2010) 94 Minn L Rev 652.

Fairfield, Joshua AT. 'Virtual Property' (2005) 85 BU L Rev 1047.

Favale, Marcella. 'Fine-tuning European Copyright Law to Strike a Balance between the Rights of Owners and Users' (2008) 33 Eur L Rev 687.

Fitzgerald, Brian F. 'Theoretical Underpinning of Intellectual Property: I am a Pragmatist But Theory is my Rhetoric' (2003) 16 Can JL & Jur 179.

Fox, Harold G, *The Canadian Law of Copyright* (Toronto: University of Toronto Press, 1944).

Frankel, Susy & Daniel Gervais, *The Evolution of and Equilibrium of Copyright in the Digital Age* (Cambridge, UK: Cambridge University Press, 2014).

Fridman, Gerald HL, *Sale of Goods in Canada*, 5th ed (Toronto: Thomson Carswell, 2004).

Geiger, Christophe. 'The Three-step Test, a Threat to a Balanced Copyright Law' (2006) 37 Intl R for Intellectual Property and Competition L 683.

Geiger, Christophe. 'The Answer to the Machine Should Not be the Machine: Safeguarding the Private Copy Exception in the Digital Environment' (2009) 30 Eur IP Rev 121.

Geiger, Christophe. 'Exploring the Flexibilities of the TRIPS Agreement's Provisions on Limitations and Exceptions' in Annette Kur & Vytautas Mizaras, eds, *The Structure of Intellectual Property Law: Can One Size Fit All?* (Cheltenham, UK: Edward Elgar, 2011) 287.

Geiger, Christophe, Reno Hilty, Jonathan Griffiths, & Uma Suthersanen. 'Declaration: A Balanced Interpretation of the "Three-Step Test" in Copyright Law' (2010) 1 JIPITEC 119, online https://www.jipitec.eu/issues/jipitec-1-2-2010/2621.

Gervais, Daniel. 'Canadian Copyright Law Post-CCH' (2004) 18 IPJ 131.

Gervais, Daniel. 'The Price of Social Norms: Towards a Liability Regime for File-Sharing' (2004) 12 J Intell Prop L 39.

Gervais, Daniel. 'Towards a New Core International Copyright Norm: The Reverse Three-step Test' (2005) 9 Marq Intell Prop L Rev 1.

Gervais, Daniel. 'Making Copyright Whole: A Principled Approach to Copyright Exceptions and Limitations' (2008) 5 U Ottawa L & Tech J 1.

Gervais, Daniel. 'A Canadian Copyright Narrative' (2009) 21 IPJ 269.

Gervais, Daniel, *The TRIPS Agreement, Drafting History and Analysis*, 4th ed (UK: Sweet & Maxwell, 2012).

Gervais, Daniel & Elizabeth Judge, *Intellectual Property, the Law in Canada* (Toronto: Carswell, 2005).

Ghidini, Gustavo, *Innovation, Competition and Consumer Welfare in Intellectual Property Law* (Cheltenham, UK: Edward Elgar, 2010).

Ginsburg, Jane C. 'A Tale of Two Copyrights: Literary Property in Revolutionary France and America' (1990) 64 Tul L Rev 991.

Ginsburg, Jane C. 'Authors and Users in Copyright' (1997) 45 J Copyright Soc'y USA 1.

Ginsburg, Jane C. 'Copyright Legislation for the Digital Millennium' (1999) 23 Colum JL & Arts 137.

Ginsburg, Jane C. 'Can Copyright Become User-Friendly? Review: Jessica Litman, Digital Copyright' (2001) 25 Colum JL & Arts 71.

Ginsburg, Jane C. '"The Exclusive Right to Their Writings": Copyright and Control in the Digital Age' (2002) 54 Me L Rev 195.

Ginsburg, Jane C. 'From Having Copies to Experiencing Works: The Development of an Access Right in U.S. Copyright Law' (2003) 50 J Copyright Soc'y USA 113.

Girot, Clarisse, *User Protection in IT Contracts: A comparative study on the protection of the user against defective performance in information technology* (The Hague: Kluwer Law International, 2001).

Goldstein, Paul & P Bernt Hugenholtz, *International Copyright Principles, Law, and Practice*, 2nd ed (Oxford: Oxford University Press, 2010).

Gordon, Wendy J. 'Fair Use as Market Failure: A Structural and Economic Analysis of the *Betamax* Case and Its Predecessors' (1982) 82 Colum L Rev 1600.

Gordon, Wendy J. 'A Property Right in Self-Expression: Equality and Individualism in the Natural Law of Intellectual Property' (1993) 102 Yale LJ 1533.

Gordon, Wendy J. 'Market Failure and Intellectual Property: A Response to Professor Lunney' (2002) 82 BU L Rev 1031.

Gordon, Wendy J. 'Harmless Use: Gleaning from Fields of Copyrighted Works' (2009) 77 Fordham L Rev 2411.

Gordon, Wendy J & Daniel Bahls. 'The Public's Right to Fair Use: Amending Section 107 to Avoid the "Fared Use" Fallacy' (2007) Utah L Rev 619.

Gray, Kevin. 'Property in Thin Air' (1991) 50 Cambridge LJ 252.

Green, Sarah & John Randall, *The Tort of Conversion* (Portland, OR: Hart, 2009).

Grunebaum, James O, *Private Ownership* (London, UK: Routledge & Kegan Paul, 1987).

Guest, Anthony Gordon, ed, *Benjamin's Sale of Goods*, 7th ed (London: Sweet & Maxwell, 2006).

Guibault, Lucie, *Copyright Limitations and Contracts: An analysis of the Contractual Overridability of Limitations on Copyright* (The Hague: Kluwer Law International, 2002).

Guibault, Lucie. 'Accommodating the Needs of iConsumers: Making Sure They Get Their Money's Worth of Digital Entertainment' (2008) 31 J Consum Policy 409.

Guilbault, Lucie & Natali Helberger. 'Copyright Law and Consumer Protection', study carried out for the European Consumer Law Group, ECLG/035/05 (2005), online: <http://www.europeanconsumerlawgroup.org/Content/Default.asp?PageID=488>.

Hadfield, Gillian K, Robert Howse, & Michael J Trebilcock. 'Information–based principles for rethinking consumer protection policy' (1998) 21 J Consum Policy, 131.

Hagen, Gregory R & Nyall Engfield. 'Canadian Copyright Reform: P2P Sharing, Making Available and the Three-Step Test' (2006) 3 U Ottawa L & Tech J 477.

Handa, Sunny, *Copyright Law in Canada* (Markham, Ontario: Butterworth Canada, 2002).

Hansmann, Henry & Reinier Kraakman. 'Property, Contract, and Verification: The Numerus Clausus Problem and the Divisibility of Rights' (2002) 31 J Legal Stud 373.

Harris, James W, *Property and Justice* (Oxford: Clarendon Press, 1996).

Harvard Law Review Note. 'A Justification for Allowing Fragmentation in Copyright' (2011) 124 Har L Rev 1751.

Hazucha, Branislav, Hsiao-Chien Liu, & Toshihide Watabe. 'Copyright, Technological Protection Measures and Their Acceptance by Consumers in Japan' (2013) SERCI, online: <http://www.serci.org/2013/Hazucha-SERCI-2013.pdf>.

Helberger, Natali. 'Making Place for the iConsumer in Consumer Law' (2008) 31 J Consum Policy 385.

Helberger, Natali & P Bernt Hugenholtz. 'No Place Like Home For Making a Copy, Private Copying in European Copyright Law and Consumer Law' (2007) 22 BTLJ 1061.

Helberger, Natali et al. 'Digital Rights Management and Consumer Acceptability: A Multi-Disciplinary Discussion of Consumer Concerns and Expectations' (2004), online: <http://www.indicare.org/tiki-download_file.php?fileId=111>.

Helberger, Natalie et al, *Digital Consumers and the Law* (Alphen aan den Rijn, the Netherlands: Kluwer Law International, 2013).

Helfer, Laurence. 'Regime Shifting: The Trips Agreement and New Dynamics of International Intellectual Property Lawmaking' (2004) 29 Yale J Int'l L 1.

Heller, Michael, *The Gridlock Economy: How Too Much Ownership Wrecks Markets, Stops Innovation, and Costs Lives* (New York: Basic Books, 2008).

Hess, Evan. 'Code-ifying Copyright: an Architectural Solution to Digitally Expanding the First Sale Doctrine' (2013) 81 Fordham L Rev 1965.

Hettinger, Edwin C. 'Justifying Intellectual Property' (1989) 18 Philosophy & Public Affairs, 31.

Hilty, Reto & Sylvie Nérisson. 'Overview of National Reports About "Balancing Copyright"' in Reno Hilty & Sylvie Nérisson, eds, *Balancing Copyright—A Survey of National Approaches* (New York: Springer, 2012) 1.

Hippel, Eric Von, *Democratizing Innovation* (Cambridge, MA: MIT Press, 2005).

Hohfeld, Wesley N. 'Some Fundamental Legal Conceptions as Applied in Judicial Reasoning' (1913) 23 Yale LJ 16.

Hohfeld, Wesley N. 'Fundamental Legal Conceptions as Applied in Judicial Reasoning' (1917) 26 Yale LJ 710.

Honoré, Tony. 'Ownership' in Tony Honoré, ed, *Making Law Bind, Essays Legal and Philosophical* (Oxford: Clarendon Press, 1987) 161.

Horovitz, Bonna Lynn. 'Computer Software as a Good Under the Uniform Commercial Code: Taking a Byte out of the Intangibility Myth' (1985) 65 BUL Rev 129.

Howe, Helena, *Concepts of Property in Intellectual Property Law* (Cambridge, UK: Cambridge University Press, 2013).

Howells, Geraint. 'The Potential and Limits of Consumer Empowerment by Information' (2005) 32 L & Soc'y 349.

Howells, Geraint & Stephen Weatherill, *Consumer Protection Law*, 2nd ed (Aldershot, UK: Ashgate, 2005).

Hugenholtz, Bernt. 'Why the Copyright Directive is Unimportant, and Possibly Invalid' (2000) 11 Eur IP Rev 501.

Hugenholtz, Bernt. 'Copyright and Freedom of Expression in Europe' in RC Dreyfuss, DL Zimmerman, & H First, eds, *Expanding the Boundaries of Intellectual Property: Innovation Policy for the Knowledge Society* (Oxford: Oxford University Press, 2001).

Hugenholtz, P Bernt & Ruth L Okediji. 'Conceiving an International Instrument on Limitations and Exceptions to Copyright', sponsored by the Open Society Institute (OSI) (2008), online: <http://www.opensocietyfoundations.org/reports/conceiving-international-instrument-limitations-and-exceptions-copyright>.

Hughes, Roger T, Susan J Peacock, & Neal Armstrong, *Hughes on Copyright & Industrial Design*, 2nd ed, loose-leaf (Toronto: Lexis Nexis Canada, 2005).

Inesi, Andrew. 'A Theory of De Minimis and a Proposal for its Application in Copyright' (2006) 21 BTLJ 945.

Issacharoff, Samuel & Ian J Samuel. 'The Intitutional Dimension of Consumer Protection' in Fabrizio Cafaggi & Hans W Micklitz, eds, *New Frontiers Of Consumer Protection: The Interplay Between Private and Public Enforcement* (Cambridge, UK: Intersentia, 2009) 47.

Izyumenko, Elena. 'The Freedom of Expression Contours of Copyright in the Digital Era: A European Perspective' (2016) 30 J of World Intel Prop 1.

Karapapa, Stavroula, *Private Copying* (Abingdon, UK: Routledge, 2012).

Katz, Ariel. 'A Network Effects Perspective on Software Piracy' (2005) 55 UTLJ 155.

Katz, Larissa. 'Exclusion and Exclusivity in Property Law' (2008) 58 UTLJ 275.

Kelke, WH Hastings, *An Epitome of Personal Property law*, 3rd ed (London, UK: Sweet & Maxwell, 1910).

Kerr, Ian. 'Digital Locks and the Automation of Virtue' in Michael Geist, ed, *From 'Radical Extremism' to 'Balanced Copyright': Canadian Copyright and the Digital Agenda* (Toronto: Irwin Law, 2010).

Keynes, AA & Claude Brunet. 'A Rejoinder to "Canadian Copyright: Natural Property or Mere Monopoly"' (1979) 40 CPR (2d) 54.

Kim, Nancy S. 'Clicking and Cringing' (2007) 43 Or L Rev 797.

Kim, Selena. 'The Reinforcement of International Copyright for the Digital Age' (2002) 16 IPJ 93.

King, Yolanda M. 'The Enforcement Challenges for Tattoo Copyrights' (2014) 22 J Intell Prop L 29.

Kretschmer, Martin. 'Digital Copyright: The End of an Era' (2003) 25 Eur IP Rev 333.

Krohn, David R Pekarek. 'Media-Rich Input Application Liability' (2010) 17 Mich Telecomm & Tech L Rev 201.

Ku, Raymond Shih Ray. 'Consumers and Creative Destruction: Fair Use Beyond Market Failure' (2003) 18 BTLJ 539.

L'Heureux, Nicole, *Droit de la consommation*, 5e ed (Cowansville, Quebec: Yvon Blais, 2000).

Lafond, Pierre-Claude. 'Le code civil du Québec et la loi sur la protection du consommateur: un mariage de solitudes' (2010) 88 CBR 407.

Lametti, David. 'Concept of Property: Relations Through Objects of Social Wealth' (2003) 53 UTLJ 325.

Lametti, David. 'The Concept and Conceptions of Intellectual Property as Seen Through the Lens of Property' in G Comandé & G Ponzanelli, eds, *Scienza e Diritto nel Prisma del Diritto Comparato* (Torino: Giappichelli, 2004).

Lametti, David. 'Coming to Terms with Copyright' in Michael Geist, ed, *In the Public Interest: The Future of Canadian Copyright Law* (Toronto: Irwin Law, 2005) 480.

Lametti, David. 'The Morality of James Harris's Theory of Property' in Timothy Endicott, Joshua Getzler, & Edwin Peel, eds, *The Properties of Law: Essays in Honour of James Harris* (Oxford: Oxford University Press, 2006).

Landes, William M & Richard A Posner, *The Economic Structure of Intellectual Property Law* (Cambridge, MA: Bellnap Press, 2003).

Lastowka, Greg, *Virtual Justice* (New Haven, CT: Yale University Press, 2010).

Lee, Edward. 'Technological Fair Use' (2010) 83 S Cal L Rev 797.

Lemley, Marc A. 'Beyond Preemption: The Law and Policy of Intellectual Property Licensing' (1999) 87 Cal L Rev 111.

Lemley, Marc A. 'Property, Intellectual Property and Free Riding' (2005) Texas L Rev 1031.

Lessig, Lawrence, *The Future of Ideas* (New York: Random House, 2001).
Lessig, Lawrence, *Free Culture: How Big Media Uses Technology and the Law to Lock Down Culture and Control Creativity* (New York: Penguin Press, 2004).
Levine, Dan (Reuters). 'Instagram Furor Triggers First Class-Action Lawsuit' (2013) 30 No 16 WL J Computer & Internet 10.
Liebowitz, Stan. 'Back to the Future: Can Copyright Owners Appropriate Revenues in the Face of New Copying Technologies?' in Wendy J Gordon & Richard Watt, eds, *The Economics of Copyright* (Cheltenham, UK: Edward Elgar, 2003).
Litman, Jessica. 'The Public Domain' (1990) 39 Emory LJ 965.
Litman, Jessica, *Digital Copyright* (Amherst, NY: Prometheus Books, 2001).
Litman, Jessica. 'Lawful Personal Use' (2007) 85 Tex L Rev 1871.
Litman, Jessica. 'Readers' Copyright' (2011) 58 J Copyright Soc'y USA 325.
Liu, Joseph P. 'Owning Digital Copies: Copyright Law and the Incidents of Copy Ownership' (2001) Wm & Mary L Rev 1245.
Liu, Joseph P. 'Copyright Law's Theory of the Consumer' (2003) 44 BC L Rev 397.
Liu, Joseph P. 'Enabling Copyright Consumers' (2007) 22 BTLJ 1099.
Liu, Joseph P. 'Two-Factor Fair Use?' (2008) 31 Colum JL & Arts 571.
Loos, Marco BM et al. 'Analysis of the Applicable Legal Frameworks and Suggestions for the Contours of a Model System of Consumer Protection in relation to Digital Content Contracts' (2011) University of Amsterdam, Centre for the Study of European Contract Law (CSECL), Institute for Information Law (IViR), Amsterdam Centre for Law and Economics (ACLE), online: <http://ec.europa.eu/justice/newsroom/consumer-marketing/events/digital_conf_en.htm>.
Lowe, Robert, *Consumer Law and Practice*, 6th ed (London, UK: Sweet & Maxwell, 2004).
Lucas, André. 'International Exhaustion' in Lionel Bently, Uma Suthersanen, & Paul Torremans, eds, *Global Copyright: Three Hundred Years Since the Statute of Anne, From 1709 to Cyberspace* (Cheltenham, UK: Edward Elgar, 2010) 304.
Lucas, André & Pierre Sirinelli. 'Exceptions de copie privée et mesures techniques de protection' (2005) 16 Propriétés intellectuelles 340.
Lucchi, Nicola. 'The Supremacy of Techno-Governance: Privatization of Digital Content and Consumer Protection in the Globalized Information Society' (2007) 15 Int'l JL & IT 192.
Lunney, Glynn S Jr. 'The Death of Copyright: Digital Technology, Private Copying and the Digital Millennium Copyright Act' (2001) 87 Va L Rev 813.
Lunney, Glynn S Jr. 'Fair Use and Market Failure: Sony Revisited' (2002) 82 BU L Rev 975.

MacMillan, Fiona. 'Copyright and Corporate Power' in Ruth Towse, ed, *Copyright and the Cultural Industries* (Cheltenham, UK: Edward Elgar, 2002).
MacMillan, Fiona. 'The Cruel C: Copyright and Film' (2002) 24 Eur IP Rev 483.
Mak, Chantal. 'Fundamental rights and the European regulation of iconsumer contracts' (2008) 31 J Cons Law Policy 425.
Martin, John V, *Copyright: Current Issues and Law* (Hauppauge, NY: Nova Science Publishers, 2002).
Masse, Claude, *Loi sur la protection du consommateur, analyse et commentaires* (Cowansville, Quebec: Yvon Blais, 1999).
Mazziotti, Giuseppe, *EU Digital Copyright Law and the End-User* (Berlin: Springer-Verlag, 2008).
McGowan, David. 'Some Copyright Consumer Conundrums' in Jane K Winn, ed, *Consumer Protection in the Age of the 'Information Economy'* (Aldershot, UK: Ashgate, 2006) 155.

McKeown, John S, *Fox on Canadian Law of Copyright and Industrial Designs*, 4th ed (Toronto: Carswell, 2003).

McManis, Charles R. 'The Privatization ("Shrink-Wrapping") of American Copyright Law' (1999) 87 Cal L Rev 173.

Menell, Peter S. 'The Property Rights Movement's Embrace of Intellectual Property: True Love or Doomed Relationship?' (2007) 34 Ecology LQ 713.

Merrill, Thomas & Henry Smith. 'Optimal Standardization in the Law of Property: the Numerus Clausus Principle' (2000) 110 Yale LJ 1.

Mezey, Naomi. 'Law as Culture' (2001) 13 Yale JL & Human 35.

Miller, CJ, Brian W Harvey, & Deborah L Parry, *Consumer and Trading Law* (Oxford: Oxford University Press, 1998).

Moon, Ken. 'The Nature of Computer Programs: Tangible? Goods? Personal Property? Intellectual Property?' (2009) 31 Eur IP Rev 396.

Mosley, C Todd. 'Mourning the Loss of Copyright's Unsung Hero: Destruction of the First Sale Doctrine' (2014) 14 Chi-Kent J Intell Prop 235.

Mossman, Mary Jane & William F Flanagan, *Property Law Cases and Commentary*, 2nd ed (Toronto: Emond Montgomery, 2004).

Mossoff, Adam. 'Is Copyright Property?' (2005) 42 San Diego L Rev 29.

Mossoff, Adam, ed, *Intellectual Property and Property Rights* (Cheltenham, UK: Edward Elgar, 2013).

Moyse, Pierre-Emmanuel. 'La nature du droit d'auteur: droit de propriété ou monopole?' (1998) 43 McGill LJ 507.

Moyse, Pierre-Emmanuel, *Le droit de distribution: Analyse historique et comparative en droit d'auteur* (Cowansville, Quebec: Yvon Blais, 2007).

Moyse, Pierre-Emmanuel. 'Kraft Canada c Euro-Excellence: l'insoutenable légèreté du droit' (2008) 53 RD McGill 741.

Munzer, Stephen R, *A Theory of Property* (Cambridge, UK: Cambridge University Press, 1990).

Nadel, Mark S. 'How Current Copyright Law Discourages Creative Output: The Overlooked Impact of Marketing' (2004) 19 BTLJ 785.

Netanel, Neil Weinstock, *Copyright's Paradox* (New York: Oxford University Press, 2008).

Netanel, Neil Weinstock, 'First Amendment Constraints on Copyright After *Golan v. Holder*' (2013) 60 UCLA L Rev 1082.

Newman, Christopher M. 'Patent Infringement as Nuisance' (2009) 59 Cath U L Rev 61.

Newman, Christopher M. 'Transformation in Property and Copyright' (2011) 56 Vill L Rev 251.

Nimmer, David. 'A Riff on Fair Use in the Digital Millennium Copyright Act' (2000) 148 U Pa L Rev 673.

Nimmer, David, Elliot Brown & Gary N Frischling. 'The Metamorphosis of Contract into Expand' (1999) 87 Cal L Rev 17.

Okediji, Ruth. 'Givers, Takers, and Other Kinds of Users: A Fair Use Doctrine for Cyberspace' (2001) 53 Fla L Rev 107.

Olivier, Alain. 'Fitness for Purpose in the Contract of Lease under the Civil Code of Quebec' (1995) 40 McGill LJ 187.

O'Regan, Karla M. 'Downloading Personhood: A Hegelian Theory of Copyright Law' (2009) 7 Can JL & Tech 1.

Pallente, Maria A. 'The Next Great Copyright Act' (2013) 36 Colum J L & Arts 315.

Parchomovsky, Gideon & Philip J Weiser. 'Beyond Fair Use' (2010) 96 Cornell L Rev 91.
Patry, William, *Moral Panic and the Copyright Wars* (New York: Oxford University Press, 2009).
Patry, William, *How to Fix Copyright* (New York: Oxford University Press, 2012).
Patterson, L Ray. 'Free Speech, Copyright and Fair Use' (1987) 40 Vand L Rev 1.
Patterson, L Ray & Stanley W Lindberg, *The Nature of Copyright: A Law of Users' Rights* (Athens, GA: University of Georgia Press, 1991).
Penalver, Eduardo Moises & Sonia K Katyal, *Property Outlaws* (New Haven, CT: Yale University Press, 2010).
Penner, James E, *The Idea of Property in Law* (Oxford: Clarendon, 1997).
Perzanowski, Aaron & Jason Schultz. 'Digital Exhaustion' (2011) 58 UCLA L Rev 889.
Perzanowski, Aaron & Jason Schultz. 'Copyright Exhaustion and the Personal Use Dilemma' (2012) 96 Minn L Rev 2067.
Perzanowski, Aaron & Jason Schultz. 'Legislating Digital Exhaustion' (2014) 29 BTLJ 1535.
Perzanowski, Aaron & Jason Schultz. 'Reconciling Intellectual Property with Personal Property' (2014) 90 Notre Dame L Rev 1211.
Peters, Marybeth. 'The Legal Perspective on Exhaustion in the Borderless Era: Consideration of a Digital First Sale Doctrine for Online Transmissions of Digital Works in the United States' in Lionel Bently, Uma Suthersanen, & Paul Torremans, eds, *Global Copyright: Three Hundred Years Since the Statute of Anne, From 1709 to Cyberspace* (Cheltenham, UK: Edward Elgar, 2010) 329.
Posner, Richard A. 'The Law and Economics of Intellectual Property' (2002) Daedalus 5.

Radin, Margaret Jane. 'Property and Personhood' (1982) 34 Stan L Rev 957.
Radin, Margaret Jane, *Boilerplate: The Fine Print, Vanishing Rights, and the Rule of Law* (Princeton, NJ: Princeton University Press, 2014).
Radin, Margaret Jane. 'Regime Change in Intellectual Property: Superseding the Law of the State with the "Law" of the Firm' (2003–2004) 1 U Ottawa L & Tech J 173.
Rahmatian, Andreas, *Copyright and Creativity: The Making of Property Rights in Creative Works* (Northampton, MA: Edward Elgar, 2011).
Ramsay, Ian. 'Consumer Redress Mechanisms for Poor Quality and Defective Products' in Ian Ramsay, ed, *Consumer Law* (New York: New York University Press, 1992) 391.
Raustiala, Kal & Jonathan Springman, *The Knockoff Economy: How Imitation Sparks Innovation* (New York: Oxford University Press, 2012).
Reed, Chris & John Angel, *Computer Law, The Law and Regulation of Information Technology*, 6th ed (Oxford: Oxford University Press, 2005).
Reichamn, Jerome H, Graeme B Dinwoodie, & Pamela Samuelson. 'A Reverse Notice and Takedown Regime to Enable Public Interest Uses of Technically Protected Copyrighted Works' (2007) 22 BTLJ 981.
Reiss, Sarah. 'Toward A "Digital Transfer Doctrine?" The First Sale Doctrine in the Digital Era' (2014) 109 Nw U L Rev 173.
Reto, Hilty. ' "Exhaustion" in the Digital Age' in Irene Calboli & Edward Lee, eds, *Research Handbook on Intellectual Property Exhaustion and Parallel Imports* (Northampton, MA: Edward Elgar, 2016), online: <SSRN:http://ssrn.com/abstract=2689518>.
Rezabakhsh, Behrang et al. 'Consumer Power: A Comparison of the Old Economy and the Internet Economy' (2006) 29 J Consum Policy 3.
Ricketson, Sam & Jane C Ginsburg, *International Copyright and Neighbouring Rights, The Berne Convention and Beyond*, 2nd ed (Oxford: Oxford University Press, 2006).
Riis, Thomas & Jens Schovsbo. 'Users' Rights: Reconstructing Copyright Policy on Utilitarian Grounds' (2007) 29 Eur IP Rev 1.

Rimmer, Matthew, *Digital Copyright and the Consumer Revolution—Hands Off My iPod* (Cheltenham, UK: Edward Elgar, 2007).
Roberts, RJ. 'Canadian Copyright: Natural Property or Mere Monopoly' (1979) 40 CPR (2d) 33.
Robinson, Glen O. 'Property Servitudes' (2004) 71 U Chicago L Rev 1449.
Rodau, Andrew. 'Computer Software: Does Article 2 of the Uniform Commercial Code Apply?' (1986) 35 Emory LJ 853.
Rosenfeld, Michel. 'Rethinking the Boundaries Between Public Law and Private Law for the Twenty First Century: An Introduction' (2013) 11 Intl J Constitutional L 125.
Rott, Peter. 'Download of Copyright-Protected Internet Content and the Role of (Consumer) Contract Law' (2008) 31 J Consum Policy 441.

Samuelson, Pamela & Jason Schultz. 'Should Copyright Owners Have to Give Notice of Their Use of Technical Protection Measures?' (2007) 6 J Telecomm & High Tech L 41.
Scassa, Teresa. 'Users' Rights in the Balance: Recent Developments in Copyright Law at the Supreme Court of Canada' (2005) 22 CIPR 133.
Schnaps, Adi. 'Do Consumers Have the Right to Space-shift, as they do Time-shift, Their Television Content? Intellectual Property Rights in the Face of New Technology' (2007) 17 Seton Hall J Sport L & Ent L 51.
Schovsbo, Jens. 'Integrating Consumer rights into Copyright Law: From the European Perspective' (2008) 31 J Consum Policy 393.
Scott, Colin. 'Enforcing Consumer Protection Laws' in Geraint Howells, Ian Ramsay, & Thomas Wihelmsson, eds, *Handbook of Research on International Consumer Law* (Cheltenham, UK: Edward Elgar, 2010).
Senftleben, Martin, *Copyright, Limitations and the Three-Step Test* (The Hague: Kluwer Law International, 2004).
Senftleben, Martin. 'The International Three-Step Test: A Model Provision for EC Fair Use Legislation' (2010) 1:2 JIPITEC 67.
Seringhaus, Michael. 'E-Book Transactions: Amazon "Kindles" the Copy Ownership Debate' (2009) 12 Yale JL & Tech 147.
Serra, Theodore. 'Rebalancing at Resale: ReDigi, Royalties, and the Digital Secondary Market' (2013) 93 BU L Rev 1753.
Siebrasse, Normand. 'A Property Rights Theory of the Limits of Copyright' (2001) 51 UTLJ 1.
Sims, Alexandra. 'The Denial of Copyright Protection on Public Policy Grounds' (2008) 30 Eur IP Rev 189.
Smith, Fiona & Lorna Woods. 'A Distinction without a Difference: Exploring the Boundary between Goods and Services in the World Trade Organization and the European Union' (2005) 12 Colum J Eur L 1.
Smith, Henry E. 'Property as the Law of Things' (2012) 125 Harv L Rev 1691.
Smith, Krysta M. 'Copyright in the Mobile Media Era' (2013) 13 U Pitt J Tech L & Pol'y 1.
Sookman, Barry B, *Computer, Internet, and Electronic Commerce Law*, loose-leaf (Toronto: Thomson Carswell, 1988).
Sookman, Barry. 'Copyright Reform for Canada: What Should We Do? A Submission to the Copyright Consultation' (2009) 22 IPJ 1.
Spence, Michael, *Intellectual Property* (Oxford: Oxford University Press, 2007).
Storella, Alison C. 'It's Selfie-Evident: Spectrums of Alienability and Copyright Content on Social Media' (2014) 94 BUL Rev 2045.
Sullivan, Ruth, *Sullivan on the Construction of Statutes*, 6th ed (Markham, Ontario: Lexis Nexis Canada, 2014).

Sun, Haochen. 'Overcoming the Achilles Heel of Copyright Law' (2007) 5 Nw J Tech & IP 265.

Sunstein, Cass R, ed, *Behavioral Law and Economics* (Cambridge, UK: Cambridge University Press, 2000).

Swan, Angela, *Canadian Contract Law*, 2nd ed (Toronto: Lexis Nexis Canada, 2009).

Takeyama, Lisa N. 'Piracy, Asymmetric Information and Product Quality' in Wendy J Gordon & Richard Watt, eds, *The Economics of Copyright* (Cheltenham, UK: Edward Elgar, 2003).

Targosz, Tomasz. 'Exhaustion in Digital Products and the "Accidental" Impact on the Balance of Interests in Copyright Law' in Lionel Bently, Uma Suthersanen, & Paul Torremans, eds, *Global Copyright: Three Hundred Years Since the Statute of Anne, From 1709 to Cyberspace* (Cheltenham, UK: Edward Elgar, 2010) 337.

Tawfik, Myra J. 'International Copyright Law and Fair Dealing as a User Right' UNESCO Copyright Bulletin (2005), online: <http://portal.unesco.org/culture/en/ev.php->.

Tawfik, Myra J. 'International Copyright Law: W[h]ither User Rights?' in Michael Geist, ed, *In the Public Interest: The Future of Canadian Copyright Law* (Toronto: Irwin Law, 2005) 66.

Tawfik, Myra J. 'No Longer Living in Splendid Isolation: The Globalization of National Courts and the Internationalization of Intellectual Property Law' (2007) 32 Queen's LJ 573

Thaler, Richard H & Cass R Sunstein, *Nudge: improving decisions about health, wealth, and happiness* (New Haven, CT: Yale University Press, 2008).

Tjong Tjin Tai, Eric. 'Exhaustion and Online Delivery of Digital Works' (2003) 25 Eur IP Rev 207.

Towse, Ruth. 'Creativity, Copyright and the Creative Industries Paradigm' (2010) 63 KYKLOS 461.

Trebilcock, Michael J. 'Rethinking Consumer Protection Policy' in Charles EF Rickett & Thomas GW Telfer, eds, *International Perspectives on Consumer Access to Justice* (Cambridge, UK: Cambridge University Press, 2003) 68.

Trosow, Samuel E. 'The Illusive Search for Justificatory Theories: Copyright, Commodification and Capital' (2003) 16 Can JL & Jur 217.

Tussey, Deborah. 'From Fan Sites to File Sharing: Personal Use in Cyberspace' (2001) 35 Ga L Rev 1129.

Tussey, Deborah. 'UCITA, Copyright and Capture' (2003) 21 Cardozo Arts & Ent LJ 319.

Twigg-Flesner, Christian, *Consumer Product Guarantees* (Aldershot, UK: Ashgate, 2003).

Tyler, ELG & NE Palmer, *Crossley Vaines' Personal Property*, 5th ed (London, UK: Butterworths, 1973).

Van Hoboken, Joris & Natali Helberger. 'Looking Ahead—Future Issues when Reflecting on the Place of the iConsumer in Consumer Law and Copyright Law' (2008) 31 J Consum Policy 489.

Van Houweling, Molly Shaffer. 'The New Servitudes' (2008) 96 Geo LJ 885.

Van Houweling, Molly Shaffer. 'Exhaustion and the Limits of Remote-Control Property' (2016) 93 Denv L Rev 951.

Vaver, David. 'Intellectual Property Today: Of Myths and Paradoxes' (1990) 69 Can Bar Rev 98.

Vaver, David, *Intellectual Property Law* (Toronto: Irwin Law, 1997).

Vaver, David, *Copyright Law* (Toronto: Irwin Law, 2000).

Vaver, David. 'Canada's Intellectual Property Framework: A Comparative Overview' (2004) 17 IPJ 125.

Vaver, David. 'Copyright and the Internet: From Owner Rights and User Duties to User Rights and Owner Duties?' (2007) Case West L Rev 731.

Vaver, David, *Intellectual Property Law: Copyright, Patents, Trade-Marks*, 2nd ed (Toronto: Irwin Law, 2011).

Vaver, David. 'Intellectual property: Still a "bargain"?' (2012) 34 Eur IP Rev 579.

Vaver, David. 'Harmless Copying' (2012) 25 IPJ 19.

Vaver, David. 'Copyright Defenses as User Rights' (2013) 60:4 J Copyright Soc'y USA 661.

Voon, Tania. 'A New Approach to Audiovisual Products in the WTO: Rebalancing Gatt and Gats' (2007) 14 UCLA Ent L Rev 1.

Waddams, Stephen M, *The Law of Contracts*, 5th ed (Toronto: Canada Law Book, 2005).

Wagner, R Polk. 'Information Wants to be Free, Intellectual Property and the Mythologies of Control' (2003) 103 Colum L Rev 995.

Waldron, Jeremy, *The Right to Private Property* (Oxford: Clarendon Press, 1988).

Waldron, Jeremy. 'From Authors to Copiers: Individual Rights & Social Values in Intellectual Property' (1993) 69 Chicago-Kent L Rev 841.

Walker, Peter, *Consumer Law*, 4th ed (London, UK: Cavendish Publishing, 2001).

Walker, Scott L & Matthew Savare. 'Foul Use? FTC Declines to Take Action against Allegedly Overbroad and Misleading Copyright Warnings' (2008) 25 WTR Ent & Sports Law 1.

Warren, Samuel D & Louis D Brandeis. 'The Right to Privacy' (1890) 4 Harv L Rev 193.

Wiebe, Andreas. 'The Economic Perspective: Exhaustion in the Digital Age' in Lionel Bently, Uma Suthersanen, & Paul Torremans, eds, *Global Copyright: Three Hundred Years Since the Statute of Anne, From 1709 to Cyberspace* (Cheltenham, UK: Edward Elgar, 2010) 321.

Winn, Jane K. 'Introduction: Is Consumer Protection an Anachronism in the 21st Century?' in Jane K Winn, ed, *Consumer Protection in the Age of the 'Information Economy'* (Aldershot, UK: Ashgate, 2006) 1.

Xifaras, Mikhaïl, *La Propriété Etude de philosophie du droit* (Paris: Presses Universitaires de France, 2004).

Yu, Peter K. 'Anticircumvention and Anti-Anticircumvention' (2006) 84 Denv UL Rev 13.

Yu, Peter K. 'Six Secret (and now open) Fears of Acta' (2011) 64 SMU L Rev 975.

Ziegel, Jacob S & Anthony J Duggan, *Commercial and Consumer Sales Transactions, Cases, Text and Materials*, 4th ed (Toronto: Edmond Montgomery, 2002).


## Government Documents and Other Reports


Austl, Commonwealth, Law Reform Commission, *Copyright and the Digital Economy* (Report No 122) (Sydney: ALRC, 2013).

Canada, Culture and Communications, Standing Committee on Communications and Culture, *The Ties That Bind* (Ottawa: The Committee, 1992) (Chair: Bud Bird).

Canada, Department of Consumer and Corporate Affairs, AA Kayes & C Brunet, *Copyright in Canada—Proposals for a Revision of the Law* (Ottawa: Government of Canada, 1977).

Canada, Departments of Consumer and Corporate Affairs and Communications, *From Gutenberg to Telidon: A White Paper on Copyright: Proposals for the Revision of the Canadian Copyright Act* (Ottawa: Supply & Services Canada, 1984).

Canada, Intellectual Property Policy Directorate Industry Canada, Copyright Policy Branch, Canadian Heritage, *Consultation Paper on Digital Copyright Issues* (2001), online: <http://www.ic.gc.ca/eic/site/crp-prda.nsf/eng/h_rp01102.html>.

Center for Democracy & Technology, 'Evaluating DRM: Building a Marketplace for the Convergent World' (2006), online: <http://www.cdt.org/copyright/20060907drm.pdf>.

EC, Commission, *The Green Paper on the Review of the Consumer Acquis* (Brussels: EC, 2006).

EC, Parliament, DG for Internal Policies, Policies Department: Citizens' Rights and Constitutional Affairs, 'The Relations between Copyright Law and Consumers' Rights from a European Perspective', by Séverine Dusollier (2010).

EC, *Proposal for a Directive of the European Parliament and of the Council on certain aspects concerning contracts for the supply of digital content*, COM (2015) 634 final.

EC, *Proposal for a Directive of the European Parliament and of the Council on consumer rights*, COM (2008) 614 final.

Economic Council of Canada, Report on Intellectual and Industrial Property, Information Canada, by BV Hindley (Ottawa: Economic Council of Canada, 1971).

Electronic Frontier Foundation. 'Unintended Consequences: Fifteen Years Under the DMCA' (March 2013), online: <https:// www.eff.org/document/unintended-consequences-fifteen-years-under-dmca>.

EU, Opinion Advocate General Bot, *UsedSoft GmbH v Oracle International Corp*, Case C-128/11, 24 April 2012.

Government of Canada, *Balanced Copyright, Copyright Modernization Act—Backgrounder*, What Will the Bill Do—Users and Consumers, online: <http://balancedcopyright.gc.ca/eic/site/crp-prda.nsf/eng/h_rp01237.html>.

Government of Canada, Competition Bureau, Intellectual Property Enforcement Guidelines (2000), online: <http://www.competitionbureau.gc.ca/eic/site/cb-bc.nsf/eng/01286.html>.

Government of Canada, 'Copyright Consultations', online: <http://www.ic.gc.ca/eic/site/008.nsf/eng/home>.

Government of Canada, 'Copyright Modernization Act Backgrounder', online: <http://balancedcopyright.gc.ca/eic/site/crp-prda.nsf/eng/h_rp01151.html>.

Government of Ontario, 'Backgrounder the *Consumer Protection Act*' (27 June 2006), online: <http://www.mgs.gov.on.ca/en/News/Print/STEL02_047088.html>.

House of Commons, Standing Committee on Communications and Culture, 'A Charter of Rights for Creators—Report of the Subcommittee on the Revision of Copyright' (Ottawa: Supply & Services Canada, 1985), the Minutes of Proceedings and Evidence of the Sub-Committee of the Standing Committee on Communications and Culture on the Revision of Copyright: Response to From Gutenberg to Telidon.

Industry Canada, New Media, Information Technologies Industry Branch, *Study on New Media and Copyright*, by NGL Nordicity Group Ltd: P Lyman, T Rajan, L Rocca, LE Harris, & T Scapillati, 1994.

Ontario, Law Reform Commission, Jacob Ziegel, *Report on Sale of Goods* (Toronto: Ministry of the Attorney General, 1979).

Organisation for Economic Co-Operation and Development (OECD) Guidelines for Consumer Protection in the Context of Electronic Commerce (1999), online: <http://www.oecd.org/document/18/ 0,3746,en_ 2649_ 34267_ 44132242_ 1_ 1_ 1_ 1,00.html>.

UK, Councillor of the Exchequer, *Gowers Review of Intellectual Property*, Andrew Gowers, 2006, online: <www.official-documents.gov.uk/document/other/.../0118404830.pdf>.

UK, Department for Business, Innovation and Skills, *Consumer Rights in Digital Products*, Robert Bradgate, 2010, online: <http://www.google.ca/search?sourceid=navclient&ie=

UTF-8&rlz=1T4ADBF_enCA275CA275&q=Bradgate%2c\+Consumer\+rights\+in\+digital\+products\+2010>.

UK, Ian Hargreaves, 'Digital Opportunity: A Review of Intellectual Property and Growth', 2011, online: <www.ipo.gov.uk/ipreview-finalreport.pdf>.

UK, Intellectual Property Office, 'Complaints to Secretary of State under s. 296ZE under the Copyright, Designs and Patents Act 1988' (17 July 2015), online: <https://www.gov.uk/government/uploads/system/uploads/attachment_data/file/440384/ipo-foi-2014-432-complaints-to-secretary-of-state-under-s_296ze-cdpa.pdf>.

UK, Intellectual Property Office, 'Guidance on the Technological Protection Measures (TPMs) complaint process' (3 November 2014), online: <https://www.gov.uk/government/uploads/system/uploads/attachment_data/file/448277/Guidance_on_the_Technological_Protection_Measures_TMPs_Complaints_Proces....pdf>.

UK, Intellectual Property Office, *Private Copying and Fair Compensation: An Empirical Study of Copyright Levies in Europe*, Martin Kretschmer, 2011, online: <www.ipo.gov.uk/ipresearch-faircomp-full-201110.pdf>.

UK, Office of Fair Trading, 'Consumer Affairs Strategy: A Consultation Paper', 1996, online: <http://www.oft.gov.uk/shared_oft/reports/consumer_protection/oft166.doc>.

UK, Strategic Advisory Board for Intellectual Property, *The Relationship between Copyright and Contract Law*, Martin Kretschmer, Estelle Derclaye, Marcella Favale, & Richard Watt, 2010, online: <http://www.ipo.gov.uk/ipresearch-relation-201007.pdf>.

UN, *Report of the Special Rapporteur in the field of cultural rights, Farida Shaheed—Copyright policy and the right to science and culture*, UNHRCOR, 28th Sess, UN Doc A/HRC/28/57 (2014).

US, Copyright Compendium, Fed Reg (2014) § 101.

US, Copyright Office, *A Report of the Register of Copyrights pursuant to section 104 of the DMCA* (2001), online: <http://www.copyright.gov/reports/studies/dmca/dmca_study.html>.

US, Copyright Office, Compendium of US Copyright Office Practices § 101 (3rd ed 2014).

US, Copyright Office, *Exemption to Prohibition on Circumvention of Copyright Protection Systems for Access Control Technologies*, 80:208 Fed Reg 65944 (2015) (to be codified at 37 CFR § 201).

US, Copyright Office, *Section 1201 Study: Notice and Request for Public Comment*, 80:249 Fed Reg 81369 (2015).

US, Embassy of the United States, Ottawa, Canada, Special 301 Report (Intellectual Property Rights), online: <http://canada.usembassy.gov/key-reports/special-301-report-intellectual-property-rights.html>.

US, Federal Trade Commission, *Computer & Communications Industry Association (CCIA), Request for Investigation and Complaint for Injunctive and Other Relief*, filed with the Federal Trade Commission 1 August 2007, online: <http://www.google.ca/search?sourceid=navclient&ie=UTF-8&rlz=1T4ADBF_enCA275CA275&q=Computer\+%26\+Communications\+Industry\+Association\+complaint\+federal\+trade\+commission\+2007>.

US, Federal Trade Commission, *Letter in Response to Computer & Communications Industry Association (CCIA) Complaint*, 6 December 2007, online: <http://www.google.ca/search?sourceid=navclient&ie=UTF-8&rlz=1T4ADBF_enCA275CA275&q=Computer\+%26\+Communications\+Industry\+Association\+complaint\+federal\+trade\+commission\+2007>.

US, House Judiciary Committee, *WIPO Copyright Treaties Implementation and On-line Copyright Infringement Liability Limitation* (HR Rep No 105-551) (1998).

US, Register of Copyrights, 'Section 1201 Rulemaking: Sixth Triennial Proceeding to Determine Exemptions to the Prohibition on Circumvention, Recommendation of the Register of Copyrights' (8 October 2015), online: <http://www.copyright.gov/1201/2015/introduction-analysis.pdf>.

## Other Materials

Amazon.com Kindle License Agreement and Terms of Use, online: <http://www.amazon.com/gp/help/customer/display.html/ref=help_search_1-1?ie=UTF8&nodeId=200506200&qid=1336750645&sr=1-1>.

Apple iTunes store terms of services for music downloads, film rentals, and iBooks, online: <http://www.apple.com/legal/itunes/us/terms.html#SERVICE>.

Arthur, Charles, 'Anti-piracy agreement rejected by European Parliament, but Acta could be revived by European Commission', *The Guardian* (4 July 2012), online: <http://www.guardian.co.uk/technology/2012/jul/04/acta-european-parliament-votes-against>.

BEUC, 'Digital Products: How to Include Them in the Proposal for a Consumer Rights Directive', Position Paper (based on a study by Peter Rott), Brussels (2010), online: <http://www.beuc.org/Content/Default.asp?PageID=2135>.

BEUC, 'Digital Products: EU consumers need clear rights', Position Paper, Brussels (2012), online: <http://www.beuc.org/Content/Default.asp?PageID=2135>.

*Black's Law Dictionary*, 10th ed.

*The Canadian Abridgment: Words & Phrases Judicially Defined in Canadian Courts and Tribunals* (Toronto: Carswell, 1993) (WL Can).

Condon, Stephanie, 'PIPA, SOPA Put on Hold in Wake of Protests', *CBS News* (20 January 2012), online: <http://www.cbsnews.com/8301-503544_162-57362675-503544/pipa-sopa-put-on-hold-in-wake-of-protests/>.

Crews, Kenneth D, 'Study on Copyright Limitations and Exceptions for Libraries and Archives: Updated and Revised' (10 June 2015), online: <http://www.wipo.int/edocs/mdocs/copyright/en/sccr_30/sccr_30_3.pdf>.

Geist, Michael, 'Copyright Users' Rights in Canada Hits Ten: The Tenth Anniversary of the CCH Decision' (4 March 2014), online: <http://www.michaelgeist.ca/2014/03/cch-anniversary>.

Goodman, Amy, 'The SOPA Blackout Protest Makes History', *The Guardian* (18 January 2012), online: <http://www.guardian.co.uk/commentisfree/cifamerica/2012/jan/18/sopa-blackout-protest-makes-history>.

Gross, Robin, 'ACTA's Misguided Effort to Increase Govt Spying and Ratchet-Up IPR Enforcement at Public Expense', *IP Justice* (21 March 2008), delivered to the Office of the United States Trade Representative on the proposed Anti-Counterfeiting Trade Agreement (ACTA), online: <http://ipjustice.org/wp/2008/03/21/acta-ipj-comments-ustr-2008march/>.

Halsbury's Laws of Canada, *Defamation*, 'Slander and Related Torts: Malicious Falsehood'.

Joel Fights Back.com, online: <http://joelfightsback.com/2012/09/myth-and-facts-the-latest-update-in-joels-case/>.

KOBO Inc Canada terms of use for the purchase of ebooks, online: <http://www.kobobooks.com/termsofuse>.

Netflix terms of use for audio-visual entertainment streaming services, online: <https://signup.netflix.com/TermsofUse>.

Vaver, David, 'Canada's IP Laws, Amiss and A Mess', *IP Osgoode* (15 October 2008), online: <http://www.iposgoode.ca/2008/10/canada%e2%80%99s-ip-laws-%e2%80%93-amiss-and-a-mess/>.

Weisman, Jonathan, 'After an Online Firestorm, Congress Shelves Antipiracy Bills', *NY Times* (20 January 2012), online: <http://www.nytimes.com/2012/01/21/technology/senate-postpones-piracy-vote.html?_r=1&>.

Wilkinson, Margaret Ann, 'Copyright Users' Rights in International Law', *Law Publications*: Paper 84 (2014), online: <http://ir.lib.uwo.ca/cgi/viewcontent.cgi?article=1083&context=lawpub>.

# *Index*

Note: *n* = footnote. *t* = table.